On Goethe

Cultural Memory | *in the Present*

Hent de Vries, Editor

ON GOETHE

WALTER BENJAMIN

EDITED BY
Susan Bernstein, Peter Fenves,
and Kevin McLaughlin

STANFORD UNIVERSITY PRESS
Stanford, California

STANFORD UNIVERSITY PRESS
Stanford, California

English translation and introduction © 2025 by the Board of Trustees of the Leland Stanford Junior University. All rights reserved.

The original writings translated in this book are available in Walter Benjamin, *Gesammelte Schriften*, ed. Rolf Tiedemann and Hermann Schweppenhäuser, 7 vols., © 1972–91, Suhrkamp Verlag.

Printed in the United States of America on acid-free, archival-quality paper

Library of Congress Cataloging-in-Publication Data available on request.

Library of Congress Control Number: 2025931295

ISBN (cloth) 9781503630963
ISBN (paper) 9781503642225
ISBN (ebook) 9781503642232

Cover design: Martyn Schmoll

Typeset by Scribe Inc. in 11/14 Arno Pro

Contents

Acknowledgments	vii
Abbreviations	ix
Note on Translation	xiii

INTRODUCTION by Peter Fenves 1

PART I

1. A Remark on Gundolf: Goethe 47
2. On a Lost Conclusion to the Note on the Symbolic in Cognition 50
3. Supplements To: On the Symbolic in Cognition 52
4. Early Romantic Theory of Art and Goethe 53
5. Life Built Up from the Elements 63
6. Purity and Rigor Are Categories of the Work 66
7. Notes toward a Work on the Idea of Beauty 67
8. Categories of Aesthetics 68
9. On "Semblance" 71
10. Beauty 74
11. Beauty and Semblance 76
12. Truth and Truths / Cognition and Cognitions 77
13. Theory of Art Critique 79
14. The More Powerfully the Expressionless Comes Forth in Poetry 82
15. The Sacramental Also Turns into the Mythic 84
16. With Reference to François-Poncet 86
17. Concerning Elective Affinities 88
18. Goethe's Elective Affinities 91

vi CONTENTS

PART II

19. Goethe	165
20. Goethe's Politics and View of Nature	194
21. Weimar	200
22. Two Dreams of Goethe's House	203
23. Goethe's Theory of Colors	204
24. Against a Masterpiece: On Max Kommerell, *The Poet as Führer in German Classicism*	207
25. One Hundred Years of Writing on Goethe	214
26. Faust in the Sample Case	227
27. Books on Goethe—but Welcome Ones	233
28. New Literature about Goethe	235
29. Popularity as a Problem: On Hermann Schneider, *Schiller's Work and Legacy*	238
30. Letters about, to, and from Goethe	240
31. Mythic Anxiety in Goethe	246
32. Two Notes from the *Arcades Project*	252

Books by and about Goethe in "Registry of Readings"	253
Further Readings	255
Guide to Names	259
Glossary	277
Notes	283
Index of Goethe Citations (English-German)	351
Name Index	355
Note on the Translators	363

Acknowledgments

The editors would like to thank Lisa-Marie Fleck and Nora Mercurio at Suhrkamp Verlag for responding quickly and graciously to our initial inquiry about this volume. The editors would especially like to thank Ursula Marx (Walter Benjamin Archive, Akademie der Künste, Berlin) for her invaluable assistance at several stages of this volume's production. We also want to express our deep gratitude for the assistance we received from Astrid Deuber-Mankowsky, Thomas Schestag, and Samuel Weber.

The volume benefited from the advice and suggestions made by two anonymous readers of earlier versions of the texts in this volume. We are also indebted to Nina Melovska for her careful review of the manuscript and Dr. Carly Bortman for compiling the "Guide to Names" as well as producing the two indices.

Abbreviations

Citations of a multivolume text in parentheses without any additional abbreviation, for example, "(2:179)," refer to the following edition, which is designated by GS whenever required: Walter Benjamin, *Gesammelte Schriften*, ed. Rolf Tiedemann and Hermann Schweppenhäuser, 7 vols. (Frankfurt am Main: Suhrkamp, 1972–91). Citations of a single-volume text in parentheses, for example, "(217)," refer to the pages in this volume.

Benjamin

Beyond GS, the following abbreviations are used for Benjamin's writings:

GB   *Gesammelte Briefe*. Ed. Christoph Gödde and Henri Lonitz. 6 vols. Frankfurt am Main: Suhrkamp, 1995–2000.

WBA   Walter Benjamin Archive (shelf-number), Akademie der Künste, Berlin. The dates of composition associated with notes and fragments derive, with a few exceptions, from the corresponding entries in the Archive catalog, available at https://archiv.adk.de/bigobjekt/19358.

WuN   Walter Benjamin, *Werke und Nachlaß. Kritische Gesamtausgabe*. Ed. Christoph Gödde and Henri Lonitz in association with the Walter Benjamin Archive. 22 vols. projected. Frankfurt am Main: Suhrkamp, 2008–.

WuN 3   *Der Begriff der Kunstkritik in der deutschen Romantik*. Ed. Uwe Steiner. Frankfurt am Main: Suhrkamp, 2008.

X ABBREVIATIONS

WuN 8   *Einbahnstraße.* Ed. Detlev Schöttker and Steffan Haug. Frankfurt am Main: Suhrkamp, 2009.

WuN 9   *Rundfunkarbeiten.* Ed. Thomas Küpper and Anja Nowak. 2 vols. Frankfurt am Main: Suhrkamp, 2017.

WuN 10 *Deutsche Menschen.* Ed. Momme Brodersen. Frankfurt am Main: Suhrkamp, 2008.

WuN 12 *Das Kunstwerk im Zeitalter seiner technischen Reproduzierbarkeit.* Ed. Burkhardt Lindner, Simon Broll, and Jessica Nitsche. Frankfurt am Main: Suhrkamp, 2012.

WuN 13 *Kritiken und Rezensionen.* Ed. Heinrich Kaulen. 2 vols. Frankfurt am Main: Suhrkamp, 2011.

*

Citations of Benjamin's writings other than those translated in this volume refer to GS, followed by the volume/page numbers of an existing translation whenever possible (except in the case of Benjamin's letters, which are identified by their dates), using the following abbreviations:

EW   *Early Writings, 1910–1917.* Ed. and trans. Howard Eiland and others. Cambridge, Mass.: Harvard University Press, 2011.

MD   *Moscow Diary.* Ed. Gary Smith, trans. Richard Sieburth. Cambridge, Mass.: Harvard University Press, 1986.

O   *Origin of the German Trauerspiel.* Trans. Howard Eiland. Cambridge, Mass.: Harvard University Press, 2019.

RB   *Radio Benjamin.* Ed. Lecia Rosenthal, trans. Jonathan Lutes, Lisa Harries Schumann, and Diana Reese. New York: Verso, 2014.

S   *Sonnets.* Ed. and trans. Carl Skoggard. Louiseville, Quebec: Pilot Editions, 2014.

SW   *Selected Writings.* Ed. Michael Jennings and Howard Eiland. 4 vols. Cambridge, Mass.: Harvard University Press, 1996–2000.

TCV *Toward the Critique of Violence: A Critical Edition.* Ed. Peter Fenves and Julia Ng. Stanford: Stanford University Press, 2021.

Goethe

In the citation of the epigraph that begins the published version of his dissertation (1:10), Benjamin refers to the recently completed Weimar Ausgabe, abbreviated as WA; it is also called the Sophien-Ausgabe in honor of Grand Duchess Sophie von Sachsen, who commissioned its production. Only rarely in the texts translated here does Benjamin conform to academic conventions and identify the version of Goethe's work from which he draws his citations. As he indicates in one of the manuscripts of "Goethe's Elective Affinities" (see 1:842) as well as in one of the fragments translated in this volume (see 78), Karl Goedeke's edition, *Sämmtliche Werke* (Stuttgart: Cotta, 1868–76), was a principal source of his citations. For the sake of both consistency and convenience—and because Benjamin describes it as both "rigorously philological" and "unsurpassable" (GB 1:433; 23 February 1918)—the endnotes to this volume uniformly refer to the (currently) 143-volume Weimar edition, that is, *Goethes Werke*, ed. Hermann Böhlau and successors under the patronage of Sophie von Sachsen (Weimar: Böhlau, 1887–1919), which includes *Goethes Gespräche*, ed. Woldemar Freiherr von Biedermann (Leipzig: Biedermann, 1889–96), and *Nachträge zur Weimarer Ausgabe*, ed. Paul Raabe (Munich: DTV, 1990). In addition to identifying a section with a Roman numeral (or, in the case of conversations, "G" for *Gespräche*), followed by a volume and page number(s), references in the endnotes describe where the text can be found in any English translation (title followed by section/chapter numbers or paragraph numbers, dates of letters, dates of conversations).

Kant

All reliable English-language translations include marginal references to the following editions:

Aka   Immanuel Kant, *Gesammelte Schriften*. Ed. Königlich Preussische (later, Deutsche) Akademie der Wissenschaften. 29 vols. Berlin: Reimer; later, de Gruyter, 1900–.

A   *Critique of Pure Reason* (1781 edition).

B   *Critique of Pure Reason* (1787 edition).

Note on Translation

Throughout the period in which Benjamin worked most intensely on Goethe, he was involved in two major translation projects—first with Baudelaire, then with Proust. And Benjamin's reflections on Goethe, from the earliest to the last, are closely connected with the essays he wrote in response to these two projects: "The Task of the Translator" (4:9–21; SW 1:253–63) in the first instance and "On the Image of Proust" (2:310–24; SW 2:237–47) in the second. The translators who worked on this volume have been ever mindful of two early attempts to bring Benjamin's work into another language, both of which involve his engagement with Goethe. The first—and this also seems to be the first translation of Benjamin's work into any language—derives from the commission he received from the editorial committee of the Большая советская энциклопедия (*Great Soviet Encyclopedia*). An article titled "Гёте (Goethe), Иоган Вольфганг" (without the "von" that marks Goethe's ascension to the minor nobility) appeared in a volume of the encyclopedia published in 1929 under Benjamin's name along with five others; but the article had almost nothing to do with the manuscript he submitted (see 165–93). This is perhaps the nadir of Benjamin-translation. The next attempt to make Benjamin's writings on Goethe available to a non-German-speaking readership was far more successful. Published in *Les Cahiers du Sud* in 1937, it was prepared by Pierre Klossowski, who left an amusing description of what it was like to attempt to fulfill the task of the translator in the vicinity of the author: "Benjamin, considering my initial version too free, had started

xiii

translating it again with me. The result was going to be a text perfectly unreadable as a result of the fact that it was closely modeled on the slightest German expressions, for which Benjamin would accept no transposition" (WuN 12:665–66). We hope that the translations in this volume retain much that is "essential in Benjamin's exposition" and are still readable enough to convey a sense of why Benjamin would at times resist certain kinds of efforts to make his work appear perfectly readable upon first glance.

The original conceptions of a collection of essays that would bring Benjamin's thoughts to the attention of a wider public in the post-WWII era included "Goethe's Elective Affinities" as a prominent element. And the essay was included in the German edition of *Illuminations* but unfortunately not in its English counterpart. This oversight—probably generated by the complexity of the essay along with the relative obscurity of Goethe's novel in the English-speaking world—was finally rectified with the inclusion of Stanley Corngold's translation in the first volume of *Selected Writings*, published by Harvard University Press. The four volumes of *Selected Writings* and the single-volume *Arcades Project* include translations of many other texts related to Goethe, some of which appear in this volume in entirely new translations. The approach here differs from the one that guides *Selected Writings*. Benjamin's writings on Goethe have been selected, edited, translated, and annotated so as to make it possible for the reader to discern the outlines and direction of a distinct and remarkable critical project that spans almost the entirety of Benjamin's literary corpus.

When Benjamin translated Baudelaire's brief collection of poems, he did so by himself. When he worked on Proust's massive novel, he did so in collaboration with a like-minded friend, Franz Hessel. This volume is conceived more along the lines of the latter than the former; that is, it is a collaborative project in which the final state of each translation is cooperatively established. The initial translator is in each case marked by his or her initials in the first (unnumbered) endnote: SB stands for Susan Bernstein; JC for Jan Cao; PF for Peter Fenves; KM for Kevin McLaughlin; and JR for Jonas Rosenbrück.

The footnotes in this volume all derive from Benjamin. The editors are responsible for the endnotes. To reduce the number of the latter, the volume includes a guide to the people who are discussed or mentioned in the translations as well as in the Introduction.

On Goethe

INTRODUCTION

by Peter Fenves

In the late 1960s, Hannah Arendt famously said of the relation between Bertolt Brecht and Walter Benjamin that it was a "unique [case] in that here the greatest living German poet met the most important critic of the time."[1] Several years later, partly in response to this remark perhaps, a volume of Benjamin's writings under the title *Understanding Brecht* was published.[2] It was the first—and still remains the only—collection of his writings in English that focus on a German writer. Though the volume was certainly welcome, it does not recognize the source of Arendt's claim, which lies in an expansive insight into the "spiritual existence" of her friend, namely, that it "had been formed and informed by Goethe."[3] It is for this reason that Arendt many years earlier had insisted that Benjamin's essay on Goethe's novel *Elective Affinities* serve as the entrance point for posthumous collections of his writings.[4] And it is for the same reason that she argued that Benjamin had a greater affinity with a poet like Brecht than a theoretician like Theodor Adorno.

Arendt began her essay on Benjamin with a reflection on the phenomenon of his posthumous fame, which has expanded and intensified in ways she probably never imagined. It would not be an exaggeration to say that he has become the most widely cited and widely read German critic of the twentieth century. One thing is clear about his role as a specifically literary critic: he engaged more often with Goethe than with any other German writer and, indeed, with any other writer apart from Baudelaire. From the essay that concluded his secondary school education to the last book that he was able

1

to publish in his lifetime, Benjamin not only wrote a vast variety of notes, fragments, essays, and articles about the supreme representative of modern German culture; he had at least two plans to write a book about Goethe. The failure of the second one—the director of Insel-Verlag turned down Benjamin's proposal to write a book for the one hundredth anniversary of his death in 1932—may have been an even more devastating blow than the failure of *Origin of the German Trauerspiel* to earn Benjamin a *venia legendi* ("license to teach") at a German university. As the final texts of this volume make clear, this blow did not stop Benjamin from reflecting on Goethe's work, life, and afterlife; on the contrary, he continued to account for their critical potential in and beyond the point where the Weimar Republic was replaced by the Nazi reign of terror.

1.

Benjamin begins the central section of "Goethe's Elective Affinities," one of the two pivotal texts around which this volume revolves, with some thoughts about the genre of introductions to classical works: "If only rarely does an edition of a classic fail to stress in its introduction that precisely its matter, more than scarcely anything else, is understandable solely on the basis of the author's life, this judgment already contains in principle the πρῶτον ψεῦδος of a method that seeks to present the development of the work in the author through a template-like image of his essence and an empty or incomprehensible lived experience" (119).[5] In his account of his friendship with Benjamin, written some fifty years after the publication of "Goethe's Elective Affinities," Gershom Scholem made the following comment about the life of its author during the period of its conception: "There developed a situation which, to the extent that I was able to understand it, corresponded to the one in Goethe's *Elective Affinities*."[6] The "situation" in question was this: the marriage between Benjamin and his wife, Dora Kellner-Benjamin, was crumbling, as Benjamin drew closer to Jula Cohn, while Dora was attracted to another of their mutual friends, Ernst Schoen. A vaguely similar situation—if one abstracts from many dissimilar details, such as, for instance, the social class of the four figures—obtains at the beginning of Goethe's novel. Without Scholem's notable hesitation about the state of his understanding, his comment, amplified by a few passages in Charlotte Wolff's *On the Way to Myself* and concretized in the decision on the part of the editors of the *Gesammelte Schriften* to place "dedicated to Jula Cohn" (1:123) directly below the title page (without indicating that she married still another mutual friend, Fritz Radt, in the year of its publication), became a widely cited "fact" about what Benjamin was doing when he set out to write an extensive study of *Elective Affinities*.[7] It would be difficult to find a more precise instantiation of the πρωτον ψευδος that Benjamin identifies. The manner in which readers are introduced to a "classical work," beginning with its title page, obstructs access to its subject-matter. Obstruction derives not from historical distance but from the presumption of sentimental proximity.

It should be emphasized, however, that the πρωτον ψευδος Benjamin discusses at the beginning of the second part of "Goethe's Elective Affinities" has nothing to do with the demand that "works" alone be examined and that "life"—along with letters and reported conversations—should be summarily ignored. For if such were the case, not only would "Goethe's Elective Affinities" be deemed invalid, so, too, would a significant share of the other writings in this volume, including and especially its other pivotal essay, namely, the article Benjamin wrote for the *Great Soviet Encyclopedia* of 1929. This collection of Benjamin's writings is broken into two parts in recognition of the difference between these two central essays. And what a difference it is! Though written only a few years apart, they seem worlds apart. A key term in Goethe's critical vocabulary, "polarity," immediately comes to mind as a description of their relation. The polarity in this case can be described in a variety of ways; but this is probably the most palpable: "Goethe's Elective Affinities" repeatedly refers to God, whereas the article written for the *Soviet Encyclopedia* does not. There is also a major difference between the two essays that has nothing to do with their author's intention. After much effort, Benjamin eventually found a publisher for "Goethe's Elective Affinities," whereas—except for a few excerpts, here translated for the first time—the article for the *Soviet Encyclopedia* never appeared in any language during Benjamin's lifetime.

The polarity that characterizes the relation between Benjamin's two longest writings on Goethe gives shape to this volume. Its intention, however, is not to capture everything Benjamin ever wrote about Goethe. This would probably be an impossible task, especially if by "everything," one wanted to include not only all of the places in his writings, published and unpublished, where he cites or refers to Goethe but also those where an allusion can be detected. This volume does not include a large number of essays, reviews, and reports where Benjamin writes something related to Goethe. And two other forms of communication are entirely absent from its table of contents: first, passages in Benjamin's correspondence that are concerned with Goethe, and second, portions of his radio programming, where Goethe becomes a partner in his attempt to popularize knowledge in a new medium.[8]

As for the texts translated in the volume, there is a simple principle of selection at work: the items in Part One converge on a project that eventually turned into a detailed discussion of *Elective Affinities*, whereas the items in Part Two develop out of the article he hoped to have translated in the *Soviet Encyclopedia*.[9] Only a single item in Part One, "Goethe's Elective Affinities," was published; the rest are notes, fragments, plans, an "outline," and several additions that Benjamin stored in an offprint of the published essay, probably with the intention of using them for its expansion into a book. Part Two, by contrast, includes only two texts whose publication Benjamin did not himself oversee: the encyclopedia article that begins Part Two and the two notes from the *Arcades Project* that conclude it. The rest of Part Two is composed of texts he published—most under his given name, one anonymously, and a few, after the Nazi seizure of power, under a pseudonym.

The aim of organizing the volume in this way is to open a door into the laboratory of Benjamin's work. The texts in Part One move toward a definitive, though not quite final, stage of completion; those in Part Two take their point of departure from a work that was not primarily intended for a German-speaking audience, appeared only in the form of a few excerpts, and was consciously undertaken as an experiment in the construction of an "object of materialist analysis" (6:321; MD 39)—where the concepts of both "object" and "analysis" derive in no small part from a Goethean theory of science. Part Two concludes with two notes that emphasize how thoroughly this theory, to borrow Arendt's apt formulation, "formed and informed" Benjamin's concept of history.

The remainder of the Introduction has no other aim than to help readers approach the texts themselves. This will be done in several ways relative to the writings under consideration. For "Goethe's Elective Affinities" and the article for the *Soviet Encyclopedia*, there are separate sections that describe the circumstances of their composition and publication (or, in the case of the article, non- or mispublication). These central sections are preceded by two that revolve around the moment Benjamin realized that he had "*much* to say about Goethe" (GB 1:442; 30 March 1918). And after a section concerned with the article Benjamin submitted to the *Soviet Encyclopedia*, there are several more that describe its effect on his later writings, including sundry contributions to the one hundredth anniversary of Goethe's death, commentaries on Goethe-related letters, a productive reencounter with "Goethe's Elective Affinities" ten years after its publication, and the return of Goethe's theory of science to the forefront of his theoretical itinerary.

2.

From the evidence of his surviving literary corpus, up until 1916, when Benjamin was beginning to decide on a theme for a doctoral dissertation, his reception of Goethe was, in blunt terms, nothing special. Of course, he, like most students who went through German educational institutions in the early twentieth century, read an assortment of Goethe's works, whose importance to German culture and the idea of Germanness during this period was inestimable. For a large segment of middle-class German Jews around 1900, Goethe's works were on the same level and even on the very same shelf as the Bible.[10] What of those works Benjamin read beyond the standards—this would include *Faust, Torquato Tasso, The Sorrows of Young Werther, Wilhelm Meister's Years of Apprenticeship*, and a variety of famous poems—cannot be determined with any degree of certainty. It is more difficult to trace the course of his reading in his earlier years than in his later ones, for the first few pages of his "Registry of Readings" have been lost. Begun around the time of his Abitur, it mostly includes books that he read from cover to cover; in a few places, he indicates where he stopped reading, and in still fewer, he gives a brief judgment on the work, such as "trash" (7:449; in this case, incidentally, referring to a book about Goethe's *Theory of Colors*). The extant pages of the registry begin with number 462, and Goethe's name first appears under 481, "Schiller and Goethe: *Correspondence*" (7:437; 253), which he probably read in 1916. (A complete list of the books and essays by and about Goethe in the registry can be found near the end of this volume.) Before 1916, four passages in his extant writings indicate that, though Goethe's work was important to Benjamin, it was nothing special. Here are the passages in chronological order:

> 1. "Sleeping Beauty," March 1911: In this contribution to the youth-movement journal *Der Anfang* (The Inception), which was also Benjamin's first published exercise in literary criticism, under the pseudonym of "Ardor-Berlin" he presents two protagonists of Goethean plays as representatives of youth. First, there is Tasso, who "stands guard over an idea—that of beauty" (2:10; EW 28)

but founders "by becoming disloyal to an aesthetic ideal" (2:11; EW 28). Then there is Faust, who can be considered "the most universal representative of youth" to the extent that his "entire life is youth" (2:11; EW 18). "In reference to Faust," Benjamin adds—and this is the conclusion of his treatment of Goethe—"it becomes clear why these heroes of youth are not allowed to 'get anywhere,' why they must perish in the moment of fulfillment or lead an eternal, unsuccessful struggle for ideals" (2:11; EW 28). Despite the exclamation mark added to the name "Goethe" when it is first introduced, the procedure Benjamin adopts for the display of a typology of youth allows no space for a Goethean difference. He is one among several major dramatists, each of whom follows Shakespeare. Thus does a discussion of a play by Schiller introduce the exposition of two by Goethe, which, in turn, leads to a reflection on three by Ibsen. All of the playwrights—but perhaps most of all Carl Spittler, with whom Benjamin concludes his essay—are counted among the "greatest in literature" (2:12; EW 29).

2. Abitur-essay, marked as "very good" (7:536), the spring of 1912: In order to receive their secondary school diploma, students were required to submit an essay on German literature in response to a prompt. For Benjamin's class, the prompt was formulated around an enigmatic (and perhaps sarcastic) remark made by Samson (Judges 14:18), here transferred to the relationship between Goethe and Franz Grillparzer: "Can It Be Said of Grillparzer's 'Sappho' That the Poet 'Plowed with Goethe's Calf'?"[11] The premise of Benjamin's essay is that both Goethe and Grillparzer are geniuses and therefore gravitate toward the portrayal of genius: "If in general it is valid to describe the works of great writers as confessions of their creators," the essay begins, alluding to a famous phrase from *Poetry and Truth*, "then we approach presentations of those who are genial as particularly intimate testimonies of poets. The problem of genius has forcefully lured almost all great dramatists out of their own nature. Aeschylus treated it in *Prometheus*, Shakespeare in *Hamlet*, Goethe in *Tasso* and *Faust*, Grillparzer in *Sappho*" (7:532).[12] The essay proceeds with a point-by-point comparison between two of these plays: "[Grillparzer] 'ploughed with Goethe's calf' by making Goethe's problem in *Tasso* into his own in *Sappho*" (7:532). What unites Tasso and Sappho is their common "prickliness" (7:533), which is rendered in several contrasting ways that are each inflected by their difference in gender. The official prompt alludes to this difference; but Benjamin, who may have calculated that this would be judged unfavorably, does not consider what Samson meant when he tells the "men of the city," "Had

you not plowed with my heifer, you would not have found out my riddle." Nor, perhaps for the same reason, does he reflect on the reason the German judges of scholastic aptitude would choose a bovine image, combined with a Sappho-themed work, to represent the relation of an Austrian writer to his German predecessor. The conclusion of Benjamin's essay is in any case that Goethe's representation of genius is considerably more complicated than Grillparzer's, and its image of genius can be seen in a range of nineteenth-century poets, including Friedrich Hölderlin and Georg Büchner, whereas "the beautiful and harmonious way in which Sappho takes charge of her problem"—an enigmatic (and perhaps sarcastic) statement in that she commits suicide at the end of the play—"may be rare or impossible in ordinary life" (7:536).

3. Italian Journey, early summer 1912: At the beginning of a diary in which Benjamin kept a record of a trip to Italy he took at the end of his secondary school education, he makes a remark that connects his journey with Goethe's: "The journey should emerge first from the diary that I intend to write. In this diary, I would like to let the collected essence, the quiet, self-evident synthesis that is required of an educational journey [*Bildungsreise*] and that constitutes its essence, develop itself. This, for me, is all the more indispensable, since no particular lived experiences stamped with any degree of power the impression of this entire journey. Nature and art uniformly culminated everywhere in what Goethe calls 'solidity.' And no adventures, no adventurous spirit of the soul presented a potent or charming background" (6:252).[13] It may be that Benjamin is alluding to a variety of Goethean themes in this brief introduction to his travel diary; but it seems more likely that Benjamin refers to the "solidity" of nature and art simply to emphasize that nothing striking or extraordinary is to be expected in the pages that follow.

4. "Teaching and Evaluation," May 1913: Instead of discussing anything by Goethe per se, another essay Benjamin published under a pseudonym in *Der Anfang* indicates the degree to which Goethe's works were treated within the sphere of secondary school education as a means of evaluation that was itself without any value. Taking *Hermann and Dorothea* as an example, Benjamin describes how students, "hour by hour," are required to outline each of its cantos without ever being asked to undertake an evaluation of the work as a whole: "For most students, however, it is evaluated. The title of the poem induces nausea" (2:36–37; EW 91–92). What remains of Goethe is a series of platitudes, beginning with his putative realism: "Goethe is by and large entirely realistic; one must only understand what he means" (2:35; EW 91).

8 INTRODUCTION

If, for Benjamin, there was anything special about Goethe, it would not find a place in this essay, which seeks to show how high school instruction, as it was configured at the time, would make anything in his work that transcended generic labels unrecognizable. The object of Benjamin's satire is, of course, his former teachers; but it also applies to his own treatments of Goethe, whom he accepts as a representative genius whose work is a "great confession" of what genius requires and entails.

3.

Sometime during the early years of the First World War, Benjamin ceased to be an acolyte of genius. This did not take the form of either a reversal of values or a leveling of differences. Rather, following a philological lead, Benjamin began to make a distinction between two words: *Genie*, which is generally translated as "genius," and *Genius*, which would in many contexts also be translated as "genius" but, for him, retains the Latin sense of the word, according to which it is associated with a localization of spirit. Here is how Benjamin describes the difference in a letter to Fritz Radt: "Genius [*Genie*] is not important but, rather, *Genius*. In the incomparable word *Genius*, the significance of which has been forgotten since around the time of Hölderlin and Wilhelm von Humboldt and Goethe, there lies in the clearest possible manner that purity of productivity that flows only from a clear consciousness of its matter-of-fact sources. Genius [*Genie*] remains problematic in a work and in creation: *Genius* is 'holy-sober'" (GB 1:298–99; 3 December 1915).[14] Benjamin draws the term "holy-sober" from Hölderlin's poem "Half of Life" and immediately thereafter directs Radt's attention to Hölderlin's "Song of the Germans," where *Genius* is said to "migrate like spring / From country to country."[15] The idea of a *Genius* that comes and goes stands, moreover, at the "center" (2:116; SW 1:28) of "Two Poems of Friedrich Hölderlin," whose introductory remarks prepare the way for "Goethe's Elective Affinities" insofar as they specify the object of analysis as the "exhibition" of a poem's "inner form," and the latter is equated, in turn, with "what Goethe designates as the matter [*Gehalt*]" (1:105; SW 1:18). When Benjamin proceeds to identify *Gehalt* with what he calls "the poetized" (*das Gedichtete*)—without noting that Goethe had used this term—he inadvertently indicates how much of Goethe's work remains, for him, terra incognita.[16]

Soon after formulating the distinction between *Genie* and *Genius* in his letter to Fritz Radt, Benjamin begins to describe conversations he conducted with a somewhat older doctoral student in philosophy whom he calls "the universal genius" (*das Universalgenie*) without ever revealing his name. This was Felix Noeggerath. It is not clear why Benjamin refuses to use Noeggerath's name in his letters from this period, nor does he ever suggest that it was "the universal genius"—often shortened to "the genius"— who helped him see the difference between *Genie* and *Genius*, but there can be little question that Noeggerath helped him gain an appreciation of Goethe's theory of science. The doctoral dissertation that Noeggerath was completing when the two of them first met, "Synthesis and System Concept in Philosophy" (University of Erlangen, 1916), begins with three carefully chosen epigraphs: the third and shortest is from Plato's *Symposium* (202 E), the middle one is a single sentence from the *Critique of Pure Reason* (B viii), while the first and longest derives from an essay Goethe wrote late in his life, "Analysis and Synthesis." It reads in full, including Noeggerath's ellipsis, "The main thing that one does not seem to consider with the exclusive application of analysis is that every analysis presupposes a synthesis. . . . A great danger that an analyst runs into is therefore this: when he applies his method where there is no underlying synthesis. His work then is altogether a labor of the Danaids, and we can find the saddest examples of this. For at bottom, he is conducting his entire enterprise only so as finally to attain once again the synthesis; but if no synthesis lies at the basis of the object on which he is working, he labors in vain to discover it" (WA II, 11:72).[17]

Guided by Goethe's theory of science, as set forth in "Analysis and Synthesis," Noeggerath seeks to radicalize the "system of philosophy" developed by Hermann Cohen, the cofounder of the Marburg school of neo-Kantianism, by showing how each part of his system has its own mode of objectivity. In the first fragment in this volume, "A Remark on Gundolf: Goethe," Benjamin can be seen to proceed along a parallel path, for his principal objection to Friedrich Gundolf's *Goethe* consists in a claim that accords with the passage from "Analysis and Synthesis" quoted above: Gundolf lacks an object, which means that his analysis is in vain, or, more exactly, that, qua analyst, he seizes on a totally "inadequate" object: "the individual Goethe" (48). The importance Benjamin ascribes to Goethe's theory of science can be gauged by the fact that he draws the sole epigraph for his own dissertation, "On the Concept of Art Critique in German Romanticism" (University of Bern, 1919), from the final paragraphs of "Analysis and Synthesis" (WA II, 11:72; 1:10; SW 1:116).

And he made a similar gesture at the end of the aforementioned letter to Radt, where he tells his friend that he and Radt's sister, Grete, are reading a book on Goethe and Plato (GB 1:292; 21 November 1915). The book Benjamin read together with Grete Radt was doubtless the doctoral dissertation that Elisabeth Rotten wrote under the directorship of Paul Natorp, the other cofounder of the Marburg school, and like Noeggerath, Rotten seeks to show in her dissertation an inner connection between Plato, Kant, and Goethe.[18]

By acknowledging Rotten's dissertation in the first footnote of the "esoteric afterword" (GB 2:26; 14 May 1919) to the published version of his own doctoral dissertation, Benjamin may have been sending something akin to a secret signal, on the one hand, to "the universal genius" and, on the other, to the siblings whose surname is contained in the suppressed name "Noeggerath," that is, Grete Radt and Fritz Radt, the latter of whom, as noted earlier, would later marry Jula Cohn, whose first name punctuates a poem Benjamin wrote around the time he was completing his dissertation, "Sonnet in the Night" (7:64–67; S 368–69). All of this is enigmatically connected with the situation in which Benjamin began to immerse himself in Goethe's scientific writings, probably for the first time, on a holiday trip in the winter of 1918. As a German national, Benjamin could not cross into Italy; but the Italian region of Switzerland was still accessible. Writing to Scholem from Locarno, he presents a comprehensive view of Goethe's life, work, and afterlife that is scarcely conceivable from the various remarks about the poet in his earlier writings:

> I must tell you that among several books that the southern climate here does not tolerate, regardless of how useful, necessary, and good they may be, I have here at least one that fits this climate exceedingly well: this is Goethe's *Maxims and Reflections*. Or, rather, one part of it in the unsurpassable, rigorously philological Weimar Sophien-Ausgabe. A precise immersion in these maxims and reflections fortifies in me the old opinion that only our generation [stands] critically over against Goethe, that only this generation gratefully follows him. The Romantics stood much too close to him for them to grasp more than a few *tendencies* of his creative work: above all, they did not see the moral dimension with which he wrung his *life* and did not know about his historical solitude. What's more, though, I am convinced that Goethe—at any rate, in his old age—was an entirely pure human being in whom no lie passed over his lips and into his pen. (GB 1:433; 23 February 1918)[19]

This is a striking passage, which can be broken down into a series of separate remarks, each more peculiar than its predecessor. And there is something strange beyond its content, namely, its recipient. As Benjamin was well aware, Scholem knew very little about Goethe: "We," Scholem writes many decades later, "had quite a number of conversations about Goethe; since I had read little of Goethe at the time, they were monologues on Benjamin's part, or at best monologues interrupted by questions."[20] Scholem's diary confirms this. He had read almost nothing of Goethe's work, and the little he did read "annoyed" him.[21] Around the time he received the letter from which the passage above is drawn, he identifies the source of this aversion to Goethe: "[He] never appealed to me. That must mean something very great, perhaps [it means] that the Jewish genius is in me somehow marked off from the Germanic world."[22] Because Scholem had so little knowledge of Goethe, he could scarcely have guessed that the book to which Benjamin refers, *Maxims and Reflections*, is not in fact the title of the book he is reading, for the Weimar Ausgabe—to which he prominently refers, even as it interrupts the flow of his discussion—breaks up the posthumously published *Maxims and Reflections* and scatters its content across ten volumes. Benjamin thus hides from his friend—who, it should be noted, was a student of mathematics and physics—the actual title of the book he is praising, *On Natural Science, General Theory of Nature*, which contains, among its many aphorisms, essays, maxims, and reflections, "Analysis and Synthesis." He may have done this so that Scholem would not respond to his remarks—if he was inclined to do so—with, say, a disquisition on the place of mathematics in contemporary natural science but would, instead, draw his response from his other field of emerging expertise, namely, Jewish traditions, especially mystical ones, where the image of "an entirely pure human being" would not be out of order.

The peculiarities of the passage go far beyond its addressee and the misidentification of the book to which Benjamin refers. Consider its localization of the reading experience—in sunny (wintertime, wartime) Locarno, where only certain kinds of books are bearable, specifically those that are not inward compensations for outward misfortune but are, on the contrary, cheerful confirmations of nature's favor. The "old opinion" to which Benjamin refers, moreover, is nowhere evident in his earlier remarks on Goethe; it seems to be a function of Benjamin's study of early German Romanticism, which, if true, belies the description of the "opinion" as "old." Or rather: the oldness of the opinion slips away from himself as opiner and becomes as old as Goethe himself. And the opinion itself is peculiar: the new generation of Goethe's readership finds itself in a position to follow him only because its members can distance themselves from his work through a critique that takes its starting point not from a review of his works but from an insight into his life that is anything but "critical" in the conventional sense of the word. Goethe, of course, had been subject to plenty of criticism about the way he conducted life, not least because he lived with Christiane Vulpius long before a marriage ceremony supposedly sanctified their union. For this reason, and many others, he was dubbed immoral, "pagan," un-Christian. As reported by Scholem, Benjamin was transfixed in his Swiss period by the inquisitorial spirit with which Alexander Baumgartner, a Jesuit priest who sought to escape the German "Kulturkampf" by taking refuge in Switzerland, meticulously prosecuted Goethe in the course of a three-volume biography.[23] And Benjamin had read those parts of Kierkegaard's *Stages on Life's Way* (7:437) in which Goethe's life, confined as it was to the "aesthetic sphere," without any awareness of its ethical, much less its religious counterpart, is presented as the paragon of modern self-deception about the nature of love.[24]

If Benjamin were simply inverting moral values and presenting Goethe as a supreme practitioner of something like "Renaissance self-fashioning" or "Nietzschean self-transcendence" in which his greatest work would turn out to be his style of life, then it would naturally follow that the rebelliousness of the young Goethe should be favored over the "renunciation" (*Entsagung*) that, according to the poet-dramatist-novelist-scientist-autobiographer-privy-councilor's own words, characterized its later half. In the passage under discussion, the opposite is true: it is the old Goethe rather than the younger one whom Benjamin is inclined to describe as "an entirely pure human being," that is, someone incapable of uttering a lie. Whatever compromises may have been required under the rubric of renunciation, there were, in other words, no consciously conceived falsehoods—for example, the falsehood that renunciation is somehow personally beneficial, socially beneficent, or artistically necessary. There is, by contrast, a kind of falsehood that reveals the characterization of Goethe qua renunciant. This Benjamin dubs "objective mendacity," a term he first formulates in response to Gundolf's widely celebrated book on Goethe's life qua work.[25] This new term obviates a well-established one: "ideology." Both terms express a distinction between lying, understood as a function of consciousness, and forms of falsehood that have little or nothing to do with the intention of an individual speaker or writer. The concept of ideology, for its part, was constructed in opposition to that of science. Correspondingly, Benjamin constructs the concept of objective mendacity in conjunction with a critical appropriation of a Goethean conception of science. Some of Goethe's currently most celebrated readers, especially Gundolf and Rudolf Borchardt, are concerned with objects that, lacking an underlying synthesis, do not really exist.[26] This is why their mendacity is "objective." And it is for this reason, too, that Benjamin seeks to develop a concept of critique that is permeated by the problem of truth.

4.

When Benjamin published his doctoral dissertation on *The Concept of Art Critique in German Romanticism*, he added an "esoteric afterword" that delineates the contrasting ways in which early German Romanticism and Goethe conceived and formulated their theories of art. In the first footnote to this afterword, he indicates that "no supporting documentation can be given within this narrow framework" (53) and directs attention to Elisabeth Rotten's dissertation while also emphasizing that his path differs from hers. Here, it seems, would be a propitious direction for a habilitation thesis: his telegraphic treatment of Goethe's theory of art could be expanded, and a seamless connection would thus be forged between the two principal items in a scholastic dossier that would lead to the acquisition of his *venia legendi*. This may have been in broad outlines Benjamin's intention: become a privatdozent through a thesis on Goethe. In the extant documentation, however, he says nothing to this effect. To be sure, the first large-scale study he undertook after the completion of his doctoral dissertation revolved around Goethe's 1809 novel, *Die Wahlverwandtschaften*, whose strange title derives from contemporaneous chemistry and is therefore generally translated as *Elective Affinities* rather than a more literal translation, which would be something like "The Kinships by Choice."[27] In his search for a position as privatdozent, the essay Benjamin eventually wrote on the novel came to be included in a dossier of his writings, and it seems as though he may have entertained some hope that this dossier would suffice for his "habilitation."[28] Even if this is so, it gives no indication as to why he focused his attention on *Elective Affinities*. There is nothing in his extant correspondence that provides even so much as a glimmer of an answer. It is in this void that readers of his work, with nothing else to hold on to, saw a "personal reason" for his otherwise inexplicable decision to write a hundred-page manuscript on a novel involving a dissolving marriage.

14   INTRODUCTION

A clue concerning the impetus for "Goethe's Elective Affinities" can be found, however, in the "Registry of Readings," where the novel is listed as 782 (253). In itself, of course, this says little; but the proximity of the entry to a slightly earlier one makes it possible to determine the approximate time when and precise place where Benjamin read *Elective Affinities*. Here is the entry, minus erroneous corrections that obscure the relevant information: "778) Alfred Seidel: The Metaphysics of Productive Forces" (7:449).[29] Seidel was a young scholar whose academic career eerily followed a trajectory akin to Benjamin's with a two- or three-year time gap. Like Benjamin, Seidel got involved in the Independent Student Association, and like Benjamin, he saw the educational theorist Gustav Wyneken as his teacher. After breaking with Wyneken because of his support of the war, Seidel, like Benjamin, became associated with Kurt Hiller's "activist" program, which, again like Benjamin, he soon found dissatisfying. Like Benjamin once again, Seidel matriculated at the University of Freiburg im Breisgau, where he studied with the neo-Kantian philosopher Heinrich Rickert, who eventually disappointed both of them.[30] In 1920—and here Seidel anticipates rather than follows Benjamin—he moved to the University of Heidelberg so that he could study under its renowned faculty of sociology, led by Max Weber, whose stature was only magnified by his untimely death in June of that year. Benjamin visited Heidelberg in the following summer at the invitation of Emil Lederer, managing editor of the *Archiv für Sozialwissenschaft und Sozialpolitik* (Archive for Social Science and Social Policy), which included Benjamin's essay "Toward the Critique of Violence" in its August issue.[31] A few weeks earlier Lederer had introduced Benjamin to the "sociological evenings" hosted by Weber's widow, Marianne, and his brother, Alfred, who was also Seidel's dissertation director. It was probably during one of these evenings that Benjamin met Seidel and soon thereafter acquired a copy of the exposé of the latter's dissertation, that is, the aforementioned "Metaphysics of Productive Forces."[32]

Heidelberg may have had no special relation to Goethe; but its university acquired such a relation to Goethe studies, not least because it was the institutional home of Friedrich Gundolf, whom Benjamin, as it happens, encountered during his visit: "Gundolf seemed to me tremendously weak and harmless in his personal impression, entirely different than in his books" (GB 2:171; 20 July 1921). The encounter with the author of *Goethe* may have been one of the reasons Benjamin decided to read *Elective Affinities*, which is the first literary text of Goethe's recorded on his register of books since number

603, namely, *Faust, Part Two* (7:443; 253), a text he read for the first time in the winter of 1919, "with eyes and ears open" (GB 2:11; 19 January 1919). There is, however, another, more direct impetus for Benjamin's choice of *Elective Affinities* as reading material. In conjunction with his visit to Heidelberg, he prepared a set of notes under the title "Capitalism as Religion" (6:100–102; TCV 90–92) that takes shape as a response to the argument Weber developed in *Gesammelte Aufsätze zur Religionssoziologie* (Complete Essays on the Sociology of Religion; listed at 6:102; TCV 92), the first chapter of which consists in his influential study of *The Protestant Ethic and the Spirit of Capitalism*. Benjamin must therefore have come across the following passage, enigmatic and yet crucial for Weber's argument, where the title of Goethe's novel—placed in quotation marks but not acknowledged as a literary work whose title is borrowed from an emergent natural science—is appropriated for the purpose of promoting a science of society that will revise and replace any program of research, especially those associated with Marx, that are based on the assumption that the relationship between economic and ideological structures is determinative, unilateral, and thus, in brief, nonelective: "In view of the prodigious confusion of interdependent influences between the material basis, the forms of social and political organization, and the spiritual subject-matter of the Reformation's cultural epochs, it is only possible to proceed at first with an investigation as to whether, and at what points, specific 'elective affinities' ['*Wahlverwandtschaften*'] between certain forms of religious belief and vocation-determinative ethics are recognizable."[33]

Prompted by this and similar passages in Weber—or perhaps the discussion of these passages during the "sociological evenings"—Benjamin read or reread *Elective Affinities* in late August or early September 1921. A response to the social-scientific appropriation of the novel's title can in any case be discerned in the opening paragraph of "Capitalism as Religion," where Benjamin proposes an image that runs counter to the one Weber appropriated from Goethe: the detachability of "affinities" or "relationships" (*Verwandtschaften*) characterized by "choice" or "election" (*Wahl*) is replaced by the tightness of an all-encompassing "net" (6:100; TCV 90). In light of *Elective Affinities* itself, detached from Weber's appropriation of the term, a new project crystallizes, one that gives Benjamin a chance to collect, develop, and systematically organize several lines of inquiry that he had pursued over the last several years. These lines move in three general directions, two of which already intersect with his reading of Goethe. The first direction centers on the relation of

16 INTRODUCTION

truth to cognition, where the Goethean idea of science forms an indispensable touchstone. The second concerns the theory of art and the corresponding problem of construing a concept of its critique: Friedrich Schlegel and Friedrich von Hardenberg (Novalis) insist on the possibility and necessity of the concept of art critique, while Goethe, as Benjamin argues in the appendix to his doctoral dissertation (53–62), does not. A third line of inquiry—which had previously been unrelated to Goethe—focuses on the relation between beauty and semblance, understood as categories of the aesthetic akin to the "pure concepts of the understanding" (A 76; B 102) that Kant had derived from a table of judgments. In reading *Elective Affinities*, Benjamin discovered a figure that allows him to advance this last line of inquiry beyond the two unpromising directions it had hitherto taken: formal-logical tables (see 66 and 68), on the one hand, and phenomenological-eidetic exercises (71–72), on the other. The figure in question is, of course, Ottilie, whose death at the end of the novel forms the focal point for the third and final part of the essay. The enigmatic theme of "expiring semblance" (154), concretized in Ottilie, disengages the evolving project from its originating impetus—so much so that the latter seems to disappear.[34]

Heidelberg is related to "Goethe's Elective Affinities" in still another way, marked in the essay perhaps by one of its final citations (159). For it was in Heidelberg that Benjamin met the publisher Richard Weißbach, who, much to Benjamin's surprise, proposed that he edit a journal. The initial proposal, it seems, was that he take over the editorship of *Die Argonauten*, which Weißbach had published since 1914 with Ernst Blass as editor. The final, much-delayed issue of "The Argonauts"—the title derives from *Faust, Part Two* (WA I, 15:126)—contained two contributions by Benjamin, "Fate and Character" (2:171–79; SW 1:201–6) and "Dostoevsky's Idiot" (2:237–41; SW 1:78–81). During his visit to Weißbach, Benjamin made a counterproposal: he would edit an entirely new journal, whose title would be *Angelus Novus*.[35] As Benjamin tells Scholem in a letter written from Heidelberg (GB 2:178; 4 August 1921), the aim of the journal originated in plans he developed with his close friend, the poet Fritz Heinle, in July 1914; a month later, in apparent protest of the general conscription order that began the First World War, Heinle and Friederike (Rika) Seligson, the sister of Benjamin's close friend, Carla Seligson, killed themselves. Despite the novelty designated by the title he chose for the journal, *Angelus Novus*, it was conceived from the beginning in recognition of its own missed beginning, evident in the absence of its coeditor, and something of this "missingness" may have been an element in the conception of Benjamin's original plan for his own contribution to the first issue of the old-new journal: "I have myself been busy," he tells Weißbach in a draft of a letter, "with a critique of the Goethean elective affinities that I am preparing for the Angelus" (GB 2:191; 15 September 1921).[36]

The metacritical distinction between critique and commentary that begins the essay Benjamin would eventually write about "the Goethean elective affinities"—minus "critique" in its title—reverberates with the concept of critique with which he introduces the task of the new journal: "Since, for almost a hundred years, every unwashed feuilleton in Germany has been allowed to dress itself up as critique, it is doubly demanded that the critical word regain its force. . . . [Critique] must give precisely that account of the truth of works that art, no less than philosophy, demands" (2:242; SW 1:293). The opening paragraph of "Goethe's Elective Affinities," whereby critique is connected to truth, can thus be seen in this context as the epitome of the program that Benjamin wanted to develop not so much for himself as for a generation of writers and thinkers whose principal organ would be a journal under his editorship. There was a practical problem, however: because the journal would not pay attention to the fluctuating tastes of the reading public (see GB 2:182–85; 8 August 1921), it would be able to distribute only a limited number of copies, and the size of each issue had to remain limited as well. With so "much" (GB 1:442; 30 March 1918) to say about Goethe, Benjamin's reflections outgrew these constraints. His reference to a "critique of the Goethean elective affinities" in a draft of a letter to Weißbach had to be replaced with a shorter contribution by the time he posted the official letter. In this case his choice was obvious: the essay he was preparing in conjunction with his translation of Baudelaire's *Tableaux parisiens*, also intended for Weißbach's press. It is at this point, moreover, that he may have drafted the opening remarks of this essay in which he formulates in a stark form the editorial guidelines for the new journal: "With respect to an artwork or a form of art, consideration of the audience never proves productive for their cognition" (4:9; SW 1:253).

In a letter to Scholem, Benjamin therefore places "The Task of the Translator" at the end of a table of contents for the first issue and then indicates why the text he had originally planned as his contribution had to be replaced. In brief, it will contain too much: "I have to draft my critique of the elective affinities [or, critique of *Elective Affinities*], which is, for me, equally important

18   INTRODUCTION

as an exemplary critique and as a groundwork for certain purely philosophical expositions, amidst which there is to be found what I have to say about
Goethe" (GB 2:208; 8 November 1921). As an addendum, a few weeks later,
he adds a further description of his critique-in-progress. Here, too, it corresponds to the plans for the new journal, even if the expanding essay cannot
find a place in the inaugural issue. In his "Announcement of the Journal," Benjamin does not shy away from calling the critique in question "annihilating"
but emphasizes that the annihilation can succeed as critique only if it looks
toward "greater contexts," on the one hand, and concentrates on "individual
works of art" (4:9; SW 1:253), on the other. The revision of "A Remark on
Gundolf: Goethe" (47–49) into the paragraph that begins the second section of the final essay (122–27) is an exemplary version of this coordination
of expansion-annihilation-concentration: "As of now, I have no rest until
I'm finished with my work on *Elective Affinities*. The legally binding conviction and execution of Friedrich Gundolf is to be found therein" (GB 2:212;
27 November 1921).

However much Benjamin may have wanted to rest at the end of November 1921, his work on *Elective Affinities* was far from over. And as he tells
Weißbach, beyond the contents of the initial issue, there is much else that he is
preparing for the new journal, including "a novella, 'The Death of the Lovers,'
and from me a large-scale and, as I hope, not only essential but also surprising
critique of the Goethean elective affinities" (GB 2:218–19; 3 December 1921).[37]
So this was still the plan: complete the essay and publish it in his own journal.
For more than a year, he gives his correspondents, principally Scholem, brief
accounts of his progress toward this goal. At the end of 1921, he emphasizes
that the work required to prepare the essay for publication will be slow and
hard going (GB 2:224; 17 December 1921). A few weeks later, he glimpses an
end to his labors and recommends that Scholem begin to read the novel so
that he will be prepared to receive its critique (see GB 2:236; 15 January 1922).
In February, however, Benjamin is so far from being finished that he emphasizes the degree to which his work impedes his ability to respond to letters in a
timely manner (GB 2:242; February 1922). Silence, then, for six months, during which time he continues to write letters but says nothing about what he is
otherwise working on. Finally, in September, he includes a manuscript of the
essay in a letter to Scholem that is primarily concerned with other potential
contributions (GB 2:266; 11 September 1922). This manuscript—designated
as M² by the editors of the *Gesammelte Schriften* (1:840; see 311)—was not,

however, a fair copy, prepared for immediate publication, and the completion process continues as Benjamin begins to look for a new publisher under an editor who would be someone other than himself.

Forced to undertake this search after Weißbach proves unwilling to support the new journal, Benjamin proceeds in two directions. On the one hand, he contacts the publishing house of Paul Cassirer. He may have asked Cassirer whether he would be interested in publishing the journal, with his own essay as a sample of the kind of work that would find a home in the journal; or—and this seems more likely—he may simply have asked whether Cassirer-Verlag would be able to publish the essay on its own (see GB 2:311; 1 February 1923). After studying it for three months, Cassirer declines, citing "technical difficulties" (GB 2:328; 2 April 1923). In this case, too, the difficulties may have been related to the essay in isolation (for it is longer than the usual contributions to a collection of essays and shorter than the usual monograph) or the production of a new journal in 1923, during a period in which Germany was suffering its year of hyperinflation; indeed, this may have been what Cassirer meant when he referred to "technical difficulties."[38] In any case, soon after Cassirer said "no," Benjamin turned his attention to a new scholarly journal, *Deutsche Vierteljahrsschrift für Literaturwissenschaft und Geistesgeschichte* (German Quarterly for Literary Studies and the History of Ideas), the first issue of which had recently appeared under the coeditorship of Paul Kluckhohn, a professor of history and literature in Münster, and Erich Rothacker, a privatdozent in the philosophy department in Heidelberg.

When, in February 1923, Benjamin left a sanatorium in Austria, he did not take the most direct route to Berlin but, instead, took something like a tour of Germany, the result of which can be found in a section of *One-Way Street* titled "Imperial Panorama: A Tour through German Inflation" (4:94–101; SW 1:450–55). Heidelberg was one of his stops, and there he met Rothacker. Beyond a letter to his friend Florens Christian Rang in which he says of the *Angelus Novus* project that it is defunct "at least for now" (GB 2:315; 23 February 1923), there is no trace of his brief layover in Heidelberg. Rothacker, though, describes the meeting in a letter to Kluckhohn: "Recently, by the way, a certain Herr Benjamin was with me. He's written a serious book on art-critique in Romanticism (a type of religious Jew, very talented, very serious), and he offered me a text on *Elective Affinities* of around 100 pages; shortening is excluded; the manuscript is still with [Franz] Schultz. He prizes it [his text] purely as a work of art and believes he has achieved a precise grasp of

Goethe's style, especially the late style, *as* style; now he's turning to [Goethe's] *Pandora*. He also has an essay on the 'art of translation' in preparation. He wanted to give me the *Elective Aff[inities]* essay at some point to see if I could do something with it. I'm very eager."[39] When Rothacker received the essay, presumably from Schultz, his eagerness was rewarded: "Yesterday, for half the night, against my usual disposition, Benjamin's work wholly captivated me, and although I admit that I did not understand everything upon the first cursory reading, I must still say: if we are to support young talents—and if ever [it is to be] Benjamin—we have a duty here. The essay made a strong impression on me."[40]

Thus Rothacker writes to Kluckhohn in a letter dated 6 April 1923. He adds a few caveats, most especially concerning the attack on Gundolf, who is, after all, his senior colleague in Heidelberg and whose position commands respect. Even as Rothacker makes clear that this attack is inappropriate in terms of modern scholarly forms, he admits that Benjamin's criticism of Gundolf's *Goethe* plays an essential function in the development of the argument. He then singles out several striking passages: "I am eager to hear what you have to say. Particularly concerning 'neglection' (15) [110], 'Olympian' (16) [111], 'fear of life' (19) [116], and I found especially significant [echoing what Benjamin must have said during the meeting] Goethe's 'late style' (29ff.) [130] and 'novella' (30f.) [130], even their formulation, though, to be sure, it is obscure." As in his previous letter, Rothacker does not fail to include a comment on Benjamin's Jewishness, this time with a sharper edge: "Strange, these altogether rigorous moral Jews (including Cohen quotes!) who have gone through Goethe and Hölderlin."[41]

Kluckhohn seems to have disagreed, and as the senior editor—he was the equivalent of an "associate" professor in contrast to Rothacker's adjunct status—his lack of enthusiasm was sufficient to keep the essay out of the journal. Writing the official letter of rejection, Rothacker keeps open the possibility that parts of the essay could be made into a publishable contribution and indicates why the attack on Gundolf's *Goethe*, which begins the second part, was not appropriate for a contemporary scholarly journal. Overall, the official verdict can be read as an elaborate version of a standard form of rejection that, as Rothacker already knew, Benjamin would immediately reject, namely, revise and resubmit.[42] Benjamin is accused of making a mistake typical of young scholars, who are always trying to cram everything they want to say into a single piece of writing. From Rothacker's slightly elevated position in the academic hierarchy, he recommends that Benjamin identify the most salient points, especially in the first part, consolidate its argument, and use the rest of the manuscript as material for future projects. There is no evidence Benjamin replied, and indeed he had no need to do so: Rothaker understood—and had told Kluckhohn as much—that he had no intention of cutting down the essay.[43]

By a curious coincidence, the letter in which Rothacker expresses his highly favorable impression of "Goethe's Elective Affinities" includes a brief remark about his most recent communications with Martin Heidegger. Rothacker was eager to enlist Heidegger for the new journal and had been in communication about a contribution to the *Deutsche Vierteljahrsschrift* for several months, if not significantly longer.[44] Apropos the letter from April 1923, Heidegger had recently told Rothacker that he was still not yet in a position to submit a contribution, whose topic varied over the course of their correspondence. He had initially proposed an essay on "The Ontological Foundations of Late Medieval Anthropology and the Theology of the Young Luther," but in late 1923, he changed course and proposed a review article about a recently published volume of the correspondence between Wilhelm Dilthey and Paul Graf York von Wartenburg. When the editors of the journal finally received Heidegger's would-be contribution, they encountered a manuscript that stretched across some seventy-five pages, thus approximating the size of Benjamin's own submission.[45] In this case, too, Rothacker was eager to accept the manuscript, but Kluckhohn apparently was not. With respect to Heidegger, Rothacker's eagerness seems to have been based more on the rumors of Heidegger's coming fame than on the quality of the manuscript's contribution to literary studies or the history of ideas; but the outcome was the same. Both essays failed to appear in the new journal.

And there are still more coincidences. In 1912 and 1913 Benjamin and Heidegger had together taken classes and seminars in Freiburg taught by Rickert, who had subsequently moved to Heidelberg, where he served as Rothacker's immediate superior in the department of philosophy.[46] While Rothacker and Kluckhohn were in the process of deciding on Benjamin's and Heidegger's submissions, Rickert submitted a long essay of his own, which was strangely like both of theirs: like Benjamin's, it was concerned with a single work of Goethe's; and it treated this work in direct correspondence with another article published in the *Deutsche Vierteljahrsschrift*, indeed its very first article, to which Heidegger, for his part, would refer in the work from which his own would-be contribution to the journal was drawn.[47] Rickert's essay had to be published, for he was a renowned professor and made clear that a much more established journal would doubtless accept it if, for some reason, the editors of the upstart publication demurred.[48] Were it not for this overlong and forgettable essay, there may have been enough room for the work of his former students, Benjamin and Heidegger. All of these overlapping coincidences pose a series of questions, beginning with ones around the interaction between Rothacker and Heidegger, especially since the correspondence of the former to the latter has been lost (or is perhaps still in the Heidegger archive, waiting to be found). Here are a few: Did Rothacker ever discuss "Goethe's Elective Affinities" with Heidegger, for instance, when the two of them were slated to meet in March 1924?[49] If so, did Rothacker communicate the positive impression it made on him or indicate something of the reason for his desire to encourage the work of its "talented" author—for instance, Benjamin's treatment of *Lebensangst* ("fear of life"), to which he had earlier directed Kluckhohn? And if so, was Heidegger then tempted to read it when it finally appeared? Regardless of the answer to these and similar questions, the paths of the two former students of Rickert, which often diverged in diametrically opposite directions, did so here as well: Heidegger absorbed his review article into his forthcoming book, whereas Benjamin had no such option, for his essay was an integral whole.

After the rejections from Cassirer as well as Rothacker, Benjamin was prepared to follow the advice of his friend Florens Christian Rang, who had been proposing that the essay would find a home with *his* friend, the esteemed poet, dramatist, and librettist Hugo von Hofmannsthal, who had successfully inaugurated a new journal under a title that, like the one Benjamin planned, heralded its novelty: *Neue Deutsche Beiträge* (New German Contributions). Thus began a delicate interplay among the four parties: Rang, Hofmannsthal, Benjamin, and the essay. The correspondence among the first three about the last one can be seen in retrospect as a process akin to the chemical reaction from which Goethe took the title of his novel: with Rang as catalyst, the essay is detached from its author and reattached to Hofmannsthal as publisher. The final stage of the process was nearly instantaneous. Hofmannsthal received the essay in early November 1923, soon after which he wrote the following to Rang: "I took a look into the manuscript on *Elective Affinities* and felt myself so powerfully attracted that I intend to use the rest of the afternoon attentively to familiarize myself with its first pages."[50]

A few weeks later, after reading the entire essay, Hofmannsthal appraises its status:

> Please do not expect me to go into much detail about the absolutely incomparable essay by Benjamin, which you were kind enough to entrust to me. I can only say that it has made an epoch in my inner life and that my thoughts have scarcely been able to detach themselves from it. What strikes me as marvelous—speaking of the seemingly "outward"—is the lofty beauty of the presentation in the context of such an unprecedented penetration into the mystery; this beauty springs from a completely secure and pure thinking, of which I know few examples. Should this man be younger, perhaps much younger than myself, I would be profoundly struck by this maturity. The connection of the deepest kind with your world seized me; what beneficence it is to become aware of such things in a world torn apart to the most frightening degree. Do I thus obtain through you the earnestly requested permission to publish this work in the *Beiträge*?[51]

Writing a few years later, near the end of life, Hofmannsthal's sense of the essay's uniqueness was undiminished. The following remarks appear in a letter of recommendation he wrote in English on Benjamin's behalf: "His strength of penetration in treating a literary subject is extraordinary. He does not try to make you *see* his object, but he instantly throws you into the dephts [*sic*] of the matter (dephts [*sic*] scarcely attainable to the spirit of an ordinary scholar) and from there he makes you feel the relationship, yea the unity of things which on the surface seem far from having to do with one another" (7:878).[52] Benjamin became aware of Hofmannsthal's eagerness to publish "Goethe's Elective Affinities" at the end of 1923, at which point their correspondence began. Hofmannsthal had promised Rang that it would appear in the next two issues of the journal, which indeed it did; the first issue, containing the first two parts of the essay, was published in April; but the second, containing the concluding part, was delayed until January of the following year. Beyond the delay of the final part, Benjamin had only one complaint: Hofmannsthal's publisher, the Munich-based Verlag der Bremer Presse, did not send him the agreed-upon number of copies (GB 2:457; 25 May 1924).

In conjunction with an attempt to procure a stipend from the newly founded Hebrew University in Jerusalem, Benjamin produced two curricula vitae in 1928 that include brief descriptions of what he sought to accomplish in "Goethe's Elective Affinities."[53] They are both worth quoting in full; at the same time, however, they should probably be understood with the

24 INTRODUCTION

same precaution that guided Benjamin in approaching the principal motivations for Goethe's later reflections on *Elective Affinities*: "He had his work
to defend—that was one. He had to preserve its secret—that was the other"
(108). Without further commentary, here are the two passages:

> Gradually, the interest in the philosophical matter of literary writing and forms
> of art came to the foreground for me and ultimately found its expression in the
> object of my dissertation. This direction also dominated my subsequent efforts,
> in which I concerned myself with an ever more concrete connection to details,
> not only for reasons of exactness but also for the subject-matter of my literary
> investigations. The thought of illuminating a work altogether from within itself is
> what I attempted to accomplish in my text, "Goethe's Elective Affinities." (6:216)

> Just as Benedetto Croce, by dismantling the doctrine of artistic forms, cleared the
> path to the individual concrete artwork, so my previous attempts have sought to
> pave the way to the artwork by dismantling the doctrine of the territorial char
> acter of art. Their shared programmatic intention is to promote the integration
> process of science, which increasingly breaks down the rigid walls between disci
> plines, as characterized by the concept of science of the previous century, through
> an analysis of the artwork that recognizes in the work an integral expression—not
> territorially restricted in any respect—of the religious, metaphysical, political, and
> economic tendencies of an epoch. . . . Such an approach seems to me, above all,
> a precondition for every emphatically physiognomic apprehension of whatever
> in works of art makes them incomparable and unique. In this respect, it stands
> closer to the eidetic than the historical approach to phenomena. (6:218–19)

The second passage, taken from the second curriculum vitae, was meant
to apply more to the *Origin of the German Trauerspiel* than "Goethe's Elective
Affinities," but even as Benjamin turned much of his attention to the longer
study, first as his habilitation thesis, then as a book that had to be prepared for
its publisher, he did not cease his work on *Elective Affinities*. Thus, for instance,
he compiled a list of relatively obscure discussions of the novel, ranging from
a book-length treatise on its "world-historical significance" from 1838 to a
brief inquiry into its sources that appeared in 1902.[54] Several sets of notes
also seem to stem from the period in which, having sent Hofmannsthal a fair
copy—which no longer survives—Benjamin was awaiting its publication.
These are to be found in the texts translated here as "The Sacramental Also
Turns into the Mythic" (84–85) and "With Reference to François-Poncet"

(86–87). The Verlag der Bremer Presse produced a few offprints of the complete essay, one of which came into Benjamin's possession. He placed the two additional notes into his copy while also making small changes in numerous places. The reason for this is clear: he expected to publish the essay in book form; he even had a contract for its publication from the Berlin-based Rowohlt publishing house, which in 1928 would release both *Origin of the German Trauerspiel* and *One-Way Street*. The back cover of both books lists all the others by the same author, including the following item: "*In preparation*: GOETHE'S ELECTIVE AFFINITIES / Berlin 1928 / Ernst Rowohlt Verlag" (WuN 8:78).[55] By this time, however, Benjamin was deeply involved in another Goethe project that had unexpectedly arisen two years earlier.

5.

The other project was prompted by a communication from Moscow. In the spring of 1926, Benjamin received an invitation to write an article on Goethe for a forthcoming volume of the Большая советская энциклопедия (*Great Soviet Encyclopedia*). The letter containing the commission has not been preserved. Nor is there any clear evidence of how and why Benjamin was chosen for this task. None of his earlier writings, least of all "Goethe's Elective Affinities," suggests that he would be well suited to present Goethe in Russian for an encyclopedia that aims to be a compendium of knowledge from A to Я in accordance with—to use Benjamin's term, perhaps taken directly from the commission—"Marxist doctrine" (GB 3:133; 5 April 1926). In 1924 and 1925, he had coauthored texts with two writers with close connections to Soviet-supported communist parties, Asja Lācis ("Naples," 4:307–16; SW 1:414–21) and Bernhard Reich ("Revue or Theater," 4:796–802), who were themselves a couple, though their marriage was not officially registered until decades later.[56] In a memoir Lācis published in the early 1970s, she indicates that Benjamin came to the attention of the officials in charge of the literary department of the *Soviet Encyclopedia* through Reich; but since at least one other element in her account of the article is erroneous, this, too, may be mistaken.[57] It is probably not a mistake, however, to say that Benjamin's interest in pursuing the commission was partly determined by his pursuit of Lācis, whose hold over this writing is etched into the dedication lines of *One-Way Street* (1828): "This street is named / *Asja Lacis Street* / After her who / *As an engineer* / Breached it in the author" (4:83; SW 1:445).

Benjamin also had other reasons to accept the commission. One of these derives from the origin of his earlier Goethe project. If, as previously proposed in this Introduction, the decision to write a critique of *Elective Affinities* emerged from the same Heidelberg-saturated circumstances that gave rise to "Capitalism as Religion," then an article for the *Soviet Encyclopedia* would represent an auspicious opportunity to return to the point where two critical projects parted ways. In other words, not only would the commission give Benjamin a chance to reexamine the material that informs "Goethe's Elective Affinities" in light of his interest in the theory of historical materialism; it would also allow him a place where he could rethink the complex of concerns that led him to identify the figure of the "Übermensch" with the "prototype of capitalist religious thought" (6:101; TCV 91) and interpret "cares" (*Sorgen*) as a "mental illness appropriate to the capitalistic epoch" (6:102; TCV 92). Though neither of these terms is directly associated with Goethe in "Capitalism as Religion," they both play pivotal roles in the construction of *Faust*—the first in its opening scene, the second in its final act.

Even if, considered solely for themselves, the two central texts in this volume, the essay published in *Neue Deutsche Beiträge* and the article destined for Большая советская энциклопедия, suggest the Goethean concept of polarity, the relation between the essay and the article might be better understood through a concept that, for Goethe, represents its own polar counterpart, namely, the concept of "elevation" or "intensification" (*Steigerung*)—which, as it happens, is also a term Benjamin introduces into his analysis of capitalism as a religion. If it is difficult to view "Goethe" as an intensification of "Goethe's Elective Affinities," this may be due in large part to a difference between their intended readerships: the article had to be written for the education of an emergent public with which Benjamin was wholly unfamiliar, whereas the essay was conceived as a contribution to a new journal that was deliberately to have paid no attention to the inclination of its readers and was published in a new journal whose educational function, signaled by the central word in its title—"German"—was far removed from the Communist International direction that was supposed to govern the new *Soviet Encyclopedia*.

Benjamin's initial response to the commission, expressed in a letter to Scholem in the spring of 1926, indicates how unexpected it was and how little prepared he was for its fulfillment: "A curious commission will soon wring from me three-hundred lines, as ordered. The new *Great Soviet Encyclopedia* wishes to hear from me with this number of lines on Goethe from the standpoint of Marxist doctrine. The divine impudence that lies in the acceptance of such a commission appeals to me, and I think myself able to make up something appropriate. We will see (yet indeed)" (GB 3:133; 5 April 1926). In a follow-up letter, Benjamin makes the impudence of his acceptance into a positive characteristic; he will not respect or abide by the scholarly protocols that guide "literary history" but will, instead, engage in a certain experimentation—he calls it "improvisation"—that, as such, has no guarantee of success: "So far as I know, 'literary history,' at least the more recent kind, has no right to make much ado about its methods, such that a 'Marxist' approach is just as much an opportunity for improvisation as any other. What this approach consists in, and what it teaches, this I will have to establish, and if (as I am inclined to assume) 'literary history' in the strict sense has as little reality from the perspective of Marxism as from any well-thought-out one, this does not preclude that my attempt to treat an object from such an angle—an object to which I will otherwise scarcely return—can result in an interesting something that in the worst case the editorial commission may then confidently reject" (GB 3:162; 5 May 1926).[58]

In the fall of 1926, Benjamin traveled to Moscow, where he met up with Lācis and Reich. He also carried along a "schema" for his article on Goethe, presumably the "three-hundred lines" that he had mentioned to Scholem. Shortly before leaving, in a letter to Hofmannsthal, he expressed both skepticism and confidence about the article-in-progress: skepticism, since, as he writes, it would be a "miracle" if his "Goethe image" were able to "capture the contemporary Russian reader," yet confidence, insofar as the project is "not only possible but also supremely productive" (GB 3:208; 30 October 1926). From the evidence of his *Moscow Diary*, his preliminary efforts at fulfilling the commission met with a chilly reception. Does this mean his confidence was misplaced? One of the early scenes in the *Moscow Diary* indicates how little hope there was for a successful reception of his article while simultaneously showing that the pursuit of the problem contained in the commission could be valuable in itself. When first visiting the offices of the *Soviet Encyclopedia*, accompanied by Reich, Benjamin encountered a "well-meaning young man" who examined his schema: "His intellectual insecurity immediately became evident. There were many things in my project that intimidated him, and he finally ended up recommending an image of life painted against a sociological background" (6:321; MD 39). Benjamin's response to this befuddled recommendation captures the outlines of the problem, the solution to which

28   INTRODUCTION

may not be successful in terms appropriate for an encyclopedia article; but the attempt may be productive nevertheless: "One cannot, however, in principle depict a writer's life in a materialist manner but, rather, only show its historical aftereffect. In fact, if one abstracts from its afterlife, an artist's existence and even his purely temporal oeuvre can offer no object whatsoever for materialist analysis" (6:321; MD 39).

Benjamin's formulation not only consists in a reiteration and transformation of what he says about "the history of works" (92) at the beginning of "Goethe's Elective Affinities"; it also alludes to a section of the book Benjamin read in Locarno in the final winter of the war, namely, Goethe's "Analysis and Synthesis," from which he drew the epigraph for his dissertation. (The epigraph to the "Cognition-Critical Preface" that begins his *Origin of the German Trauerspiel* is also drawn from one of Goethe's contributions to the theory of science; see 1:207; O 1.) Analysis, Goethe argues, can proceed only on the basis of a genuine synthesis, which must be categorically distinguished from agglomeration: "If no synthesis lies at the basis of the object on which [the analyst] is working, he labors in vain to discover it" (WA II, 11:72).[59] Benjamin alludes to this conception of the relation between synthesis and the object of a genuine analysis near the beginning of "Goethe's Elective Affinities," where he locates a "new approach" in late Goethe, beginning with the 1809 novel, an approach that turns toward "a synthetic intuition of subject-matters" (93). In working out the preliminary draft of the encyclopedia article, Benjamin follows Goethe in this respect: he is trying out a "new approach," associated with Marxism, which is turned not toward "synthetic intuitions of subject-matters" but, rather, toward a single theory: historical materialism. One thing, for Benjamin, is clear about this theory: it is not, like intuition, characterized by immediacy. For this reason, he completes his account of the altercation with the "young man" at the offices of the *Soviet Encyclopedia* as follows: "Here [in the young man's recommendation that he paint a picture of Goethe with a sociological background] is probably the same unmethodological universality and immediacy that characterizes the totally idealistic, metaphysical formulations in Bukharin's *Introduction to Historical Materialism*" (6:321; MD 39).

Several weeks later, Benjamin returned to the encyclopedia offices, again accompanied by Reich. They inadvertently encountered a man who is neither young nor particularly "well meaning," namely, Karl Radek. At that moment—January 1927, a few months before Radek would publicly mock

Stalin for proposing "Socialism in One Country" and soon thereafter suffer the consequences—he enjoyed a wide range of influence, far wider, it seems, than anyone else Benjamin met during his trip to Moscow.[60] Benjamin had revised and expanded his initial "schema" into what he called his "exposé," which Radek happened to read: "By accident, it was precisely Radek who had come by [the offices of the encyclopedia], had seen the manuscript on the table and picked it up. Suspicious, he inquired as to who had written it. 'The phrase "class conflict" occurs ten times on every page,' [he said]. Reich pointed out that this was not the case and said that it is impossible to deal with Goethe's activity, which had developed during a time of intense class conflict, without using the term. Radek: 'The point is to introduce it at the right moment.' The prospects for the acceptance of the exposé are hereafter extremely slim" (6:366; MD 81).

As Benjamin immediately adds, Radek's negative assessment was far worse for Reich than it was for him, for Radek could damage Reich's position, whereas he could only cancel Benjamin's commission. Later that day, Benjamin told Lācis about Radek's response. He was annoyed that she assumed that Radek must somehow be right: "Her words," Benjamin explains, "merely expressed a cowardice and a need unconditionally to bend, at whatever cost, in whatever direction the wind may be blowing" (6:366; MD 81). Benjamin left Lācis, who was expecting Reich and did not want to overhear his description of what happened in the offices of the encyclopedia; she then returned to Benjamin, who finally read her the exposé. She responded favorably, judging it "clear and matter-of-fact"—at which point Benjamin described the source of his abiding interest in Goethe, reiterating in effect what he had said to Scholem when he was in Locarno, this time, however, in a far clearer and more matter-of-fact manner: "I spoke with her about what constituted, for me, the interesting thing in the theme of 'Goethe': how a man who had existed so thoroughly in compromises could nevertheless have accomplished something so extraordinary" (6:367; MD 82). In this way, the two of them were reconciled—but only briefly, for Lācis soon began to emphasize how little Benjamin understood the people for whom he was supposedly writing an article about Goethe.

As unpleasant as this encounter with Radek's wit may have been, it nevertheless seems to have had a positive effect on Benjamin's conception of what, after all, he sought to accomplish. For even if, as Reich insists, Radek exaggerates the frequency with which the exposé invoked "class conflict," it

30 INTRODUCTION

is nevertheless clear that Benjamin reduced the number of times he used this term. In the extant typescripts, it occurs only once, and this occurrence can be seen as a commemoration of Radek's directive, which was itself modeled on the last of Marx's "Theses on Feuerbach" ("the point is to change it"). Without engaging in any compromise generated by the fear of a high-level official—for no one could see what he was doing, and Radek was no longer in a position to lord over the offices of the *Soviet Encyclopedia*—Benjamin converts a sardonic remark into productive advice. Here, then, is where Benjamin finds "the right moment to introduce 'class conflict'": "While Schiller wanted to take up class conflict all down the line, Goethe had long before drawn a fortified line of retreat from which the offensive could still be launched only into the cultural arena; all political activity of the bourgeois class, by contrast, remained limited to the defensive" (181). This residue of the exposé in which Goethe is seen to assume a leadership position among the bourgeoisie under the stringent condition that its domination be restricted to the sphere of culture not only clarifies Goethe's relation to the conflict between the nobility and bourgeoisie; it also explains how a seemingly unlimited willingness to make political compromises goes hand-in-glove with extraordinary cultural accomplishments.

The two visits to the offices of the *Soviet Encyclopedia* were not very encouraging. Even so, Benjamin does not seem to have altogether abandoned work on the article upon his return to Germany. And then, some fifteen months after leaving Russia, he received a letter renewing the commission, which he accepted with alacrity (see GB 3:368; 23 April 1928). The completion of "Goethe" required the entire summer, during which time he would tell his correspondents that, though it certainly had to be completed, the task to which it was devoted could not really be accomplished. It involved "an unsolvable antinomy" (GB 3:392; 18 June 1928), as he tells Scholem; it was "impossible and contradictory," as he tells Siegfried Kracauer (GB 3:400; 21 July 1928); and it left him in a situation where there is no "help" to be found, as he again informs Scholem (GB 3:406; 1 August 1928). The terms differ, but the impasse in question is the same as the one Benjamin had earlier described to Hofmannsthal: a popular discussion of an artist is supposed to be combined with a treatment that derives from a theory and correspondingly aims for its advancement. In combination with his work on radio broadcasting, which began with a 1927 program, now lost, about the situation of "Young Russian Writers" to a German audience, Benjamin's work on the

Soviet Encyclopedia article issued into a series of reflections on the conditions under which advancements in a field of knowledge can be communicated to a popular audience.[61] He would soon argue that a body of knowledge that derives from specialized training—"science," in short—can be most successfully popularized under two independent conditions: on the one hand, the popularizer must be familiar with the intended audience; on the other, the field of knowledge must be at a point where its governing theory is becoming unfamiliar to expert and layperson alike. In other words, a science is well positioned for popularization when it is in the process of being revolutionized.[62] The conditions under which Benjamin produced "Goethe" are the opposite of those that are conducive to successful popular science: the popularizer in this case knows little about the target audience, while the governing theory, that is, historical materialism, is—at least in Russia—becoming ever more firmly established as epistemic orthodoxy.

Yet would it be possible to imagine another target audience as well as a situation in which historical materialism was advancing by becoming unfamiliar to both experts in the study of history and a laity that saw themselves in this advancement? A question along these lines may have sustained Benjamin in his persistent work on "Goethe" despite one discouraging episode after another. There is no direct evidence that Benjamin raised a question like this, as he prepared a draft of an article in the fall of 1928 that, once translated into Russian, would become unintelligible to him. There is no question, however, that he was simultaneously preparing versions of his work that would be directed toward a different—that is to say, a university-trained—German-speaking audience. Two typescripts of the article are extant, one of which was sent to Scholem, accompanied by a remark that indicates that its publication in German may be unlikely but is nevertheless not only possible but also—though this is only implicit—intended: "'Goethe,' in the form that it appears before your fortunate eyes, will probably see the light of day neither in Russia nor in Germany" (GB 3:421; 30 October 1928).

With respect to Russia, Benjamin's prognosis was largely accurate. In 1929 an article titled "Гёте (Goethe), Иоган Вольфганг" appeared in volume 16 of the *Great Soviet Encyclopedia*, where it is attributed to six authors.[63] The editors of the *Gesammelte Schriften* asked Wolfgang Kasack, an esteemed scholar and translator, to compare their edition of "Goethe" with the article in Russian. Kasack's conclusion: "Only 12% of the published Russian version shows parallels to the Benjamin manuscript; but one can scarcely call these parallels

32 INTRODUCTION

'translations'. . . . Decisive for the divergence is the fundamentally different intellectual conception, to which was sacrificed, above all, the interpretation of individual works and Benjamin's attempt to understand intellectually Goethe's uniqueness as a poet and human being. Everything essential from Walter Benjamin's exposition was eliminated" (2:1472). This was the end of the matter in Russia. Not so in Germany: one of the two extant typescripts seems to have been designed for the purpose of producing excerpts, with certain paragraphs marked out under a series of headings. *Die Literarische Welt* (The Literary World) published three excerpts in November 1928 under the title "Goethe's Politics and View of Nature." The typescript identified several more potential excerpts, though none was published, perhaps because, from Benjamin's perspective, they had not been sufficiently developed for a German audience.[64] In any case, the experimental "improvisation" that gave rise to a (lost) "schema," a (lost) "exposé," two typescripts, and a (lost) fair copy did not simply end with a single issue of *Die Literarische Welt*; on the contrary, its effects range far and wide in Benjamin's subsequent writings.

6.

The first five texts that follow "Goethe" in Part Two of this volume can be described as its direct byproducts. This is obvious in the case of "Goethe's Politics and View of Nature," which, as the editors of *Die Literarische Welt* explain in their preamble (194), comes from the article intended for the *Great Soviet Encyclopedia*. And Benjamin uses this word in a letter to Hofmannsthal to describe an essay he wrote in response to a recent visit to the small city where Goethe passed much of his adult life: "'Weimar' is a byproduct of my 'Goethe' for the Russian encyclopedia. . . . I was in Weimar a year ago. The impression benefited in some places the essay for which the stay was intended. On these two pages, though, I sought to retain the essence, untroubled by the context of a presentation" (GB 3:472; 26 June 1929). In a letter to Scholem, he says something similar, though in writing to a friend rather than a fellow writer, he discusses not literary technique but, rather, the double-sided character of his gaze, which forms the "January" of a new era in his work: "'Weimar' . . . represents in the loveliest manner the side of my Janus-head that turns away from the Soviet state" (GB 3:438; 14 February 1929).

The two dreams of Goethe's house that Benjamin originally published in Ignaz Ježower's *Das Buch der Träume* (Book of Dreams) are not byproducts—in the sense of "day residues"—of the visit to Weimar that resulted in the like-named essay, for the visit occurred in June 1928, several months after the publication of Ježower's volume. He had visited the city at least twice before, first in July 1910 on a school holiday and again in June 1914 as a speaker at a student-association conference. The two dreams, especially the second, may have been informed by what he experienced during the holiday vacation; both dreams at any rate allude to his work on *Elective Affinities*, especially the second through its invocation of his own *Verwandtschaft*, here translated as "relatives," which stand in contrast to Goethe's relatives, who project a spectral presence through the absent *Ahnen* ("ancestors") that are thus intimated ("ahnen" = "to intimate").[65] And both dreams can be seen as byproducts of Benjamin's effort to discover the source of Goethe's productivity. In both Benjamin is seeking permission to gain proximity: in the second dream, permission to enter Goethe's house; in the first, permission to touch him once there. Because entrance precedes contact, the second dream, so it seems, should come first—as indeed it does, when Benjamin reprints the two dreams in *One-Way Street*, both prefaced by a third dream that is itself prefaced by a reflection on "the house of our life." The key feature of such a house is that its underground layer be a place where permission to enter can never be peacefully granted; on the contrary, it can be reached only after "enemy bombs" (4:86; SW 1:445) have destroyed the upper layers. Once those parts of Benjamin's house have been laid bare and the incomparable thing that lies below has been summarily exposed—so the sequence of dreams in *One-Way Street* suggests—he can enter Goethe's.

Still another byproduct of "Goethe"—different in both style and substance from those described above—is Benjamin's review of a new and rather dubious edition of *Goethe's Theory of Colors*, produced by Hans Wohlbold, who was a prolific propagandist for Rudolf Steiner. Though few readers of *Die Literarische Welt* would have noticed this, the review, published in a November 1928 issue, prepares the way for one of the extracts from the encyclopedia article that appeared a few weeks later. In the latter, under the heading "Goethe's Natural-Scientific Studies," Benjamin identifies the source of Goethe's "refractory" (177) attitude toward new technical innovations that had expanded the scope of human perception, preferring instead to see the unaided human body as the only valid proving ground for a science that wants to be true to the idea of genuine knowledge. Correspondingly, the review focuses on the conflict between Newton and Goethe. Benjamin insists that it cannot be blandly brushed aside, above all because it is a conflict

Goethe himself stages and, as Benjamin emphasizes, very much wants to win. Benjamin closes the review with an image of how this victory can be accomplished; the basis of the image is drawn from Salomo Friedländer's *Creative Indifference*; but it should be noted that the image, that of the Trojan horse, is conspicuously hollow.[66] Goethe will defeat Newton, Friedländer proposes, through the invention of a "Goethean mathematics" (206) to make up for what is missing in the original. The term, however, says little—and even as Benjamin ends his review with Friedländer's quotation, he does not give any indication of what it could be said to mean. What is clear, however, from both the November review and the December extract is that Goethe's scientific studies and his reflections on the methodology of science remain "relevant beyond the context of Goethe-related research" (205).

Another review of Benjamin's also counts as a direct byproduct of the article for the *Great Soviet Encyclopedia*.[67] Max Kommerell's *Poet as Führer in German Classicism* was published in 1928 by Bondi-Verlag, the house press of the George circle, which had earlier brought out Gundolf's *Goethe*. Kommerell's book is as monumentalizing as Gundolf's, and as the first word in the title of Benjamin's review indicates, "Against a Masterpiece," he will not recommend that readers should rush out and consume their copy without a grain of salt; at the same time, however—and this is obviously very different from his attitude toward Gundolf—the review recognizes from the outset the book's magisterial quality.[68] Where is this quality to be found? A more direct answer to this question can be found in the opening sentence of the original draft of the review than in the sentence that begins the published version: "This book is a new and noteworthy demonstration as to how a view that derives from fullness by itself teaches something methodologically important. This presentation contributes more to a materialist history of literature [*Dichtung*] than many guild-oriented literary histories" (WuN 13.1:732). Kommerell, regardless of his own intentions, can be seen as a comrade in the construction of a historical object that becomes analyzable when viewed under a theoretical optic. In other words—which are clearer and more matter-of-fact—Kommerell does not produce an image of a group of artists set off against a sociological background but, instead, through the "fullness" of the exposition, facilitates a synthetic intuition through which a certain object, here called "German classicism," becomes available for analysis.

To say the same in still other words: if it were not for Kommerell's fascist tendencies, signaled by the Führer principle that guides the book from its title onward, his approach would shadow the one Benjamin sought to develop in response to the commission issuing from the Soviet Union. The rest of the review, especially its description of the notion of "renunciation" by which Goethe at once exposes and conceals the nature of his late work (see 209–10), derives from a divergence in approach: for Kommerell, the object is established so that it can be followed; for Benjamin, it is to be constructed so that it can be analyzed. This difference is then reflected in Benjamin's enigmatic conclusion, where he sharpens the distinction between what he called "synthetic intuition" in "Goethe's Elective Affinities" and now calls "theory." Kommerell, for his part, avoids both the word "synthesis" (too techno-scientific) and the word "intuition" (too philosophico-plebeian); instead, he goes to the root of the latter, *Anschauung*, and thus speaks of the poet's *Schau* ("vision"), which is supposed to be set apart from mere "show," which is the plebian understanding of *Schau*.[69] Benjamin, in response, introduces the word *theory*, which, of course, like *theater*, derives from an ancient Greek word for "vision." Here it means—as those familiar with Benjamin's recent work would know—historical materialism. Benjamin proceeds to show that Kommerell's *Schau* is but a "show," after all. *Schau*, like *Anschauung*, has the deceptive lure of immediacy, whereas theory does not. And the relation between "synthetic intuition" (in the guise of *Schau*) and theory (as shorthand for "historical materialism") is precisely formulated as follows: the latter "leaves behind the spellbinding circle" (213) of the former.

7.

"Weimar" originally appeared in a Swiss journal in 1928. It also appeared unaltered in a German newspaper four years later. Why the republication? The year 1932 was the one hundredth anniversary of Goethe's death, and it unleashed a commemorative flurry in Germany. Benjamin, whose livelihood largely derived from the payments he received from journals, newspapers, and radio programs, participated in the commemoration. His most substantial contribution was a radio play, "What the Germans Were Reading While Their Classical Authors Were Writing," that, as the title indicates, has far less to do with Goethe's work than with the absence of a receptive public: "Do you know how many subscriptions Göschen got for the Goethe edition he published between [17]87 and '90? I have the figure from the man himself: six hundred. As for individual volumes, sales were supposed to have been much worse" (4:666–67; RB 330).[70] Benjamin's second substantial contribution

36   INTRODUCTION

to the "Goethe Year" is similarly askew from the common patterns of com-memoration: it appears at first sight as though it were nothing more than an annotated bibliography that, strangely enough, excludes not only Goethe's own works but also everything written by both his closest associates and "classical writers" (214). As a contribution to the Goethe centenary, "One Hundred Years of Writing on Goethe" is not to be mistaken for a contribu-tion to Goethe scholarship. Still less is the poet monumentalized amid its brief remarks about sixty-some books, collected under an apparently random assortment of headings. The final two sections, however, are different—and are marked as such. Directly following a discussion of six books that seek to produce a "popular image of Goethe," Benjamin turns to the "philosophical image." The six books under discussion are ordered in a systematic manner. The principle of selection is neither Goethean polarity nor dialectical devel-opment but, rather, strict opposition between claim and refutation. This pro-ceeds in the following order: Carl Rosenkranz vs. Hermann Grimm (Hegelian philosophizing vs. retention of a "lively tradition"); Houston Stewart Cham-berlain vs. George Simmel (anti-Semitic propaganda vs. proof of its nullity); and Max Kommerell vs. Franz Mehring (George school vs. Marxism). And even though "One Hundred Years of Writing on Goethe" appeared anony-mously, it culminates in a reference to an article on "Goethe" in the *Great Soviet Encyclopedia* by "Walter Benjamin" (226), which, though unavailable to readers, still forms the culmination of the "Philosophical Goethe Image," insofar as it retains Mehring's lively tradition, just as Hermann Grimm had retained Goethe's.

In the same commemorative issue of the *Frankfurter Zeitung*, Benjamin published under his own name a review of a two-volume book published by Insel-Verlag under the title *Goethe*, though it is largely a commentary on *Faust* alone. Its author, Eugen Kühnemann, had been a visiting professor at vari-ous universities around the world, including Harvard. Hence, the title Benja-min chose for his review, "Faust in the Sample Case." In Kühnemann's hands, *Faust* becomes a marketable item. This is done, as Benjamin demonstrates, by ignoring the scholarly literature and, above all, by failing to read the text itself, including its revisions and fragments. By quoting the following passage, Benjamin demonstrates that Kühnemann's view of *Faust* is based on a look at its table of contents: "Part Two . . . is divided in the clearest way into five acts and is thus closer to a regular play than Part One" (228). Benjamin contrasts Kühnemann's treatment with a recently published collection of essays by

INTRODUCTION   37

Gottfried Wilhelm Hertz, about which he expressed enthusiasm in a letter to the sociologist Albert Salomon (GB 4:81–82; 5 April 1932), who had himself recently written an essay on Goethe, which he had sent to Benjamin, probably in connection with a conversation the two of them had about the theory of history. The outlines of that conversation can be found in a notebook Benjamin titled "Diary of the Seventeenth of August, Nineteen-Thirty, until the Day of My Death" (6:442–43).[71] While mocking Kühnemann, Benjamin brings attention to the fine philological work of the less well-traveled Hertz and makes several striking observations about what Goethe was doing in the first act of *Faust, Part Two* that recall certain remarks he made about its compositional principle in "Goethe's Elective Affinities" (see 141 and 157). But is this separation of good from bad philology enough to generate the energy required to go through a thousand-page nullity? Unlike Gundolf's similarly titled tome, whose success both Kühnemann and the editors at Insel-Verlag had probably hoped to repeat, *Goethe* was never reprinted and generated few responses beyond Benjamin's.

At the beginning of "Faust in the Sample Case," Benjamin quotes Gottfried Keller's attack on the "sanctimoniousness" (227) of the Goethe cult. The beginning of a brief review he wrote for *Die Literarische Welt* in 1932 takes up where the Keller citation leaves off: "Every word not spent on speaking about Goethe this year is a blessing, and so nothing is more welcome than laconic anniversary books" (233). He briefly discusses two such books. He is silent, however, about another—his own, which never appeared and can therefore be classified as laconic to a point of perfection. There is no question that Insel-Verlag had been in contact with Benjamin about a Goethe book and had presumably done so in connection with the 1932 commemoration. But there is little else that is certain about this unwritten book. The following three documents are, it seems, all there remains:

1. In one of the curricula vitae Benjamin wrote in 1928 he does not specifically speak of a separate book on Goethe but indicates that he has plans to expand his current work, and the natural form of this expansion would be a separate book: "I hope I will have the opportunity to complete the image of Goethe, as I sketched it in the work on *Elective Affinities*, through two studies, one of which is to make *Pandora* its object, the other 'The New Melusine'" (6:219).[72]

2. In a letter to Scholem from 1932, Benjamin begins to discuss the expected content of the book; but he cuts himself off in midsentence and introduces an ellipsis

38   INTRODUCTION

as a sign of the book's demise: "Have I—apropos 'Goethean' things—written to you that in the previous year I was close to a Goethe-book which the Insel publishing house would have commissioned me to write, if only . . . I fear that I've lost the exposé for this book; I always knew enough about it, however, to draw up a report that would elicit the astonishment of the University of Muri's teaching faculty, especially its professors of Kabbalistics and Jewish philosophy of the Middle Ages" (GB 4:106; 25 June 1932).[73]

3. The third document captures the precise moment when Benjamin's hopes for a Goethe book were dashed. It is recorded at the beginning of the aforementioned notebook, ominously titled "Diary of the Seventeenth of August, Nine-Hundred-and-Thirty-One until the Day of Death": "This diary does not promise to be very long. Today, I received the rejection letter from Kippenberg, and my plan thus gains all the urgency that only hopelessness [*Ausweglosigkeit*] can provide" (6:441). Anton Kippenberg was the founder and director of Insel-Verlag. The end of Benjamin's effort to produce a Goethe book is thus designated as the beginning of the end of his life.[74]

A few addenda to this dismal affair are worth adding: (1) in 1939 Goethe's hometown, Frankfurt am Main, awarded Kippenberg its annual Goethe-Badge; (2) in 1955 Insel-Verlag published a book titled *Goethes Wahlverwandtschaften* by Walter Benjamin; (3) sales of *Goethes Wahlverwandtschaften* were brisk enough for Insel-Verlag to release a second printing a few years later.[75]

8.

One of Benjamin's contributions to the commemoration of Goethe's death appeared in the pages of the *Frankfurter Zeitung* under his own name; another, published anonymously, concluded with his name associated with an article soon to be published in Moscow. A year later, after the Nazi seizure of power, he could still publish reviews in the *Frankfurter Zeitung*, though it had to be done under a pseudonym. This was because the Nazi regime, wanting to show foreign powers that it respected press freedom, allowed the *Frankfurter Zeitung* some slight leeway from the otherwise mandatory policy of "Gleichschaltung," a euphemism for total acquiescence to regime-generated propaganda.[76] It is in this context that Benjamin reviewed two more books about Goethe under the name Detlev Holz. The review is notable, above all, for its discussion of class conflict, telegraphed—it could not be otherwise in Nazi Germany—via the Goethe family, whose late nineteenth-century

INTRODUCTION   39

descendants, unlike their illustrious ancestor, who rose to nobility by his own bootstraps, wanted to make themselves into seamless members of the upper-aristocracy. The review enigmatically refers to a "tensile force requisite for cognition" (237)—this is what the book under review misses because of its categorical confusion. Benjamin does not end his review with this diagnosis; rather, he proposes that the "root of the evil" lies deeper, namely, in an "apologetic intention" (237), which is a widespread evil. The defense of Goethe makes his "shape . . . subservient" not only to a set of confused categories, aesthetic as well as social, but also to a form of *Gleichschaltung*—though the word, of course, is not used—that pretends to be a free exchange of ideas.

Benjamin published one further review in the *Frankfurter Zeitung*. Although it does not refer to Goethe by name, it can be read, and may have been intended to be read, as a short goodbye to the study of Goethe in Germany "today" (239). The repeated use of the word "today" is an emphatic feature of the single page of newsprint on which this 1935 review is published. Its belated occasion is the publication a year earlier of a book about Goethe's partner in the construction of Weimar classicism, that is, Friedrich Schiller, about whom Benjamin rarely has anything to say except in combination with other writers, most notably Goethe, of course, beginning with their much-cited volume of correspondence. Just how little the review has to do with Schiller can be discerned in its title, "Volkstümlichkeit als Problem" (Popularity as a Problem), which itself signals a problem in the context of Nazi Germany, insofar as it puts into question, however tangentially, the value of the Volk. As if this were not enough, the review opens with a discussion of contemporary physics, referring not to "German" or "Aryan physics," which was then at the apex of its influence, but on the contrary, to its adversary, signaled by the seemingly off-hand reference to "the theory of relativity" (238).[77] Had Benjamin, under the pseudonym of Detlev Holz, referred directly to Einstein, the vilified paragon of "Jewish science," it is unlikely that even the *Frankfurter Zeitung* would have allowed the review to reach the German public.

All of this, moreover, is connected to the commemoration of the one hundredth anniversary of Goethe's death—not directly, of course, but through the book under review, which was written in 1934 as a contribution to the commemoration of the 175th anniversary of Schiller's birth. The author's explicit goal is to make Schiller's dramas accessible to the German people of today. Citing the example of a successful popularization of "Jewish" physics, the author of the review states unequivocally that this goal is blocked by a certain "historical constellation" (238). And this conclusion can be read as a retrospective verdict on the far more momentous commemoration that took place a mere two years earlier under a far different circumstance. Just as Einstein's name is implied in the reference to Arthur Stanley Eddington that sets the review in motion, so Goethe's name, beyond its close association with Schiller, is hidden under a name with which it concludes: Julian Hirsch, author of *The Genesis of Fame*, which consists in a careful dismantling of the adoration accorded to certain "glorious" personalities, beginning with Goethe.[78] It's surprising that the editors of the *Frankfurter Zeitung* allowed Detlev Holz to refer to a Jewish-socialist-émigré sociologist whose scholarship showed in detail the process through which certain German men, with Goethe qua "genial poet" as prime example, were raised to the status of immortal individualities. It is no surprise, however, that this review—with its references to "relativity," "revolution," "bourgeois science," and Julian Hirsch—was the last publication to appear in Germany under the name Detlev Holz or any of Benjamin's other pseudonyms until the end of the Nazi regime.

Detlev Holz, however, did continue to publish outside of Germany. It was under this name that a Swiss publisher produced and distributed a small book that developed out of the letters by eighteenth- and nineteenth-century writers and scholars Benjamin had begun in the *Frankfurter Zeitung* in the spring of 1931. In the original preface to the publication of this letter, which is translated here, Karl Friedrich Zelter's announcement of Goethe's death to Chancellor von Müller resonates with the upcoming commemoration of the one hundredth anniversary of his death while at the same time serving as a warning about the very real possibility of a certain "epoch" (240) coming to an end. One could say in retrospect that the epoch to which Benjamin refers is the one now associated with Goethe's adopted hometown; but in the original introduction to the series of letters, he means something else. The epoch that is in imminent danger of coming to a close is that of "German humanism," and the danger derives in large part from a "one-sided" (240) attack from scholars who are fully aware of what they are doing. He is referring, of course, to writers and scholars who side with fascism, including—to name some of the people discussed above—Erich Rothacker, Martin Heidegger, Franz Schultz, Max Kommerell, and Eugen Kühnemann. In transforming the series of articles into a book, Benjamin expanded the opening remarks into a one-page preface (4:151; SW 3:167) that is no longer concerned with the end of German humanism.

A trace of the original introduction is retained, however, in the title of the book: *Deutsche Menschen*, which is best translated as "German Human Beings." *Menschen* ("human beings") is not a neutral word that can be replaced *salva veritate* by a list of various kinds of humanity. In conjunction with "German," *Menschen* in this context suggests a humanism that once was to have characterized a sphere—however thin it may have been—of German letters that gave insight into certain forms of life, buoyed by the back-and-forth of communication, where the pluralization of *Mensch* was an indispensable feature. The book, in other words, is not to be mistaken for one more glorification of a German-inflected *singulare tantum*: "der deutsche Geist" (the German spirit), "die deutsche Seele" (the German soul), or "das deutsche Dasein" (German existence). At the same time, *Menschen* in Detlev Holz's title stands in stark contrast with two terms of contemporaneous discourse in Nazi Germany, *Übermensch* and *Untermensch*.

Among the configuration of "German human beings" in Benjamin's collection, it is Goethe, above all, who is most intimately connected with the end of the epoch of German humanism: first, through the announcement of his death, which begins the collection, as it began the series of newspaper articles; then—in the second letter translated in this volume—as the addressee of a letter written by the same associate, Karl Friedrich Zelter, who had earlier responded to this announcement; and finally—in the last of the letters translated here—as the author of a letter addressed to the son of a recently deceased scientist with whom Goethe once worked and from whom he distanced himself to the point of "neglection" (243). Benjamin's remarks on one of Goethe's last letters are unlike anything else in *German Human Beings*, for they include a "commentary" that seeks to bring out the peculiar characteristics of the poet's late style (244–45). This addendum to his recollection of "German Human Beings" casts a retrospective light on the distinction between commentary and critique with which "Goethe's Elective Affinities" begins. In its discussion of the phrase through which Goethe refers to his tendency toward "neglection"—"the human in its peculiarities" (245)—commentary reveals itself as critique.

9.

Around the same time as Benjamin was putting together *German Human Beings*, he was drawn back to "Goethe's Elective Affinities" several times. The first of these appears in one of the many footnotes he added to the original versions of "The Artwork in the Age of Its Technical Reproducibility," where the following passage can be found: "Beautiful appearance as auratic reality altogether fulfills Goethean creativity. Mignon, Ottilie and Helen take part in this reality: 'For the beautiful is neither the cover nor the covered object but, rather, the object in its cover' [155]—that is the quintessence of the Goethean as well as the ancient view of art. Its decay doubly suggests that a look be directed back at its origin. This lies in mimesis as the urphenomenon of all artistic actuation" (7:368; SW 3:127). Even as Goethe's view of art is said to be antiquated—doubly so, indeed, for, according to this passage, it was old even when Goethe was himself young—the word he invents for viewing the deepest strata of nature, namely, "urphenomenon," not only remains part of the current vocabulary for grasping the work of art, therefore outliving such terms as form and content; it lets us see anew the oldest enactment of art as such.

Benjamin again returned to "Goethe's Elective Affinities" when, sometime in the fall of 1935, a representative of the Sorbonne's l'Institut d'Études germaniques invited him to give a lecture in the following February.[79] No topic seems to have been specified. He tells Scholem that he intends to discuss *Elective Affinities* (GB 5:190; 24 October 1935). When he writes to Jean Ballard, however, the topic has changed. Ballard was an editor of the Marseilles-based journal *Cahiers du Sud*, as was Marcel Brion, with whom Benjamin had been in correspondence since the latter published a review of his translation of Baudelaire's *Tableaux parisiens* some ten years earlier.[80] In his letter to Ballard, Benjamin indicates that he has been in conversation with Jean Cassou, still another editor of the journal, about an upcoming "lecture on Goethe and Romanticism" (GB 5:197; 23 November 1935). The apparent change in topic coincides with Cassou's plans for a special issue of *Cahiers du Sud* on German Romanticism. As Benjamin tells Ballard, certain "fragments" of his lecture may be appropriate for the special issue. The lecture never seems to have taken place. Instead of publishing the fragments of a lecture that failed to take place, the editors of the journal, doubtless under Benjamin's guidance, published a portion of "Goethe's Elective Affinities" with an editorial preface that referred to his book on "The Notion of Art-Criticism in German Romanticism" (246). The translator was Pierre Klossowski, who had previously produced the French version of "The Artwork in the Age of Its Technical Reproducibility" that the editors of the *Zeitschrift für Sozialforschung*, oddly enough, wanted for its initial publication. "Goethe's Mythic Anxiety" turned out to be the only contribution to the issue on "le Romantisme allemand" written by a German—if, that is, Benjamin was still to be counted as "a German" in 1937.

In writing to Ballard, Benjamin expresses his appreciation for the special issue as a whole: "You have put the spotlight back on a literary tradition that, at present, is scarcely in favor in its own country" (GB 5:577; September 1937). He was not pleased, however, by a review of the issue that Alfred Kurella produced for a newly founded communist journal *Internationale Literatur*. According to Kurella, "Mythic Anxiety in Goethe" is evidence that Benjamin is a "follower of Heidegger" (GB 6:138; 20 July 1938). Kurella was confused, of course; but neither he nor Benjamin knew how very confused he was. Not only was Benjamin's essay written before Heidegger's book; as noted earlier in this Introduction, it is not out of the question that Heidegger learned something about the essay, including its analytic of *Angst*, before he completed the version of *Being and Time* that he sent off to the publisher. It is therefore more illuminating to see Heidegger as a "follower" of Benjamin than the other way around.

10.

In the aforementioned letter to Ballard, immediately after praising the special issue, Benjamin expresses his desire to read a recently published book by one of the other contributors to the special issue, specifically Albert Béguin's *L'âme romantique et le rêve* (GB 5:577; September 1937).[81] His reading resulted in a review that was eventually published in Thomas Mann's exile journal *Maß und Wert* (Measure and Value, 3:557–60; SW 153–57). The review is noteworthy for several reasons, not least its critique of Béguin's haphazard historical methodology that takes its primary point of orientation from Goethe's "Analysis and Synthesis," which Benjamin quotes from memory: "Whoever undertakes an analysis, Goethe reminds us, should see to it that a genuine synthesis also underlies it. However attractive the object treated by Béguin may be, there remains the question as to whether the attitude whereby the author approaches this object is compatible with Goethe's advice. To carry out the synthesis is the privilege of historical cognition" (3:559; SW 4:154). Benjamin immediately adds a trenchant remark whose applicability goes far beyond Béguin's book and encompasses his own major projects of the period: "The object, as it is outlined in the title of the book [*The Romantic Soul and the Dream*], can in fact expect a historical construction" (3:559; SW 4:154).

In the folder of his *Arcades Project* designated "Cognition-Theoretical, Theory of Progress," Benjamin outlines what it means for an object to expect its historical construction. This problem draws him back to Goethe's theory of science, just as his attempt to outline the book he planned to write on Baudelaire returns him to the "dialectical rigor" (see GB 6:62; 16 April 1938) of "Goethe's Elective Affinities," as expressed in its thesis-antithesis-synthesis structure. Unless the synthesis lies at the beginning, it cannot stand in the end. To quote again the passage of "Analysis and Synthesis" that seems to have punctuated the conversations Benjamin and Noeggerath conducted in Munich during the winter of 1915–16 and then again on Ibiza just before and after the Nazi seizure of power: "A great danger that an analyst runs into is therefore this: when he applies his method where there is no underlying synthesis. His work then is altogether a labor of the Danaids, and we can find the saddest examples of this" (WA II, 11:71).

In the context of the numerous folders of the *Arcades Project*, each of which looks like an aggregate that is juxtaposed with the others, the corresponding passage from "Analysis and Synthesis" that Benjamin uses for the epigraph for his doctoral dissertation becomes especially pertinent: "Above all, . . . the analyst should inquire, or rather direct his special attention toward, whether he is really dealing with a synthesis full of secrets, or whether he is only busying himself with an aggregate, a juxtaposition, . . . or how the whole thing could be modified" (WA II, 11:71; 1:10; SW 1:116). This is how Benjamin comes to see what he calls "the dialectical image": "that form of the historical object which satisfies Goethe's requirements for the object of an analysis: to exhibit a genuine synthesis" (252). The name Goethe gave to this form is "urphenomenon."[82] The writings collected into this volume can be understood as a series of ever so many attempts on Benjamin's part to make the concept of urphenomenon effective, beginning with the reconstruction of a lost note on the function of symbolism in cognition (50) and concluding with its transference (252) from a single natural nexus to historical ones, which is to say, in brief, its rigorously constructed pluralization.[83]

Part I

1

A REMARK ON GUNDOLF: GOETHE

[1:826] At the beginning of the book, there is to be found the distinction among three concentric life circles of a creative person and, in particular, Goethe.[1] These are: work, letter, conversation (if I remember correctly; or does Gundolf put the last two into one single category and insert another intermediate circle? No matter).[2] He makes the work the central circle to which one must in essence refer. He guards himself against any other testimonials and sources that might significantly contribute to the evaluation of Goethe's essence. The objective mendacity of the said separation rests on the following: its analogy is useful and required in the large historical presentation, where it presents a methodical and source-critical point of view as a separation between what has been written and what has been passed on orally, and enables different scales of transition between written and oral tradition.[3] Above all, this true analogue of the false Gundolfian distinction is important, where there exists the most essential difference between the two kinds of tradition, namely, in the religious and mythic region of history—where the balancing and struggle between the two regulate humanity's relationship to its ultimate foundation (revelation). The difference, wherever it is legitimate, may never be conceived by the historian as a difference of value, only as a difference of meaning. In Gundolf's case, this is reversed: the two peripheral circles are considered to have almost negative value for historical presentation; they have, for him, no deeper difference of meaning. In fact, their only legitimate objective basis, the divorce between speech and writing, is not present at all. This means: all conceivable "oral tradition" (letter, conversation, etc.) concerning Goethe would have to be essentially transformed into a written tradition, and the entire influx of oral speech (and what's more, of *private life*) into writing creates a completely different concept of the written word than the mythic-religious concept; and the work, to be sure, also belongs within the scope of this new concept, but it does not belong within the mendacious exclusivity and monumentality in which Gundolf seeks to present it.

Without dwelling on the question concerning the possibility of a book on Goethe, some negatively critical things are to be established: Gundolf has two things before his eyes. The first [is] a worthy, serious, and great concept of history [1:827] (pragmatic history, in short) to which something like the separation between written and oral sources also methodologically belongs.[4] The second [is] an imposing feeling of Goethe's appearance. Both [are] altogether unclear because both far exceed his capacities. But how does he assimilate these great objects? (A concept of this assimilation [is] the same as the fundamental critical concept of objective mendacity.) He applies the categories of history *without an object* by giving them an object that is *toto coelo* inadequate: the individual Goethe. From this he drafts an apparently forceful—in reality, however, altogether objectless—image. For, does Gundolf have an image, in other words, an idea of Goethe? Nothing less.[5] He seeks simply to verify through him a methodological idea that he is unable to develop in a pure conceptual manner. And he is sneaky about his verification: he does not apply his idea to Goethe (since it is impossible for him to do, lacking concepts or, to speak subjectively, by virtue of intellectual unscrupulousness); instead, he seeks to install Goethe as the empirical (!) sum total of this methodological idea.[6] Seen from the other side, the moral repugnancy of this business presents itself as the falsification of the life of a historical individual, Goethe, into a mythic hero, whose existence would be presentable in obscure outline under the broadest historical categories only from his work, since sparse sources yield only obscure tidings. This semblance is occasioned by the fact that the object is conceptually and formally evacuated and made into the emptiest scheme of mere presentability, which an individual can never be. All the more welcome to the reader is the optical illusion by which the empty scheme is mistaken for a demigod conjured up by the author. In fact, Gundolf does not finally know anything conclusive to say about Goethe;

individual insights evaporate into catchphrases when they should be related to the whole, and at every point the simplest concepts have been replaced by the most horrible words. The whole thing blasphemies the concept of the idea, to which he gives no object, and it blasphemies the object [of the study], whom he turns into a puppet because he attempts to present him directly in terms of his idea. (In this nothingness he finds space for all his velleities, his arbitrary and empty linguistic hodgepodge.) Above all, the biographer (or if you prefer: the historian) of Goethe must be a backward-turned prophet: but how cold is Gundolf wherever it's a matter of seeing Goethe's work and existence symbolically as something specific and yet surely as a life and *sorrow* to come.[7] He contents himself with spinning a tiny thread between Goethe and some modern literature, because, for him, the sense of everything Goethean for the most specific and deepest tasks of contemporary life is closed [1:828]. No wonder: he has closed himself off from these tasks. (And in this respect, one can say that even the most insignificant scrivener of literary history has a more correct feeling when he registers his little judgments about the value and valuelessness, transience and immortality, of poets and their works. Although Gundolf's striving apparently arose from his opposition to the poverty of such procedure, his weakness has not allowed him actually to annihilate it via action.)

After one has clarified the methodology of such a formation, there remains the question of its possibility. This leads to the deepest and still completely unresolved metaphysical riddles. In other words, there must lie in *language* the possibility out of which such a book can contest its semblance. This semblance is something objective, just as the (false) contents of the judgment "$2 + 2 = 5$" is something logically objective. From the side of the philosophy of language as well as the theory of cognition there arises the question concerning the objective possibility of semblance and error. Gundolf's language derives its possibility from semblance and error; his book is a veritable falsification of cognition.

2

ON A LOST CONCLUSION TO THE NOTE ON THE SYMBOLIC IN COGNITION

[6:38] The Goethean study of nature was conceived in this conclusion as a representative of a genuine theoretical cognition carried out in symbols. The symbols in which nature is cognizable disclosed themselves to Goethe not in poetic analogies but, rather, in visionary insights. The urphenomenon ~~represents~~ is a systematic-symbolic concept.[1] It is, as an ideal, a symbol.

In the lost conclusion, it was furthermore designated as an idea. But in what sense? In the purely theoretical sense in which concepts derive from the idea. In the sense of the idea as task. The ideal, by contrast, presents the relation to art or, speaking more accurately, to perception.[2] New:

In the descriptive natural sciences, perception is constitutive. That is to say: within the theoretical region, with respect to physics and chemistry, it is possible to abstract from intuitability; not so in the biological sciences. When it is a matter of life, it is a matter of ~~its~~ intuitability, [that is,] perceptibility. A moment of irreducible perception lies in life, in contradistinction from physical and chemical phenomena.

Also with regard to Goethe's study of nature and poetry, nature was designated as the chaos of symbols, which is not permeated and ordered in a religious, apocalyptic manner. So [it is] especially with respect to the second part of *Faust*.

[6:39] ~~In general~~ To that essay, this is to be added:

The system {Ontology} does not at all serve to gain cognition of the true insofar as one understands by "truth" something within this system {ontology} or within an external world. In order to clarify this, it is decisive to comprehend the radical difference between truth and truths or, better yet, [truth and] cognitions. Truth is nothing caught and enclosed in ontology; rather, it rests on the relation of ontology to the other two members of the system. The system has the following structure: the cognitions of ontology hang on its walls. Ontology is not the palace. To stay with this image: the cognitions of ontology must preserve the dimension of the paintings. To explain the image: via their latent symbolic matter, all cognitions must be adapted be bearers of a forceful symbolic intention that, under the name of "ontology," orders them into the very system whose decisive category is doctrine, also truth, not cognition.[3] The task of ontology is to charge cognitions with symbolic intention so that they lose themselves in truth or doctrine, coming up and undone in it, nevertheless without grounding or justifying it, for its justification is revelation, language.

To return to the image: to so fulfill fill out the walls of the palace with images, until the images appear to be the walls.

The forceful intention toward a symbolic impregnation of all cognitions is the basis of Kant's mysticism. His terminology is mystical; it is absolutely determined by the striving from origin onward to give the concepts located therein a symbolic charge, to give them the invisibly glorifying dimension of genuine cognition, of pictures in the palace. All scrupulousness is only the pride in this birth the mysterium of this, its birth, which critique extinguish is not capable of blotting out, though critique does not comprehend the mysterium. This is Kant's esotericism. // The place {role} of the system, whose necessity is evident only to philosophers who know that truth is not a cognitive nexus but, rather, a symbolic intention (that of its members of the system toward one other)—this role is played in Plato precisely by dialogue DIALOGUE.

3

SUPPLEMENTS TO:
ON THE SYMBOLIC IN COGNITION

[6:40] To be distinguished in principle from the domain of philosophy and philosophical cognition, which radically aims for truth and, indeed, for its totality, is the insight into truths or into a single truth that not only lawfully and infallibly discloses itself to every precise approach to a work of art but will also presumably, now and then, become apparent to every artist in the act of creating.[1] Those truths contain "truth," specifically the one for which the philosopher aims; but these truths do not point to "truth" in the same way as philosophical truths (~~toward~~ in the lower intention) point to truth ~~and~~ {through} philosophical systematicity (in the higher ~~level~~ {intention}). Goethe's world of thought is representative of that nonphilosophical, specifically artistic or, in the strict sense, muse-related insight into truth.[2] With equal justification, however, it may recall Jean Paul, or, in another sense, Balzac's maxims concerning men and women; but Humboldt's ~~thoughts about~~ {insights into} language, Kandinsky's insights into color emerge from a specifically "theoretical" yet nonetheless nonphilosophical intention.[3]

4

EARLY ROMANTIC THEORY OF ART AND GOETHE

[1:110] The theory of art of the early Romantics and that of Goethe are opposed to one another in their principles.* And indeed the study of this opposition expands considerably the knowledge of the history of the concept of the critique of art. For this opposition signifies at the same time the critical stage of this history: the pure problem of art critique comes immediately to light in the problem-historical relation of the Romantics' concept of critique to that of Goethe. The concept of art critique itself, however, stands in a [relation of] univocal dependency on the center of the philosophy of art. This dependency is formulated most incisively in the problem of the criticizability of the artwork. Whether this is denied or asserted is thoroughly dependent on the basic philosophical concepts that found the theory of art. The entire art-philosophical labor of the early Romantics can be thus summarized in that their labor sought to prove in principle the criticizability of the artwork. Goethe's entire theory of art supports his intuition of the

---

* For the following conception of the Goethean theory of art, no supporting documentation can be given within this narrow framework, because the relevant passages as well as the propositions of the early Romantics require in-depth interpretation. This is to be given some other place in the broad context it demands. For the general way of posing the question in the following exposition, see in particular Elisabeth Rotten, *Goethes Urphänomen und die platonische Idee* [Goethe's Urphenomenon and the Platonic Idea] (Gießen, 1913), chap. 8; its way of posing the question altogether corresponds to this one, though its way of answering the question diverges from it.

uncriticizability of works. It's not as though he emphasizes this view otherwise than occasionally; it's not as though he wrote no critiques. He was not interested in the conceptual elaboration of this intuition, and in the later period, which primarily comes under consideration here, he composed more than a few critiques. In many of these, however, one finds a certain ironic reserve with regard not only to the work [under review] but also to his own activity, and in any case the intention of these critiques was only exoteric and pedagogical.

*The category under which the Romantics grasp art is the idea. The idea is the expression of the infinity of art and of its unity. For Romantic unity is an infinity. [1:111] Everything that the Romantics state about the essence of art is a determination of its idea, thus also the form, which, in their dialectic of self-limitation and self-elevation, brings to expression the dialectic of unity and infinity in the idea. The *a priori* of a method in this context is understood under the term "idea"; there corresponds to it the ideal as the *a priori* of the coordinated matter.[1] The Romantics know nothing of an ideal of art. They gain merely a semblance of it through the things that cover over the poetic absolute, such as morality and religion. All determinations that Friedrich Schlegel gave about the matter of art, especially in the "Dialogue on Poetry," lack—in contrast to his conception of form—any more precise relation to what is peculiar about art, let alone that he had found an *a priori* of this matter. Goethe's philosophy of art issues from such an a priori. Its driving motif is the question concerning the ideal of art. The ideal is also a supreme conceptual unity, that of the matter. Its function is therefore one that is completely different from the function of the idea. It is not a medium that contains within itself and forms out of itself the nexus of forms but, rather, a unity of another kind. It is graspable only in a limited multeity of pure contents into which it decomposes itself. The ideal, therefore, manifests itself in a limited, harmonious dis-continuum of pure contents. Goethe makes contact with the Greeks in this conception. Interpreted by and through the philosophy of art, the idea of the muses under the supremacy of Apollo is the idea of the pure contents of all art. The Greeks counted nine such contents, and it is certain that neither the kind nor the number was arbitrarily determined. The sum total of pure contents—the ideal of art—may therefore be designated as the muse-related [*das Musische*]. Just as the inner structure of the ideal is a discontinuous one in

---

* Idea and Ideal

contrast with the idea, so the connection of this ideal with art is not given in a medium but, rather, through a refraction. The pure contents are, as such, to be found in no work. Goethe calls them archetypes. The works cannot attain these invisible—but intuitable—archetypes, whose protectresses the Greeks knew under the name of the muses; they can only equal them to a greater or lesser degree. This "equaling," which [1:112] determines the relation of works to archetypes, is to be preserved from a pernicious materialistic misunderstanding. It cannot in principle lead to equality, and it cannot be achieved through imitation. For the archetypes are invisible, and "equaling" designates simply the relation of what is most perceptible to what is intuitable only in principle. An object of intuition is thereby the necessity that any content that purely announces itself in feeling become completely perceptible.[2] Hearing [*Vernehmen*] this necessity is intuition.[3] The ideal of art as an object of intuition is therefore a necessary perceptibility—which never purely appears in the artwork itself, as that which remains an object of perception.— For Goethe, the works of the Greeks were, among all works, the ones that came closest to archetypes; they became, as it were, relative archetypes or models. As works of the ancients, these models exhibit a double analogy to the archetypes themselves; the former are, like the latter, completed in the double sense of the word; they are perfect, and they are finished.[4] For only the completely concluded formation can be an archetype. The primal source of art does not lie, according to Goethe's conception, in eternal becoming, in the creative movement in the medium of forms. Art itself does not create its archetypes—these rest, prior to all created work, in that sphere of art where art is not Creation but, rather, nature. To grasp the idea of nature and thereby to make it suitable for an archetype of art (for a pure content)—this was in the final instance Goethe's endeavor in the identification of urphenomena.[5] The contention that the artwork reproduces nature can be correct in a deeper sense, therefore, only if it is understood simply as a content of the artwork's nature itself—not, however, as a truth of nature. It follows thereupon that the correlate of the content, [namely,] that which is presented (therefore nature), cannot be made equal to the content.[6] The concept of "that which is presented" has a double sense. It does not here have the meaning of "the depiction," for this is indeed identical with the content. This place otherwise contains the concept of true nature—following what was said above about intuition—as indiscriminately identical with the domain of archetypes or urphenomena or ideas, without worrying over the concept [1:113] of nature as an object of science. It is, however, not a matter of defining in a totally naive manner the concept of nature pure and simple as an art-theoretical concept. On the contrary, the question of how nature appears to science is an urgent one, and the concept of intuition perhaps accomplishes nothing by way of an answer.[7] For it remains within the theory of art (here in the place where the relationship between work and archetype is treated). What is presented can be seen only in the work; outside of the work, it can be only intuited. A content of the artwork that is true to nature would presuppose that nature be the standard against which the work would be measured; this content itself, however, should be visible nature. Goethe thinks in terms of the sublime paradox of that old anecdote, according to which the sparrows flew to the grapes of the great Greek master.[8] The Greeks were no naturalists, and the excessive verisimilitude reported in this story seems only a splendid circumlocution for true nature as content of works themselves.[9] Here, though, everything would depend on the more narrow definition of the concept of "true nature," such that this "true" visible nature, which is supposed to constitute the content of the work of art, not only must not be indiscriminately identified with the visibly appearing nature of the world but must, on the contrary, be at first differentiated in a rigorously conceptual way from this world, such that the problem would be of a deeper, essential identity of the "true" visible nature in the artwork with the (perhaps invisible, only intuitable, urphenomenal) nature present in the appearances of visible nature. And this problem would in a possible as well as paradoxical way solve itself, such that only in art—not, however, in the nature of the world—the true, intuitable, urphenomenal nature would become reproducibly visible, whereas in the nature of the world, it would be present, to be sure, but concealed (faded by appearance).

*With this way of seeing, however, it is posited that every individual work exists contingently, to a certain extent, vis-à-vis the ideal of art, regardless of whether one calls its pure content the muse-like moment or nature, since, like Goethe, one seeks a new muse-like canon in it. For this ideal is not created [1:114] but, rather, according to its cognition-theoretical determination, an idea in the Platonic sense; unity and the absence of a beginning, the Eleatic resting point in art, is resolved in its sphere. Individual works may well have a share in the archetypes, but there is no transition from their realm to the

---

*   The Muse-Related

works; none like the one that definitely exists in the medium of art from absolute form to individual forms. In relation to the ideal the individual work remains, as it were, a torso.* It is an isolated endeavor to present the archetype, and the archetype can endure with others of its kind only as a model; never, however, are they capable of vitally coalescing into the unity of the ideal itself.

†Goethe thought about the relationship of works to the unconditioned and thus to each other in a renunciatory manner. Everything in Romantic thinking, however, rebelled against this solution. Art was the region in which Romanticism strove to carry out most purely the immediate reconciliation of the conditioned and the unconditioned. Admittedly, in his first period, Friedrich Schlegel still stood close to Goethe's conception and formulated it very pithily when he designated Greek art as that "whose particular history would be the universal natural history of art," and immediately continues: "... the thinker ... requires ... a perfect intuition. Partly as an example and proof for his concept, partly as a fact and certification of his investigation. ... The pure law is empty. For it to be filled out ... it requires ... a supreme aesthetic archetype ... no word other than imitation for the action of one ... who dedicates himself to the lawfulness of that archetype."‡ But what forbade Schlegel this solution, the more he came to himself, was that it led to a highly conditional estimation of the individual work. In the same essay in which his developing standpoint strives to find its destination, when he says the following, he basically contrasts necessity, infinity, and idea with imitation, perfection, and ideal: "The purposes of human beings are partly infinite and necessary, partly [1:115] limited and contingent. Art is therefore ... a free art of ideas."§ It is then said about art much more decisively around the turn of the century: It "wants ... every part in this highest formation of the human spirit to be at the same time the whole, and were this wish really unattainable,

---

* A form, which for its part only within this intuition of art, becomes comprehensible and belongs to it as the fragment belongs to the Romantic [intuition of art].

† The Unconditional Work

‡ [Friedrich Schlegel, *Seine prosaischen*] *Jugendschriften* [*1794–1802*, ed. J. Minor, 2nd ed., 2 vols. (Vienna: Konegan, 1906)], I, 123ff. ["On the Study of Greek Poetry"]. See also [Novalis] *Briefwechsel* [ed. J. M. Raich (Mainz: Kirchheim, 1880)] 83.—Also here, with the concept of imitation, Schlegel overstrains the original thought.

§ [F. Schlegel] *Jugendschriften* I, 104 ["On the Study of Greek Poetry"]; "Free art ideas," also *Jugendschriften* II, 361 ["Dialogue on Poetry"].

58 WALTER BENJAMIN

as sophists . . . would have us believe, then we would rather give up on the null and perverse beginning* once and for all."† "Every poem, every work should mean the whole, really and in fact mean and through the meaning . . . also really and in fact be."‡ The intention in Friedrich Schlegel's concept of form is the sublation of the contingency, the torso-character of works. Vis-à-vis the ideal, the torso is a legitimate shape; it has no place in the medium of forms. The artwork is not allowed to be a torso; it must be a moving, transitory moment in the vital transcendental form. By limiting itself in its form, it makes itself transitory in a contingent shape; eternal, however, in a transient shape, by critique.§

§The Romantics wanted to make the lawfulness of the artwork into an absolute. The moment of contingency, however, is dissolved or, on the contrary, transformed into a lawfulness only with the dissolution of the work. That is why, for the sake of consistency, the Romantics had to conduct a radical polemic against the Goethean doctrine of the canonical validity of Greek works. They could not recognize models, self-sufficient, self-contained [1:116] works, formations that are definitively stamped and exempted from eternal progression. Novalis turned against Goethe in the most high-spirited and wittiest way: "Nature and insight into nature arise at the same time,** like antiquity and knowledge of antiquity; for one very much errs, when one believes that antiquities are given. Only now does antiquity begin to

---

* Referring to poesy.

† [F. Schlegel] *Jugendschriften* II, 427 ["Conclusion to the Lessing Essay"].

‡ [F. Schlegel] *Jugendschriften* II, 428 ["Conclusion to the Lessing Essay"].

§ The prescriptions and techniques of poetics were given with reference to the contingent, torso-character of individual works. Goethe studied the law of the artistic genres, to some extent, not without reference to these prescriptions and techniques. The Romantics also explored them—not, however, in order to hold in place such artistic genres but, rather, with the intention of finding the medium, the absolute into which the works would critically dissolve. They set up these investigations on analogy with morphological studies that are suitable for the exploration of the relations of beings to life, whereas cognitions of normative poetics can be compared to anatomical studies, which have as their object less immediately life than the rigid structure of individual organisms. For the Romantics, the exploration of the artistic genres refers only to art, whereas, with Goethe, it additionally pursues normative, pedagogical tendencies with regard to the individual work and its fabrication as well.

§ Antiquity

** Cf. Part I, Chap. IV [see 1:53–61; SW 1:143–48].

arise. . . . It is with classical literature as with antiquity; it is not actually given to us—it is not here and now; rather, it first has to be brought forth by us. A classical literature—which the ancients themselves did not have—first arises for us through diligent and spirited study of the ancients—."* "Only let us not believe all too firmly that antiquity and the perfected would be made—made in the sense that we say something is made. They are made as the beloved is made by the agreed-upon sign of the friend in the night, as sparks are made by contact with the conductor or the star by a movement in the eye."† That is to say, it arises only where a creative spirit recognizes it; it is not a fact in the Goethean sense. The same assertion is read in another place: "Antiquities are at the same time products of the future and of prehistory."‡ And immediately afterward: "Is there a central antiquity or a universal spirit of antiquity?" The question touches on Schlegel's thesis about the work-like unity of ancient poetry, and both are understood to be anticlassical.—As with ancient works, it is also a matter for Schlegel of dissolving the ancient genres into one another. "It was in vain that individuals completely expressed the ideal of their genre, if the genres themselves were not also . . . rigorously and sharply isolated. . . . But arbitrarily to transpose oneself now into this sphere, now into that sphere . . . this is only possible for a mind that . . . contains an entire system of persons in himself, and in whose interior the universe . . . is . . . ripe."§ Therefore: "All classical modes of poetry in their rigorous purity are now ridiculous."¶ And finally: "One can compel no one [1:117] to take the ancients for classic or for ancient; that depends in the end on maxims."**

††The Romantics determine the relation of works of art to art as infinity in totality—that is: the infinity of art fulfills itself in the totality of the works; Goethe determines this relation as unity in multeity—that is: the unity of art is to be found again and again in the multeity of the works. The infinity of the former is that of pure form, the unity of the latter is that of the pure

---

* [Novalis] *Schriften* [*Kritische Neuausgabe*, ed. Ernst Heilborn, 2 vols. (Berlin: Reimer, 1901)], [2:] 69ff. [Fragmente 1797].

† [Novalis] *Schriften* [2:]563 [General Draft for an Encyclopedia, 1798–1799].

‡ [Novalis] *Schriften* [2:]491 [General Draft for an Encyclopedia, 1798–1799].

§ [F. Schlegel] *Athenäum* [*Fragment #*] 121.

¶ [F. Schlegel] *Lyceum* [*Fragment #*] 60.

** [F. Schlegel] *Athenäum* [*Fragment #*] 143.

†† Style

content.* The question of the relationship between the Goethean and the Romantic theory of art coincides with the question concerning the relationship between the pure content and the pure (and, as such, rigorous) form. The question concerning the relationship between form and content, which is often erroneously posed with a view toward the individual work and is never precisely solvable in such a context, arises in this sphere. For form and content are not substrates in the empirical formation but, rather, relative distinctions in it, encountered due to necessary, pure art-philosophical distinctions. The idea of art is the idea of its form, just as its ideal is the ideal of its content. The fundamental systematic question of the philosophy of art can therefore also be formulated as the question concerning the relationship between the idea and the ideal of art. The present investigation cannot transgress the threshold of this question; it could only lay out a problem-historical nexus up to the point where it indicated the systematic nexus with full clarity. This status of German philosophy of art around 1800, as it presents itself in the theories of Goethe and the early Romantics, is still legitimate today. The Romantics did not resolve, or indeed even simply pose, this question, any more than Goethe did. They work together to pose this question for [1:118] problem-historical thinking. Only systematic thinking resolves it.—As was already emphasized, the Romantics were not capable of grasping the ideal of art. It remains to be noted that Goethe's solution to the problem of form did not attain in philosophical scope his determination of the content of art. Goethe interpreted artistic form as style. Yet he saw in style the form-principle of the artwork only by placing before his eyes a more or less historically determined style: the presentation of a typifying kind. For the plastic arts, the Greeks represented to him style; for poetry, he himself strove to set up its model. However, despite the fact that the content of the work is the

---

* Here, to be sure, there exists an equivocation in the term "pure." More exactly, it designates, first, the methodological dignity of a concept (as in "pure reason"); thereafter, it can have a meaning that is positive with regard to content, one that is, if you will, morally colored. In the above, both of these meanings are intended in the concept of "pure content" as the muse-element, whereas absolute form should be designated as pure only in the methodical sense. For its matter-of-fact [*sachliche*] determination—which corresponds to the purity of the content—is presumably rigor. The Romantics did not develop this in their theory of the novel wherein the perfectly pure, but not rigorous form was elevated to the absolute form (see *Athenäum* [*Fragment #*] 107); here, too, is a circle of thought in which Hölderlin towered over them.

archetype, the type nevertheless does not have any need to determine its form. Goethe did not thus provide a philosophical clarification of the problem of form in the concept of style but only an indication of that which is authoritative in certain models. The intention that thereby disclosed to him the depths of the problem of content in art became the source of a sublime naturalism in advance of the problem of form. While an archetype, a nature, was also supposed to show itself in contrast with form, an art-nature, as it were—for such is style in this sense—had to be made into the archetype of form—since nature could not in itself be this. Novalis saw this very clearly. Rejecting it, he calls it Goethean: "The ancients are from another world; it is as if they fell from the sky."* He thereby designates in fact the essence of this art-nature that Goethe represents in style qua archetype. The concept of the archetype, however, loses its meaning for the problem of form as soon as it is conceived as its solution. The problem of art, circumscribed by its entire scope, by form and content through the concept of the archetype, is the privilege of the ancient thinkers, those who sometimes pose the deepest questions of philosophy in the shape of mythic solutions. Goethe's concept of style in the end recounts a myth. The objection to it may also be raised on the basis of the lack of distinction between form of presentation and absolute form that runs through it. For the question concerning the presentational form remains to be differentiated from the already considered problem of form as a question concerning absolute form. It scarcely needs [1:119] to be emphasized, incidentally, that the presentational form has an entirely different meaning for Goethe than for the early Romantics. It is the measure establishing the beauty that makes its appearance in the matter. The concept of measure is remote from Romanticism, which paid no attention to an a priori of content, nothing up against which art is to be measured. By rejecting beauty, it also rejected not only rules but also measure, and its poetry is not only without rule but also without measure.

†Goethe's theory of art leaves unresolved not only the problem of absolute form but also that of critique. Whereas it acknowledges the former in veiled form and is summoned to express the magnitude of this question, it appears, however, to deny the latter. Critique in relation to the artwork is in fact, according to Goethe's ultimate intention, neither possible nor necessary.

---

*   [Novalis] *Schriften*, [2:]491 [General Draft for the Encyclopedia, 1798–1799].

†   Critique

A notice of the good or a warning about the bad may at most be needed, and for the artist who has an intuition of the archetype, apodictic judgment about works is possible. But Goethe refuses to acknowledge criticizability as an essential moment of the artwork. From his standpoint, methodical critique, that is, one that is factically necessary, is impossible. In Romantic art, however, critique is not only possible and necessary; in their theory, rather, there inevitably lies the paradox of a critique esteemed more highly than the work. In their critiques the Romantics are also therefore unfamiliar with any consciousness of rank that the poet occupies over the reviewer. The cultivation of critique and forms, in which, on both accounts, they acquired the greatest merits, are set into their theory as deepest tendencies. In this, therefore, they fully achieved unanimity in deed and thought and fulfilled precisely what, according to their convictions, counted as the highest for them. The lack of poetic productivity, with which one sometimes depicts Friedrich Schlegel in particular, does not belong in the strict sense within the scope of his image. For he did not primarily want to be a poet in the sense of one who makes a work. The absolutization of the work in its creation, the critical procedure, was for him the highest. This can be made sensuous in an image: as the generation of bedazzlement in the work. This bedazzlement—the sober light—makes the multeity of works fade away. It is the idea.

5

LIFE BUILT UP FROM THE ELEMENTS

[7:732] {Life   built up from the elements
   Outward expressions   Historical}[1]

     Life   Object
   built up from the elements   of a biography
          As the essence determines itself
             and
         for which its manifestations
           are determined

     Expressions
Works   manifestations
Total   partial
"Nature"*   character
Unfathomableness   freedom
Evincing   determining

---

* "our most inner essence, the common substratum of us all," Nietzsche I, p. 21, that is "nature." [The passage is drawn from the opening section of Nietzsche's *Birth of Tragedy*, which is a description of the dream state, associated with Apollo.]

In the majority [of cases]

Existence ◄

Differentiating tendency	Integrating tendency
reactive (contemplative)	active
Experience	Lived experience
of one's own essence	of one's own essence

Essence
determined through elements

Determinable but not definable,
Therefore, neither works nor manifestations
synthetically derivable from it

Mythic

Work and fate	character	life
↑ totality ↓	integrability	singularity

[7:733]

	Historical		Mythic
Work		Manifestation	Works
Freedom			Destining [*Schickung*]
Creation			Fulfillment

Conjuring character of mythic poetry
Particular *life contents* of the artist

Essence	Work	Life
Daemon	Shape	Fate

Non-separation

Banal biography ◄————————► mythic conception

↓

By contrast, true artwork

↓

Poet in the George school[2]

{Totality}

A problematic of scientific dignity

| The mythic work | Destiny |
| | Fulfillment |

| The artwork | Freedom |
| | Creation |

6

PURITY AND RIGOR ARE
CATEGORIES OF THE WORK

[6:128] Purity and rigor are categories of the work.
Beauty and the expressionless [are] those of art.

Purity is the purity of the matter	Universality
Rigor is the rigor of the form	Limitation
Beauty is beauty of what is perceived	Totality
Expressionless is expressionless of the symbol	Singularity[1]

NOTES TOWARD A WORK ON THE IDEA OF BEAUTY

[6:128] Not every form is beautiful. Form is (probably) earlier, certainly also later than beauty.

The authentic time of beauty is defined by the decay of myth until its demolition. Such a demolition first occurred during the time of the migration of peoples.[1] Before its decay and after its demolition, myth is foreign to beauty.

Beauty has the latent working of myth as its presupposition. The beauty of a poem asserts itself *despite* an exhibition of mythic elements. But it would not be "beautiful" without such elements.

A new framework inserted itself through Christianity around the world of myth, as it was demolished during the time of the migration of peoples.[2] The stretto of the Gothic, like myth, fits into the prickly framework: beauty as the framework that again holds together the world of myth that had been demolished from within. Thereby the Gothic, the Baroque, etc. correspond to the Greek time when beauty formed itself in the decay of myths.

How did mythological motifs become "beautiful"? The problem of Homeric poetry is thus posed.

8

CATEGORIES OF AESTHETICS

[1:828] I
  I. Form—Content   to be interpreted as rigor and purity
  II. Intuition—Perception
  III. Beauty—Expressionless   to be interpreted as perception and symbolic
  IV. Creation—Formation

The concept of Creation does not enter the philosophy of art as the concept of a cause. For "Creation" develops the *virtus* of cause in general only in a single domain, namely, in "something created." The artwork, however, is not a "created thing." It is something sprung forth; those without insight may call it something arisen or something that came into being; in any case, it is not something "created." This is because the created thing is defined such that its life—which [1:829] is higher than the life of something sprung forth—shares in the intention of redemption. An uninhibited share. Even nature (as a setting of history), to be sure, has such a share, to say nothing of the human being, but not the work of art.—The relation of Creation to the work of art cannot be comprehended through the schema of cause-and-effect. Nevertheless, not infrequently Creation has a connection to the great work of art. Specifically, as content. Creation is one of the most forceful themes of art. An entire class of forms that deal with "Creation" would have to be called a kind of form in which the theme of Creation comes into view after enduring the variations of intuition. These works distinguish themselves perhaps through an especially high measure of the expressionless in them; perhaps, however, Creation can come to light only in the slightest things and the most colorful things. One can designate the form of works whose theme is "Creation" as a "punched-out form." These are forms that seemingly salvage so much shadow and turmoil, like the hollow punched-out or hammered-out inside of metallic relief-work. Such forms are, however, not Creation; they are not even "created"; rather, they present Creation, or, on the contrary—this is their essence, properly speaking—they present its content in the high and sublime rank of Creation. All forms perhaps actually have something of the punched-out form, insofar as all works of art still somehow have Creation for their content.

Works of art, and forms, too, are not created. This stamps itself in the essence of works and their forms. Mörike's profound verse, "Whatever is beautiful is (!), however, blissful in itself,"[1] connects semblance with beauty, here understood, to be sure, as the beauty of art. The beauty of art is in fact bound up with semblance. [It is] bound up with the semblance of totality and perfection; and therefore bound precisely through semblance. The higher the beauty, the higher the kind of perfection and totality that it seems to conduct with itself. At the lowest level, it is the totality and perfection of sensible reality; at the highest, it is that of blessedness. All the same, these categories remain limited within certain boundaries. Never can the beauty of art be called holy. *Nonsemblant beauty is no longer essentially beautiful but something greater. Correspondingly, however, a beauty whose semblance no longer seeks to be bound up with perfection and completion but, rather, remains free by, as it were, intensively strengthening this beauty is no longer a beauty of art but, instead, a daemonic beauty. The seductiveness of beauty* [1:830] *rests on shamelessness, the nakedness of semblance that sheathes it (The Temptation of St. Anthony).*[2]

A form is the law according to which beauty connects itself to totality and perfection. All form is mysterious and enigmatic, because it ascends from the unfathomableness of beauty, where it is arrested by semblance. This is why Goethe says, "Beauty can never become clear about itself."[3] Form springs forth in the unfathomable, but the creature is created from nothingness.

Creature and shape—construction and form are to be distinguished from each other as something created and something sprung forth. Without the Creator there is eidetically no Creation and no creature; construction and form, by contrast, eidetically persist even without the artist.

It is decisive, however, that the act of Creation concerns the persistence of Creation, the persistence of the world. The origin of the work, though, concerns its perceptibility from inception onward. This is located in the primordial tendency of semblance. The life of Creation remains in obscurity, in the shadow of the Creator, until the Creator releases himself from Creation. This release of the Creator is a moral act.[4] It constitutes the sphere of perception in an unbroken, rectilinear intention from the Creation that in this sphere is good, which is seen as "good" only because it constitutes "seeing."[5]

The *intentio* of beauty, by contrast, breaks through the resistance of intuition in order to break into the sphere of perception as a shape of Creation, yet not completely. Rather, the work is weakened by the necessity of its purity and rigor.[6]

The essence of Creation is exemplary for the moral conditionality of utopian perception. To the extent that a work penetrates the circuit of art and is a utopian perception, it is a Creation; it is subjected to moral categories not only in relation to the human being who receives it but also in relation to its persistence in the circuit of perception. The morality of Creation imprints the stamp of the expressionless on the work. The order according to which Creation is capable of being morally perceptible is to be set forth with reference to the opening of Genesis.

9
ON "SEMBLANCE"

[1:831] "Not everything is possible, but the semblance of everything is." Hebbel[1]

A semblance that one must fathom (e.g., an error)
        that one must flee from (e.g., Sirens)
        that one is allowed to take no notice of (e.g., a will-o'-the-wisp)

Another classification of semblance:

Semblance behind which something is concealed (e.g., the seductive: the Lady World of medieval legend whose back is eaten away by worms, while her front looks beautiful).[2]
    behind which nothing is concealed
    (e.g., fata morgana
        Also, chimera?)

Connection of semblance with the world of the visual.—Eidetic experiment: a man crosses the street, and a coach with four horses, coming down to him, appears from out of the clouds.[3] On another walk, a voice from the clouds resounds to the same person with the words, "You left your cigarette case at home." Now, in the analysis of both cases, once the possibility of hallucination—therefore, a subjective basis for the semblance—is left aside, this yields the following: in the first case, it is conceivable that nothing stands behind the appearance; in the second, this is inconceivable. The semblance in which nothingness appears is the more forceful, the more authentic. This is therefore conceivable only in the visual.

Does the intentional object that appears as semblance on the basis of a subjective cause (such as hallucinations) have a genuine semblance character?—And if "yes," is it the same character as a pure objective semblance?

"Going there, [we] perceived at the end of the rue des Chanoines, [as if] forming an optical image, the twin towers of the old Saint (?)-Étienne (l'Abbaye-aux-Hommes), veiled in a mist that made them more beautiful; for veils embellish all that they conceal and all that they reveal: women, horizons, and monuments!" D'Aurevilly, *Memoranda*, p. 227.[4]

Nietzsche's determination of semblance in *The Birth of Tragedy*.[5]

[1:832] ~~In every work and in every genre of art beautiful semblance is present; everything beautiful in art is there on account of beautiful semblance.~~ Among all kinds of semblance this beautiful semblance is to be a precisely distinctive kind. Not only is it found in art; but all authentic beauty in *art* is there on its account. On the other hand—inside as well as outside of art—only the beautiful and nothing ugly is to be attributed to this kind of semblance; regardless of whether it be found in art or elsewhere, it belongs to beautiful semblance, even if it is a semblance. There are different degrees of beautiful semblance, a scale that is determined not by the greater or lesser beauty in it but, rather, by its more or less semblance-like character. The law of this scale is not only fundamental for the theory of beautiful semblance but also essential for metaphysics in general. It states that in every formation of beautiful semblance, the greater the semblance, the livelier it appears. It is thereby possible to determine the essence and the boundaries of art as well as a possible hierarchy of its kinds of semblance.

No work of art can appear thoroughly alive without becoming mere semblance and ceasing to be a work of art. The life trembling in it must appear rigidified and spellbound as in an instant. The life trembling in it is the beauty, that harmonia that suffuses chaos and—only seems to tremble. That which puts a stop to this semblance, spellbinds life, and stops harmonia in midphrase is the expressionless.[6] Such trembling constitutes beauty, such rigidification the truth of the work. For, just as the interruption of a liar's speech by a commanding word can extract the truth where speaking stops, so the expressionless compels the quivering harmonia to come to a halt and eternalizes its trembling through its protest. In this eternalization, the beautiful must answer for itself, but now it appears as though it were interrupted in this, its taking-responsibility. The expressionless is that critical force that cannot, to be sure, separate semblance from truth in art but refuses the mixing of one with the other. It has this force, however, as a moral word. In the expressionless, the sublime force of the true appears as it determines the symbolism of the existing world according to the laws of the moral one. Trembling life is never symbolic, for it is formless; still less is it beautiful life, for it is semblance. Precisely spellbound life, however, as rigidified and mortified, can indeed point to the symbolic. This it does by the force of the expressionless.—The expressionless, more exactly, shatters whatever in all beautiful semblance still endures as the heritage of chaos: the false, the mendacious, the errant totality, in short, the absolute totality. The latter first completes the work by smashing it into piecework, into the *smallest* totality of semblance, which [is] a great fragment of the true world, a fragment of a symbol.

10

BEAUTY

[6:128] Its idea   Its ideal
        The intuition of the secret   Beautiful nature (the living body)

[6:129] Art seeks to satisfy the idea of beauty and attain its ideal. Beauty presents itself in the ideal as a living body; in art it does so as a sharing. Art shares only a part of beauty.[1]

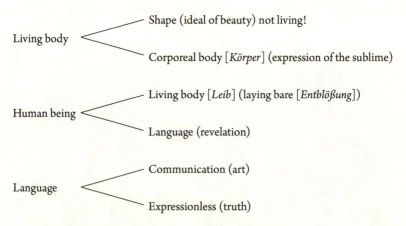

Nothing authentically alive is truly beautiful. Therefore, the essentially beautiful is semblance wherever it attaches itself to whatever is authentically alive.

[6:706]² First Part: The Mythic as Thesis, ["]Whoever chooses blindly is struck in the eyes by the smoke of sacrifice["]³

Threefold meaning of Ottilie's sacrificial death

1) A sacrifice for the de-expiation⁴ of others

innocence
relics

2) A sacrifice of destiny

guilty-innocent

3) An expiation of her own guilt

purification
suicide [*Freitod*]

11

BEAUTY AND SEMBLANCE

[6:129] I. Every<thing>[1] living that is beautiful is semblant
  II. Every <thing> artificial that is beautiful is semblant
      because [it is] somehow lively
  III. There remains, therefore, only natural dead things that can be beautiful without perhaps being semblant.

12

TRUTH AND TRUTHS / COGNITION AND COGNITIONS

[6:46] Cognition in an objective sense is defined as the sum total of all cognitions. Just as the concept of this totality in this definition [6:47] should be stringent and absolute and refer to the totality of cognitions in general, not only the complete cognitions of a specific region, so does *the concept of cognition* designate a chimerical site of unification. Only the concept of cognitions in their multeity is cogent; a multeity whose unity does not lie in their own sphere is not a sum total, not a judgment. If one means by unity a unity not only of cognitions but also of cognition, there is no unity of cognitions.

Truth takes the place in the system that is so often usurped by a chimerical sum total of cognition. Truth is the sum total of cognitions as symbol. It is not, however, the sum total of all truths. Truth expresses itself in the system or in its conceptual title. Truths, however, express themselves neither systematically nor conceptually, let alone like cognitions in the form of a judgment but, instead, in art. Artworks are the site of truths. So many genuine works, so many ultimate truths. These ultimate truths are not elements but, rather, genuine parts, pieces, or fragments of truth, which, on their own accord, however, afford no possibility of composition and on their own account do not complement one another. Cognitions, on the other hand, are not pieces, not fragments of truth, and are therefore not of the same essence as these ultimate truths but, rather, deeper, as it were, less organized material out of which the higher <part> constructs itself (as from elements?).

The chimerical nature of a sum total of cognitions is to be demonstrated.

On the relation of cognition to truth, Goethe: Materials for the History of Theory of Colors, First Section, Greek and Roman, Reflections . . . "Since in knowledge as in reflection no whole can be brought together, because the former lacks the inner, while the latter lacks the outer, we must conceive of science necessarily as an art if we expect from it any kind of whole. And indeed we have to seek this not in something universal, not in something overwhelming but, rather, just as art always presents itself completely in individual artworks, so science should also demonstrate itself completely in every individual thing with which it is concerned."[1] Immediately thereafter science in the sense [6:48] of an artwork, "whatever the matter may be,"[2] comes under discussion (Goedeke X 361).[3]

An accurate judgment is designated as a cognition. I am allowed to judge this cognition as "correct." I am not allowed, however, to judge as "true" the same thing that I judge as "correct." If I can call a judgment correct, I mean the judgment as a whole, unaltered, as it stands. If I say, however, it is true, I mean that it is true that this judgment is correct. The correctness of a judgment has a relation to truth, and this is what I mean when I say "this proposition is true." The correctness of a cognition is never identical with truth, but every correctness has a relation to truth. And indeed, all cases of correctness are as such homogenous. The judgment "every fly has six legs" is correct precisely in the same way that the judgment "$2 \times 2 = 4$." The truth of these propositions, however, is a heterogeneous one. For the truth of the second judgment stands in a deeper relation to truth than that of the first.

Cognition and truth are never identical: there is no true cognition and no cognized truth. Nevertheless, cognitions are indispensable for the presentation of truth.

13

THEORY OF ART CRITIQUE

[1:833] The unity of philosophy, its system, is, as an answer, of a higher cardinality than the infinite number of finite questions that can be posed. It is of a higher kind and cardinality than that which the sum total of all these questions can ask, because the *unity* of the answer cannot be inquired into.[1] It is therefore also of a higher cardinality than any individual philosophical question or problem can inquire into.—If there were such questions that nevertheless inquire into the unity of the answer, these would stand in a fundamentally different relationship to philosophy than its problems. In the answer to these problems there always again arises the tendency of questioning further, a tendency that has given occasion to shallow interpretations of a phrase in which philosophy is said to be an infinite task.[2] The thus-disappointed longing after unity that cannot be inquired into expresses itself in another tendency in the answer, which can be designated as its return-questioning: a return-questioning aimed at the lost unity of the question or at a better question in which the unity of the answer would at the same time be inquired into.—So, if there were such questions in which the unity could be inquired into, then in advance of answering them, there would exist in this unity no further-questioning and no return-questioning as tendency. There are no such questions; the system of philosophy can in no sense be inquired into. And to this virtual question (which is glimpsed only from the answer) there is, it goes without saying, precisely a single answer: the system of philosophy itself. There are, however, formations that—without being able to be philosophy itself, that is, without the answer to that virtual question and without being virtual, that is, without being able to be the question—nevertheless have the deepest affinity [*Affinität*] with philosophy, or rather, with the ideal of its problem; [these are] real, not virtual formations, which are neither answers nor questions. They are works of art. The work of art does not compete with philosophy itself; rather, it simply enters into the deepest relationship with philosophy through its affinity [*Verwandtschaft*] with the ideal of the problem. The ideal [of the] problem is an idea, which is designated as an ideal because [1:834] it refers not to the immanent form of the problem but, rather, to the content of its answer that transcends it, although only through the concept of the problem itself, as to the concept of the unity of its answer. According to a lawfulness that probably lies in the essence of the ideal as such, the ideal of the problem can present itself only in a plurality (just as the idea of the pure content in art presents itself in the plurality of muses). Therefore, only in a plurality or multeity of ~~virtual~~ questions is the unity of philosophy in principle to be inquired into.[3] This multeity lies locked up in the multeity of true works of art, and its extraction is the business of critique.[4] What critique finds there to be exposed in the work of art is at bottom the virtual formulability of its content as a philosophical problem, and it is at the formulation of the problem that it comes to a halt out of respect, so to speak, for the work of art, to be sure, even more so, however, out of respect for truth. For critique always and constantly demonstrates the aforementioned formulability under the never fulfilled presupposition that the philosophical system would in general be capable of inquiring into. In other words, critique asserts that the philosophical system, completed, would in this or that problem show itself as inquired into. Critique allows the ideal of the philosophical problem to come to light in the work of art, in one of its appearances; if, however, it wants to speak of the work of art as such, it can say only that it symbolizes this problem. The multeity of artworks is, as the Romantics already saw, harmonious, and indeed it is so, as the early Romantics also already intimated, not from some vague principle belonging only to art and immanent only in art. It is harmonious with reference to the appearances of the ideal of the problem.

When one says that all beauty somehow refers to the true, and its virtual place in philosophy is determinable, this means that an appearance of the ideal of the problem can be located in every true work of art. And a remark is to be added to this: an appearance of the ideal of the problem is assigned to every philosophical problem as, so to speak, its radiant circle; the virtual direction toward the to-be-inquired-into unity is everywhere possible, and the work of art in which it lies enclosed is therefore related to certain genuine philosophical problems, even if it is also precisely separated from them.

Another yet-to-be-determined appearance of the beautiful in the true corresponds to this appearance of the true as well as the individual truth in the individual beautiful formation; the appearance of the enclosed harmonious totality of the beautiful in the unity of the true. At its summit Plato's *Symposium* is concerned with this totality. Beauty, so it is taught there, virtually appears only in the whole of truth.

[1:835] This remains to be investigated: which common ground for these two relations between art and philosophy can be found.

(The true: unity
The beautiful: multeity, condensed into totality)
(Perhaps a relationship of virtuality also exists between other regions. Cannot
morality appear virtually in freedom?)

A comparison: One gets to know someone who is young, beautiful, and attractive but who seems to hold a secret. It would be indelicate and reprehensible to want to press him, so as to snatch it away. It is, however, certainly allowed to find out whether this person has siblings and whether their kind and essence would in some way clarify for us the mysterious essence of the stranger. Altogether in this way does the true critic conduct research into the siblings of artworks. And every great work has its sibling (brother or sister?) in a philosophical sphere.

Just as philosophy draws morality [*Sittlichkeit*] and language into the theoretical sphere in symbolic concepts, so, in reverse, the theoretical (logical) can be drawn into morality and language in symbolic concepts. Then, moral and aesthetic critique emerges.

14

THE MORE POWERFULLY THE EXPRESSIONLESS COMES FORTH IN POETRY

[7:733] [...] may be. (The linguistic side to the moral nature of the expressionless obviously remains to be illuminated with some clarity.)¹—The more powerfully the expressionless protrudes into poetry, the more all beauty and all semblance must disappear into the fleeting remainder. Such protruding has scarcely been clearer than in Greek tragedy, on the one hand, and in Hölderlin's hymns, on the other—perceptible in tragedy as the falling silent of the hero, in the hymns as the protest in the rhythm. Indeed, one cannot more precisely designate such rhythm than with the statement that something beyond the poet stops the poetry in midphrase.² Just as the expressionless protrudes into Hölderlin's lyric, so does beauty protrude into Goethe's at the very limit of what can compose itself in the artwork. With the former, chaos almost passing into harmony; with the latter, the world almost persisting in symbols.

In this respect, German poetry cannot venture a step beyond Goethe without mercilessly succumbing to an illusory world. Whereas [7:734] Goethe did everything so that he would not have to do this, his epigones stopped at nothing so as to be able to do so. And unlike Goethe, Hölderlin had necessarily set the limit of his poetry with his life.³

Every hierarchy concerning artistic kinds that is determined by the share that the arts take in beautiful semblance would at the same time express the measure of liveliness that inheres in the kinds of art. Poetry would find its

THE MORE POWERFULLY THE EXPRESSIONLESS COMES FORTH IN POETRY   83

place at the deepest stratum of that order: in it the liveliness of the beautiful is at its most powerful. In accordance with its form, it discloses the fact that it always remains accessible to the human voice. One would have to seek the essential basis of this liveliness in language. Next, there would be a place for painting, whose greater distance from liveliness is indicated only through the fact that its beauty is a material appropriate to it. This material, furthermore, is for it and it alone. Only painting, not poetry, may choose a Mona Lisa as its motif without succumbing to semblance. In this hierarchy music would presumably assume the highest position, whereas, concerning architecture, it will also be suggested in this reflection that it is not an art but, rather, according to its essence, a certain, difficult-to-fathom marking out of a place.

—Supplement: beautiful semblance is the semblance of totality. The more beautiful the semblance, the higher the kind of totality, which at first appears as empirical being, lastly as blessed being. By contrast, the more semblance-like the beautiful, the weaker its degree of totality, which at first appears to establish itself uniformly in everything, lastly only in a moment of the work.—The law according to which beautiful semblance is bound to the maximal degree of totality is called form.

The relation of the expressionless to the sublime in its ancient sense, to which a tendency opposing the beautiful inheres, stands in need of an exposition.—It must unconditionally be brought to evidence that the region of the validity that accrues to the judgment "this is beautiful" is infinitely greater than the region in whose appearances the beautiful is present. Thus, works of architecture lie perhaps in the first, certainly not in the second region. Here should be added a fundamental remark for which confirmations everywhere offer themselves in metaphysical lines of thought. The more precisely thought grasps the linguistically plain formulations of fundamental metaphysical insights, the more it becomes clear which extraordinary and almost unforeseeable tasks of logic arise in the logical, categorial illumination of these insights.

15

THE SACRAMENTAL ALSO TURNS INTO THE MYTHIC

[1:837] The sacramental also turns into the mythic. For the following lies [1:838] at the basis of this peculiar state of affairs: two couples get to know each other, and the old bonds are loosened; where two of the individuals who earlier did not know each other are mutually attracted to each other, the other two very soon enter into the closest relationship. It seems as though the simplest things proceed arduously and with difficulty as long as the Good Lord is concerned with them; but the most difficult things come off easily and happily if only the devil has a hand in them. The banal explanation for this occurrence lies close at hand. And yet, there is something to this matter, which may be explained by the "need for consolation," by the "common plight," by the "desire to exact revenge," but it is so forcefully and triumphantly beautiful, so little a makeshift and subterfuge, that such explanations become entirely vacuous. From the magic of mirrors there arises a flame that trembles in the triumphant encounter of the forsaken. For, to them, love is not original; what is original to them is the situation in which the ancient sacramental forces of marriage, which are decaying, seek to nest themselves among them as mythic, natural forces. This, and not love, is the authentic, silenced interior side of that symbiosis, that "common" situation in which those who are forsaken find themselves. The new day-to-day life, which falls into their lap, lays bare the sacrament of marriage: one sees oneself constantly, effortlessly, like a married couple; the previous spouses promote to the best of their ability the new interaction among those from whom they distanced themselves. Here, love is nothing more than the semblance of life, as it lends itself to the blind, death-defying passion of alchemical research, still more to the discovered, the uncovered sacrament of marriage. The spirit of the Black Mass here returns: the sacrament takes the place of love, while love takes the place of the sacrament. The spirit of satanic success prevails and shows marriage reflected as in a mirror. For Satan is dialectical, and a kind of deceitful, fortunate success—the semblance to which Nietzsche deeply succumbed—gives him away, just as the spirit of gravity betrays him.[1]

16

WITH REFERENCE TO FRANÇOIS-PONCET

[1:838] [François-Poncet's book][1] represents an incomprehensible, purely intellectual view, which, so to speak, sees a fabric of didactic moments in the novel. [1:839] This corresponds to the superficial view of the details: the novella is, despite some analogically important features, at bottom only an "interesting digression." It is supposed to have been written long before and thereafter worked into the novel. What significance—as the nucleus of the novel—it could possibly claim there escapes the author's mind.—In the novella, is the Captain really the rescuer, not the rejected one (pp. 184-88)?[2]

The diary is equally regarded in a superficial way as Goethean wisdom of life, which would be introduced without a true connection with the nature of Ottilie, whereas, in truth, Goethe lends his thought to this figure out of love and thereby animates her in accordance with her weak, fading type (pp. 200–203).[3]

The Nazarene moments are in need of the most rigorous critique. Poncet has rightly emphasized Goethe's inability to confront naked death. Death either remains almost imperceptibly gentle, or it is confronted with beautifying cheerful splendor. The Nazarene moment here contains a deep, soothing cheerfulness, and the Catholic tendency therein is related to—but not in accordance with—its otherwise deeply pagan tendency (pp. 233–35).—Poncet also notes that Goethe avoided the burial and, later, the grave of his mother.

Natural-scientific orientation of the Goethean approach to miracles. Its religious moments are secondary (pp. 231–32). This noticeably distinguishes such a viewpoint from the Romantic one by making it appear illegitimate. And this also belongs to the critique of the Nazarene moments.

The mute appearance of the architect at Ottilie's grave, to which Poncet refers (p. 229), is essential. This indicates the pure intention of that love, which had to be directed toward Ottilie. Such love would relinquish [any attempt] to draw this figure into the circle of human existence, a figure that in her beauty is, as it were, the very secret of being alive.

It is noted how Ottilie's wish to commit suicide is nowhere expressively admitted by herself and thus is not in the proper sense a resolution (p. 224).

This occurrence is quite wrongly claimed to be conceivable as similar to a tragic performance (pp. 236, 251–53, 256). The tragic, however, can solely and uniquely accrue to actions in the sense of drama—that is, the contestation of persons carried out in words; in the wordless realm of a merely reported occurrence to which the events of this novel belong like no other, there is nothing [1:840] tragic. The tragic, in other words, appears not in fantasy but only in the bodily shape of the hero and thus asserts its extra-aesthetic, historical-philosophical form of existence.

Burning of the manuscripts (p. 54).

Goethe gives no physiognomic details of his characters in the novel (p. 95).

The Masonic character of the speech at the ceremony where the foundation stone is set (pp. 104–11).

[1:855][4] Ottilie is an orphan. In the moment when her mother left her, she shows herself in the half-wakened state in which she overhears the conversation about her, [where she is] destined, like plants, for telluric powers.[5] In the same moment, in her interior, there forms a refusal of waking and conscious life without which there can be no morality [*Sittlichkeit*]. (The analogy to this occurrence can be found very precisely after the death of Charlotte's child.)

17

CONCERNING ELECTIVE AFFINITIES

[1:835] Outline[1]

First Part: The mythic as thesis
  I. Critique and commentary
     A. Truth-of-the-matter and subject-matter
     B. Subject-matters in the Enlightenment
  II. The meaning of the mythic world in *Elective Affinities*
     A. Marriage as mythic order of law
        1. Marriage in the Enlightenment
        2. Marriage in *Elective Affinities* [1:836]
     B. The mythic natural order
        1. The telluric
        2. Water
        3. Human beings
     C. Fate
        1. The names
        2. The symbolism of death
        3. Inculpated life
        4. The house
        5. Sacrifice
  III. The meaning of the mythic world for Goethe
     A. According to his words

88

1. Contemporary criticism of *Elective Affinities*
2. The fable of renunciation
  B. According to his life
    1. The Olympian or mythic life-forms of the artist
      a. Relationship to critique
      b. Relationship to nature
    2. Fear, or mythic life-forms in the existence of the human being
      a. The daemonic
      b. The fear of death
      c. The fear of life

Second Part: Redemption as antithesis
  I. Critique and biography
    A. The traditional conception
      1. The analysis of the works
      2. The presentation of essence and work
    B. The heroizing conception
  II. Gundolf's *Goethe*
    A. Methodological debilitation
      1. The poet in the George school
        a. As hero
        b. As Creator
      2. Life as work
      3. Mythos and truth
    B. Matter-of-fact debilitation, the later Goethe
  III. The novella
    A. Its necessity in the composition
      1. The novel form of *Elective Affinities*
      2. [1:837] The form of its novella
    B. Its matter-of-fact meaning
      1. The correspondences in detail
      2. The correspondences in their entirety

Third Part: Hope as synthesis
  I. Critique and philosophy
  II. Beauty as semblance
    A. Virginity
    B. Innocence

1. In death
2. In life
C. Beauty
    1. The Helen motif
    2. Conjuration
    3. The expressionless
    4. Beautiful semblance

III. The semblance of reconciliation
    A. Conciliation and being touched
        1. Harmony and peace
        2. Passion and inclination
            a. Ottilie, Luciane, the young woman in the novella
            b. The pair of lovers
            c. Marriage in the novel
            d. The trilogy of passion
    B. Redemption
        1. Shattering
            a. Expiring semblance
            b. The cover of beauty
            c. Laying Bare
        2. Hope

GOETHE'S ELECTIVE AFFINITIES

by

Walter Benjamin[*][1]

I[†][2]

Whoever chooses blindly is struck in the eyes by the smoke of sacrifice.

—(Klopstock)[3]

[1:125][‡] The existing writings on literary works suggest that the level of detail in such investigations owes more to philological than to critical interest. The following exposition of *Elective Affinities*, which also goes into some detail, could therefore easily be misleading as to the intention with which it is given. It could appear as commentary; it is meant, however, as critique. Critique seeks the truth-of-the-matter with regard to an artwork; commentary, its subject-matter.[4] The relationship between the two determines that fundamental law of literature according to which the more significant a work, the more invisibly and intensely the truth-of-the-matter is bound up with its subject-matter. If, accordingly, the works that prove themselves enduring are precisely those whose truth is most deeply sunken into their subject-matter, then in the course of this duration, the *realia* in the work appear all the more clearly to the eyes of the beholder the more they die out in the world. In accordance with appearances, however, the subject-matter and

---

[*] Dedicated to Jula Cohn
[†] I. The Mythic as Thesis
[‡] I. Critique and Commentary / A. Truth-of-the-Matter and Subject-Matter

92 WALTER BENJAMIN

the truth-of-the-matter, which are united in the work's early period, thereby come apart with its duration, for the latter always keeps itself equally concealed, even as the former emerges. Increasingly therefore the interpretation of what is striking and disconcerting—the subject-matter—becomes a precondition for every later critic. One may compare such a critic to a paleographer before a parchment whose faded text is covered by the traits of a more robust writing that refers to it. Just as the paleographer would have to begin by reading the later writing, the critic would have to begin by engaging in commentary. And from this, with a single stroke, an invaluable criterion of a critic's judgment issues from him: he can now for the first time pose the fundamental critical question as to whether the semblance of the truth-of-the-matter is due to the subject-matter, or the life of the subject-matter is due to the truth-of-the-matter. For, as they diverge in the work, they decide on its immortality. In this sense, the history of works prepares their critique [1:126], and as a result, historical distance thus increases their force. If, for the sake of a simile, one views the growing work as a flaming funeral pyre, then the commentator stands before it as a chemist, the critic like an alchemist.[5] Whereas, for the former, wood and ashes alone remain the objects of his analysis, for the latter, only the flame itself preserves an enigma: the enigma of whatever is alive. The critic, therefore, asks about the truth whose living flame continues to burn over the weighty foundering of what once was, as well as the light ashes of what was lived through.

*The meaning, though not of course the existence, of the *realia* in the work will mostly conceal itself from the poet as from the public of his time. Because, however, the eternal element of the work emerges only on the basis of the *realia*, every contemporaneous critique, however elevated it is, comprehends in the work moving more than reposing truth, temporal effect more than eternal being. Nevertheless, as valuable as the *realia* may always be for the interpretation of the work, it scarcely needs to be said that the creative work of Goethe cannot be seen in the same way as that of a Pindar. Rather, there was certainly never a time more foreign than Goethe's to the thought that the most essential contents of existence are stamped onto the world of things, indeed that these contents are incapable of fulfilling themselves without such a stamp. Kant's critical work and Basedow's *Elementary Work*—the one dedicated to the meaning, the other to the intuition of the experience of that

---

*   B. Subject-Matters in the Enlightenment

time—testify in very different yet equally definitive ways to the poverty of its subject-matter. An indispensable precondition of Kant's lifework, on the one hand, and Goethe's creative work, on the other, can be glimpsed in this constitutive feature of the German, if not the entire European, Enlightenment. For precisely at the time that Kant's work was completed and the map showing the way through the barren forest of the real was drafted, Goethe's search for the seeds of eternal growth began. There came the tendency of classicism that sought to grasp less the ethical and the historical than the mythical and the philological. This thinking was directed not at the emerging ideas but rather at the formed matters, as they preserved life and language. After Herder and Schiller, it was Goethe and Wilhelm [1:127] von Humboldt who took the lead. If the renewed subject-matter that exists in the literary works of Goethe's old age escaped his contemporaries—when it did not emphasize itself, as in the *West-Eastern Divan*—this derived from the fact that, entirely in contrast to the corresponding phenomenon in the life of antiquity, the very search for such a renewed subject-matter was foreign to them.

* * *

*How clear was the intimation of the matter, or the insight into the subject, within the most sublime minds of the Enlightenment, and yet how incapable even they were of elevating themselves to the intuition of the subject-matter—this becomes compellingly clear in view of marriage. A new approach of the poet, one turned toward a synthetic intuition of subject-matters, makes its earliest manifestation yet in the Goethean elective affinities, and it does so around marriage, as one of the most rigorous and most matter-of-fact characteristics of what matters in human life.[6] Kant's definition of marriage in *The Metaphysics of Morals*, which is every now and then considered only an example of a rigid template or a curiosity of his late-life senility, is the most sublime product of a *ratio* that, incorruptibly loyal to itself, penetrates infinitely deeper into the state of affairs than a sentimental ratiocination. To be sure, the subject-matter itself, which surrenders only to philosophical intuition—more precisely, philosophical experience—remains inaccessible to both *ratio* and ratiocination; but whereas the one leads into the abyss, the other touches precisely on the ground where true cognition

---

* II. The Meaning of the Mythic World in *Elective Affinities* / A. Marriage as Mythic Order of Law / 1. Marriage in the Enlightenment

is formed. It accordingly explains marriage as "the connection between two persons of different sexes for lifelong possession of each other's sexual properties.—The purpose of begetting and bringing up children may be a purpose of nature, for which it implanted the inclination of the sexes for each other; but for the legitimacy of this connection, it is not required that the human being who gets married must set this purpose for itself, for otherwise the marriage would dissolve by itself at the very moment when the production of children stops."[7] Of course, this was the most prodigious error of the philosopher: he thought he could expound the moral possibility, indeed necessity, of marriage through a derivation from this definition that he gave of its nature and, in such a way, confirm its legal reality. Derivable from the matter-of-fact nature of marriage would obviously be only [1:128] its depravity—and it unintentionally boils down to this in Kant. This alone is decisive: the matter of marriage never relates to its fact by way of a derivation; on the contrary, the former must be grasped as the seal that presents the latter. Just as the form of a seal is not derivable from the material of the wax, nor is it derivable from the purpose of the fastener, nor even from the signet, where one side is convex, the other concave, and just as it is ascertainable only by someone who at some time had the experience of the seal, and evident only to someone who knows the name that the initials only suggest, so the matter of the fact is to be derived not from an insight into its existence, nor from an investigation into its determination, nor even from an intimation of the matter; rather, it is ascertainable only in the philosophical experience of its divine imprint, evident only in the blessed intuition of the divine name.[8] In this way, the consummated insight into the subject-matter of existing things coincides in the end with a consummated insight into its truth-of-the-matter. The truth-of-the-matter proves itself such [viz. true] as that of the subject-matter. Nevertheless, their difference—and with it, the difference between a commentary and a critique of works—is not idle, insofar as striving for immediacy is nowhere more confused than where the study of the fact and its determination, like the intimation of its matter, must precede every experience. In such a matter-of-fact determination of marriage, Kant's thesis is consummated, and in the consciousness of its lack of any intimation, it is sublime. Or, finding amusement in his sentences, does one forget what precedes them? The beginning of the paragraph reads: "Sexual community (*commercium sexuale*) is the reciprocal use that one human being makes of the sexual organs and faculties of another (*usus membrorum et facultatum sexualium alterius*) and is either a natural use (by which procreation of a being of the same kind is possible) or an unnatural use, and of the latter, either with a person of the same sex or with an animal that is different from the human species."[9] Thus Kant. If one places this segment of *The Metaphysics of Morals* side by side with Mozart's *Magic Flute*, the most extreme and at the same time most profound intuitions that the age possessed of marriage thus appear to present themselves. For, to the extent that this is at all possible for an opera, *The Magic Flute* takes precisely conjugal love as its theme. This is something that does not seem [1:129] to have been thoroughly recognized even by Cohen, in whose late study of Mozart's libretti the two above-named works meet one another in such a dignified spirit.[10] The content of the opera is less the longing of lovers than the steadfastness of the couple. It is not only that they should go through fire and water to win each other, but it is so that they may remain forever united. However much the spirit of freemasonry had to dissolve all matter-of-fact bonds, the intimation of the matter here arrived at its purest expression in the feeling of fidelity.

*Is Goethe in *Elective Affinities* really any closer to the subject-matter of marriage than Kant and Mozart? One would have to deny this altogether if, in the wake of Goethe philology in its entirety, one seriously wanted to take Mittler's words about this for those of the poet. Nothing allows for this assumption; too much explains it. After all, the dizzying sight would look for something to hold on to in this world, which is sinking in circles, as happens in whirlpools. Here were only the narrow-minded blusterer's words, which one was glad to be able to take at face value: "'Anyone who attacks the state of marriage,' Mittler cried, 'whoever undermines this foundation of all ethical society by word or deed, he will have to reckon with me; or else, if I cannot get the better of him, I will have nothing to do with him. Marriage is the basis and summit of all culture [*Kultur*]. It makes those who are rough gentle, and it gives the most cultivated man [*Gebildetste*] an opportunity to demonstrate his gentleness. It must be indissoluble, for it brings so much happiness that all individual misfortune cannot at all be counted against it. And what does one mean by misfortune? Impatience is what seizes a person from time to time, and then he is pleased to find himself unfortunate. Let the moment pass, and one will extol oneself fortunate that something that has stood so long still stands. There is absolutely no sufficient reason to separate

---

*   2. Marriage in *Elective Affinities*

oneself. The human condition is so charged with sorrow and joy that what a spousal couple owe each other cannot at all be calculated. It is an infinite debt [*Schuld*] that can be paid off only by eternity. It may be unpleasant at times, this I can well believe, and that is precisely right. Are we not also married to conscience, of which we would often like to rid ourselves, since it is more disagreeable to us [1:130] than any husband or wife could ever be?'"[11] It would have been necessary here even for those who did not see the cloven hoof of the Puritan to pause for a moment and think: not even Goethe, who often showed himself scrupulous enough, when warranted, to tell off those who said worrisome things—not even he succumbed to interpreting Mittler's words. Indeed, it is highly significant that someone who, himself living unmarried, appears as the lowest-ranking among all of the men of his circle, blasts out this philosophy of marriage. Whenever on important occasions Mittler lets his words flow, they are out of place, whether at the baptism of the newborn or in the last moments Ottilie spends with her friends. And while in these instances the tastelessness of his words becomes sufficiently perceptible through their effects, after Mittler's famous apologia for marriage Goethe concluded as follows: "He thus spoke in a lively manner and would have very well gone on speaking for a long time."[12] Such talk can indeed be pursued indefinitely—talk that, to speak with Kant, is a "nauseating mishmash," "patched together" out of baseless humanitarian maxims and turgid, fallacious legal instincts.[13] The impurity should escape no one—the indifference to the truth in the life of the married couple. It all comes down to the claim of the statute. Yet in truth, marriage never has justification in law, as would an institution, but solely as an expression of the persistence of love that by nature would seek expression sooner in death than in life.[14] For the poet, however, the imprint of the juridical norm remained indispensable in this work. Nevertheless, he did not, like Mittler, want to justify marriage but rather to show the forces that emerge from it in its decay. These, though, are surely the mythical forces of law, and marriage is only the dispatching in these forces of a demise that it does not decree.[15] For the dissolution of marriage is pernicious only because it is not the highest powers that bring it about. And the inescapable horror of the proceedings lies solely in the misfortune that is stirred up. In fact, however, Goethe thereby touched on the factual matter of marriage. For, even if he did not mean to show this in an undistorted way, his insight into the foundering relationship remains forceful enough. In its demise, the relationship becomes, for the first time, the one Mittler upholds.

It never occurred to Goethe, however, to establish a foundation for marriage in matrimonial law, even if he certainly never did gain [1:131] a pure insight into the moral substance of this bond. For him, the morality of marriage at its most profound and reticent foundation was the least indubitable thing. What he wishes to portray in the life-form of the count and the baroness, as opposed to the morality of marriage, is not so much its immorality as its nullity. This is attested precisely by the fact that they are conscious neither of the moral nature of their present relationship nor of the juridical nature of the relationships from which they are separated.—The object of *Elective Affinities* is not marriage. Nowhere are the moral forces of the latter to be sought in the former. From its inception, they are disappearing, as the beach disappears under water at high tide. Marriage here is not a moral problem, and it is also not a social one. It is not a bourgeois life-form. In its dissolution, everything human becomes appearance, and the mythical remains alone as essence.

*A superficial glance contradicts this, of course. According to it, a higher spirituality is conceivable in no marriage other than in one where even its decay is not capable of diminishing the morals of those thereby affected. In the realm of mores, however, nobility is bound to the relation of person to outward expression. Wherever a noble outward expression is not appropriate to the person, nobility is in question. And this law, whose validity may not, of course, be called unlimited without great error, extends beyond the realm of mores. If there are, without any question, realms of outward expression whose contents are valid regardless of who gives them their characteristic stamp—if indeed these are the highest ones—then this binding condition remains inviolable for the domain of freedom in the widest sense. The individual stamp of what is appropriate, the individual stamp of spirit, belongs to this domain: everything that is called culture. Those who trust one another manifest culture, most of all. Is this truly appropriate to their situation? Less hesitation might bring freedom; less silence, clarity; less indulgence, decision. Culture thus preserves its value only when the fact that it would manifest itself lies open to it. The action [of the novel] also shows this clearly in other ways.

Its bearers are, as cultured human beings, almost free from superstition. If now and again superstition appears in Eduard, it is at first merely in the

---

* B. The Mythic Natural Order / 1. The Telluric

endearing form of a clinging to lucky portents, whereas only the banal character of [1:132] Mittler, despite his self-satisfied gestures, shows traces of the genuinely superstitious fear of evil omens. He is the only one who refrains from walking on the cemetery grounds as on any other, not out of pious, but rather superstitious, trepidation, while strolling there does not seem offensive to the friends, nor does it seem forbidden to do as they please. Without a single concern, indeed without any regard, the gravestones are lined up along the church wall, and the leveled ground traversing a footpath is left to the minister for his clover patch. It is impossible to think of a more concise separation from what has come before than one executed over the ancestral graves that, in the sense not only of myth but also of religion, establish the ground under the feet of the living. Where does the freedom of the agents lead them? Far from disclosing new insights, it blinds them to what is inherently real in whatever may be dreadful. And this is precisely because freedom is ill suited to them. Only rigorous binding to ritual—which may be called superstition solely when, torn from its nexus, it survives in a rudimentary manner—can promise to preserve such people from the nature in which they live. Charged with superhuman forces, as only mythic nature is, the latter comes menacingly into play. Whose power, if not mythic nature's, calls down the minister who cultivates his clover on the graveyard? Who, if not this nature, sets the embellished setting in a pallid light? For such a light pervades—understood in a literal or a more extended manner—the entire landscape. At no point does it appear in sunlight. And, though much is also said about the estate, never is there talk of its crops or the rural affairs that are in service to sustenance rather than ornament. The only allusion of this sort—a prospect of the vintage—leads away from the setting of the action to the estate of the baroness.[16] The magnetic force of the earth's interior speaks much more clearly. Goethe said of this force in his *Theory of Colors*—possibly around this same time—that to those who are attentive, nature is "never dead or mute; indeed, it even gave the rigid terrestrial body a certain confidant, a metal, the tiniest piece of which is supposed to make us aware of what is happening in the entire mass."[17] Goethe's people commune with this force, and they enjoy themselves in playing with whatever lies below, as they do in their games with [1:133] whatever lies above. And yet, what finally are their inexhaustible preparations for the embellishment of this ground-above other than a transformation of the backdrop for a tragic scene. Thus does a hidden power ironically manifest itself in the existence of the landed gentry.

*Water bears the expression of this power, as the tellurian bears the waters. Nowhere does the lake deny its ominous nature under the dead surface of the mirror. An older critical work speaks significantly of the "daemonic fate that holds sway around the pleasure lake."[18] Water, as the chaotic element of life, does not threaten here with a rough wave that brings human beings down but, rather, with the enigmatic calm that lets them go to ruin.[19] To the extent that fate holds sway, the lovers go to their ruin. When they spurn the blessings of firm ground, they succumb to the unfathomable, which appears as something primeval in stagnant water.[20] In a literal sense, one sees its ancient power conjuring them. For ultimately the unification of the water, as it gradually breaks down the firm ground, leads to the restoration of the erstwhile mountain lake that was found in the region. In all of this, it is nature itself that under human hands stirs in a superhuman manner. In fact: even the wind "that drives the boat toward the plane trees rises up"—as the reporter of the *Evangelische Kirchen-Zeitung* [Reform-Church newspaper] scornfully surmises—"probably by order of the stars."[21]

†Human beings themselves must manifest the force of nature. For they have never outgrown it. With respect to them, this constitutes the particular justification of that more general cognition according to which the characters in a literary work can never be subjected to moral judgment. And indeed not because, like the moral judgment of human beings, it would surpass all human insight. Rather, the grounds of such judgment already irrefutably prohibit its application to literary characters. Moral philosophy has to prove stringently that the fictionalized person is always too poor and too rich to come under moral judgment. This can be executed only on human beings. Characters in a novel are to be distinguished from human beings in that the former are fully arrested by nature. And what is required is not to sit in judgment about their mores but to comprehend what happens in a moral manner. It remains foolish, as was done by Solger and later also by Bielschowsky, to take a fuzzy moral judgment of taste that should [1:134] never have been ventured and yet put it on display, so that it can catch the first applause.[22] The figure of Eduard acts to no one's satisfaction. But how much deeper is Cohen's vision than that of those two; for him—according to the expositions in his *Aesthetics* [*of Pure Feeling*]—it counts as nonsense to isolate Eduard's appearance from the totality of the novel. Eduard's unreliability, indeed his coarseness, is the expression of fleeting despair in a lost life.

---

*   2. Water

†   3. Human Beings

He appears "in the overall configuration of the relationship exactly as he characterizes himself" to Charlotte: "'For actually, though, I depend only on you!' He is the plaything—not, to be sure, of moods, which Charlotte does not have at all but, rather, of the final goal of the elective affinities toward which her central nature, with its firm center of gravity, notwithstanding all fluctuations, strives."[23] From the inception of the novel onward, the characters stand under the spell of the elective affinities. But their wondrous stirrings, according to Goethe's deeper intuition, full of intimation, do not serve as the basis for an intimate-spiritual accord among those who are there but, rather, only for the particular harmony of deeper natural layers. These, more exactly, are meant with the faint falseness that adheres without exception to those joinings. Ottilie, to be sure, adjusts herself to Eduard's flute playing, but it is false. Reading with Ottilie, Eduard, to be sure, tolerates what he refuses to Charlotte, but it is a nuisance. To be sure, he feels wonderfully entertained by her, but she remains silent. The two of them, to be sure, suffer in common, but it is only a headache. These characters are not natural, for children of nature—in a fabulous state of nature or a real one—are human beings. At the height of culture, however, they are subject to the forces that culture represents as mastered, though it may also prove itself always powerless to suppress them. These forces left them a feeling for what is appropriate; they have lost it for what is right.[24] Here is meant a judgment not on their actions but on their language. For, seeing yet dumb, feeling yet deaf, they go their way. Deaf before God and dumb before the world. Accountability eludes them, not through their actions but through their being. They are stupefied.

*Nothing binds the human being to language more than his name. Hardly any literature, however, offers a narrative with the scope of *Elective Affinities* in which so [1:135] few names are to be found. This sparseness of naming is open to an interpretation other than the customary one that refers to Goethe's inclination for typical characters. Rather, it belongs in the most intimate way to the essence of an order whose members live out their lives under a nameless law, a disaster that fills their world with the pallid light of a solar eclipse. All the names, up until Mittler's, are mere baptismal names. There is nothing ludic in the name Mittler [mediator], thus no allusion by the poet that is to be seen; it is, rather, a turn of phrase that designates with incomparable certainty the essence of its bearer. He has to be regarded as a man whose self-love allows for no abstraction from the suggestions that seem to be given in

---

* C. Fate / 1. The Names

his name, and it is a name that thereby debases him. Six names, besides his, are to be found in the narrative: Eduard, Otto, Ottilie, Charlotte, Luciane, and Nanny. The first of these, however, is not genuine, so to speak. It is arbitrary, chosen for its sound, a feature in which an analogy with the displacement of the gravestones may certainly be seen. A portent also attaches itself to the double name, for it is his initials, E and O, that ordain one of the glasses from the count's youth into the pledge of his fortune in love.

*The fullness of premonitory and parallel features in the novel has never escaped the critics. It is already sufficiently acknowledged as the nearest expression of the novel's character. Nevertheless, wholly apart from the interpretation of this expression—how deeply it penetrates the entire work does not seem fully ascertained. Only when this stands brightly in the field of vision does it become clear that here lies neither a bizarre propensity on the part of the author nor simply an intensification of suspense. Only then does it also come to light in a more precise manner what these features contain most of all. It is a symbolism of death. "One sees, indeed, at the very start that it must end in fiasco," reads a strange turn of phrase in Goethe. (It is possibly of astrological origin; Grimm's *Dictionary* does not take note of it; Hebel includes it in one of his rogue stories.[25]) On another occasion the poet referred to the feeling of "anxiety" that is supposed to arise in the reader with the moral decay in the elective affinities.[26] It has also been reported that Goethe laid weight on "how swiftly and irresistibly he brought about the catastrophe."[27] In its most hidden features [1:136] this symbolism is woven throughout the entire work. Where, however, only selected beauties offer themselves to the objective conception of the reader, only a feeling familiar with this symbolism takes in its language without any effort. In a few places Goethe gave a clue to this symbolism, and they have remained, on the whole, the only ones that have gained notice. They are all connected with the episode of the crystal glass, which, destined to shatter, is caught in midfall and preserved. It is the building-inaugural sacrifice that is rejected during the consecration of the house in which Ottilie dies. Here too, though, Goethe keeps the procedure hidden, since he derives the gesture that completes this ceremony from joyous ebullience. Clearer is a sepulchral warning contained in the Masonic-inflected[28] words at the laying of the foundation stone: "It is a serious business, and our invitation is serious, for this ceremony is celebrated

---

*   2. The Symbolism of Death

in the depths. Here within this narrow, hollowed-out space you do us the honor of appearing as witnesses to our secretive business."[29] The great motif of bedazzlement emerges from the preservation of the glass, greeted with joy. Eduard seeks by all means to secure for himself precisely this sign of scorned sacrifice. He acquires it at a high price after the banquet. With good reason an old review says: "But how strange and shocking! Whereas the unheeded portents all come to pass, the one that is heeded turns out to be deceptive."[30] And such unheeded portents are in fact not lacking. The first three chapters of the second part are altogether filled with preparations for, and conversations about, the grave. In the course of the latter, the frivolous, indeed banal interpretation of the dictum *mortuis nihil nisi bene* is remarkable.[31] "I heard it asked why one speaks well of the dead so uninhibitedly, of the living always with a certain caution. It was answered: because we have nothing to fear from the dead, and the living could still somehow come our way."[32] How a fate seems ironically to betray itself here too: one through which the speaker, Charlotte, learns how firmly two of the deceased do stand in her way. The days that prefigure death are the three on which the birthday celebration of the friends falls. Like the laying of the foundation stone on Charlotte's birthday, the roofing ceremony must take place under inauspicious signs on Ottilie's birthday [1:137]. No blessing is promised to the dwelling. On Eduard's birthday, however, his female friend serenely consecrates the completed tomb. It is altogether appropriate that her relationship to the chapel under construction, whose purpose is of course still undeclared, is juxtaposed with Luciane's relationship to the Mausoleum at Halicarnassus.[33] Ottilie's essence powerfully moves the architect; Luciane's effort on a related occasion to arouse his interest remains impotent. The playfulness is thereby visible and the seriousness secretive. Such hidden parity, which, when discovered, is still more striking for having been hidden, is also present in the motif of the little chest. This gift to Ottilie, which contains the material for her shroud, corresponds to the architect's container with its findings from prehistoric graves. The former comes from "tradespeople and milliners," while it is said of the latter that its content took on the look of "something fine" through its arrangement and that one "would look at it with enjoyment, as one does at the little chests of a milliner."[34]

*The things that correspond to one another this way—always symbols of death in those mentioned above—are also not simply to be explained by

---

*   3. Inculpated Life

the typic of the Goethean configuration, as R. M. Meyer tries to do.[35] This approach is on target only when it recognizes this typic as fateful. For the "eternal return of all the same," as it rigidly asserts itself through the most inwardly varied feelings, is the sign of fate, whether it likens itself in the life of the many or repeats itself in the life of the individual.[36] Twice Eduard offers his sacrifice to destiny: the first time, with the drinking glass, thereafter—though no longer willingly—with his own life. He recognizes this connection himself: "A glass marked with our monogram that was thrown in the air at the laying of the foundation stone did not shatter; it was caught and is again in my hands. So, I shouted to myself, I myself, who have spent so many dubious hours in this lonely spot—I therefore want to make myself into a sign in place of the glass, a sign of whether our union may be possible or not. I go forth and seek death, not as one who is raving mad but as one who hopes to live."[37] One has also rediscovered the inclination toward the typic as a principle of art in the depiction of the war into which he hurls himself. Even here, however, questions would arise as to whether Goethe, also for this reason, [1:138] treated the war in such a general manner because he had in mind the hated war against Napoleon. Be that as it may: not only a principle of art but, above all, a motif of fateful being is ascertained in the aforementioned typic. Throughout the work the poet unfolded this fateful kind of existence, which encompasses living natures in a single nexus of guilt and expiation. The kind in question is not, however, as Gundolf claims, to be compared with that of plant existence. A more exact contrast to this kind is inconceivable. No, not "by analogy to the relationship of seed, flower, and fruit is Goethe's concept of law, his concept of fate and character in *Elective Affinities*, to be interpreted."[38] This would be as little the case with Goethe's concepts as with any other valid ones. For fate (character is something else) does not affect the life of innocent plants.[39] Nothing is further from this. On the contrary, fate inexorably unfolds itself in inculpated life. Fate is the guilt-nexus of the living. Zelter touched upon it in this work when, comparing it to the comedy *The Accomplices*, he said of the latter: "Yet precisely for this reason it has no pleasant effect, because it arrives at everyone's door, because this includes those who are good; and so I compared it with *Elective Affinities*, where even the best have something to hide and must blame themselves for not keeping to the right way."[40] That which is fateful cannot be designated with greater certainty. And so it appears in *Elective Affinities*: as the guilt that in life passes itself on. "Charlotte is delivered of a son. The child is born from the lie. As a sign of this, it bears the features of the Captain and Ottilie. As a creature of the lie, it is condemned to death, for only truth is essential. Guilt for his death must fall on those who, by overcoming themselves, have not expiated their guilt for the child's inwardly untrue existence. These are Ottilie and Eduard.—This is roughly how the natural-philosophical-ethical schema that Goethe had drafted for the final chapters would have run."[41] This much is incontrovertible in Bielschowsky's conjecture: it corresponds entirely to the order of fate when the child, who enters this order as a newborn, does not de-expiate the old turmoil; rather, its guilt passing onto him, he must pass away.[42] Under discussion here is not moral guilt—how could the [1:139] child acquire it?—but, rather, natural guilt, into which human beings fall not through resolution and action but through negligence and ceremony. When, failing to heed the human, they succumb to the power of nature, it is then that natural life, which preserves innocence in human beings no longer than its attachment to a higher life, draws everything human downward. With the vanishing of supernatural life in the human being his natural life turns into guilt, without this life committing an act contrary to morality. For natural life stands then in league with mere life, which manifests itself in the human being as guilt. The human being does not escape the bad luck that guilt conjures upon him. Just as every movement stirs fresh guilt in him, so every one of his deeds draws misfortune upon him. This the poet picks up in that material of ancient tales that concerns those who are burdened with too much, tales in which the fortunate man, by giving too abundantly, indissolubly chains *fatum* to himself.[43] This, too, [is] the behavior of someone who is bedazzled.

*Once the human being has sunk to this level, even the life of seemingly dead things gains power. Gundolf very rightly pointed to the significance of thingliness in the events of the novel.[44] Such inclusion of all facts into life is indeed a criterion of the mythic world. From time immemorial, the first among them was the house. So it is here—fate coming closer, the closer the house comes to completion. The laying of the foundation stone, the roofing ceremony, and the inhabiting of the house mark so many stages of demise. The house stands alone, without a view of any settlements, and it is occupied almost unfurnished. On its balcony, while Charlotte is absent, she appears in a white dress to her woman friend. Also to be remembered is the mill in the shady bottom of the woods, where the friends gathered together in the

---

*   4. The House

open air for the first time. The mill is an ancient symbol of the underworld. It may be that this derives from the decomposing and transforming nature of grinding.

*The forces that come to light in the collapse of the marriage must necessarily triumph in this circle. For they are precisely those of fate. The marriage seems a destiny, one that is more powerful than the choice in which the lovers indulge. "One must persevere where destiny places us more than choice. To cling to a people, a city, a prince, a friend, a wife; to relate everything to this and therefore to have an effect; to deprive [1:140] oneself of everything and suffer everything: that is esteemed highly."[45] This is how Goethe in his essay on Winckelmann grasps the opposition under discussion. Measured from the perspective of destiny, every choice is "blind" and blindly leads to misfortune. The violated statute stands powerfully enough opposed to choice as to demand sacrifice from the troubled marriage as a form of expiation.[46] Under the primal-mythic form of sacrifice, therefore, the symbolism of death fulfills itself in this destiny. Ottilie is predestined for it. As a reconciler, "Ottilie stands there in the magnificent 'tableau (vivant)'[47]; she is the one rich in pain, the one grieving, the one whose soul is pierced by the sword," says Abeken in the review so admired by the poet.[48] Similar is Solger's equally leisurely essay that was equally esteemed by Goethe: "She is indeed the true child of nature and at the same time its sacrifice."[49] Yet the matter of the proceedings had to escape completely both reviewers, because they started out, not from the whole of the presentation, but from the essence of the heroine. Only in the first case does Ottilie's passing away unmistakably offer itself as a sacrificial action. That her death is a mythic sacrifice—if not in the mind of the poet, then certainly in the more decisive direction of his work—this becomes evident in two ways. At first: it runs counter not only to the meaning of the novel form to shroud in darkness the resolution from which Ottilie's deepest essence speaks as it does nowhere else; no, also the unmediated, almost brutal way that the work of her resolution comes to light also appears foreign to the tone of poetry. Thereupon: what this darkness conceals nevertheless emerges more clearly from everything else—the possibility, indeed the necessity, of sacrifice in accordance with the deepest intentions of this novel. Not only, therefore, as a "sacrifice of destiny" does Ottilie fall—never mind that she truly "sacrifices herself"—but rather, she falls inexorably, more

---

*   5. Sacrifice

precisely, as the sacrifice for the de-expiation of the guilty ones. For expiation in the sense of the mythic world conjured by the poet is always the death of the innocent. That is why Ottilie, despite her suicide, dies a martyr, leaving her miracle-working mortal remains behind.

* * *

*Nowhere, to be sure, is the mythic the highest subject-matter, but the former is everywhere a rigorous index of the latter. As such, Goethe made it into the basis of his novel. The mythic is the subject-matter of this book: its content appears as a mythic shadow play in [1:141] costumes of the Goethean age. What Goethe thought about his work suggests such a strange conception. It is not as though the path of critique has to be mapped out for it by the poet's statements; yet the more critique distances itself from these statements, the less it will want to evade the task of understanding them from the same hidden sector as the work.[50] This cannot be the sole principle for such an understanding, of course. That is to say, the biographical, which does not at all enter into commentary and critique, has its place here. Some of the things Goethe let on about this literary work are codetermined by a striving to counter contemporary judgments. Hence, a glance at these would be advisable, even if a much closer interest than the one designated by the aforementioned index did not also steer the approach in their direction. Among contemporaneous voices with little weight—mostly anonymous judges—are those that greet the work with the conventional respect that at the time was already owed to everything of Goethe's. What retains weight are the propositions of a distinctive stamp as they are preserved under the names of prominent individual correspondents. They are for this reason not untypical. Rather, there were precisely among the writers of these propositions at first those who dared to say outright what lesser ones did not wish to admit out of respect for the poet. He nevertheless had a feeling for the attitude of his public, and in a bitter, unadulterated recollection he reminds Zelter in 1827 that, as the latter will well recollect, with regard to his *Elective Affinities*, the public "reacted as if to the robe of Nessus."[51] Unnerved, numb, as if it had been struck, it stood before a work in which it thought that it was only supposed to seek help in escaping the confusions of its own life, without wanting selflessly to immerse itself in

---

*   III. The Meaning of the Mythic World for Goethe / A. According to his Words / 1. Contemporary Criticism of *Elective Affinities*

the essence of another's. The judgment of Madame de Staël's *De l'Allemagne* [On Germany] is representative. It reads: "On ne saurait nier qu'il n'y ait dans ce livre . . . une profonde connaissance du coeur humain, mais une connaissance décourageante; la vie y est représentée comme une chose assez indifférente, de quelque manière qu'on la passe; triste quand on l'approfondit, assez agréable quand on l'esquive, susceptible de maladies morales qu'il faut guérir si l'on peut, et dont il faut mourir si l'on n'en eut guérir."[52] More emphatically [1:142] Wieland's laconic phrase seems to signify something similar—it is taken from a letter whose addressee, a woman, is unknown—: "I admit to you, my friend, that I have read this truly terrifying work not without taking a warm interest."[53] The matter-of-fact motivations for a rejection that may have been scarcely conscious to anyone who was mildly taken aback—these come blatantly to light in the verdict of the ecclesiastical faction. The overtly pagan tendencies in the work did not escape its more gifted fanatics. For, even if the poet offers up all happiness of the lovers to those dark powers, an unerring instinct would feel the lack of the divine-transcendent element in the execution. Yet, if their demise in this existence could not suffice— what would guarantee that they would not triumph in a higher one? Indeed, is not this just what Goethe seemed to want to indicate in the concluding words? For this reason, F. H. Jacobi called the novel a "heavenly ascension of evil pleasures."[54] Just a year before Goethe's death, Hengstenberg leveled the most massive critique of all in his Protestant newspaper. His stirred-up sensibility, which is rescued by no *esprit* of any kind, offered a model of malicious polemic.[55] All this, however, remains far behind. Zacharias Werner, who at the moment of his conversion was least likely to lack an eye for the somber ritualistic tendencies in this sequence of events, sent to Goethe—simultaneously with news of his conversion—a sonnet of his, "Elective Affinities"—a piece of prose that even a hundred years later Expressionism would be unable to match with anything more accomplished both as a letter and as a poem.[56] Goethe noticed soon enough what he was doing and let this noteworthy document form the conclusion of their correspondence. The enclosed sonnet reads:

Elective Affinities

Past graves and tombstones,
That, beautifully masked, await the certain prey,

Snakes the path to Eden's garden
Where the Jordan and the Acheron unite.

Built on quicksand, Jerusalem wants to appear
Towering; only the terribly tender [1:143]
Sea-nixes, who have already waited for six thousand years,
Thirst to purify themselves through sacrifice in the lake.

There comes along a sacredly insolent child,
The angel of salvation bears him, the son of sins,
The lake swallows everything! Woe is us!—It was a joke!

Does Helios want therefore to set the earth on fire?
Indeed, he only glows lovingly to embrace it!
You are allowed to love the demigod, trembling heart![57]

One thing seems to shine through such mad, undignified praise and blame: that the mythic matter of the work was present to Goethe's contemporaries not through insight but through feeling. Apropos of this matter, it is different today, since the hundred-year-long tradition has executed its work and almost buried the possibility of original cognition. If a work of Goethe's strikes its readers today as alien or hostile, numb silence will soon take possession of them and smother the true impression.—With unconcealed joy Goethe welcomed the two who let themselves be heard, however faintly, in contrast with such judgments. Solger was one, and Abeken the other. Concerning the well-meaning words of the latter, Goethe did not rest until they were given the form of a critique, in which they would appear in a visible place.[58] For he found the human element emphasized in these words, an element that the work puts so systematically on display. No one's glimpse of the fundamental matter seems to have become more turbid than Wilhelm von Humboldt's: "Above all, I feel the lack of fate and inner necessity in it" was his judgment, strangely enough.[59]

    *Goethe had dual motives for not following the conflict of opinions in silence. He had his work to defend—that was one. He had to preserve its secret—that was the other. The two work together to give his explanation an entirely different character from that of an interpretation. It has an apologetic and mystifying trait, which perfectly unite in its main point. One could call it

---

*   2. The Fable of Renunciation

the fable of renunciation. Goethe found in this the ready-made support for denying knowledge a deeper point of entry. At the same time, it also served as a reply to so many [1:144] philistine attacks. Goethe thus proclaimed it in the conversation that, in Riemer's rendition, henceforth determined the traditional image of the novel. There he says: the struggle of morality with inclination is "displaced behind the scenes, and one sees that it must have gone on before. The human beings carry themselves like people of rank who, for all of their inner strife, nevertheless maintain their outward decorum.— The struggle of morality is never appropriate for an aesthetic presentation. For, either morality triumphs, or it is defeated. In the first case, one does not know what was presented and why; in the second, it is disgraceful to look at it. For in the end, at some moment or another, preference must be given to the sensual over the moral, and the spectator does not precisely admit to this moment but, rather, demands a more striking one that a third person keeps eluding, the more moral he himself is.—In such presentations the sensual must always become master; but be punished by fate, that is to say, by the moral nature that salvages its freedom through death. Thus, Werther must shoot himself after he has allowed sensuality to gain mastery over him. Thus, Ottilie must καρτερ-ize, and Eduard the same, after they allowed their inclination free rein.[60] Only now does morality celebrate its triumph."[61] Goethe liked to insist on these ambiguous sentences as well as on every sort of draconianism that he loved to emphasize in conversation about this topic, since, with the demise of the hero, expiation was so richly awarded for the juridical offense in the violation of marriage, [that is,] for the mythic inculpation. Except that, in truth, this was not expiation of a violation but, rather, redemption from the entrapment of marriage. Except that, despite all these words, no struggle between duty and inclination plays out either visibly or secretly. Except that morality never triumphantly lives here but, rather, singularly and alone lives in defeat. The moral matter of this work thus lies in much deeper layers than Goethe's words let one guess. Their evasiveness is neither possible nor necessary. For his discussions are not only insufficient in their opposition between sensuality and morality; they are obviously untenable in their exclusion of inner ethical struggle as an object of poetic construction. What [1:145] else would presumably remain of drama, of the novel [form] itself? However the matter of this literary work is to be grasped in a moral manner, it nevertheless does not contain a *fabula docet*,[62] and it is not remotely touched by that feeble admonition to renounce with which learned criticism from the very beginning leveled its abysses and peaks. In addition, Mézières has already correctly noted the epicurean tendency that Goethe lends to this attitude.[63] Because of this, the admission in the *Correspondence with a Child* strikes much deeper, and one is only reluctantly persuaded by the probability that it was fabricated by Bettina, who took her distance from this novel in many respects. There it states that he "set for himself here the task of gathering into a fabricated destiny, as into a funerary urn, the tears for many neglected things."[64] One does not, however, call what one has renounced a neglected thing. It is not, therefore, renunciation that was foremost for Goethe in many a relationship in his life but, rather, neglection. And when he recognized the irretrievability of what was missed, the irretrievability due to neglection, only then may renunciation have made itself available to him and is only the last attempt still to embrace in feeling what is lost. This may also have applied to Minna Herzlieb.

*To want to develop an understanding of *Elective Affinities* from the poet's own words about the novel is wasted effort. Precisely these words have the aim of hindering access to critique. The ultimate reason for this is not the inclination to ward off foolishness. The reason, rather, lies in an endeavor to leave unnoticed precisely what the poet's own explanation denies. Its secret was to be preserved by the technique of the novel, on the one hand, and the circle of motifs, on the other. The domain of poetic technique forms the boundary between an upper-exposed and a deeper-hidden stratification of works. What the poet is conscious of as his technique; what is also already in principle recognizable as such to contemporaneous critique touches on the *realia* in the subject-matter, to be sure; but it forms the boundary around the truth-of-the-matter, of which neither the poet nor the critique of his day can be entirely conscious. Subject-matters are necessarily observable in the technique, which—in contrast to the form—is alone decisively [1:146] determined by them, and not by the truth-of-the-matter. For, to the poet, the presentation of subject-matters is the enigma, the solution to which he has to seek in technique. Goethe could thus secure for himself through technique an emphasis on mythic powers in his work. What ultimate meaning these powers have—this had to escape him, as it did the zeitgeist. The poet, though, sought to guard this technique as his artistic secret. When he says that he worked out the novel

---

*   B. According to his Life / 1. The Olympian or Mythic Life-Forms of the Artist / a. The Relation to Critique

according to an idea, there seems to be an allusion to this. The idea may be conceived as a technical one. Otherwise, the additional comment calling into question the value of such a procedure would scarcely be understandable.[65] It is quite conceivable, however, that the infinite subtlety that the referential fullness concealed in the book could at some point appear dubious to the poet. "I hope that you shall find my old methods in it. I have inserted many things; hidden much. May this open secret joyously redound in you."[66] Thus Goethe wrote to Zelter. In the same sense, Goethe insists on the proposition that there is more contained in the work "than anyone would be capable of apprehending in a single reading."[67] The destruction of the drafts, however, speaks more clearly than anything else. For it could hardly be an accident that not even a fragment of these was preserved.[68] On the contrary, it's apparent that the poet altogether deliberately destroyed everything that would have shown the thoroughly constructive technique of the work.—If the existence of subject-matters is hidden in this way, then their essence conceals itself. All mythic meaning seeks secrecy. Therefore, Goethe could confidently say precisely of this work: the poetized asserts its right, as does the occurrence.[69] Such a right is here indeed to be thanked, in the sarcastic sense of the phrase, not for the poetic work but, rather, for the poetized—for the mythic material stratum of the work. In this consciousness Goethe could aloofly tarry not actually above yet still in his work, as per the words that conclude Humboldt's critical remarks: "One is not permitted to say some things to him. He has no freedom over his own facts, and he becomes mute when one reproaches him in the least."[70] This is how Goethe in his old age stands in relation to all critique: as an Olympian. Not in the sense of *epitheton ornans* or the beautifully appearing shape that moderns give him. This [1:147] word—it is ascribed to Jean Paul—designates the obscure mythic nature, sunken into itself, which in speechless rigidity inheres in Goethean artistry. As an Olympian, he laid the foundation of the work and with scant words sealed the vault.[71]

*In the twilight of this vault the eye lands on whatever rests most concealed in Goethe. Features and connections that do not show themselves as such in the light of everyday observation become clear. And it is alone through these that the paradoxical semblance of the preceding interpretation, in turn, disappears more and more. A primal basis for Goethean research into nature thus appears only here. This study is founded on a sometimes naive

---

* b. The Relation to Nature

but also sometimes more thoughtful double sense in the concept of nature. For this concept designates in Goethe the sphere of perceptible appearances as well as that of intuitable archetypes. Never, however, was Goethe able to produce an account of this synthesis. Instead of engaging in a philosophical fathoming, his research seeks in vain empirical proof of the identity of the two spheres by conducting experiments. Since he did not determine "true" nature in a conceptual manner, he never penetrated to the productive center of an intuition that called upon him to seek the presence of "true" nature as urphenomenon in its appearances, as he presupposed them in works of art.[72] Solger notices this connection, which especially exists between *Elective Affinities* and Goethean natural research, something also emphasized in the book's advertisement copy.[73] Solger writes: "The *Theory of Colors* ... surprised me to a certain extent. God knows I had formed beforehand absolutely no specific expectation of its content; for the most part, I thought I'd find mere experiments in it. Now comes this book in which nature becomes alive, human, and companionable. It seems to me that it also sheds some light on *Elective Affinities*."[74] The emergence of the *Theory of Colors* is also close in time to that of the novel. All of Goethe's research on magnetism clearly intervenes in the work itself. This insight into nature, through which the poet thought he could always carry out the verification of his works, consummated his indifference to critique. They did not need it. The nature of urphenomena was the standard, legible in every [1:148] work's relationship to it. On the basis of the double sense in the concept of nature, however, it all too often turned from urphenomena as archetype into urphenomena as model. This view would never have become powerful if in the resolution of the aforesaid equivocation it had been disclosed to Goethe that only urphenomena—as ideals—present themselves adequately to intuition, whereas in science they are replaced by the idea, which is capable of irradiating the object of perception but never transforming it in intuition. Urphenomena are not there before art; they subsist within it. By rights, they can never yield standards. If, with this contamination of the pure and empirical domains, sensuous nature already seems to demand the highest place, then its mythic visage triumphs in the total appearance of its being. It is, for Goethe, only the chaos of symbols. As such, then, with him, sensuous nature's urphenomena make their appearance in common with the others, as it is so clearly presented among the poems in the book *God and World*.[75] Nowhere did the poet ever attempt to establish a hierarchy of urphenomena. The fullness of their forms presents itself to his mind no differently than the confused world of sound to the ear. It may be permitted to enfold into this simile a portrayal he gives of such fullness, because it, like little else, announces so clearly the spirit in which he regards nature. "Let us shut our eyes, let us open and sharpen our ears, and from the softest breath to the wildest noise, from the simplest sound to the most elevated harmony, from the most violent, most passionate cry to the gentlest words of reason, it is only nature that speaks, revealing its existence, its force, its life, and its relationships, so that a blind man, to whom the infinitely visible is denied, can apprehend an infinitely living element in the audible."[76] If, therefore, in the most extreme sense, even the "words of reason" are pummeled into possessions of nature, it is no wonder that, for Goethe, thought never entirely shone through the realm of urphenomena. But he thereby deprived himself of the possibility of drawing boundaries. Lacking all distinctions, existence succumbs to the concept of nature, which grows into the monstrous, as the fragment from 1780 teaches. And Goethe remained faithful to the propositions in this fragment—"Nature"—even in advanced old age.[77] [1:149] Its conclusion reads: "It has installed me; it will also lead me forth. I entrust myself to it. It may do as it likes with me; it does not hate its work. I did not speak of it; no, what is true and what is false—it has spoken all. All is its fault; all is to its credit."[78] In this way of approaching the world is chaos. For the life of myth eventually issues into it, a life that imposes itself without ruler or boundaries as the sole power in the domain of beings.

*The renunciation of all critique and the idolatry of nature are the mythic life-forms in the existence of the artist. That they acquire in Goethe a supreme pithiness—this one will be permitted to see signified in the name Olympian. It at once designates light in its mythic essence. An obscurity corresponds to it, however, one that in the gravest way shadowed human existence. Traces of this are recognizable in *Poetry and Truth*.[79] The least of them surely penetrated Goethe's confessions. Only the concept of the daemonic stands like an unpolished monolith on their surface. Goethe introduced the last section of the autobiographical work with this concept: "In the course of this biographical presentation one has seen at length how the child, the boy, and the youth tried to approach the supersensuous by various paths—first, looking with an inclination to a natural religion, then attaching himself lovingly to a positive religion; next testing his own powers by contracting within himself,

---

* 2. Fear, or Mythic Life-Forms in the Existence of the Human Being / a. The Daemonic

and at last joyously giving himself over to the universal faith. While wandering back and forth in the interstices between these regions, seeking, looking about, much came upon him that could belong to none of all these, and he believed he understood more and more that it would be better to turn his thoughts away from the prodigious, the incomprehensible.—He believed that he discovered something in nature, whether living or lifeless, animate or inanimate, that manifested itself only in contradictions and therefore could be grasped under no concept, much less under a word. It was not divine, for it seemed irrational; not human, for it had no intelligence; not devilish, for it was beneficent; and not angelic, for it often betrayed Schadenfreude. It was like [1:150] chance, for it showed no consequence; it resembled providence, for it suggested connection. Everything that limits us seemed penetrable by it; it seemed to do as it pleased with the necessary elements of our existence; it contracted time and expanded space. It seemed to find pleasure only in the impossible and scornfully to push away the possible with contempt.—This being, which seemed to infiltrate all others, separating and combining them, I called 'daemonic' after the example of the ancients and those who had perceived something similar. I sought to save myself from this fearful being."[80] It hardly needs to be pointed out that in these words, written more than thirty-five years after the famous fragment ["Nature"], the same experience of the incomprehensible ambiguity of nature proclaims itself. The idea of the daemonic, which is again found as a conclusion in the *Egmont* quotation from *Poetry and Truth* and at the beginning of the first stanza of "Primal Words. Orphic," accompanies Goethe's intuition throughout his life.[81] It is this that makes its appearance in the idea of fate in *Elective Affinities*; and if mediation between the two were needed, then that, too, which for millennia has been closing the ring, is not lacking in Goethe. The primal words refer palpably, the memoirs of his life allusively, to astrology as the canon of mythical thinking. *Poetry and Truth* concludes with reference to the daemonic; with reference to the astrological, it begins. And this life does not seem entirely deprived of an astrological approach. Goethe's horoscope, as it was cast half-playfully, half-seriously in Boll's *Belief in the Stars and Astrology*, points, for its part, to the turbidity of this existence.[82] "Also, the fact that the ascendant closely follows Saturn and thereby lies in ominous Scorpio casts some shadows onto this life; the zodiacal sign functioning as 'enigmatic,' in conjunction with the hidden nature of Saturn, will at the very least cause a certain reticence in the later stages of life; but also"—and this anticipates what follows—"functioning as an earth-crawling zodiacal creature in which the 'telluric planet' Saturn stands, [it will cause] that strong worldliness which clings to the earth 'in crude love lust, with clinging organs.'"[83]

*"I sought to save myself from this fearful being." [1:151] Mythic humanity pays with fear for associating with daemonic forces. This fear often spoke out unmistakably in Goethe. Its manifestations are to be taken out of the anecdotal isolation in which they are remembered almost with disgust by the biographers and placed in the light of an examination that, it must be admitted, shows with terrible clarity the violence of primeval powers in the life of this man, who, however, would not have become the greatest poet of his nation without them. The fear of death, which includes all others, is the loudest one. For death threatens the shapeless panarchy of natural life most of all, the panarchy that forms the spell of myth. The poet's aversion to death and to everything that designates it bears all the features of the most extreme superstition. It is known that around him no one was ever permitted to speak of anyone who died; less known is that he never approached the deathbed of his wife. His letters disclose the same attitude toward the death of his own son. Nothing indicates this more than the letter in which he reports this loss to Zelter and its truly daemonic concluding formulation: "And so onward, over graves!"[84] The truth of the words placed in the mouth of the dying man affirms itself in this sense. Mythic vitality ultimately replies in these words to the nearing darkness with their impotent desire for light.[85] The matchless cult of the self in the last decades of his life was also rooted in this attitude. *Poetry and Truth, Daybooks and Yearbooks,* the edition of his correspondence with Schiller, and the care expended on the correspondence with Zelter are so many efforts to foil death. Everything he says of the continued existence of the soul voices still more clearly the heathen concern that, instead of harboring immortality as a hope, demands it as a pledge.[86] Just as the idea of immortality that comes from myth was shown to be an "incapacity to die," so in Goethean thought this idea also is not the drawing of the soul into its homeland but, rather, a flight from the limitless into the limitless. Above all, the conversation after the death of Wieland, transmitted by Falk, wants immortality to be granted in conformity with nature and also, as if to emphasize the inhuman element in immortality, wants to know that it is actually granted to great minds alone.[87]

---

*   b. Fear of Death

*No feeling is richer in variants than fear. To the fear of death there is joined that of life, as to a keynote its [1:152] innumerable overtones. Moreover, the tradition neglects and conceals the Baroque play around the fear of life. It is concerned with erecting a norm in Goethe, and it is thereby far removed from recognizing the struggle of life-forms that he carried out in himself to its full term. Goethe locked this struggle too deeply within himself. Hence, the loneliness in his life and—sometimes painfully, sometimes defiantly— the muteness. In *On Goethe's Correspondence* Gervinus showed in its portrayal of the early Weimar period how soon muteness sets in. Gervinus was the first and the surest among all others to draw attention to these phenomena in the Goethean life; he, perhaps alone, intimated their significance, regardless of how erroneously he passed judgment on their value. Neither Goethe's silent self-absorption in his later period nor his interest, intensified into a paradox, in the subject-matters of his own life therefore escaped Gervinus. The fear of life, however, speaks from them both: from his brooding, fear of its power and breadth; from his embracing, fear of its flight. In his text, Gervinus determines the turning point separating the creative work of the older Goethe from that of the earlier periods, and he sets it at the year 1797, the time of the projected journey to Italy.[88] In a contemporaneous letter written to Schiller Goethe deals with objects that, without being "wholly poetic," would have awakened in him a certain poetic mood. He says: "I have therefore precisely examined the objects that elicit such an effect and, to my surprise, noted that they are properly symbolic."[89] The symbolic, however, is that in which the indissoluble and necessary binding of a truth-of-the-matter with a subject-matter appears. "If one," as it is written in the same letter, "henceforth, with the further progress of the journey, were to direct one's attention not so much toward what is noteworthy as toward what is significant, then one would ultimately have to reap a fine harvest for oneself and for others. While still here I want to try to take note of what I can of the symbolic, but especially to train myself in foreign places that I am seeing for the first time. If that should succeed, then one would necessarily, without wanting to pursue the experience across the board, yet by going into depth at every place, at every moment, to the extent it was granted to one, carry off still enough plunder from familiar lands and regions." "One may well say," [1:153] Gervinus adds, "that this is almost continuously the case in his later poetic productions and that in

---

*   c. Fear of Life

them he measures experiences that he had formerly presented in sensuous breadth, as art demands, according to a certain spiritual depth, whereby he often loses himself in the abyss. Schiller very astutely sees through this new experience, which is so mysteriously veiled; . . . a poetic demand without a poetic mood and without a poetic object would seem to be his case. In fact, what would matter here, if the object is to mean something to him, is much less the object itself than the mind." (And nothing is more characteristic of classicism than this striving, in the same phrase, to grasp and to relativize the symbol.) "It would be the mind that sets the boundary here; and here too, as everywhere, he can find the common and the spiritually rich only in the treatment, and not the choice, of material. What those two places were to him, he believes—every street, bridge, and so on would have been to him in an excited mood. If Schiller had been able to have an intimation of the consequences of this new approach in Goethe for his subsequent undertakings, the former would hardly have encouraged the latter to give himself over to it entirely, because through such a vision of objects a world would be set into the individual thing. . . . For this is thus the next consequence: Goethe begins to accumulate bundles of travel folders and files into which he puts all official papers, newspapers, weekly journals, excerpts from sermons, theater programs, decrees, price lists, and so on, adding his comments, comparing them with the voice of society, adjusting his own opinion accordingly, once again taking the new instruction *ad acta*, and thus hoping to preserve the materials for future use!! This already prepares the way for the momentousness developed later to an entirely ridiculous point, with which he holds diaries and notes in the highest esteem and considers the most miserable thing with the pathetic mien of a sage. From then on, every medal bestowed on him, every piece of granite bestowed by him, is for him an object of the highest importance; and when he drills rock salt, which Friedrich the Great despite all of his orders had not succeeded in finding, Goethe sees in this I know not what miracle and sends a symbolic knife-point, replete with it, to his friend Zelter in Berlin. There is nothing more [1:154] characteristic of this later way of thinking, which develops steadily as he grows older, than the fact that he makes it his principle to contradict with zeal the old *nil admirari* and, instead, to admire everything, to find everything 'meaningful, wonderful, incalculable.'"[90] Astonishment certainly has a share in this attitude, which Gervinus, without any exaggeration, paints so exquisitely; but so does fear. The human being solidifies in the chaos of symbols and loses the freedom unknown to the ancients. In acting, he turns to signs and oracles. These were not lacking in Goethe's life. Such a sign showed him the way to Weimar. Indeed, in *Poetry and Truth* he recounted how, while on a walk, divided between his calling to poetry or painting, he made use of an oracle.[91] Fear of responsibility is the most spiritual among all those with which Goethe was arrested by his essence. It is the foundation for the conservative ethos he brought to the political, the social, and—in his old age—the literary sphere as well. It is the root of the neglection in his erotic life. It's certain that it also determined his interpretation of *Elective Affinities*. For precisely this literary work casts a light into such grounds of his own life that, because his confession does not betray them, also remained hidden from a tradition that has not yet freed itself from the spell of this life. This mythic consciousness, however, cannot be addressed via the trivial catchphrase under which one was often pleased to recognize something tragic in the life of the Olympian. There is something tragic only in the existence of drama, that is to say, in the performing person, never in the existence of a human being. Least of all, though, in the quiescent existence of a Goethe, in whom such performing moments are scarcely to be found. What matters, then, for this life, as for every human life, is not the freedom of the tragic hero in death but, rather, redemption in eternal life. [1:155]

II[*]

Since there, all 'round, are heaped, for clarity,
The peaks of time,
And the most beloved live near, growing weak on
Most separated mountains,
Give, therefore, innocent water,
Oh, give us wings, from sense most loyal,
Hither-beyond to go and back to turn.

—Hölderlin[92]

[†]If every work is able to shed light on the author's life and on his essence, as *Elective Affinities* does, the usual approach misses this essence, the more so as it believes that it is adhering thereto. For, if only rarely does an edition of a classic fail to stress in its introduction that precisely its matter, more than

---

*   II. Redemption as Antithesis

†   I. Critique and Biography / A. The Traditional Conception / 1. Analysis of Works

scarcely anything else, is understandable solely on the basis of the poet's life, this judgment already contains in principle the πρῶτον ψεῦδος[93] of a method that seeks to present the development of the work in the poet through a template-like image of his essence and an empty or incomprehensible lived experience. As it takes its point of departure from the essence and life of the author, this πρῶτον ψεῦδος in nearly all modern philology—that is, in such philology that is not yet determined by verbal and factual inquiry—aims, if not to deduce the literary work as a product of the life, then nevertheless to bring the life closer to lazy comprehensibility. However, in as much as it is unquestionably appropriate to base cognition on what is certain and demon-strable, wherever insight directs itself toward a matter and an essence, the work must stand thoroughly in the foreground. For nowhere do these lie in a more enduring, more impressive, and more comprehensible way than in the work. The fact that even there they appear difficult enough and, for many, are never accessible may be sufficient ground for those who find them inaccessible to base the study of art on an inquiry into people and their relationships rather than on a precise insight into the work; but this should not move anyone who is judging the work to grant them credence, let alone to follow them. On the contrary, the one judging will keep in mind that the only rational con-nection between creative artist and work consists in the testimony that the latter gives of the former. There is knowledge of the essence of a human being not only through his outward expressions, to which in [1:156] this sense his works also belong—no, the essence is determined first and foremost by the works. Works, like deeds, are underivable, and every reflection that accepts this proposition in its entirety only to oppose it in individual cases has lost its claim to matter.

*What in this way escapes the banal presentation is insight not only into the value and kind of works but equally into the essence and life of their author. In the first place, every cognition of a writer's essence in its totality, that is, every cognition of his "nature," is rendered vain through the neglected interpretation of the works. For, even if interpretation is not in a position to yield a final and complete intuition of the writer's essence, which is indeed, for certain reasons, always unthinkable, yet when the work is disregarded, this essence remains completely unfathomable. But insight into the life of a cre-ative artist is also closed off to the traditional method of biography. Clarity

---

*   2. The Presentation of Essence and Work

about the theoretical relation between essence and work is the fundamental condition for any intuition of a creative artist's life. So little has happened up until now to achieve such clarity that psychological concepts generally count as the best means of insight, whereas one must renounce all intimation of the true state of affairs here more than anywhere else so long as the terms of psychology remain in style. This much, in sum, can be asserted: the primacy of the biographical in the image of the life of a creative artist—that is, the presentation of the life as that of a human, with the double emphasis on what is decisive and what is undecidable for human beings in matters of morality—would be found only where knowledge of the unfathomability of the origin of every work, delimited according to both its value and its matter, is excluded from the ultimate sense of his life. For, even though the great work does not form itself in common existence; indeed, if the former is actually the guarantor of the latter's purity, nevertheless the great work is ultimately only one among the other elements of common existence. And thus it can clarify the life of an image-maker only in a way that is entirely fragmentary—according more to the course than to the matter of this life. The entire uncertainty about the meaning that the works can have in the life of a human being has led to this: peculiar types of contents are attributed to the life of creative artists, reserved for it, and justified in it alone. Such a life is not [1:157] only supposed to be emancipated from moral maxims; no, it is supposed to be partaking of a higher legitimacy and more clearly open to insight. No wonder that for such a view every genuine content of life, which always emerges in the works as well, has very little weight. Perhaps this view has never been more clearly presented than with regard to Goethe.

*In the interpretation according to which the life of creative artists is supposed to have autonomous contents at its disposal, a trivial habit of thought touches so precisely on a much deeper one that it may be assumed that the former is a deformation of this deeper, more original habit of thought, which, of late, has again come to light. If, to be more precise, following the traditional view, work, essence, and life mingle equally without any determinations of one with respect to the others, this view also explicitly attributes unity to the three. It thereby constructs the appearance of the mythic hero. For, in the realm of myth, essence, work, and life do indeed form the unity that is otherwise granted to them only in the mind of a member of the lazy literati. Here,

* B. The Heroizing Conception

the essence is daemon; the life is fate; and the work, which only embosses the other two, is a living shape. Here, the work retains within itself the ground of the essence and at the same time the content of the life. The canonical form of mythic life is precisely that of the hero. At the same time, the pragmatic is therein symbolic; therein alone, in other words, the symbolic shape and, with it, the symbolic matter of human life is adequately given to insight. This human life, however, is in fact a superhuman life and therefore different from the properly human not only in its existing shape but decisively in its essential matter. For, while the hidden symbolism in human life stringently rests as much on the individual element of the animate being as on its human element, the manifest symbolism in the life of the hero extends neither to the sphere of individual particularity nor to that of moral uniqueness. Type, that is, norm, even if superhuman, separates the hero from the individual; his role as representative separates him from the moral uniqueness of responsibility. For he is not alone before his god but is, rather, representative of humanity before its gods. All representation in the moral realm is of a mythic nature, from the patriotic "one for all" to the sacrificial death of the redeemer.— Typology and representation in the life of the hero [1:158] culminate in the concept of its task. The presence of this task and of its obvious symbolism distinguishes superhuman from human life. It marks Orpheus's descent into Hades no less than Hercules with his twelve tasks: the mythic bard as much as the mythic hero. One of the most powerful sources for this symbolism flows from astral myth: in the superhuman type of the redeemer, the hero represents humanity through his work on the starry sky. The Orphic primal words apply to him: it is his daemon, the sunlike one; his Tyche, changing like the moon; his fate, ineluctable like astral $αναγκη$. Not even Eros points beyond them—only Elpis does.[94] It is thus no accident that the poet came upon Elpis as he sought something humanly close in the other primal words and that, among them all, she alone was found to need no explanation. It's no accident either that, instead of her, the rigid canon of the four others provided the schema for Gundolf's *Goethe*.[95] Accordingly, the question of method applied to biography is less doctrinaire than this, its justification, would lead one to suppose. For in Gundolf's book, the attempt has indeed been made to present Goethe's life as a mythic one. And this conception not only demands attention because something mythic lives in the existence of this man; it demands attention doubly so in approaching a work to which the conception in question could be appealing on account of its mythic moments. For, should this conception succeed in corroborating the claim, this means that a lifting of the layer in which the meaning of this novel independently presides would be impossible. Where the existence of no such separated domain can be demonstrated, it can no longer be a matter of literature but, rather, only of its forerunner, magical script. Every thoroughgoing approach to a work by Goethe, but most especially *Elective Affinities*, therefore depends on the repudiation of this attempt. In doing so, there is at the same time an indication of insight into a luminous kernel of redemptive matter that in *Elective Affinities*, as everywhere else, eluded the attitude just described.

* * *

*The canon corresponding to the life of the demigod appears in a peculiar displacement in the conception of the poet proclaimed by the George school. [1:159] It assigns the poet, like the hero, his work as a task, and his mandate is thereby considered divine. From God, however, human beings receive not tasks but only demands, and thus before God no special value is ascribed to the poetic life. The concept of the task is, therefore, also inappropriate from the perspective of the poet. The poetic work in the most proper sense arises only where the word liberates itself from the spell of even the greatest task. Such poetry does not descend from God but rather ascends from what is unfathomable in the soul; it has a share in the deepest self of the human being. Because poetry's mission appears to the George circle to stem directly from God, it grants the poet not only an inviolable, though merely relative, rank among his people but also a completely problematic supremacy as a human being pure and simple, and in this way, the mission grants the life of the poet a problematic supremacy before God, to whom he, as a superhuman, appears to be equal.[96] The poet, though, is not by degrees but in kind a more provisional appearance of human essence than the saint. For a relationship of the individual to the national community is determined in the essence of the poet, while in that of the saint, it is the relationship of the human being to God.[97]

   †Along with the heroizing view of the poet that can be found in the reflections of the George circle, which stand in a highly confusing and disastrous

---

*   II. Gundolf's *Goethe* / A. Methodological Debilitation / 1. The Poet in the George School / a. As Hero

†   b. As Creator

way at the foundation of Gundolf's book, a second error of no lesser importance can be found, an error that emerges from the abyss of thoughtless linguistic confusion. Even if the title of Creator certainly does not belong to the poet, it has nevertheless devolved to him in the spirit that does not perceive the tone of the metaphorical that admonishes one to remember the true Creator. And in fact, the artist is less primal ground or Creator than origin and image-maker, and certainly, the artist's work is by no means his creation but, rather, his formation. A formation, to be sure, not only a creature, has a life. But what establishes the definitive difference between the two is this: only the life of the creature, and never that of something formed, has an unimpeded share in the intention of redemption. However the creativity of the artist may be discussed by way of likeness, Creation is able to unfold its ownmost *virtus*—namely, that of cause—not through the works of the artist but singularly and [1:160] alone through creatures. Hence the careless use of language that is based on the word "Creator" leads all by itself to considering the life and not the works as the artist's ownmost product. But whereas what presents itself in the life of the hero by virtue of his full symbolic luminosity is something fully shaped, whose shape is the struggle, a univocal task, much less a univocal and clearly demonstrable struggle, is not to be found in the life of the poet any more than in the life of any human being. Since the shape in question must still be conjured up, what is offered beyond the one that lives in struggle is only the one that stiffens into scripture. Thus comes to completion a dogma that enchants the work into life; that has the work, as life, stiffen back into a work through an equally misleading error; and that presumes to grasp the much-invoked "shape" of the poet as a hermaphrodite combining hero and Creator in view of which nothing more can be distinguished and yet about which everything is asserted with the semblance of profundity.

*The most thoughtless dogma of the Goethe cult, the palest avowal of its adepts, is that among all of Goethe's works, the greatest is his life—this Gundolf's *Goethe* has adopted. Goethe's life is therefore not rigorously divorced from that of his works. Just as the poet in a clearly paradoxical image called colors the deeds and the sufferings of light,[98] so Gundolf, in a highly turbid vision, makes the Goethean life into such light, a light in which his works would ultimately be nothing other than its colors. This attitude accomplishes two things for Gundolf: it removes every moral concept from

---

*   2. Life as Work

the horizon, and at the same time, in attributing to the hero, as Creator, the shape that befits him as victor, it achieves a level of blasphemous profundity. Thus, it is said of *Elective Affinities* that Goethe therein "pondered the legal procedures of God."[99] But the life of a human being, even if it should be that of a creative artist, is never that of the Creator. Just as little can it be interpreted as the life of the hero who gives shape to himself. It is in this sense that Gundolf engages in commentary on a human life. For the subject-matter of this life is not grasped with the faithful attitude of the biographer even and precisely for the sake of what is not understood in it; it is not grasped with the [1:161] great modesty of a true biography as the very archive of indecipherable documents of this existence.[100] Rather, the subject-matter and the truth-of-the-matter are supposed to lie plainly in the open and correspond to one another, as in the life of a hero. Only, however, the subject-matter of life lies plainly in the open, and its truth-of-the-matter is hidden. The single trait, single link, certainly can be illuminated, but not the totality, unless it, too, is grasped only in a finite linkage. For in itself the linkage is infinite. Hence, in the realm of biography, there is neither commentary nor critique. In violation of this principle, two books, which may be called the antipodes of Goethe scholarship, encounter each other in a strange way: the work by Gundolf and the presentation by Baumgartner.[101] Whereas the latter directly undertakes a fathoming of the truth-of-the-matter without so much as an intimation of the place where it is buried and therefore must pile up critical failures beyond measure, Gundolf immerses himself in the world of the subject-matters of the Goethean life in which, though, he can present their truth-of-the-matter only in vain. For a human life does not allow itself to be considered by analogy to a work of art. Gundolf's source-critical principle, however, shows that his decision in favor of just such a distortion is fundamental.[102] If, in the hierarchy of sources, the works are consistently placed in the first position and the correspondence, not to mention the conversation, is subordinated to them, this attitude can simply be explained by his view that the life itself is a work. For only over against such a work does the commentary derived from this ordering of sources possess a higher value than those derived from any other one. But this is only because the concept of work specifies a proper and strictly circumscribed sphere into which the poet's life is incapable of penetrating. If, moreover, the aforementioned sequential order was perhaps supposed to attempt a separation of extant materials that were originally written from those that were initially oral, this, too, is only a vital issue of history as it actually happens, whereas biography must hold on to the full breadth of a human life even with the highest claim to matter. The author, to be sure, dismisses biographical interest at the beginning of his book; but the lack of dignity that often characterizes more recent biography should not cause one to forget that a canon [1:162] of concepts lies at its basis, a canon without which every historical approach to a human being succumbs to the loss of its object. No wonder, therefore, that with the inner deformity of this book a formless type of poet takes shape, a type that recalls the monument sketched out by Bettina [von Arnim] in which the prodigious forms of this revered man dissolve into the shapeless, the hermaphroditic.[103] This monumentality is mendacious, and—to speak in Gundolf's own language—it shows that the image emerging from feckless logos is not so dissimilar to the one created by boundless eros.[104]

*Only the persistent pursuit of its methodology stands up against the chimerical nature of this work. Without this weapon it is wasted effort to deal with its individual passages. For an almost impenetrable terminology is their armor. The fundamental significance for all cognition in connection with the relationship between myth and truth manifests itself in association with this terminology. The relationship in question is that of mutual exclusion. There is no truth in myth, for there is no univocity and therefore not even any error in it. Since, however, there can be just as little truth about myth (for there is truth only in facts, just as matter-of-factness lies in the truth), there is, so far as the spirit of myth is concerned, singularly and alone a cognition.[105] And where a presence of truth should be possible, it can be so only under the condition of cognizing myth, that is to say, recognizing its annihilating indifference to truth. This is why in Greece authentic art and authentic philosophy—as distinct from their inauthentic stage, the theurgic—arise with the ending of myth, because art is no less based on truth than philosophy, and philosophy is no more based on truth than art. So unfathomable is the confusion established by the identification of truth and myth, however, that this initial distortion, with its hidden efficacy, threatens to shield almost every single sentence of Gundolf's work from all critical suspicion. And yet the whole art of the critic here consists in nothing other than snatching up, like a second Gulliver, a single one of these Lilliputian minisentences in spite of its wriggling sophisms and contemplating it in total calm. "Only" in marriage "were united . . . all

---

*   3. Mythos and Truth

the attractions and [1:163] repulsions that arise out of the suspension of the human being between nature and culture, out of his duality—that, with his blood, he borders on the animal, with his soul on the divine. . . . Only in marriage does the fateful and the instinctive unification or separation of two human beings . . . through the begetting of a legitimate child become in pagan language a mystery and in Christian language a sacrament. Marriage is not only an animal act, but also a magical one, an enchantment."[106] This statement is distinguished from the kind of thinking found in a message contained in a Christmas cracker only by the bloodthirsty mysticism of its expression. How securely stands, by contrast, the Kantian explanation, whose rigorous reference to the natural moment of marriage—sexuality—does not obstruct the path to the logos of its divine aspect—fidelity. This is because logos is suited to the truly divine; it does not establish life without truth, nor does it ground ritual without theology. By contrast, what is common to all pagan vision is the primacy of cult over a doctrine that shows itself to be pagan most assuredly in that it is exclusively esoteric. Gundolf's *Goethe*, this ungainly pedestal for the author's own statuette, marks him [Gundolf] in every sense as the initiate of an esotericism, which only out of forbearance tolerates the attempt on the part of philosophy to trouble itself with a secret whose key he holds in his hands. Yet no mode of thinking is more disastrous than one that disconcertedly bends back into myth the very thing that had begun to grow out of it, a mode that, sure enough, through this forced submersion in the monstrous, would have immediately alerted every intellect for whom it is not quite right to reside in the wilderness of tropes, in a primeval forest, where words swing like chattering monkeys from bombast to bombast so as not to be required to touch the very ground that would betray their inability to stand, namely, logos, where words are meant to stand and constitute a speech. They avoid logos, however, with so much show, because, in the case of all mythic thinking, even when surreptitious, the question concerning the truth therein becomes null and void. To mythic thinking, in other words, it makes no difference whether or not the blind terrestrial stratum of the mere subject-matter is taken for the truth-of-the-matter in Goethe's work, and instead of purifying a true matter out of a notion like that of fate by means of cognition, it is spoiled by a sentimentality that, by means of its capacity to smell, empathizes with such notions. [1:164] Along with the mendacious monumentality of the Goethean image, there thus appears the counterfeit legality of its cognition, and along with the insight into the methodological frailty of this monumentality, the investigation into its logos bumps up against its linguistic presumption and, therefore, encounters its center. Its concepts are names, its judgments formulas. For, in this monumentality, language, the radiance of whose *ratio* even the poorest wretch could not fully suffocate, is precisely what had to diffuse a darkness that it alone could illuminate. The last shred of belief in the superiority of Gundolf's work over the Goethe literature of earlier schools must thereby vanish; an intimidated philology—intimidated not only for the sake of its bad conscience but also because it could not measure this book against its own root concepts—let it stand as their rightful and grander successor. Yet even the almost unfathomable perversion of this work's mode of thinking does not remove from the philosophical approach an endeavor that, unless it bore the depraved appearance of success, would therefore pass judgment on itself.

*Wherever an insight into Goethe's life and work is in question, a mythic element—regardless of how visibly it may be manifested in them—can never form the ground of cognition. Although it may very well be an object of the approach in the case of a certain detail, when it comes to the essence and the truth in the work and in the life, insight into myth, even in the case of an objective linkage, is not the final one. For neither Goethe's life nor any one of his works is fully represented in the domain of myth. Whereas this is simply guaranteed by his nature as a human being so far as the life is in question, this is what the works teach in detail, inasmuch as a struggle that was kept secret in life manifests itself in the last of them. And only in these last works does one encounter the mythic element also in the matter, not just in the material. They can probably be viewed in the context of this life as a valid testimony of its final course. Their testimonial force applies not only, and not at the deepest level, to the mythic world in Goethe's existence. There is in him a wrangling to loosen its clutches, and the Goethean novel testifies to this wrangling, no less than it testifies to the essence of that mythical world. In the prodigious experience of mythical powers—a fundamental experience that reconciliation [1:165] with them is not to be obtained except through the continuity of sacrifice—Goethe revolted against these powers.[107] Whereas in the years of his manhood there was an attempt on Goethe's part, constantly renewed and undertaken with despondency yet also with an iron will, to surrender to those mythic orders wherever they still rule, indeed, to reinforce their

---

*   B. Matter-of-Fact Debilitation / The Later Goethe

rule, just as a servant always only reinforces the powers that be, this attempt broke down after the last and most difficult submission of which Goethe was capable—after, that is, in his more than thirty-year struggle against marriage, which appeared menacingly to him as the emblem of mythic arrest, his capitulation; and one year after his marriage, which had been imposed on him during the days of fateful pressure, Goethe began *Elective Affinities*, through which he lodged a protest against the world with which his years of manhood had concluded a pact, a protest that unfolded with increasing power in his later work.[108] *Elective Affinities* is a turning point in this work. With it begins the last series of his productions, not from a single one of which he was completely able to detach himself because, until the end, their heartbeat remained alive in him. Understandable, therefore, is the gripping character of the diary entry from 1820 stating that he "had begun reading *Elective Affinities*"[109] and also the speechless irony of a scene transmitted by Heinrich Laube: "A lady addressed Goethe with regard to *Elective Affinities*: 'I cannot approve of this book at all, Herr von Goethe; it is really immoral and I do not recommend it to any woman.'—In response to which Goethe kept silent very seriously for a while and then finally said with great intensity: 'I am sorry; it is nevertheless my best book.'"[110] This last series of his works attests to, and accompanies, a purification that was no longer allowed to be a liberation. Perhaps because his youth had often taken all-too-swift flight from the emergencies of life into the domain of poetic art, age, via a terribly punishing irony, made poetry into the master of his life. Goethe submitted his life to the orders that made this life an occasion for his literary works. His contemplation of subject-matters in his later years has much to do with this moral circumstance. *Poetry and Truth*, *West-Eastern Divan*, and the second part of *Faust* became the three great documents of such masked penance. [1:166] The historicization of his life, as it devolved first to *Poetry and Truth* and later to his diaries and annual notebooks, had to verify and poetize how much this life had been an urphenomenon of one poetically full of matter, an urphenomenon of a life full of material and occasions for "the poet." The occasion for poesy that is here under discussion is not only something other than the lived experience that more recent convention makes the basis of poetic invention; it is, rather, its exact opposite. What is handed down through histories of literature as the catchphrase that Goethean poesy was supposed to be "occasional poetry," meaning "poetry of lived experience," spoke the opposite of the truth with regard to his last and greatest works. For the occasion provides the matter, and the lived experience leaves behind only a feeling. Related and akin to the relationship between occasion and lived experience is the relationship between the words *Genius* and *Genie*. In the mouths of the moderns, *Genie* [generally translated as "genius"] amounts to a title that, no matter how they position themselves, will never be suitable for capturing the relationship of a human being to art as an essential one. The word *Genius* achieves this, and Hölderlin's verses vouch for it: "Are not many of those alive known to you? / Does not your foot stride upon the true, as upon carpets? / Therefore my Genius! step only / Nakedly into life and have no care! / Whatever happens, let it all be occasional [*gelegen*] for you!"[111] This is precisely the ancient vocation of the poet, who, from Pindar to Meleager, from the Isthmian Games to an hour of love, found only distinctly high, yet as such always worthy, occasions [*Gelegenheiten*] for his song, which could therefore never have struck him as based on lived experiences. This is why the concept of lived experience is nothing other than a circumlocution for the lack of consequence in poetry that is longed for even by the loftiest—because equally still cowardly—philistinism, one that, robbed of a relation to truth, is incapable of arousing accountability from its sleep. In his old age, Goethe had penetrated deeply enough into the essence of poesy to feel with horror the absence of every occasion for song in the world that surrounded him and still to want only to stride on that carpet of the true. It was late when he stood on the threshold of German Romanticism. To him, access to religion in the form of a conversion—the turning toward a community—was not allowed, as it was not allowed to Hölderlin. Goethe abhorred [1:167] conversion among the early Romantics. But the laws, which the Romantics sought in vain to satisfy through conversion and thereby through the extinguishing of their lives, sparked in Goethe, who also had to submit to these laws, the very highest flame of his life. In this flame, the dross of every passion burned off; and thus in his correspondence up to the end of his life, he was able to keep his love for Marianne [von Willemer] so painfully close that more than a decade after the time in which their inclination to each other came to light, perhaps the most forceful poem of the [*West-Eastern*] *Divan* could emerge: "No longer on a page of silk / Do I write symmetrical rhymes."[112] And the latest phenomenon of such poetry, which commanded life and, indeed, finally even its duration, was the conclusion to *Faust*. If, in the series of works of his old age, *Elective Affinities* is the first, then a purer promise must be visible there, no matter how darkly myth may also hold sway therein. But the promise will not be disclosed by the Gundolfian approach. No more than that of all the other authors does it take into account the novella, the "queer childhood neighbors."[113]

* * *

*Elective Affinities was itself planned in the beginning as a novella within the orbit of Wilhelm Meister's Journeyman Years, but its growth drove it out of this orbit.[114] Traces of this original conception of its form have preserved themselves, however, despite everything that led the work to become a novel. Only the complete mastery of Goethe, which is displayed at its highest point in this work, was able to prevent the innate tendency of the novella from shattering the novel form. The discord appears to be subdued through force, and unity achieved by his ennobling, so to speak, of the novel form through the form of the novella. The compelling device that made this possible and that imposed itself from the side of the matter in an equally peremptory manner lies in this: the poet forgoes summoning the sympathy of the reader into the center of the action. Inasmuch as this, the center of the novel, remains so thoroughly inaccessible to the immediate intention of the reader, which can be seen most clearly with the unexpected death of Ottilie, the influence of the novella form betrays itself in the novel, and a break most likely betrays itself, too, precisely in the presentation of this death, when that center, which persistently keeps itself closed in the [1:168] novella, makes itself at last perceptible with redoubled force. It may belong to the same tendency of form, as R. M. Meyer has already pointed out, that the story delights in arranging groups.[115] And indeed its imagistic quality is fundamentally unpainterly; it may be called plastic, or perhaps stereoscopic. This quality also appears novella-like. For if, like a maelstrom, the novel draws the reader irresistibly into its interior, the novella imposes distance, driving every living being out of its magic circle. In doing so, Elective Affinities remained novella-like despite its breadth. In the sustainability of its expression, it is not superior to the authentic novella it contained. A boundary form has been created in it, and by virtue of this form, it stands further removed from other novels than they do from one another. In "[Wilhelm] Meister and in Elective Affinities the artistic style is thoroughly determined by the fact that we feel the narrator everywhere. Missing here is the formal-artistic realism . . . , which makes events and human beings

---

*   III. The Novella / A. Its Necessity in the Composition / 1. The Novel Form of Elective Affinities

independent, such that they produce their effect as an immediate presence, as if from the stage; on the contrary, these really are a 'story,' which is produced by a palpable narrator who stands in the background. . . . The Goethean novels unfold within the categories of the 'narrator.'"[116] Elsewhere Simmel describes them as "recited."[117] But whatever the explanation for this phenomenon in *Wilhelm Meister*, which does not appear further analyzable to Simmel, in *Elective Affinities* it stems from the fact that Goethe jealously reserves it entirely for himself to take charge of the living sphere of his poetic work. The very same limits on the reader are characteristic of the classical form of the novella: Boccaccio gives his novellas a frame; Cervantes writes a prologue for his. However much the form of the novel is emphasized in *Elective Affinities*, precisely this emphasis and this excess of type and outline betrays it as novella-like.

*Nothing could make more invisible the residual remains of ambiguity in the form of the novel than the insertion of a novella, which, the more the principal work stood in contrast to it, understood as a pure model of its kind, the more this work would have to seem like an authentic novel. Thereupon rests the significance that, for the composition [of the novel], accrues to "The Queer Childhood Neighbors" [1:169], which must count as a paradigmatic novella, especially when reflection is restricted to form. Goethe wanted to propose this novella as exemplary no less, and, to a certain extent, even more, than the novel. For, although the event that it relates is conceived in the novel as a real one, the story is nevertheless designated as a novella.[118] It is supposed to count as "a novella" just as decisively as the main work is supposed to count as "a novel." In the novella, the intended lawfulness of its form, the inviolability of the center, which means the secret, emerges in the clearest way possible as an essential trait. For, in this form, a secret is the catastrophe placed in the middle as the animating principle of the story, whereas, in the novel, the meaning of the catastrophe, as the concluding event, remains merely phenomenal. Although so much in the novel corresponds to this catastrophe, its enlivening force is so difficult to fathom that, for an unguided reflection, the novella appears no less independent and yet also scarcely less enigmatic as "The Foolish Pilgrim."[119] And yet, in this novella, a brilliant light reigns. From the beginning, everything, sharply outlined, is at an apex. It is the day of decision that shines into the dusky Hades of the novel. The novella is therefore

---

*   2. The Form of Its Novella

more prosaic than the novel. It confronts the novel in a prose of a higher degree. Corresponding to this is the genuine anonymity of the novella's characters and the partial, undecided anonymity of those in the novel.

*Whereas in the life of the characters of the novel there prevails a seclusion that completes the guaranteed freedom of their activity, the characters in the novella appear narrowly circumscribed on all sides by their surrounding world, by their relatives. Indeed, if in the novel Ottilie relinquishes not only her father's medallion at the urging of her beloved but even the memory of her home so that she can be entirely consecrated to love, in the novella even the two who are united do not feel themselves independent from parental blessing. This little detail designates the pair most deeply. For it is certain that the lovers emerge as mature from the ties of their parental home, but it is no less certain that they transform its inner power, since each of them carries the other out of and beyond their homes, even if one of them would be obliged to remain within their own. If there is otherwise in general a sign for a pair of lovers, still there is this: not only the abyss of sex has been closed for each other [1:170], so, too, has that of the family.[120] For a loving vision of this kind to be valid, it is not allowed faintheartedly to withdraw from the sight, much less the knowledge, of one's parents, as Eduard requires of Ottilie. The force of the pair in love triumphs by fading out even the full presence of the parents among the lovers. The extent to which the lovers in their radiance are capable of releasing one another from all ties is expressed in the novella by the image of the garments in which the children are scarcely recognized anymore by their parents. The lovers in the novella enter into a relation not only with their parents but also with the rest of their surrounding world. And whereas, for the novel's characters, independence seals all the more rigorously the temporal and spatial fallenness unto fate, for the novella's characters, it holds the most invaluable guarantee that their traveling companions are in danger of foundering at the highpoint of their own distress. This shows that even the most extreme situation does not expel the pair from their own circle, whereas the perfectly formed kind of life evident in the novel's characters can do nothing against the fact that, until the sacrifice occurs, every single moment excludes them ever more inexorably from the community of the peaceful. The lovers in the novella do not obtain their peace through sacrifice.

---

*   B. Its Matter-of-Fact Meaning / The Correspondences in Detail / a. The Lovers and the Surrounding World [crossed out]

That the fatal leap of the girl does not have this significance is meant by the poet in the most delicate and precise way. For this alone is the secret intention with which she throws the garland to the boy: that she does not want "to die in beauty" and to be crowned in death as someone who has been sacrificed.[121] The boy, for his part, whose eyes are only on steering, whether it is knowingly so or without the slightest intimation, vouches for the fact that he is not participating in a performance that would be a sacrifice. Because these human beings do not risk everything for the sake of a falsely conceived freedom, no sacrifice occurs among them; rather, the decision occurs within them. In fact, freedom is as clearly removed as fate from the two youths' rescuing resolution. It is the chimerical striving for freedom that conjures fate onto the characters of the novel. The lovers in the novella stand beyond both, and their courageous resolve suffices to rend a fate that would gather over them and to see through a freedom that would draw them down into the nullity of choice. This is [1:171] the sense of their actions during the seconds of decision. Both of the lovers dive down into a living current whose force, rich with blessing, appears no less great in this event than the death-dealing power of stagnant waters in the other, that of the novel.[122] The strange mummery in the wedding clothes found by the two lovers in the novella is fully illuminated by an episode in the novel. This is where Nanny refers to the shroud prepared for Ottilie as her bridal gown. It is therefore surely allowed that the strange feature of the novella be interpreted accordingly and that—even without the mythic analogies that can perhaps be discovered in it—the wedding garments of the lovers be recognized as transformed burial shrouds that are henceforth immune to death. The complete security of existence that is ultimately disclosed to them is also indicated otherwise. Not only by their garments concealing them from their friends but, above all, through the great image of the boat landing at the site of their union, there arises the feeling that they no longer have a fate and that they stand at the place where others should one day land.

*Through all of this, it may certainly be considered incontrovertible that in the structure of *Elective Affinities* a dominant meaning accrues to this novella. Even if it is only in the full light of the main story that all its details are disclosed, those discussed above are unmistakably made manifest: to the mythic motifs of the novel, there correspond those of the novella as a

---

*   2. The Correspondences in Their Entirety

motif of redemption. If, therefore, in the novel, the mythic may be described as the thesis, the antithesis can be seen in the novella. Its title points to this. Those childhood neighbors must appear "queer," most of all, to the characters in the novel who, for this reason, also turn away from the neighbors with deeply injured feeling.[123] It is an injury that, in accordance with the secret and in many respects hidden mobilization of the novella, perhaps hidden even to Goethe, he outwardly set into motion, without thereby taking from it the inner meaning. Whereas the characters in the novel remain before the gaze of the reader more feebly and more mutely, yet in full life-size, the united couple in the novella disappears under the arch of a final rhetorical question as though in an infinitely distant perspective.[124] Should not a blessedness be implied in a readiness to clear out and disappear, the blessedness in everything small that Goethe later made into the sole motif of "The New Melusine"?[125] [1:172]

III*

Before you grasp the living body on this star,
I invent the dream for you on eternal stars.

—George[126]

[+]The offense taken at every critique of art under the pretext that it treads too closely to the work by those who do not find in the critique of art an afterimage of their own narcissistic dreaminess testifies to so much ignorance about the essence of art that a time when its rigorously determined origin is becoming increasingly vital owes it no refutation. Nevertheless, an image that grants an ultraconcise reply to this sentiment is perhaps allowed. Suppose that one makes the acquaintance of someone who is beautiful and attractive but closed off because he carries a secret within himself. It would be reprehensible to want to press him. It is, however, certainly allowed to undertake an investigation into whether he has siblings and whether their essence might explain in some way the enigmatic character of the stranger. Exactly in this way does critique investigate the siblings of the artwork. And all genuine works have siblings in the realm of philosophy. They are precisely

---

* ["Third Part: Hope as Synthesis," according to the outline, 89; Benjamin left this out of M¹, having forgotten perhaps about hope for a moment.]

+ I. Critique and Philosophy

the shapes in which the ideal of its problem appears.—The entirety of philosophy, its system, is of a higher cardinality than that which the sum total of all these problems can demand, because the unity in the solution to them all cannot be inquired into. If, more exactly, the unity in the solution to all of the problems could itself be inquired into, then, with respect to the question about which it asks, new questions would immediately impose themselves, questions upon which would rest the unity of the answer to them, along with all remaining ones. It follows from this that there is no question that spans the unity of philosophy by way of inquiry. The ideal of the problem designates in philosophy the concept of this nonexistent question, into which the unity of philosophy inquires. Even if, however, the system of philosophy can in no sense be inquired into, there are still formations that, without being questions, have the deepest affinity [*Affinität*] with the ideal of the problem. These are artworks. The artwork does not compete with philosophy itself; it simply enters into the most precise relationship with philosophy through its affinity [*Verwandtschaft*] with the ideal of the problem. And indeed, according to a lawfulness [1:173] grounded in the essence of the ideal as such, the ideal of philosophy can present itself only in a multeity. The ideal of this problem does not, however, appear in a multeity of problems. Rather, it lies buried in a multeity of works, and its promotion is the business of critique. The latter allows the ideal of the problem to enter into appearance—into one of its appearances—in the artwork. For, what critique ultimately shows in the artwork is the virtual formulability of its truth-of-the-matter as that of the highest philosophical problem; where critique pauses, however, as if in awe of the work but equally out of respect for the truth, is this formulation itself. If nevertheless that formulability alone were to be redeemed, if the system could be inquired into, it would thereby be transformed from an appearance of the ideal into the never-given existence of the ideal itself. Critique thus only says that the truth in a work would be recognized not, to be sure, as an object of inquiry but as demanded still. If, therefore, it is permitted to say that everything beautiful is somehow related to the true and that the virtual site of the true in philosophy is determinable, this then means that an appearance of the ideal of the problem can be located in every true artwork. It follows as a result that philosophy rather than myth is called upon to guide the approach that ascends from the foundations of the novel to the intuition of its perfection.—

*The shape of Ottilie thereby emerges. It is in her figure, after all, that the novel appears most visibly to outgrow the mythic world. For, even if she falls victim to obscure powers as a sacrifice, it is still precisely her innocence that determines this terrible destiny in keeping with the ancient claim that demands the irreproachability of whomever is sacrificed. To be sure, in the figure of this girl, chastity, to the extent that it might derive from intellectuality—the latter kind of untouchability constitutes almost a reproach in the case of Luciane—does not present itself; nevertheless, Ottilie's entirely natural demeanor, despite the complete passivity that characterizes her in the erotic as well as in every other sphere, makes her unapproachable to the point of madness. Werner's sonnet announces this in its impertinent way: the chastity of this child harbors no consciousness. But is its merit not thereby all the greater? Just how deeply chastity is grounded in the natural essence of the [1:174] girl—this Goethe presents in the images in which he shows her with the Christ child and with Charlotte's dead child in her arms. Both come to Ottilie without a spouse. Nevertheless, the poet said still more with this. For the "living" image[127] presenting the grace and the purity of the mother of God that is superior to all rigid morality is precisely the artificial one. The image that nature offers only a little later shows the dead boy. And precisely this unveils the true essence of that chastity whose sacral infertility is in no way superior in itself to the impure confusion of sexuality that draws the lapsed spouses to one another and whose law holds sway only to hinder a union in which husband and wife would have to lose each other. In the appearance of Ottilie, however, this chastity lays claim to far more. It calls forth the semblance of an innocence of natural life. The pagan, if not also the mythic, idea of this innocence at least owes its most extreme and consequential formulation to Christianity in the ideal of virginity. If the grounds of a mythic primal guilt are to be sought in the bare life-drive of sexuality, then Christian thought sees the counterpart of this guilt where that drive is most distant from its drastic expression: in the life of the virgin. But this clear, even if not clearly conscious, intention contains a momentous error. There is, to be sure, a natural innocence of life, just as there is a natural guilt of life; but the former is not tied to sexuality—not even in the form of a denial—but, rather, solely to its polar opposite: equally natural spirit. Just as the sexual life of a human being can become the expression of a natural guilt, so his spiritual

---

* II. Beauty as Semblance / A. Virginity

life, which is related to the unity of his individuality, however it may be constituted, can become the expression of a natural innocence. This unity of individual spiritual life is character.[128] Univocity, as its constitutive-essential moment, differentiates character from the daemonic element of all purely sexual phenomena. Attributing a complex character to a human being can only mean denying him character—whether this be truthful or unjust—just as, for every appearance of bare sexual life, the seal of its knowledge remains insight into the ambiguity of its nature. This is also demonstrated in the case of virginity. [1:175] Above all, the ambiguity of its untouchability lies in plain sight. For precisely that which is thought to be the sign of inner purity is the most welcoming sign of desire. But even the innocence of ignorance is ambiguous. For on its basis inclination passes over unexpectedly into the desire that is thought to be sinful. And precisely this ambiguity recurs in a highly significant way in the Christian symbol of innocence, the lily. The rigorous lines of the plant, the whiteness of the calyx, is combined with the numbingly sweet, scarcely any longer vegetal scents. The poet gave this dangerous magic of innocence to Ottilie, and it is very closely related to the sacrifice that celebrates her death. For, to the precise extent that she appears innocent, she does not leave the spell out of its execution. With such innocence, not purity but, rather, its semblance spreads over her figure. It is the untouchability of the semblance that transports her away from her lover. The same semblant nature is also suggested in the essence of Charlotte, who only appears completely pure and unassailable, whereas, in truth, her infidelity to her friend disfigures this essence. Even in her appearance as mother and housewife, where passivity ill suits her, she seems shadowy. And yet, in her, nobility presents itself only at the price of this indeterminacy. Hence, at the deepest level, she is not unlike Ottilie, who is the sole semblance among shadows. For insight into this work, it is therefore indispensable in general to search for its key not in the contrast among the four partners but, rather, in the way in which they are similarly distinguished from the lovers in the novella. The figures in the main story have their contrast less as individuals than as pairs.

*Does Ottilie's essence share in the genuine natural innocence that has as little to do with ambiguous untouchability as with blessed guiltlessness? Does she have character? Is her nature clearly before our eyes, not so much thanks to her own openheartedness as on the strength of a free and open expression?

---

*   B. Innocence / 1. In Death

She designates the opposite of all this. She is closed off—more than that: all her actions and words are incapable of divesting her of her closure. Plant-like muteness, as it is so clearly enunciated by the Daphne-motif of the hands upraised in supplication, lies over her existence and [1:176] obscures it even in the most extreme emergencies that otherwise, in all such cases, set existence in a clear light. Her resolution to die not only remains a secret to her friends until the end; in its total concealment it seems to form itself incomprehensibly for her as well. And this touches on the root of its morality. For, if anywhere the moral world shows itself illuminated by the spirit of language, it is in resolution. No moral resolution can enter life without a linguistic shape and, in the strict sense, without having become the object of communication. That is why the morality of the will to die that animates Ottilie becomes questionable in her complete silence. In truth, it is grounded not in a resolution but in a drive. That is why her death is not sacred, as she appears ambiguously to express it. If she herself recognizes that she has strayed from her "path," then this phrase can only mean in truth that death alone can preserve her from an inner demise.[129] And thus this death is indeed expiation in the sense of fate—not, however, the sacred de-expiation that, for human beings, death freely chosen can never become, only a death divinely imposed upon one. Ottilie's death, like her untouchability, is the last way out for a soul in flight from fallenness. A longing for rest speaks in her death-drive. Goethe does not fail to indicate how entirely it arises from what is natural in her. If Ottilie dies by depriving herself of food, he nevertheless made it clear in the novel how often she resisted nourishment, even in happier times. Ottilie's existence, which Gundolf calls sacred, is unsanctified, not so much because she would have transgressed against the disintegrating marriage, as because she lives out her life indecisively, subjected unto death to a fateful force in her appearance and in her development. At first glance, this lingering in the sphere of fate—at once guilty and guiltless—lends her an air of the tragic. Gundolf can thus speak of the "pathos of the work, no less tragically sublime and shattering than that from which Sophocles' *Oedipus* stems."[130] Before him, André François-Poncet had already spoken similarly in his vapid, bloated book on the "*affinités électives.*"[131] And yet this is the falsest judgment. For, in the tragic words of the hero, the decision is raised, a ridge beneath which the guilt and innocence of myth [1:177] entwine themselves as an abyss. The worldliness of good and evil, their this-sidedness, which can be reached only by the hero, never the hesitant girl, is grounded outside of inculpation and innocence.

It is empty talk, therefore, to extol her "tragic purification." Nothing more untragic than this mournful end could ever be thought up.[132]

*But it is not only in this that the speechless drive lets itself be recognized; her life also appears to lose its hold whenever it comes into contact with the luminous circle of moral orders. Yet only a complete lack of sympathy for this work appears to have opened the critic's eyes to this. It was thus reserved for the dowdy intellect of Julian Schmidt to pose the question that should have immediately imposed itself upon those who are unbiased with regard to this event.[133] "There would have been nothing to say against it if the passion had been stronger than the conscience, but how is the muting of the conscience to be conceived?" "Ottilie does something blameworthy; afterward, she feels it very deeply, more deeply than necessary. But how does it come about that she does not feel it earlier? . . . How is it possible that a soul as well constituted and as well brought up as Ottilie is not supposed to feel that the nature of her behavior toward Eduard wrongs Charlotte, her benefactor?"[134] No insight into the innermost connections of the novel can invalidate the plain legitimacy of this question. Misrecognizing its compulsory nature leaves the essence of the novel in obscurity. For this silence of the moral voice is not to be grasped like the muted language of the affects as a feature of individuality. It is not determined within the boundaries of a human being. With this silence semblance has consumptively settled into the heart of the noblest being. And strangely, this calls to mind the silent character of Minna Herzlieb, who died mentally ill in old age.[135] All speechless clarity in action is semblant, and the interiority of those who preserve themselves in this way is in truth no less obscure to them than it is to others. Only in her diary does Ottilie's human life seem in the end still to stir. All of her existence, to the extent that it is endowed with language, is to be sought more and more in these mute transcriptions. Yet they, too, construct only a memorial for one who is deceased. Their revelation of secrets that only death is allowed to unseal [1:178] inures one to the thought of her passing away; and by manifesting the silent quality of the living person, they also foreshadow her total muteness. The semblant element that prevails in the life of the diary writer penetrates even into her spiritual, enraptured mood. For, if it is the danger of the diary in general to disclose prematurely the seeds of recollection in the soul and to prevent the ripening of its fruits, then this danger must necessarily become disastrous

---

*   2. In Life

when spiritual life expresses itself only in a diary.[136] And yet, all the force of the most internalized existence finally stems from recollection. It alone guarantees love its soul. It breathes in the Goethean act of recollecting: "Oh, you were in lived out times / My sister or my wife."[137] And just as in such a covenant even beauty outlasts itself as recollection, so with regard to its blossoming, the former also lacks essence without the latter. The words of Plato's *Phaedrus* testify to this: "When one who is freshly initiated and is among those who gazed upon much in the beyond beholds a divine countenance or a bodily figure that truly forms an image of beauty, he at first shudders as something of the awe he experienced comes over him, then stepping right up before that image he recognizes its essence and reveres it like a god, for, recollection, elevated to the idea of beauty, sees it once again standing with discretion on sacred ground."[138]

*Ottilie's existence does not awaken such recollection; beauty really remains primary and most essential in this existence. All her favorable "impression emerges exclusively from appearance; despite the numerous pages from her diary, her inner essence remains closed off—more closed off than any of the female characters of Heinrich von Kleist."[139] With this insight Julian Schmidt joins an old critique that says with odd exactitude: "This Ottilie is not a legitimate child of the poet's spirit but is, rather, sinfully generated in a doubled recollection of Mignon and an old painting by Masaccio or Giotto."[140] The boundaries between epic and painting are in fact crossed in the shape of Ottilie. For the appearance of the beautiful as the essential matter in one who is alive lies beyond the sphere of epic material. And yet this appearance stands at the center of the novel. For if one designates the [1:179] conviction that Ottilie is beautiful as the fundamental condition for any engagement with the novel, there is no exaggeration. This beauty is not allowed to disappear as long as the world of the novel endures: the coffin in which the girl rests is not sealed. Goethe distanced himself very far in this work from the famous Homeric paradigm for the epic presentation of beauty. For not only does Helen in her mockery of Paris show herself in a more decisive way than Ottilie ever does in her words; but in the presentation of her beauty, above all, Goethe did not follow the famous rule that is drawn from the admiring speeches of the old men gathered on the wall.[141] The distinctive epithets lent to Ottilie, despite being against the laws of the novel form, serve

---

*   C. Beauty / 1. The Helen Motif

only to remove her from the epic plane in which the poet reigns and impart to her a strange vitality for which he is not responsible. The more distantly she thereby stands from the Homeric Helen, the more closely she approaches the Goethean Helen. Like the latter, she stands in ambiguous innocence and semblant beauty, and like Helen, she stands in expectation of an expiatory death. And conjuration is also at play in her appearance.[142]

*With regard to the episodic shape of the Greek heroine, Goethe maintained perfect mastery, for in the form of the dramatic presentation he suffused even conjuration with light—how little it seems an accident, with this in mind, that the scene in which Faust was supposed to implore Persephone to release Helen was never written.[143] In *Elective Affinities*, however, the daemonic principles of conjuration protrude into the very center of the poetic formation. Conjuring, in other words, consistently becomes only a semblance—the vital beauty that starkly, mysteriously, and crudely intruded into Ottilie as "material" in the most vehement sense. The Hades-like character that the poet lends to the event is thus confirmed: he stands before the depths of his poetic gift like Odysseus with his bared sword before the pit full of blood and, like him, fends off the thirsty shades in order to suffer only those from whom he seeks a meager report.[144] The report is a sign of her ghostly origin. It is this origin that spawns the peculiarly diaphanous, sometimes precious quality in the layout and execution. The formulaic character that is to be found, above all, in the construction of the second [1:180] part—which was significantly expanded in the final stages after the completion of the basic conception—nevertheless emerges implicitly in the style, with its countless parallelisms, comparatives, and qualifications, all of which suggest the mode of writing characteristic of late Goethe. In this sense Görres declared to Arnim that much in *Elective Affinities* seemed to him "polished rather than carved."[145] A phrase that might especially be applied to *Maxims and Reflections*. More problematic still are the features that cannot at all be disclosed to the purely receptive intention: those correspondences that can be disclosed only to a philologically investigative approach that turns entirely away from aesthetics. It is quite certain that in such correspondences the presentation reaches over into the domain of conjuring formulas. This is why it so often lacks the ultimate instantaneousness and finality of artistic vitalization: that is, form. In the novel, form does not so much construct shapes—which often

---

*   2. Conjuration

enough formlessly impose themselves as mythic shapes with their own plenipotent authority—as timidly, consummately, and with supreme justification dissolve them, playing with these shapes, as it were, in the manner of an arabesque. One may view the effect of the novel as an expression of an inherent set of problems. It is distinguished from other novels that find the greatest part of their effect, if not always its highest level, in the impartial feeling of the reader, in that it must affect such feeling in a very confusing way. A turbid influence was always peculiar to this novel, an influence that could prompt an engagement bordering on fanaticism in kindred minds and a reluctant distress in more alien ones. Only incorruptible reason, under whose protection the heart may abandon itself to the prodigious, conjured beauty of this work, is equal to it.

*Conjuration wants to be the negative counterimage to Creation. It, too, claims to bring forth the world from nothingness. The artwork has nothing in common with either. It comes forth not from nothingness but from chaos. It will nevertheless not wrest itself from chaos, as, according to the idealism of the doctrine of emanation, the formed [*geschaffene*] world does. Artistic formation [*Schaffen*] "makes" nothing out of chaos and does not penetrate it; just as little will semblance let itself mingle with elements of that chaos, as happens in fact with conjuration. The formula achieves this. Form, however, for an instant, enchants chaos [1:181] into the world. No artwork may therefore seem alive in a way that is entirely nonspellbound without becoming a mere semblance and ceasing to be an artwork. The life trembling in it must appear rigidified and, as for an instant, spellbound. This, which is becoming what it is in the work,[146] is a mere beauty, a mere harmony that suffuses chaos—and in truth only this, not the world—but in suffusing only seems to enliven. What calls a halt to this semblance, bans the movement, and stops the harmony in midphrase [*ins Wort fällt*] is the expressionless. Trembling life founds the secret in the work; its rigidification establishes the matter therein. Just as the interruption by the commanding word has the power to retrieve the truth from the prevarication of a woman precisely there, where it interrupts, so the expressionless compels the trembling harmony to come to a halt, and through this protest eternalizes its quaking. In this eternalization the beautiful must take responsibility, but it seems now interrupted in this answering-for-itself, and it therefore possesses the eternity of its matter just by

---

*   3. The Expressionless

grace of this protest. The expressionless is the critical force, which, to be sure, is unable to separate semblance from essence in art but prevents them from mingling. The expressionless has this force as a moral word. In the expressionless, the sublime force of the true appears as it determines the language of the real world according to the laws of the moral one. It therefore shatters that which in all beautiful semblance still survives as the legacy of chaos: false, errant totality—the absolute one. Only the expressionless completes the work by shattering it into patchwork, into the fragment of the true world, into the torso of a symbol. As a category of language and art, and not of the work or of genres, the expressionless cannot be more rigorously defined than through a passage from Hölderlin's "Remarks on Oedipus," which seems not yet to have been recognized for its fundamental significance not only for the theory of tragedy but for the theory of art pure and simple. It reads: "Tragic transport is, properly speaking, empty, and the most unrestrained.—Through it, in the rhythmic sequence of the representations in which the transport presents itself, that which one calls the caesura in meter—the pure word, the counter-rhythmic interruption—becomes necessary in order, namely, to meet the rending alteration of representations at its [1:182] highest point, such that thereupon no longer the alteration of representations but, rather, representation itself appears."[147] The "occidental Junonian sobriety" that Hölderlin represented as the almost unattainable goal of all German artistic practice several years before he wrote this passage is only another designation of the caesura in which, along with harmony, every expression simultaneously subsides in order to make room for an expressionless force within all artistic means.[148] Such force has scarcely become clearer than in Greek tragedy, on the one hand, and in Hölderlinian hymns, on the other. Perceptible in tragedy as the falling silent of the hero, in the hymns as a protest in the rhythm. Indeed, one could not designate such rhythm more precisely than by stating that something beyond the poet stops the poetry in midphrase. Here lies the reason "why a hymn will seldom (and by all rights perhaps never) be called 'beautiful.'"[149] If, in Hölderlin's lyric poetry, it is the expressionless, in Goethe's it is the beautiful that comes forth at the boundary of what can be grasped in the artwork. What stirs beyond this boundary is, in one direction, the monstrosity of madness and, in the other, conjured appearance. And in the latter case German poetry may not venture one step beyond Goethe without mercilessly falling victim to a world of semblance, the most alluring images of which Rudolf

Borchardt evoked. Yet even in the work of his master [Goethe] there is no lack of evidence that it did not always avoid the temptation that was closest to his genius, namely, to conjure semblance.[150]

*He thus, on occasion, remembers the work on the novel with these words: "One finds oneself happy enough when, in this agitated time, one can flee into the depths of tranquil passions."[151] If the contrast here between agitated surface and tranquil depths only fleetingly calls to mind a body of water, such a simile is found more expressly in Zelter. In a letter dealing with the novel he writes to Goethe: "What ultimately remains peculiar to it is a writing style that is supplied like a clear element whose nimble inhabitants swim among one another, going back and forth, now brightening, now dimming, without straying or getting lost."[152] What is enunciated in Zelter's manner, which is never sufficiently appreciated, is thus a clarification of the way in which the style of the poet, which is spellbinding through its formulaic manner, has affinities with the spellbinding character of a reflection in water. And beyond stylistics it points to the meaning [1:183] of that "pleasure lake" and ultimately to the semantic matter of the entire work. Just as, to be more precise, the semblant soul ambiguously shows itself in the work, luring with innocent clarity and leading downward into the deepest darkness, so does water partake of this strange magic. For, on the one hand, it is black, obscure, unfathomable; on the other, reflecting, clear, and clarifying. The power of this ambiguity, which had already been a theme of "The Fisherman," became dominant in the essence of passion in *Elective Affinities*.[153] If this ambiguity leads into the novel's center, it also points back to the mythic origin of its image of beautiful life and allows that image to be recognized with complete clarity. "In the element from which the goddess"—Aphrodite—"emerged, beauty seems actually to be right at home. She is praised in flowing rivers and springs; one of the Oceanides is called 'beautiful flow'; among the Nereids, the beautiful shape of Galatea comes forth and beautifully-footed daughters emerge in large number from the gods of the sea.[154] The mobile element, as it washes at first around the foot of the walker, wets the feet of the goddesses bestowing beauty, and the silver-footed Thetis remains for all times the model according to which the poetic fantasy of the Greeks depicts this part of the body in their images. . . . Hesiod attributes beauty to no man or any god considered masculine; here, too, beauty still designates no inner value whatever. It

---

*   4. Beautiful Semblance

appears predominantly in the external shape of the woman bound to Aphrodite and the Oceanian life forms."[155] If, therefore—as stated in Walter's *Aesthetics in Antiquity*—the origin of a mere, beautiful life according to the suggestions of myth lies in the world of harmonious-chaotic stirring, this is where a more profound sensibility sought the provenance of Ottilie. Where Hengstenberg spitefully gets wind of the "nymph-like meal" of Ottilie[156] and Werner tentatively comes up with his "hideously tender sea-nixies,"[157] Bettina touched with incomparable sureness on the innermost connection: "You are in love with her, Goethe—I have suspected it for a long time; that Venus rose out of the roaring sea of your passion, and after she sowed the seeds for a harvest of teardrops, she vanishes back into it in a celestial shine."[158]

* * *

[1:184] *Under the semblance character that determines Ottilie's beauty, an inessentiality still threatens the salvation that the friends in the novel gain from their struggles. For, if beauty is semblant, so, too, is the reconciliation that it mythically promises in life and in death. The sacrifice of this beauty, like its blossoming, would be in vain; its reconciling would be a semblance of reconciliation. There is true reconciliation in fact only with God. While in the latter the individual reconciles himself with God and only thereby conciliates other human beings, it is peculiar to semblant reconciliation that the individual wants human beings to conciliate one another and only thereby to reconcile with God. This relation of semblant reconciliation to true reconciliation touches once again on the opposition between novel and novella. For this is what the queer conflict entangling the lovers of the latter in their youth ultimately wants to achieve: their love, because it risks life for the sake of true reconciliation, attains it and, with it, the peace in which their bond of love endures. Because true reconciliation with God is attained by no one who does not destroy everything in it—so far as it concerns him—in order only then to find everything rising again before God's reconciled countenance: this is why a death-defying leap designates that instant when they, each entirely alone before God, for the sake of reconciliation take a stand. And in such readiness for reconciliation, already conciliated, they gain each other. For reconciliation, which is entirely beyond this world and which is

---

*   III. The Semblance of Reconciliation / A. Conciliation and Being Touched / 1. Harmony and Peace

scarcely objective for the work of art, has its worldly reflection in the conciliation among fellow human beings. Measured against this reconciliation, how far does noble indulgence, with its tolerance and delicacy, fall short, an indulgence that still serves in the end only to increase the distance in which the characters in the novel come to know themselves. For, because they always avoid open quarrels—even though Goethe did not hesitate to depict the excessiveness of this even in the violent act of a girl—conciliation must remain foreign to them. So much suffering, so little struggle. Hence, the silencing of all affects. These never come forth externally as enmity, revenge, envy, but they also do not live internally as lamentation, shame, and despair. For how could the desperate actions of those who have been spurned compare with Ottilie's sacrifice, which places in the hands of God, not the most precious good, but the heaviest burden, and anticipates his decree. Thus, just as everything annihilatory in true reconciliation is missing from her semblance; so [1:185] everything painful and violent is kept as far away as possible from the manner in which Ottilie dies. And it is not only with this that an impious caution imposes the threatening peacelessness on those who are all too ready for peace. For what the poet keeps silent about a hundred times over emerges simply enough from the course of the whole: according to moral laws, passion loses all its legitimacy and happiness where it seeks to make a pact with bourgeois, wealthy, and secure life. This is the chasm over which the poet wants, in vain, to allow his characters to stride with somnambulistic certainty along the narrow path of pure human mores. Their noble restraint and composure cannot replace the clarity that the poet certainly knew how to keep away from himself as well as from them. (Here Stifter is his perfect epigone.)[159] In the mute inhibition that encloses these people in the sphere of human, indeed of bourgeois, custom and that hopes to save the life of passion for them, there lies the obscure transgression demanding its obscure expiation. These people are, strictly speaking, fleeing from the verdict of the law that still has authority over them. If, by all appearances, they are exempted from it by their aristocratic nature, only sacrifice in reality is able to save them. For this reason, they have no share in the peace that harmony is supposed to bestow on them; their *art de vivre* of the Goethean school only makes the swelter more stultifying. For here reigns the calm before the storm; in the novella, though, it is thunderstorm and peace. Whereas love leads those who are reconciled, only beauty remains as a semblance of reconciliation among those who are not.

*For the true lover, the beauty of the beloved is not decisive. If it was, the beauty that at first attracted the one to the other will be forgotten repeatedly in favor of greater glories in order, admittedly, to become internalized repeatedly in remembrance until the end. It is otherwise with passion. Even the most fleeting disappearance of beauty makes passion despair. This is because the one who is beautiful is called the most precious good only through love; for passion, the one who is most beautiful is this good. Passionate, therefore, is also the disapproval with which the novel's friends turn away from the novella. For them, abandoning beauty is, after all, unbearable. The wildness that disfigures the young woman in the novella is not the empty, corrupting kind of Luciane but, rather, the urgent, salutary [1:186] wildness of a noble creature: no matter how much grace is combined with it, this wildness is enough to give her an estranging essence that robs her of the canonical expression of beauty. This young woman is not essentially beautiful; Ottilie is. In his own way, even Eduard himself is, too: it is not for nothing that the beauty of this couple is praised. Goethe himself not only expended all the conceivable power of his gifts—beyond the limits of art—to cast the spell of this beauty; but with the lightest touch he comes close to intimating that the world of this gentle, veiled beauty is the center of poetry. With the name "Ottilie" he alludes to the saint to whom a convent on the Odilienberg in the Black Forest was dedicated as the patron of people suffering from eye diseases.[160] Regarding the men who see her, he calls her a "consolation for the eyes," and indeed her name may even recall the mild light that is a blessing for sick eyes and the home per se of all semblance. To this light he contrasted the luster that painfully radiates from the name and appearance of Luciane—contrasting the latter's sunny, broad circle of life to the secretive-lunar one of the former. Just as, however, he juxtaposes Ottilie's gentleness not only with Luciane's false wildness but also with the correct wildness of the lovers in the novella, so the mild shimmer of Ottilie's essence is placed squarely in the middle between hostile brilliance and sober light. The furious attack recounted in the novella was directed at the eyesight of the beloved; the character of this love, which is averse to all semblance, could not be indicated more rigorously. Passion remains trapped in the spell of semblance and is in itself incapable, even in fidelity, of lending support to those who are enflamed by it. Unless a more spiritual element, one able to soothe semblance, finds its way to beauty, the

---

*   2. Passion and Inclination / a. Ottilie, Luciane, the Young Woman in the Novella

chaotic character of passion—which, as it is, succumbs to the beauty beneath every semblance—must break out in a devastating way. This element is inclination.[161]

*In inclination the human being becomes detached from passion. It is in essence a law that determines this detachment like every detachment from the sphere of semblance and every transition into the realm of essence; the law is that the transformation transpires gradually, even indeed under a final and extreme intensification of semblance. In the emergence of inclination, passion thus also seems to turn more than before and completely into love. Passion [1:187] and inclination are the elements of all semblant love that shows itself to be different from true love not in the failure of feeling but, rather, only in its powerlessness. And it must therefore be stated that true love does not reign in the case of Ottilie and Eduard. Love becomes perfect only where, raised above its nature, it is saved by God's reigning. The obscure end of love whose daemon is Eros is thus not a naked foundering but the true release from the deepest imperfection that characterizes the nature of the human being itself. For it's this imperfection that denies a human being the consummation of love.[162] That's why what determines only it, inclination, as the authentic work of Ἔρως θάνατος enters all acts of love: the admission that the human being could not love. Whereas in all rescued, true love, passion, like inclination, remains secondary, their history, and the transition from one into the other, constitutes the essence of eros. Of course, blaming the lovers in the novel, as Bielschowsky dares to do, does not lead in this direction. Nonetheless, even his banal tone does not fail to appreciate the truth. After hinting at the bad behavior—indeed, the unbridled selfishness—of the lovers, he goes on to say of Ottilie's unswerving love: "In life, such an abnormal phenomenon may be encountered here and there. But then we shrug our shoulders and say: we don't understand. Such an explanation of a poetic invention amounts to its gravest condemnation. In poetry we want and need to understand. For the poet is a creator. He creates souls."[163] To what extent this can be conceded will doubtless remain highly problematic. Unmistakable, however, is that these Goethean characters can appear neither created nor purely formed but, rather, spellbound. From this, there arises the kind of obscurity that is alien to artifacts and can be fathomed only by someone who senses its essence in something yet semblant. For semblance is not so much presented

---

*   b. The Loving Couple

in this literary work as in the presentation itself. This alone is why semblance can mean so much; this alone is why the presentation means so much. The breakdown of that love is disclosed more concisely by the fact that every love that has grown within itself must become master of this world: be it in its natural outcome, in common—that is to say, strictly simultaneous—death; be it in its supernatural [1:188] duration, in marriage. Goethe stated this expressly in the novella, for the instant of shared readiness for a death by divine will grants the lovers a new life over which old rights lose their claim. Here he shows the life of the two who are saved in the precise sense in which it preserves marriage for the pious; in this couple, he presented the power of true love that he refused to state expressly in religious form. In the novel, by contrast, there is a twofold failure in this domain of life. While some pass away in isolation, the survivors are denied marriage. The novel's ending leaves the Captain and Charlotte like shadows in limbo. Because the poet could not allow true love to preside over either of the couples, in which case this world would have had to explode, he inconspicuously yet unmistakably gave the emblem of such love to his work in the characters of the novella.

*The legal norm makes itself master over wavering love. The marriage between Eduard and Charlotte, even while decaying, puts such love to death, because the magnitude of a decision—even if in a mythical distortion—is embedded in it, a decision to which choice qua election is never equal. And the title of the novel thus pronounces—to Goethe, half-unconsciously, it seems—judgment on them. For he seeks to save the concept of choice for moral thinking in the advertisement he wrote for the novel: "It seems that the prolonged physical-scientific labors the author carried out suggested this strange title to him. He may have noticed that ethical similes are very often used in the theory of nature so as to bring nearer to the circle of human knowledge something far removed from it. And so, in a moral case, he may well have been able to trace a chemical simile back to its spiritual origin, all the more so since there is everywhere only One Nature, and since running inexorably through the serene realm of rational freedom are the traces of a turbid, passionate necessity that can be completely erased only by a higher hand, and perhaps not in this life."[164] But what speaks more clearly than these sentences—which vainly seem to seek in the realm of serene rational freedom that realm of God, where

---

*   c. Marriage in the Novel

lovers dwell—is the mere word: "affinity" is already in and of itself the purest conceivable word to designate [1:189] the closest human connectedness in accordance with not only value but also rational foundations.[165] And in marriage this word becomes strong enough to make literal its metaphorical sense. This word cannot be strengthened through choice, nor in particular would the spiritual character of such [elective] affinity be based on choice. But this rebellious presumption is most irrefutably demonstrated by the double meaning of the word, which does not cease to mean, along with what or who is grasped in the act, the act of choice itself. Only in every case where affinity becomes the object of a resolution does it pass over from the stage of choice to decision. This annihilates choice in order to establish fidelity: only decision, not choice, is recorded in the book of life. For choice is natural, and may even accrue to the elements; decision is transcendent.—Because the highest right still does not yet befit that love, only for this reason, therefore, does the greater power still accrue to this marriage. But the poet never wanted in the least to attribute to the perishing marriage a right of its own. Marriage can in no sense be the center of the novel. Like countless others, Hebbel found himself in complete error when he said: "In Goethe's *Elective Affinities*, one aspect has remained abstract: the immeasurable importance of marriage for the state and for humanity is, to be sure, suggested at the level of the argument, but it has not been made visible in the framework of the presentation, which would have very well been possible and which would have greatly reinforced the impression of the entire work."[166] And earlier in the foreword to *Maria Magdalene* Hebbel writes: "How Goethe, who was so thoroughly an artist, a great artist, could commit such a violation of the inner form in *Elective Affinities*—that he, not unlike a distracted dissector, brought an automaton to the anatomical theater instead of a real body, that he placed at the center of his presentation an inherently null, even immoral marriage like the one of Eduard and Charlotte and treated and used this relation as if it were entirely the contrary (a perfectly legitimate one)—this I could not explain to myself."[167] Apart from the fact that marriage is not at the middle but is, rather, the means of the action, Goethe did not, and did not want to, have it appear as Hebbel conceives it. For he would have felt too deeply that there was "inherently" nothing at all to be said [1:190] about it, that its morality could show itself only as fidelity pure and simple, its immorality only as infidelity. To say nothing of the fact that something like passion could form its foundation.

The Jesuit Baumgartner says tritely but not incorrectly: "They love each other, but without the passion that constitutes the only charm of life for sickly and sentimental souls."[168] For this reason, though, marital fidelity is no less conditioned. Conditioned in the double sense: by what is necessarily as well as by what is sufficiently conditioning. The former lies in the foundation of decision. The decision is certainly no more arbitrary because passion is not its criterion. On the contrary, this criterion stands before the decision all the more unambiguously and rigorously in the character of the experience. For only experience can bear the decision—that experience that, in accordance with its essence, beyond all later occurrences and comparisons, shows itself singularly and only to the one who undergoes the experience, whereas every attempt by upstanding people to found decision on lived experience sooner or later goes awry. If this necessary condition of marital fidelity is given, then its sufficient condition is called fulfillment of duty. Only if one of the two conditions can remain free of doubt as to whether it was present can the reason for the breakup of the marriage be stated. Only then is it clear whether the breakup is "inherently" necessary, whether there is still hope for a rescue through a reversal. And the prehistory Goethe devised for the novel thereby gives evidence of the most unerring feeling. In earlier times, Eduard and Charlotte loved one another; yet, regardless of this, both concluded an empty marriage bond before uniting with each other. Only in this way, perhaps, with the false step embedded in the life of both spouses, could it be left up in the air: whether this step lay in the earlier irresoluteness or in the present infidelity. For Goethe had to hold out the hope that a victorious bond would be destined to last forever. It had scarcely escaped the poet, however, that this marriage, as both a juridical and even a bourgeois form, could not confront the semblance ensnaring it. This would be given to it only in the religious sense in which "worse" marriages than it have their inviolable persistence. Accordingly, the failure of all attempts at union is deeply motivated, above all, by the fact that they issue from a man who, with the consecration of the clergyman, has himself cast aside the power [1:191] and the right that alone can justify such attempts. Since, however, a union is no longer granted to the couple, a question in the end remains triumphant, the question that apologetically accompanies everything: was this not just the liberation from what was, from the start, a flawed beginning? Be this as it may—these human beings are torn from the path of marriage in order to find themselves essentially under other laws.

*More healing than passion yet no more helpful, inclination ruins only those who renounce passion. But inclination, unlike passion, does not destroy those who are solitary. Inclination leads the lovers inseparably downward; conciliated, they reach the end. On this final path, they turn to a beauty that is no longer arrested by semblance, and they stand in the realm of music. Goethe called the third poem of the "Trilogy" in which passion comes to rest, "Conciliation." It is "the double happiness of tones and of love"[169] that shines here on those who are tormented—glowing by no means as crowning glory but as a first faint intimation, as an almost hopeless glimmer of dawn. Music, of course, knows conciliation in love and, for this reason, the last poem of the trilogy is the only one that bears a dedication,[170] whereas the "leave me alone" of passion drops out of the "Elegy" in its motto as well as in its end.[171] Reconciliation, however, which remained in the realm of the mundane, therefore already had to unveil itself as semblance and, indeed, did so to the passionate person for whom semblance finally grew turbid. "The exalted world, how it vanishes before the senses!" "Music hovers now on angelic wings," and so only now does semblance promise to give way altogether; only now does it long for turbidity and become perfect. "The eye moistens, feels in loftier longing / The divine value of the tones as of tears."[172] These tears, which fill the eyes when listening to the music, withdraw the visible world from them. This indicates the deep connection that appears to have led to a fleeting remark by Hermann Cohen, who had a sense for the mind of the aged Goethe that was perhaps better than all of his mere interpreters: "Only the lyric poet who comes to completion in Goethe, only the man who sows tears—the tears of infinite love—only he could establish this unicity in the novel."[173] This, of course, is no more than simply intimated; from here, no path leads interpretation any further. For this can be done only by recognizing that the "infinite" love in question [1:192] is far less than the simple love about which one says that it lasts beyond death—it is recognizing that inclination is what leads to death. But the essence of inclination is therein at work and announces, if one wants to speak in this way, the novel's unicity: inclination, like the veiling of the image through tears in music, provokes the decline of semblance through being touched in conciliation. For being touched is precisely the transition in which semblance—the semblance of beauty as well as the semblance of reconciliation—once again dawns most sweetly before passing away. Neither

---

*   d. The Trilogy of Passion

humor nor tragedy can grasp beauty in language; beauty cannot appear in an aura of transparent clarity. Its most exact opposite is being touched. Neither guilt nor innocence, neither nature nor the beyond, apply to being touched in rigorously distinguishable ways. Ottilie appears in this sphere: this veil must lie over her beauty. For the tears of being touched in which the gaze is veiled are at the same time the ownmost veil of beauty itself. But being touched is only the semblance of reconciliation. And how inconstant and touching is that deceptive harmony in the lovers' flute playing. Their world is completely deserted by music. How semblance, to which being touched is connected, can therefore become so powerful in those who, like Goethe, have not from the beginning been touched in their innermost being by music and who are immune to the force of living beauty. To save what is essential to it is Goethe's struggle. The semblance of this beauty becomes more and more turbid within this struggle, like the transparency of a liquid that forms crystals through the process of being thoroughly shaken. For it is not the slight state of being touched that delights in itself but only the great touch of being shattered in which the semblance of reconciliation overcomes beautiful semblance and with this, finally, itself. Tearful lamentation: such is being touched. And in this way, the space of Dionysian shattering even gives resonance to this lamentation, as it does to tearless wailing. "The mourning and the pain in the Dionysian, as the tears that are shed for the constant decline of all life, form a gentle ecstasy; it is 'the life of the cicada, which without food or drink sings until it dies.'"[174] So writes Bernoulli about the one hundred and forty-first chapter of *Matriarchy*, where Bachofen deals with the cicada, the animal that originally belonged only to the dark earth but was elevated by the mythic profundity of the Greeks [1:193] to the league of Uranic emblems.[175] What else did Goethe's ruminations on Ottilie's departure from life mean?

*The more deeply that state of being touched understands itself, the more it is a transition; for a true poet, it never means an end. This is exactly what is indicated when shattering shows itself to be the best part of being touched, and it is also what Goethe means, albeit in a strange way, when he says in reference to Aristotle's *Poetics*: "Whoever advances now on the path of a truly moral, inner development will feel and will concede that tragedies and tragic novels, far from mollifying the spirit, make the mind and what we call the heart restless, and introduce a vague and indeterminate state; youth

---

*   B. Redemption / I. Shattering / a. Expiring Semblance

loves this and is therefore passionately drawn to such productions."[176] "On the way toward a truly moral . . . development," however, being touched will be a transition from the confused intimation only to the singularly objective theme of shattering, to the sublime. It is precisely this transition that is carried out in the demise of semblance. The semblance that presents itself in Ottilie's beauty is the kind that is dying. For it is not to be understood as if external hardship and violence were bringing about the demise of Ottilie; on the contrary, it is grounded in the very character of her semblance that it must expire and that it must do so soon. This semblance is entirely different from the triumphant one of dazzling beauty, the kind that is Luciane's or Lucifer's. And whereas, for the figure of Goethe's Helen and for the still more famous figure of the Mona Lisa, the enigma of their glory derives from the conflict between these two kinds of semblance, the figure of Ottilie is permeated only by a single kind of semblance, the one that expires. The poet has put this into every one of her movements and gestures so as to let her finally, in her diary, in the gloomiest and at the same time most tender way, increasingly lead the existence of a woman who is fading away. In Ottilie, therefore, the semblance of beauty pure and simple, which manifests itself in a twofold manner, has not appeared; rather, only that vanishing semblance, the one that is hers alone. This semblance, surely enough, discloses insight into beautiful semblance as such and therein, for the first time, lets it be recognized. Every view that grasps the figure of Ottilie therefore sees arising before its own eyes the old question: whether beauty is semblance.

[1:194] *Everything essentially beautiful is always and intrinsically connected to semblance yet in infinitely different degrees. This connection reaches its highest intensity in whatever is manifestly alive, and it is precisely here that there is a clear polarity between a triumphant and an expiring semblance. For everything alive is elevated above the realm of the essentially beautiful—the higher its life is ordered, the more this is so—and accordingly, something essentially beautiful manifests itself most of all as semblance in its shape. Beautiful life, the essentially beautiful, and semblant beauty—these three are identical. The Platonic theory of the beautiful is in this sense connected with the even older problem of semblance: in accordance with *The Symposium*, the theory is, first, directed at the living beauty of the body. If this problem still remains latent in Platonic speculation, it is because, to Plato, as

---

* B. The Cover of Beauty

a Greek, beauty is represented at least as much in the young man as in the young woman; but fullness of life is greater in the feminine than in the masculine. An aspect of semblance remains preserved, however, even in what is least alive in the event that it is essentially beautiful. And such is the event with all works of art—least among them, however, with music. Accordingly, the semblance in question, which is to say, the one brushing up against and bordering on life, remains in all beauty of art, and without this semblance beauty is not possible. Semblance, though, does not encompass its essence. Rather, this points deeper down to what in the work of art may be designated in contrast to semblance as the expressionless; outside of this contrast, however, it neither occurs in art nor can be univocally named. That is to say, the expressionless stands in such a necessary relation to semblance, although opposed, that the beautiful, even if it is not itself semblance, ceases to be something essentially beautiful when semblance disappears from it. For semblance belongs to something essentially beautiful as a cover and shows itself as the essential law of beauty through the fact that beauty appears as such only in that which is covered. Beauty itself is not therefore, as banal philosophemes teach, semblance. Rather, the famous formula that Solger eventually developed in the most superficial way—beauty is truth become visible—contains the most fundamental distortion of this great theme. Nor should Simmel have taken this theorem so casually [1:195] from Goethe's remarks, which often recommend themselves to the philosopher by everything other than their wording.[177] Since truth is not visible in itself, and since it could rest only on a trait that is not its own, this formula, which makes beauty into a semblance, ultimately amounts to a philosophical barbarism, quite apart from its lack of method and reason. For nothing else is meant if the thought is nourished in this formula that the truth of beauty lets itself be uncovered. Beauty is not semblance, not a cover for something else. It is itself not an appearance but thoroughly an essence, one such that it remains intrinsically "equal to itself" only under a covering. Semblance may therefore be deception everywhere else—beautiful semblance is the cover of what is necessarily most covered. For the beautiful is neither the cover nor the covered object but, rather, the object in its cover.[178] Uncovered, however, it would prove infinitely invisible. This is the basis of the age-old view that what is covered is transformed in the uncovering, that it will remain "equal to itself" only under a covering. With regard to everything beautiful, the idea of uncovering therefore turns into that of nonuncoverability. This is the idea of art critique. The critique of art does not have to lift the cover; on the contrary, it has to lift itself up to the true intuition of the beautiful through its most precise recognition as a cover. Up to the intuition that will never be open to so-called empathy and only imperfectly open to a purer approach of the naive: up to the intuition of the beautiful as a secret. A true artwork was never yet grasped other than where it presented itself ineluctably as a secret. The object for which the cover is in the last instance essential is to be designated in no other way. Because only the beautiful and nothing besides can be essentially covering and covered, the divine basis of the being of beauty lies in the secret. So, in sum, semblance in beauty is just this: not the superfluous covering of things in themselves but the necessary covering of things for us. Such covering is divinely necessary at times, just as it is therefore divinely determined that, when uncovered at the wrong time, that invisible factor by which revelation supersedes secrets evaporates into nothing. Kant's doctrine that the foundation of beauty is a relational character [1:196] thus triumphantly asserts its methodical tendencies in a very much higher sphere than that of the psychological.[179] Like revelation, all beauty contains within itself philosophical-historical orders. For it makes not the idea visible but, rather, its secret.

*For the sake of the unity that cover and covering form in beauty, it can essentially apply only where the duality of nakedness and covering does not yet exist: in art and in the appearances of mere nature. Conversely, the more distinctly this duality expresses itself, such that it finally affirms itself to the highest degree in the human being, the more the following becomes clear: in nakedness without cover the essentially beautiful has gone away, and in the naked human body a being above all beauty is attained—the sublime—and a work beyond all formations—that of the Creator. The last of the saving correspondences in which the delicately formed novella matches the novel with incomparably rigorous precision is thereby disclosed. When the young man undresses his beloved, it is not for the sake of pleasure; it is for the sake of life. He does not consider her naked body, and it is precisely for this reason that he perceives its highness. The poet did not choose idle words when he says: "Here the desire to save overcame every other consideration."[180] For such consideration cannot dominate in love. Love did not spring from the will to happiness, as it fleetingly lingers unbroken only in the rarest acts of contemplation, in the "halcyon" stillness of the soul. Its origin is the intimation of

---

*   c. Laying Bare

the blessed life. But where love as the bitterest passion is thwarted, where in love the *vita contemplativa* is nevertheless the most powerful, the intuition of the most glorious, more longed for than union with the beloved—this *Elective Affinities* presents in the fate of Eduard and Ottilie. In this way, no feature of the novella is gratuitous. In accordance with the freedom and necessity that it shows in relation to the novel, the novella is comparable to an image in the darkness of a cathedral that presents the cathedral itself and that thus imparts an intuition of the site in the midst of its interior that is otherwise denied. At the same time, the novella thereby brings inside a reflection of the bright, indeed the sober, day. And if this sobriety seems sacred, the most wondrous thing is that perhaps only [1:197] for Goethe is it not so.[181] For his poetic composition remains devoted to the interior space in the veiled light refracted in motley panes. Shortly after completing the novella, he wrote to Zelter: "Wherever you come across my new novel, take it up in a friendly manner. I am convinced that the transparent and nontransparent veil will not prevent you from seeing into the shape that is actually intended."[182] The word "veil" was more to him than an image—it is the cover that always again had to move him wherever he struggled for insight into beauty. Three figures in his life's work grew out of this struggle, figures that shook him like no other: Mignon, Ottilie, Helen. "Let me seem like that until I become / Do not take off my white dress! / I hurry from the beautiful earth / Down into that strong house. / There I rest a little in quiet / Then the fresh view opens / I leave then the pure cover / The belt and the wreath behind."[183] And Helen also leaves the cover behind: "The dress and veil remain in [Faust's] arms."[184] Goethe knows what was fabulated about the deceit of this semblance. He has Faust admonished: "Hold on to everything that is, above all, left to you. / Do not let go of the dress, already tugging / at the ends, daemons would like / To snatch it down to the underworld. Hold tight! / It is no longer the divinity that you lost / Yet it is divine."[185] As her living body, however, Ottilie's cover remains different from these. Only with her does the law that is announced more haltingly through the others express itself clearly: the more life leaks away, the more all semblant beauty, which is indeed singularly able to cling to whatever is alive, must pass away, until at the very end of one, that of life, the other must pass away, too. Therefore, nothing mortal is nonuncoverable. If, as a result, *Maxims and Reflections* truthfully designates the extreme degree of such nonuncoverability with the profound words: "Beauty can never become clear about itself," then a God still remains before whom there is no secret, and all is life.[186] The human being appears to us as a corpse and the life of the human being as love once they are before God. Therefore, death, like love, has a power to denude. Only nature, which preserves a secret as long as God allows it to exist, is nonuncoverable. Truth is discovered in the essence of language. The human body denudes itself, a sign that the human being itself appears before God.—[1:198] Beauty that does not surrender itself to love must fall victim to death. Ottilie knows her pathway to death. Because she recognizes it prefigured in the innermost core of her young life, she is—not in action but in essence—the most youthful of all the characters created by Goethe. It is true that old age confers a readiness to die, but youth is readiness for death. How hidden was Goethe's statement about Charlotte that she "would like to live."[187] Never in a work did he give to youth what he conceded to it in Ottilie: life in its entirety, which, from its own duration, has its own death.[188] Indeed, one may say that in truth, if he was blind to anything, it was precisely to this. If Ottilie's existence, in the pathos that distinguishes it from all others, nevertheless points to the life of youth, Goethe could be conciliated with this vision, which his essence refused, only through the destiny of her beauty. There is a peculiar and, to a certain extent, well-sourced reference for this. In May 1809, Bettina [von Arnim] sent a letter to Goethe touching on the Tyrolean Rebellion in which one reads: "Yes, Goethe, during this, things took a completely different shape in me . . . gloomy halls enclosing prophetic monuments of mighty heroes of death are the focus of my weighty forebodings. . . . Oh, in remembering" the Tyroleans, "join with me . . . this is the poet's renown—that he secures immortality for heroes!"[189] In August of the same year, Goethe wrote the last draft of the third chapter in the second part of *Elective Affinities,* where one reads in Ottilie's diary: "An idea of ancient peoples is serious and can seem terrible. They thought of their ancestors as sitting in silent conversation in great caves on thrones arranged in a circle. When a newcomer entered, if he was worthy enough, they stood up and bowed to him in welcome. Yesterday, as I sat in the chapel and saw several carved chairs placed in a circle opposite my own, that thought struck me as very friendly and charming. Why can you not stay seated, I thought to myself—stay seated silently and withdrawn into yourself, for a long, long time, until finally your friends come, before whom you stand up and show them their places with a friendly bow."[190] It is reasonable to understand this allusion to Valhalla as an unconscious or cognizant [1:199] recollection of the passage from Bettina's letter. For the affective affinity between these short sentences is striking; striking, too, the thought of Valhalla in Goethe; striking, finally, how abruptly it is introduced into Ottilie's notes. Would it not be an indication that Goethe brought himself closer to Bettina's heroic behavior in those gentler words of Ottilie?

*One may judge, after all of this, whether it is truth or vain mystification when Gundolf asserts with feigned liberal-mindedness, "The character of Ottilie is neither the main subject-matter nor the actual problem of *Elective Affinities*," and whether it makes any sense when he adds, "but without the moment when Goethe saw what appears in the work as Ottilie, neither the subject-matter would have been consolidated nor the problem shaped in this way."[191] For what, if not this one thing, is clear throughout all of it: that the character, indeed, the name of Ottilie is what bound Goethe to this world as by way of a spell, bound him so as truly to rescue a woman who is passing away, to redeem a loved one in this world. He confessed as much to Sulpiz Boisserée, who captured this with wonderful words in which, thanks to his most intimate view of the poet, he at the same time points toward the secret of Goethe's work more deeply than he could have foreseen. "During the journey we came to speak of *Elective Affinities*. He emphasized how swiftly and relentlessly he brought about the catastrophe. The stars had risen; he spoke of his relation to Ottilie, how he had loved her and how she had made him unhappy. In the end he became almost enigmatically full of foreboding in his speech.—Now and then, nevertheless, he said a cheerful verse. Weary, stimulated, half-full of foreboding, half-sleepy, in the most beautiful starlight we thus came . . . to Heidelberg."[192] If it did not escape the reporter's attention that, with the rising of the stars, Goethe's thoughts were directed toward his work, then Goethe himself perhaps hardly knew—his language bears witness to this—how elevated beyond mere atmosphere the moment was and how clear the admonition of the stars.[193] What long ago was obliterated as a lived experience persisted in this admonition as experience. For the hope Goethe must have conceived for the lovers appeared to him once under the symbol of the star. The sentence that, to speak with Hölderlin, contains the caesura of the work—a sentence in which, as the embracing [1:200] couple seal their end, everything comes to a halt—reads: "Hope went away, over their heads, like a star that falls from the sky."[194] They are not aware of this, of course, and it could not be said more clearly that the last hope is never for the one who

---

*   2. Hope

harbors it but only for those for whom it is harbored. The innermost ground for the "narrator's stance" thereby comes to light. It is he alone who, in the feeling of hope, can fulfill the sense of what is happening, just as Dante takes upon himself the hopelessness of the lovers when he falls, according to the words of Francesca da Rimini, "as a corpse would fall."[195] The most paradoxical, most fleeting hope emerges at last from the semblance of reconciliation, just as, to the extent that the sun fades away, the evening star, which outlasts the night, arises at twilight. Venus, of course, provides its shimmer. And upon the slightest such shimmer rests all hope; even the richest hope comes only from it. Hope in the end thus justifies the semblance of reconciliation, and Plato's claim that it is nonsensical to desire the semblance of the good suffers its only exception. For the semblance of reconciliation may, and indeed should, be willed: it alone is the house of utmost hope. At last, hope thus wrests itself from the semblance of reconciliation, and the "how beautiful" at the end of the book, like a trembling question, resounds with the dead, who, if they ever awaken, do so not in a beautiful world but in a blessed one. Elpis comes last in the "Primal Words": the hope for redemption we harbor for all the dead responds to the certainty of the blessing that the lovers in the novella take home with them.[196] This hope is the only justification for the belief in immortality, a belief that must never burnish one's own existence.[197] Precisely because of this hope, however, the mystical-Christian elements that arrived at the end, emerging from an endeavor—altogether different from that of the Romantics—to ennoble everything mythical at the ground level, are out of place. Not this Nazarene being,[198] therefore, but the symbol of the star gliding over the lovers is the appropriate form of expression for the mystery that in the precise sense resides within the work. The mystery in the sphere of the dramatic is the moment in which it protrudes from the realm of its own language into a higher realm, one that this language cannot attain. This moment can therefore never be expressed in words but uniquely and only in the [1:201] presentation: it is the "dramatic" in the most exact sense. In *Elective Affinities*, an analogous moment of the presentation is the falling star. Alongside its epic foundation in the mythic, its lyrical breadth in passion and inclination, there enters its dramatic crowning in the mystery of hope. If music includes authentic mysteries, this remains nevertheless a mute world out of which its sound will never climb. Yet to what world is this sound well suited if not this one, the one that promises it more than conciliation:

redemption. This is inscribed in the "Tafel" (Tablet) that George placed over the house in Bonn where Beethoven was born:

> Before you grew strong for the struggle on your star
> I sing conflict to you and victory on higher stars.
> Before you grasp the living body on this star
> I invent the dream for you on eternal stars.[199]

This "before you grasp the living body" seems to be destined for a sublime irony. Those lovers never grasp it—what does it matter if they never grew strong for the struggle? Only for the sake of the hopeless is hope given to us.

Part II

19

GOETHE

[2:705] When Goethe came into the world on the 28 of August 1749 in Frankfurt am Main, the city had 30,000 inhabitants. In Berlin, the biggest city in the German Empire, 126,000 were to be counted at that time, while Paris and London at the same time each already had over 500,000. These numbers are characteristic of the political condition of Germany of that time, for in all of Europe, the bourgeois revolution was dependent upon the big cities. On the other hand, it is significant for Goethe that he had a strong revulsion his whole life to staying in large cities. He never set foot in Berlin[1] and later in life sought out his hometown of Frankfurt only twice and against his will; he spent the largest part of his life in a small ducal seat of six thousand inhabitants and got to know more closely only the Italian centers of Rome and Naples.

In its maturation, the new bourgeoisie, of which the poet was the cultural carrier and initially also the political advocate, marked itself off clearly in the poet's family tree. The male members of Goethe's ancestral lineage worked themselves up out of the circles of crafts and trade, and they married women from old, learned families or ones that were socially higher. In the father's line, the great-grandfather was a farrier, the grandfather first a tailor and then an innkeeper, the father, Johann Caspar Goethe, originally a simple attorney. Soon he attained the title of Imperial Counsel, and when he succeeded in winning the hand of Katharina Elisabeth, daughter of the mayor Textor, he finally entered the ranks of the ruling families of the city.

Spending his youth in the patrician house of a free imperial city fixed in the poet the basic Rhenish-Franconian trait: reservations about any political tie and an all-the-more vigilant sense for what was individually appropriate and beneficial. The narrow family circle—Goethe had only one sister, Cornelia—allowed the poet to be already very early on concentrated in himself. But despite that, the dominant views in his family home naturally forbad him to envision an artistic profession. The father compelled Goethe to study law. He entered [2:706] first the University of Leipzig at sixteen and at twenty-one came to Strasbourg as a student in the summer of 1770.

In Strasbourg, for the first time, the cultural circle out of which Goethe's youthful poetry emerged clearly stands out. Goethe and Klinger from Frankfurt; Bürger and Leisewitz from central Germany; Voß and Claudius from Holstein; Lenz from Livonia; Goethe as patrician; Claudius as bourgeois; Holtei, Schubart, and Lenz as teachers' or preachers' sons; the painter Müller; Klinger and Schiller as sons of the petit bourgeoisie; Voß as the grandson of a serf; and finally counts like Christian and Fritz von Stolberg; they all worked together to usher the "new" in Germany into ideological pathways. But it was the fateful weakness of this specifically German revolutionary movement that it was never able to reconcile itself with the original slogans of the bourgeois emancipation—those of the Enlightenment. The bourgeois mass, the "Enlightened ones," remained separated from its avant-garde by a prodigious chasm. The German revolutionaries were not enlightened; the German Enlightened were not revolutionary. The former grouped their ideas around revelation, language, society; the latter around the doctrines of reason and state. Later, Goethe took on the negative aspect of both movements: with the Enlightenment, he stood against revolt, with the Sturm und Drang, against the state. This split in the German bourgeoisie was the reason that it could never find an ideological connection with the West; and never was the understanding of Frenchness further from Goethe than during his time in Strasbourg, though he later took up Voltaire and Diderot in depth. Especially characteristic is his declaration about the famous manifesto of the French materialist, Holbach's *System of Nature*, in which the piercing draft of the French Revolution already blows. It appeared to him "so gray, so Cimmerian, so deathlike," that he drew back shuddering from it as from a ghost. It seemed to him to be the "downright quintessence of senility, tasteless, even vulgar." Everything became hollow and empty for him in this "sad atheistic semi-night."[2] These were the feelings of the creative artist but also of the Frankfurter patrician's son. Later, Goethe gave the Sturm und Drang movement its two most powerful manifestos, [2:707] *Götz* [*von Berlichingen*] and [*The Sorrows of Young*] *Werther*. But it has Johann Gottfried Herder to thank for the universal shape in which the movement came together as a world picture. In his letters and conversations with Goethe, Hamann, Merck, he issued the watchwords of the movement: "original genius"; "language: revelation of the spirit of the people"; "song: the first language of nature"; "unity of earth-and human history." In these years, under the title "Voices of the Peoples in Songs," Herder prepared his anthology of folk songs that spanned the globe from Lapland to Madagascar and had the greatest influence on Goethe. For in his youthful lyric, the renewal of the song form by the folk song unites with the great emancipation brought about by the Grove League in Göttingen. "Voß emancipated the peasants of the marshland for poetry. He drove out the conventional rococo images in poetry with the pitchfork, the threshing flail, and the lower-Saxon dialect that only half tips its cap to the lord of the manor."[3] Because, however, for Voß, description still forms the fundamental tone of lyric (just as, for Klopstock, rhetoric still underlies the hymnal movement), one can speak of the emancipation of German lyric from the spheres of description, didacticism, and plot only with Goethe's Strasburger poems ("Welcome and Farewell," "With a Painted Ribbon," "May Song," "Rose on the Heath"). An emancipation that, granted, could still only be a precarious transitory stage and, while leading German lyric toward its decay in the nineteenth century, was consciously restricted in the work of his old age, *West-Eastern Divan*. In cooperation with Herder, Goethe composed in 1773 the manifesto "On German Manner and Art" with that study of Erwin von Steinbach, the builder of the Strasbourg Cathedral, which later made Goethe's fanatical classicism so especially repellant to the Romantics as they rediscovered the Gothic.

Götz von Berlichingen emerged out of the same creative sphere in 1772. The split in the German bourgeoisie came clearly to expression in this work. The cities and courts, as representatives of the principle of reason made crude as realpolitik, [2:708] must embody the host of spiritless Enlightenment thinkers to which, in the leader of the rebelling peasant population, the Sturm und Drang is opposed. The historical background of this work, the German Peasant War, could mislead one to see in it a genuinely revolutionary confession.

But that it is not; for at bottom, it is the pains of the imperial knighthood succumbing to the rising princes, the pains of the old ruling class, that are vented in Götz's rebellion. Götz fights and falls first of all for himself, then for his class. The play's kernel of thought is not revolt but, rather, persistence. Götz's deed is regressive in terms of knighthood, in a finer and more endearing way the deed of a ruler, an expression of an individual drive, not to be compared with the brutal torch works of the robbers. In this material, for the first time, the procedure plays itself out that will become typical for Goethe's writing: as a dramatist, he continually succumbs to the attraction that revolutionary materials exert on him, only then to bend away from the matter at hand or to leave it lying as a fragment. To the first type belong *Götz von Berlichingen* and *Egmont*, to the second *The Natural Daughter*. The way that Goethe, already with this first drama, fundamentally withdrew from the energy of the Sturm und Drang movement emerges most clearly in comparison with the dramatic works of his contemporaries. In the year 1774, Lenz published his *Hofmeister or the Advantages of Private Education*, which mercilessly illuminates the social conditioning of contemporary literary life that was also consequential for Goethe's development. The German bourgeoisie was indeed not nearly strong enough to be able to support an extensive literary market by its own means. The consequence of these conditions was that the dependence of literature on feudalism persisted even when the sympathy of the writer rested with the bourgeois class. His meager circumstances forced him to accept free meals, to instruct noble squires as a private tutor, and to travel with young princes. Finally, this dependence even threatened to deprive him of the earnings from his literary creation, for only those works that were expressly designated by the permission of the cabinet were protected from reprinting [2:709] in the countries composing the German imperial realm.

In the year 1774, after Goethe's appointment to the Imperial Chamber Court in Wetzlar, *The Sorrows of Young Werther* was published. The book was perhaps the greatest literary success of all time. Here, Goethe perfected the type of genial authorship. If the great author makes his inner world into a public affair from the beginning and makes the questions of the times into questions of his personal world of experience and thought, Goethe represents in his youthful works the type of the great author in unmatched perfection. In Werther's sorrows, the bourgeoisie of that time found its pathology sketched harshly and flatteringly at the same time, much as does today's bourgeoisie in Freudian theory. Goethe wove together his unhappy love for Lotte Buff, the bride of a friend, with the amorous adventures of a young writer whose suicide had garnered attention. In Werther's moods the Weltschmerz of the epoch unfolds in all its nuances. Werther—this is not only the unhappy lover who in his emotional tremors finds pathways into nature that no lover since Rousseau's *Nouvelle Heloise* had sought; he is also the bourgeois whose pride is wounded by the constraints of class and who demands recognition in the name of human rights, indeed even in the name of creaturely existence in general. In him, for the last time for a long time, Goethe gives the revolutionary element in his youth a chance to speak. In a review of a work by Wieland, Goethe had written: "The marble nymphs, the flowers, the vases, the colorfully embroidered linens on the tables of this small people, what a high level of refinement don't they presuppose? What inequality of the classes; what lack, where there is so much enjoyment; what poverty, where there is so much property";[4] now, however, he writes a bit more mildly: "One can say much about the advantages of rules, more or less what one can say in praise of bourgeois society."[5] In *Werther* the bourgeoisie finds the demigod who sacrifices himself for its sake. It feels redeemed without being liberated; such is the reason for the protest of the incorruptibly class-conscious Lessing, who misses here bourgeois pride in opposition to the nobility and demanded a cynical end of *Werther*.

[2:710] After the hopeless complications of his love for Charlotte Buff, the prospect of a bourgeois marriage with a beautiful, important, and well-regarded Frankfurt girl could have seemed like a solution to Goethe. "It was a strange decision of the high one holding sway over us that I should also experience, in the course of my wondrous life, how a bridegroom feels."[6] But the engagement with Lili Schönemann was still only a stormy episode in his more than thirty years' battle against marriage. That Lili Schönemann was probably the most significant, but certainly the freest woman to step into Goethe's closest vicinity could only increase in the end his resistance to bind himself to her. He fled in May 1775 via a voyage to Switzerland undertaken with Count Stolberg. This voyage was marked for him especially by the acquaintance with Lavater. In the latter's physiognomy, which was making a sensation in Europe at the time, Goethe recognized something of the spirit of his own approach to nature. Later, the close connection between Lavater's study of the creaturely world and pietism must have disgruntled Goethe.

On the return trip, a coincidence brought about the acquaintance with the hereditary prince, later Duke Karl August of Sachsen-Weimar. Shortly thereafter followed the prince's invitation of Goethe to his court. What was intended to be a visit became a lifelong residency. On November 7, 1775, Goethe arrived in Weimar. In the same year, he became legation counselor with a seat and a vote in the state council. From the very beginning Goethe himself felt the decision to join the service of Duke Karl August to be a consequential commitment of his whole life. Two things were determinative for this resolution. In a time of increased political activity by the German bourgeoisie, his position allowed him to attain close contact with political reality. On the other hand, because the position categorized him as a highly ranked member of a civil service apparatus, he was able to avoid the necessity of a radical decision. In the face of his internal discord, this position gave his actions and his stance at least external support. How dearly this was bought—if his own uncorruptedly wakeful consciousness had not made it present to him—Goethe could have gathered from the questioning, disappointed, and indignant voices of his friends. [2:711] Klopstock, and even Wieland, were annoyed, as later was Herder, at the wholeheartedness with which Goethe approached the demands of his position and even more those made on him by the way of life and the person of the Grand Duke. For Goethe, the author of *Götz*, of *Werther*, represented the bourgeois Fronde. All the more was riding on his name as at that time the tendencies of these works hardly found any expression other than personal ones. In the eighteenth century, the author was still a prophet, and his writing was the supplement to a gospel that seemed to express itself most completely through his very life. The immeasurable personal validity that Goethe's first works had lent him—they were proclamations of the gospel—was lost to him in Weimar. Since, however, only the prodigious was expected of him, the most absurd legends began to form. Goethe, it was said, got drunk daily on brandy, and Herder preached in boots and spurs while riding around the church three times after the sermon—this was how the activities of genius were imagined in those first few months. What was in truth the basis of these exaggerations was more consequential: the friendship between Goethe and Karl August, the foundation of which was laid at that time, and which later gave Goethe the guarantees of a widely inclusive intellectual and literary regency: the first such universal European regency since Voltaire. "As far as the judgment of the world is concerned," wrote the then nineteen-year-old Karl August, "which would disapprove of the fact that I placed Dr. Goethe in my most important Collegium without his first being a civil servant, professor, chamber- or state-counsel, this changes nothing at all."[7]

The suffering and inner turmoil of these first Weimar years molded themselves and found new nourishment in Goethe's love for Charlotte von Stein. The letters that he sent her in the years 1776–86 make recognizable the steady transition in style from Goethe's early revolutionary prose, "cheating language of its privileges," to the great, calm rhythm the letters breathe that he dictated to her from 1786 to 1788 in Italy. In terms of subject-matter, they are the most important sources for the young poet's struggle with administrative affairs [2:712] but above all with courtly sociality. Goethe was by nature not always easily adaptable.

He wanted to learn and adapt "to the so-called sophisticated people, wherever it actually suits them."[8] And indeed, no harder school was possible than this highly exposed situation, one under the constrained living conditions of a small city. Additionally, Charlotte von Stein, even in the years in which she communicated with Goethe's world with such incomparable depth, never snubbed the concepts of propriety of courtly society for his sake. It took Goethe years until this woman acquired such an unshakable and beneficent position in his life that her image could issue into the figures of Iphigenia and Eleonore von Este, Tasso's beloved. The fact that he put down roots in Weimar, and the way he did it, is thoroughly tied to Charlotte von Stein. She familiarized him not only with the court but also with the city and the landscape. Alongside all official memos run those more fleeting or more expansive notes to Frau von Stein in which Goethe appears in the full breadth of his gifts and activities, as draftsman, painter, gardener, architect, etc., as he always did as a lover. When Riemer in the year 1779 tells how Goethe roamed through the duchy for a month and a half, selected young men for war service in the guild halls, evenings and nights stopped in small inns and worked on his *Iphigenia* [*in Tauris*] he gives a miniature of this entire, critical, variously threatened Goethean existence.

The poetic yield of these years are the beginnings of *Wilhelm Meister's Theatrical Mission, Stella, Clavigo, Werther's Letters from Switzerland, Tasso,* and above all, a large part of the most forceful lyric: "Winter Journey in the Harz Mountains," "To the Moon," "The Fisherman," "Only He Who Knows Yearning," "Over All Peaks," "The Mysteries." Goethe also worked on *Faust* in those years, even laying the inner foundation for parts of the second Faust, at least insofar as the origin of the Goethean state nihilism, which is there [in *Faust, Part Two*] brusquely established in the second act, begins to form in the experiences of the first Weimar years. In 1781 Goethe writes: [2:713]

"Our moral and political world is mined with underground passageways, cellars, and sewers the way a big city usually is; no one thinks or reflects on its network and the relationships among its inhabitants. It becomes much more comprehensible only to the one who has some awareness of it when, if sometime the surface of the earth collapses, here a puff of smoke . . . arises, and there fantastical voices are heard."[9]

Every turn with which Goethe solidified his position in Weimar distanced him further from the creative and friendship circle of his Strasbourg and Wetzlar beginnings. The incomparable authority he brought to Weimar and knew how to validate before the Duke rested on his leadership role in the Sturm und Drang. In a provincial city like Weimar, however, this movement could appear only fleetingly and remained stuck in tumultuous extravagances without ever becoming productive. Goethe even recognized this from the outset and countered all attempts to resume the whole Strasbourg business. When Lenz appeared in Weimar in 1776 and behaved in the court in the style of the Sturm und Drang, Goethe had him removed. The reason was political. But even more an instinctive defense against the limitless impulsivity and pathos that lay in the lifestyle of his youth and for which he did not feel prepared in the long run. In these circles, Goethe lived through the most frightful examples of outrageous geniality; a contemporaneous statement by Wieland shows how shaken he was by the company of such natures. Wieland writes to a friend that he wouldn't buy Goethe's fame for the price of his bodily suffering. Later, the poet then used the most stringent preventative means against this constitutional sensitivity. Indeed, when one sees how Goethe avoided certain tendencies whenever he could—for example, all nationalistic tendencies and most Romantic ones—one must believe that he feared an immediate infection from them. He considered it the fault of this same constitution that he did not write any tragic poetry.

The more Goethe's life in Weimar approached a certain state of balance—externally, his assimilation into the court society in 1782 was accomplished through his elevation into the noble class—[2:714] the more the city became insufferable to him. Impatience took on the form of a pathological ill temper toward Germany. He speaks of wanting to compose a work that the Germans would hate. His disinclination reaches even further. After two youthful years' enthusiasm for German landscape, knighthood, and Gothic, by the time he was twenty-five, he gradually discovered in himself and cultivated a resistance to the climate and landscape, history, politics, and essence of his people, a resistance that came from his utmost interiority; this happened at first vaguely and unclearly, gradually becoming more distinct, passionately demanding by his midthirties, and then systematic and principled. This temper irrupted in 1786 with Goethe's abrupt departure for Italy. He himself labeled the trip a flight. Superstitions and tensions overcame him so oppressively that he dared let no hint of his plan slip to anyone.

During this two-year-long voyage, which took him from Verona, Venice, Ferrara, Rome, and Naples all the way to Sicily, two things came to be decided. For one, Goethe renounced the hope of basing his life on the visual arts. He had played with this thought again and again. If Goethe had stepped into his attitude toward the nation unconsciously and for a long time would not rid himself of the physiognomy of a dilettante, his vacillation about the destiny of his genius was jointly to blame, along with the many distractions and insecurities of his literary creation. This genius bore all too often the traits of talent in order to make the poet's way easy. Goethe saw the great art of the Italian Renaissance through Winckelmann's eyes and tended not to differentiate it from that of antiquity. This art was, for him, first of all, the basis for the certainty that he wasn't born to be a painter; secondly, for the constricted classicizing doctrine of aesthetics that represents perhaps the only sphere of thought in which Goethe stood behind his time rather than led it. Nevertheless, in a second sense, Goethe found his way back to himself. He writes home with reference to the Weimar court: "The delusion that the beautiful seeds ripening in my existence and that of my friends had to be sown in this ground, and that those heavenly jewels could be grasped in the earthly [2:715] crowns of these princes—this has left me completely, and I find my youthful happiness restored."[10]

In Italy the final composition of *Iphigenia* emerged from the prose version. In the next year, 1787, the poet finished *Egmont*. *Egmont* is not a political drama but, rather, a characterology of the German tribune for which Goethe, acting as the advocate of the bourgeoisie, would have liked to make a case, probably out of necessity. Except that this image of the fearless man of the people floated away superciliously into the light, and political realities gained so much clearer expression in the mouths of Oranien and Alba.[11] The phantasmagoria of the ending—"Freedom, in a heavenly garment, surrounded by illumination, rests on a cloud"[12]—lays bare the supposedly political idea of Count Egmont as the poetic inspiration that it is after all. In his conception of the revolutionary liberation movement that broke out under the leadership of Count Egmont in 1566 in the Netherlands, narrow restrictions were drawn for the poet: firstly, by a social circle of artistic activity and a predisposition that were inseparably connected with conservative thought about tradition and hierarchy; secondly, by his fundamentally anarchistic stance, his inability to acknowledge the state as a historical factor. For Goethe, history represented an incalculable sequence of governing forms and cultures to which great individuals, Caesar and Napoleon, Shakespeare and Voltaire, offered the only clue. He was never able to admit to national and social movements. To be sure, in principle he never expressed himself in a coherent fashion about these things; but such is the doctrine that results from his conversations with the historian Luden as well as from [*Wilhelm Meister's*] *Journeyman Years* and *Faust*. These convictions also determine his relationship to the dramatist Schiller. For Schiller, the problem of the state had always been central. The state in its relation to the individual was the material of his youthful dramas; the state in its relation to the bearer of power was that of his mature ones. The driving force in the Goethean dramas is not confrontation but, rather, unfolding.—The major lyrical work of the time in Italy are the *Roman Elegies*, which [2:716] hold fast the memory of manifold Roman nights of love with a definitiveness of antiquity and a perfection of form. The intensified sensual decisiveness of his nature brought him to the decision to draw his life situations closer together and yet to act outwardly only from a limited central point. Still in Italy, Goethe made a request of the Duke in a letter that shows his diplomatic style at its highpoint; in it he asked that the Duke free him from all administrative and political duties. His request was granted, and if Goethe nevertheless found his way back to an intensive poetic production only through broad detours, his altercation with the French Revolution was the most important cause. To grasp this altercation, it is necessary to take into consideration—as with all of his scattered, fragmentary, opaque utterances about politics—less the sum of his theoretical improvisations than their function.

It is beyond doubt that Goethe experienced the enlightened despotism of the eighteenth century as problematic long before the irruption of the French Revolution, based on his experiences as a Weimar legation counselor. He was unable to reconcile himself to the Revolution not only as a consequence of his inner connections with the feudal regime and not only as a consequence of his fundamental rejection of all violent disruptions of public life but above all because it went against his grain; indeed, it was impossible for him to reach any fundamental views in matters of state life. If he never expressed himself about the "limits of the effectiveness of the state" as clearly as, for example, Wilhelm von Humboldt,[13] it was because his political nihilism went too far for him to dare do more than hint at it. Suffice it to say that, later on, Napoleon's program to destroy the German people at its roots had nothing monstrous about it for Goethe, who precisely in such explosions glimpsed the external appearance of a community in which great individuals could draw their circles of activity—circles of activity in which they could patriarchally switch on and send out to each other their spiritual signals over centuries and across state borders. It has been said correctly that the Germany of Napoleon was [2:717] the epitome of Romanesque-French inflected Franconia—for him, the most fitting place to maneuver. But the prodigious sensitivity, the pathological shattering into which the great political events of his time transposed him also worked its way into his relationship to the Revolution. This shattering, in which the poet was struck by certain episodes of the French Revolution as though they were personal blows of fate, made it just as impossible for him to regulate in general the world of the political purely on the basis of principles, as it was completely impossible to make this possible for the private existence of the individual human being.

In light of the class contradictions of the Germany of that time, the situation can be represented in this way: Goethe felt himself to be not, like Lessing, a champion of the bourgeois classes, but much more their deputy, their ambassador to German feudalism and princedom. His permanent wavering can be explained by the conflicts of this representative position. Still, the greatest representative of classical bourgeois literature—which formed the only unassailable claim of the German people to its reputation as a modern nation of culture—could not conceive of bourgeois culture in any other framework than an ennobled feudal state. If Goethe rejected the French Revolution, this occurred not only in the feudal sense—out of the patriarchal idea that any culture, including one that is bourgeois, could flourish only under the protection and in the shadow of absolutism—but just as much in the sense of the petty bourgeoisie, that is, the private man who anxiously seeks to shore up his existence against the political disruptions all around him. Neither in the spirit of feudalism nor in the spirit of the petty bourgeoisie was, however, this rejection univocal and total. That is why not a single one of the literary works, in which for an entire decade he tried to sort out and come to terms with the Revolution, could capture a central place in the total context of his oeuvre.

There are no fewer than seven works in which, from 1792 to 1802, Goethe undertook again and again to gain a compelling formulation or a conclusive image of the French Revolution. These were, first of all, either [2:718] side products, which, with *The Grand Cophta* and *The Excited Ones*, mark the lowest point that Goethe's productions ever reached, or, like *The Natural Daughter*, they were experiments condemned to remain fragments. Finally, however, Goethe came closest to the goal in two works, both of which, in their own way, knew how to treat the Revolution *en bagatelle*, so to speak. *Hermann and Dorothea* makes it into a dark background against which a small-town German idyll endearingly distinguishes itself; "Reineke Fox" dissolves the pathos of the Revolution into the form of a verse satire that not for nothing withdraws into the medieval artform of the animal epic. The Revolution as background of a moral illustration—so it appears in *Hermann and Dorothea*; the Revolution as comic Haupt- und Staatsaktion, as intermezzo in the animal history of mankind—so it appears in "Reineke Fox."[14] The poet thereby overcomes the traces of *ressentiment* that are still perceptible in the early efforts at giving shape to the material, above all in the *Conversations of German Emigrees*. The fact, however, that the story, at its true human level, is grouped around the king—this hierarchical, feudal maxim ultimately has the last word in this circle of production. But precisely the king in *The Natural Daughter* makes palpably manifest Goethe's inability to grasp political history. It is Thoas in *Iphigenia in Tauris* in a new shape, the king as a species of "the good man," who, displaced into the tumult of the Revolution, is here irrefutably destined to failure.

The political problems that burdened Goethe's production in the [eighteen] nineties were the reason he tried to withdraw from this production in manifold ways. His great asylum was the study of natural science. Schiller recognized the escapist character that inhabited the natural-scientific occupations of these years. In 1787 he writes to Körner: "Goethe's spirit has molded all the people who count themselves among his circle. A proud philosophical contempt for all speculation and investigation, with an attachment to nature driven to affectation and a resignation to the five senses; in short, a certain childlike simplicity of reason characterizes him and [2:719] his whole present sect. There, one would rather look for herbs or practice mineralogy than be caught up in empty demonstrations. The idea can be completely healthy and good, but one can also exaggerate a great deal."[15] This natural-scientific study made Goethe only more aloof from political events. He conceived of history only as natural history, grasped it only insofar as it remained bound to the creature. That is why the pedagogy that he later developed in the *Journeyman Years* was the most advanced post that he was able to attain in the world of the historical. This natural-scientific direction went against politics, but it went against theology, too. In the poet's Spinozism, hostile to the church, it found its most fruitful formation. While he goes against the pietistic writings of his friend Jacobi, because the latter puts forth the thesis that nature conceals God, the most important thing about Spinoza, for Goethe, is that nature as well as spirit are a revealed aspect of the divine. That is what is meant when Goethe writes to Jacobi: "God has punished you with metaphysics . . . but me he has blessed with physics."[16]—The concept under which Goethe represents his revelations of the physical world is the urphenomenon. It was originally formed in the context of his botanical and anatomical studies. In 1784 Goethe discovers the morphological formation of the skull bones out of modified bones of the spinal column, one year later *The Metamorphosis of Plants*. Under this designation he understood the circumstance that all organs of the plant, from the roots to the stamen, are only modified forms of the leaf. He thus arrived at the concept of the "urplant," which Schiller declared to be an "idea" in his first famous conversation with the poet but which Goethe would not allow to stand without attributing to it a certain sensuous intuitability. Goethe's natural-scientific studies occupy the position in the context of his works often taken up by aesthetics among lesser artists. One can understand precisely this side of Goethe's creativity only by realizing that he, in contrast to almost all the intellectuals of this epoch, never made peace with "beautiful semblance." Not aesthetics but rather the intuition of nature [2:720] reconciled poetry and politics for him. For this very reason, however, it cannot be denied how refractory the poet was toward certain innovations even in these natural-scientific studies—in the sphere of the technical as well as the political. On the threshold of the natural-scientific age, which would broaden the acuity and the sphere of sensuous perceptions so prodigiously, he leads back again to the old forms of exploring nature and writes: "The human being in himself, insofar as he uses his healthy senses, is the greatest and most accurate physical apparatus that can exist, and it is precisely the greatest harm of the new physics that the experiments have become divided off, as it were, from the human being and . . . one is only willing to recognize nature in what is shown by artificial instruments."[17] Science, as he conceives it, has as its foremost natural task to sort and clean up the human being in his activity and his thinking. The alteration of the world through technology was not really his concern, even though in his old age he gave an astonishingly clear account of its unavoidable significance. The highest usefulness of knowledge about nature, for him, was determined in the form that it gives to a life. He developed this intuition into a rigorous pragmatism: "Only what is fruitful is true."[18]

Goethe belongs to the family of those great spirits for whom there is at bottom no art in the stripped-down sense. For him, the doctrine of the urphenomenon as natural science was at the same time the true doctrine of art, just as, for Dante, it was scholastic philosophy and, for Dürer, the technical arts. Only the discoveries of his botany were pathbreaking for science in the strictest sense. The osteological writings are also important and recognized: the reference to the human intermaxillary bone, though it was not really a discovery. Largely ignored remained the *Meteorology*, sharply contested the *Theory of Colors*, which, for Goethe, crowned his natural-scientific work; indeed, according to certain statements one might think it crowned his lifework in general. The discussion of this most comprehensive document of the Goethean natural science has for some time now been again renewed. The *Theory of Colors* stands in sharp opposition to Newtonian optics. The fundamental opposition, from which [2:721] Goethe's sometimes extremely bitter and decades-long polemic takes its point of departure, is this: Newton explains white light to be a compositum of colored lights; Goethe, by contrast, explains it as the simplest, most indivisible, most homogenous thing we know. "It is not composed, . . . least of all, of colored lights."[19] The *Theory of Colors* takes colors to be metamorphoses of light, phenomena that form themselves in the struggle of light with darkness. Alongside the thought of metamorphosis, that of polarity, which runs through all his research, is decisive for Goethe. Dark is not a mere absence of light—for then it would not be noticeable—but is, rather, a positive counterlight. In his later years the thought occurs to him in this context that animal and plant perhaps developed out of the primal condition through light or darkness respectively.[20] It is a peculiar trait of these natural-scientific studies that in them Goethe accommodates the spirit of the Romantic school just as much as he opposes its spirit in his aesthetics.—Goethe's philosophical orientation is understood much less from his poetic than from his natural-scientific writings. From the time of his youthful epiphany, which is recorded in the famous fragment "Nature," Spinoza remained, for him, the patron of his morphological studies. Later, these made it possible for him to engage in a confrontation with

Kant. While Goethe had no relation to the major critical work—the *Critique of Pure Reason*—and equally the *Critique of Practical Reason*—the ethics—he had the highest admiration for the *Critique of Judgment*. This is because in the latter work Kant discarded the teleological explanation of nature that was a pillar of Enlightenment philosophy, of Deism. Goethe had to agree with him on this point, for his own anatomical and botanical researches represented far more advanced positions in the attack of bourgeois natural science against teleological natural science. Kant's definition of the organic as a purposiveness whose purpose lies not outside but inside of the purposive creature itself corresponded to Goethe's concepts. The unity of whatever is beautiful, including whatever is naturally beautiful, is always independent of purposes—in this, Kant and Goethe are in unison.

[2:722] The more deeply Goethe was drawn into sympathy with European conditions, the more comprehensively he sought support for his private life. This is how one must understand that the relationship to Frau von Stein was dissolved very soon after his return from Italy. Goethe's connection to the woman who would later be his wife, Christiane Vulpius, whom he got to know soon after his return from Italy, was, for fifteen years, a grave offense to the bourgeois society of the city. Nevertheless, one must not consider this relationship to a proletarian girl, a worker in a flower factory, as testimony of the poet's especially free social views. In these questions of the formation of private life, too, Goethe knew of no maxims, to say nothing of revolutionary ones. Christiane was at first simply his relationship. What is remarkable about this connection is not its origin but, rather, the course it took. Although Goethe was never able and perhaps never tried to bridge the prodigious difference in status between this woman and himself; although Christiane must have caused offense to the petty bourgeois society of Weimar, even among the freer, significant spirits, not only because of her parentage but also because of her way of life; although marital fidelity was not taken seriously by either partner, Goethe ennobled this connection and with it the woman herself through an unwavering cast of mind, a magnificent perseverance in a most difficult position, and in the year 1807, fifteen years after their first acquaintance, through a church wedding he forced court and society to acknowledge the mother of his son. But with Frau von Stein, there came to be a bland reconciliation only after years of a deep disinclination.

In the year 1790, Goethe, as state minister, took over the Department for Culture and Education, a year later the court theater. His efficacity in these areas cannot be overlooked. It expanded from year to year. All scientific institutes, all museums, the University of Jena, the technical institutes of instruction, the singing schools, the art academy, all stood under the immediate influence of the poet that often extended to the remotest details. The development of his household into a European cultural institute went hand in hand with this. [2:723] His collecting activity extended to all the areas of his research and hobbies. The Goethe-National Museum in Weimar consists of these collections—with its painting gallery, its rooms of hand drawings, faience, coins, stuffed animals, bones and plants, minerals, fossils, chemical and physical apparatuses, to say nothing of the book and autograph collection. His universality was boundless. Where being an artist was denied him, he at least wanted to be an amateur. At the same time these collections were the framework of an existence that played itself out in a more and more representative manner before the eyes of Europe. Further, they lent the poet the authority he needed as the greatest organizer of princely patronage that Germany ever had. In Voltaire, a literatus knew for the first time how to secure European authority and how to represent the prestige of the bourgeoisie to the princes through an existence that was great both intellectually and, in equal measure, materially. In this regard, Goethe is Voltaire's immediate successor. Just as Voltaire's position should be understood politically, so should Goethe's. And even if he rejected the French Revolution, he nevertheless evaluated with more awareness of purpose and more virtuosity than anyone else the increase of power that the existence of a literatus experienced through it. While Voltaire achieved princely wealth in the second half of his life, Goethe's financial situation cannot be compared to it. To understand, however, the poet's remarkable doggedness in business questions, especially in dealings with Cotta, one has to consider that, from the turn of the [eighteenth] century, he viewed himself as the founder of a national bequest.

Throughout this decade,[21] it was Schiller who again and again called Goethe to poetic production out of the distraction of the statesman's activities and the absorption in the observation of nature. The first encounter between the poets, which took place soon after Goethe's return from Italy, remained without consequence. This corresponded completely to the two men's stance toward each other. Schiller, at that time the author of the dramas *The Robbers, Intrigue and Love, Fiesco, Don Carlos*, represented with the brusqueness of his class-conscious [2:724] formulations the strongest conceivable contrast with Goethe's attempts at a moderate mediation. While

Schiller wanted to take up class conflict all down the line, Goethe had long before drawn a fortified line of retreat from which the offensive could still be launched only into the cultural arena; all political activity of the bourgeois class, by contrast, remained limited to the defensive. The fact that it came down to a compromise between these two men bespeaks clearly how poorly fortified the class consciousness of the bourgeoisie was. This compromise came about under the sign of Kantian philosophy. For the sake of his interest in aesthetics, Schiller, through his *Letters on the Aesthetic Education of Humanity*, deprived the radical formulations of Kantian morality of their aggressive sharpness and transformed them into an instrument of historical construction. This allowed a common understanding, or better said, a truce with Goethe. In truth, the social interaction between the two men remained forever characterized by the diplomatic reserve that this compromise required of them. Their discussion remained limited, with almost anxious precision, to formal problems of literary art. To be sure, in this respect it was epochal. The correspondence between them is in its every detail a well-balanced and redacted document and, for tendentious reasons, has always enjoyed more attention than the deeper, freer, and more lively correspondence in which Goethe in his old age engaged with Zelter. The "Young German" critic Gutzkow spoke correctly about the "hair-splitting of aesthetic tendencies and artistic theories" that moves in a perpetual circle throughout this correspondence.[22] And in making responsible for this hair-splitting the screaming dissonance with which art and history here encounter each other as enemies, he also saw correctly. The two poets did not therefore always find a common understanding even for their greatest works. "He was like all people," Goethe wrote in 1829, "who proceed too much from the idea. He was never at rest and could never come to terms with things. . . . I was always making certain that I stood firm, protecting his as well as my own affairs and keeping them clear from such influences."

Schiller was an important impetus, first of all, for Goethe's [2:725] ballads ("The Treasure Hunter," "The Sorcerer's Apprentice," "The Bride of Corinth," "The God and the Bajadere"). *Xenia*, though, became the official manifesto of their literary alliance. The almanac appeared in 1795. Its front line was directed against the enemies of Schiller's [journal] *Horae*, the vulgar rationalism that had its center in Nicolai's Berlin circle. The attack worked. The literary punch was intensified by anecdotal interest: the poets jointly took responsibility for the whole, without giving away the authorship of the individual distichs.

Despite all the verve and elegance of the attack, however, there was a certain desperation in this procedure. The time of Goethe's popularity was past, and though he gained authority from decade to decade, still he was never again a popular poet. The late Goethe especially has that decided contempt for the reading public common to all the writers of [German] classicism with the exception of Wieland, a contempt that now and then finds its strongest expression in the Goethe-Schiller correspondence. Goethe stood in no rapport with the public. "If his effect was immensely forceful, yet he never himself lived or continued to live where his beginning ignited the whole world."[23] He did not know what his gift positively offered Germany. Least of all did he know how to bring himself into harmony with any direction or tendency. His attempt to form one with Schiller remained in the end an illusion. To destroy this illusion was the justified motive of the nineteenth-century German public, which tried again and again to put Goethe and Schiller into opposition and to measure them against each other. Weimar's influence on the great German masses lay not with the two poets but, rather, in Bertuch and Wieland's magazines, in the *Allgemeine Literatur-Zeitung* [General literary newspaper] and *der Teutsche Merkur*. In 1795 Goethe wrote, "We don't want the radical upheavals that could prepare for classical works in Germany."[24] This radical change—it is the emancipation of the bourgeoisie that occurred in 1848, too late to still bring forth any classical works. A German essence, a German spirit of language, those were, to be sure, the strings on which Goethe played his powerful melody; but the sounding board [2:726] of this instrument was not Germany but, rather, Napoleon's Europe.

The same thing hung before Goethe and Napoleon's eyes: the social emancipation of the bourgeoisie under the political form of despotism. This emancipation was the "impossible," the "incommensurate," the "unattainable," which sat in them as the deepest thorn.[25] It wrecked Napoleon. In contrast, one can say about Goethe that, the older he became, the more he formed his life according to this political idea, consciously stamping it as the incommensurate, the unattainable, and elevating it into the microarchetype of his political idea. Assuming that fully distinct lines could be drawn, poesy could represent the bourgeois freedom of this state, while the regime completely corresponded to the despotism characteristic of his private affairs. At bottom, however, the intertwining effect of these incompatible strivings can be pursued just as much in his life and in his writing: in his life, as the freedom of erotic breakthrough and as the most rigid regime of "renunciation," in the writing nowhere so much as in the second part of *Faust* whose political dialectic gives the key to Goethe's position. Only in this context can it be understood how in his last thirty years, Goethe was able to subordinate his life completely to the bureaucratic categories of balance, mediation, postponement. It is senseless to judge his actions and his gestures according to an abstract standard of morality. The absurdity of the attacks that Börne directed at Goethe in the name of Young Germany lies in this abstraction. Precisely in his maxims and in the most remarkable peculiarities shown by the regime of his life, Goethe can be understood only from the political position that he created for himself and in which he immersed himself. Its hidden but all the deeper affinity with Napoleon's position is so decisive that the post-Napoleonic era, the power that brought down Napoleon, could no longer understand it. The son of bourgeois parents ascends, leaves everything behind, becomes the heir of a revolution before whose power everything in his hands trembles (French Revolution, Sturm und Drang), and at the moment when he has most profoundly [2:727] shaken the rule of the surviving forces, founds via a coup d'état his own rule in the same old, the very same feudal forms (Empire, Weimar).

Goethe's animosity toward the Wars of Liberation, which posed an insurmountable obstacle to the bourgeois history of literature, is perfectly self-evident in the context of his political limitations. For him, Napoleon, before founding the European imperium, was the founder of his European public. When, in the year 1815, the poet finally let himself be convinced by Iffland to write a celebratory play for the entrance of the victorious troops in Berlin, namely, *Epimenides' Awakening,* he could tear himself away from Napoleon only by holding on to that chaotic element, a nocturnal primal violence that shook Europe in the form of this man. He could not rouse any feeling for the victors. On the other hand, an idiosyncrasy comes to expression in the suffering firmness with which he sought to protect himself from the spirit that moved Germany in 1813; the same idiosyncrasy made it insufferable for him to remain in sickrooms in the vicinity of dying people. From his revulsion to everything soldierly there certainly speaks less of his rejection of military compulsion, even drilling, than his disgust for everything done to impair the human appearance, from uniform to wound. His nerves were severely put to the test when in 1792 he had to accompany the Duke during the invasion of the allied armies in France. At that time, Goethe displayed a great artistry by poetizing himself against the events he witnessed through observations of nature, optical studies, and drawings. As a contribution to an understanding of the poet, the *Campaign in France* is important; it is equally turgid and vague as an altercation with world-political events.

The European and political turn—this is the signature of Goethe's last poetic creativity. Yet Goethe felt this most stable ground under his feet only after Schiller's death. In contrast, the great prose work that was undertaken after a long pause still under Schiller's immediate influence and brought to completion, *Wilhelm Meister's Years of Apprenticeship*, designates Goethe's hesitant tarrying in the idealistic vestibule [2:728], in German humanism, out of which Goethe later forced himself into an ecumenical humanism. The ideal of the *Years of Apprenticeship*—education qua culture—and the social environment of the hero—the actors—: these are, in fact, strictly coordinated with each other; they are both exponents of that specifically German realm of thought concerning "beautiful semblance," about which the bourgeoisie, just ascending into its dominance, had little to say. In fact, it was almost a poetic necessity to place actors in the middle of a German bourgeois novel. Goethe thereby got all political conditionality out of the way only to make up for it all the more ruthlessly twenty years later in the continuation of his *Bildungsroman*. The fact that the poet made a half-artist into the hero in *Wilhelm Meister* guaranteed this novel its decisive influence precisely because it was conditioned by the German situation of the closing century. The artist novels of Romanticism, from Novalis's *Heinrich von Ofterdingen*, Tieck's *Sternbald*, to Mörike's *Painter Nolten*, emanate from it. The style of the work corresponds to its subject-matter. "Nowhere does logical machinery or a dialectical struggle of ideas with the material betray itself; rather, Goethe's prose is a perspective on the theater, a sheltered, learned piece, quietly whispered for creative thought construction. Things do not speak themselves in his works; rather, they must address themselves to the poet in order to come into speech. That is why this language is distinct yet modest, clear without sticking out, diplomatic in the extreme."[26]

It lay in the nature of the two men that Schiller's influence was exerted in essential matters as development, as incitement to the Goethean production, without fundamentally influencing the direction of Goethean creativity. It is perhaps owing to Schiller that Goethe turned to the composition of lyric ballads, to *Wilhelm Meister's Years of Apprenticeship*, and picked up the *Faust* fragment again. But almost always, the actual exchange of thoughts about these works revolved around craftsmanlike and technical issues. Goethe's inspiration remained undistracted. It was a friendship with Schiller the man and Schiller the author. But it was not the poetic friendship that one often believed was to be seen here. The extraordinary charm and the forcefulness of Schiller's person [2:729] did nonetheless disclose themselves to Goethe in their greatness, and he erected a monument to them after his death in his "Epilogue to Schiller's Bell." After Schiller's death, Goethe undertook a new organization of his personal relations. There was, moreover, no one around him whose validity anywhere approached that of his own name. And there hardly lived anyone in Weimar itself who could have been drawn into his confidence in any special way. At the same time, the significance of Zelter, the founder of the Berlin Singing Academy, had grown, for Goethe, in the course of the new century. With time, Zelter took on for Goethe the rank of an ambassador who represented him in the Prussian capital. In Weimar itself, the poet gradually founded a whole staff of assistants and secretaries without whose cooperation the prodigious legacy that he edited in the last thirty years of his life could never have been secured. Finally, the poet placed his whole life in an almost Chinese manner under the category of script. The huge literature and press office is to be approached in this sense—with its assistants, ranging from Eckermann, Riemer, Soret, Müller, down to the clerks Kräuter and John. Eckermann's *Conversations with Goethe* have become the main source for these last decades and, moreover, one of the best prose books of the nineteenth century. What bound the poet to Eckermann was perhaps more than anything else his unconditional inclination toward the positive as is never found in superior minds and only seldom even in lesser ones. Goethe had no relationship to critique in the more narrow sense. The strategy of the art business, which now and again captivated even Goethe, played itself out, for him, in dictatorial forms: in manifestos, as he sketched them out alongside Herder and Schiller, and in instructions he composed for actors and artists.

More independent than Eckermann and therefore, of course, less exclusively subservient to the poet was Chancellor von Müller.[27] His *Conversations with Goethe* also belong among the documents that determined Goethe's image as it came down to posterity. Not as a conversational partner but certainly through his great and acute characterization of Goethe, the professor of ancient philology, Friedrich Riemer, is to be placed at their side. [2:730] The first great document that emerged from the literary organism that the aging Goethe created is the autobiography. *Poetry and Truth* is a preview of Goethe's late life in the form of a retrospective recollection. This look back on Goethe's active youth first gives access to one of the most important principles of this life. Goethe's moral activity is in the last resort a positive riposte to the Christian principle of repentance: "Seek to give a consequence to everything in your life." "He is the happiest man who can connect the end of his life with the beginning."[28] In all this, the drive was at work in his life to form and bring into appearance the image of the world with which he had gotten comfortable in his youth, the world of unattainability, of compromises, of contingencies: of erotic indecision, of political wavering. On this basis alone does the Goethean "renunciation" attain its proper sense, that of its terrible ambiguity: Goethe renounced not only desire but also greatness, heroism. This is perhaps the reason that this autobiography breaks off before he achieved his position. The memorabilia of the late life show up scattered throughout the *Italian Journey*, *The Campaign in France*, and *Daybooks and Yearbooks*. In his representation of the years 1750–75, Goethe inserted a series of character studies of the most significant contemporaries of his youth, and Günther, Lenz, Merck, Herder entered literary history in part as stamped by Goethean formulae. The poet made vivid not only these figures themselves in their representation but also at the same time his own persona in its polarity, a persona who comes to grips through either enmity or affinity with those friends or competitors. In this, the same coercion is at work that moved him as a dramatic poet to set Egmont against Oranien, man of the people against man of the court; Tasso against Antonio, poet against courtier; Prometheus against Epimetheus, creative man against lamenting dreamer; Faust against Mephisto—all of these at once as personae of his own self.

[2:731] Around this first, subservient circle, there gathered another circle in these later years. The Swiss Heinrich Meyer, Goethe's source in questions of art, strictly classicistic, level-headed, assistant in the editing of the Propyläen and later in the leadership of the magazine, *Kunst und Altertum* [*Art and Antiquity*]; the philologist Friedrich August Wolf, who moved Goethe in conflicting ways through his proof that the Homeric epics stemmed from a whole series of unknown poets whose songs were only later edited together and disseminated under the name of Homer and who, along with Schiller, had a part in the effort to continue the *Iliad* in an "Achilleïs" that remained a fragment; Sulpiz Boisserée, the discoverer of the German Middle Ages in painting, the inspiring advocate of the German Gothic, and as such, friend to the Romantics and chosen by all of Romanticism to make himself the advocate of its artistic conviction to Goethe. (His efforts, which lasted many years, had to be satisfied with a half victory; Goethe finally found himself ready to present to the court a collection of documents and plans for the history and completion of the Cologne Cathedral.) All these relationships as well as countless others are the expression of a universality for the sake of which Goethe consciously let the borders between artist, researcher, and amateur flow into one another: no genre of poetry and no language became popular in Germany if Goethe did not take it on. What he achieved as translator, travel writer, even biographer, art connoisseur and art judge, physicist, educator, even theologian, theater director, court poet, society man, and minister, all this served to increase the reputation of his all-sidedness. But the life space of this universality became more and more Europe and indeed in opposition to Germany. With passionate admiration he encountered the great European spirits who showed up toward the end of his life, Byron, Walter Scott, Manzoni; in Germany, by contrast, not seldomly he advanced the mediocre and had no sense for the genius of his contemporaries Hölderlin, Kleist, Jean Paul.

In 1809, *Elective Affinities* was written, at the same time as *Poetry and Truth*. While Goethe was writing this novel, he achieved for the first time a secure feeling for the [2:732] European nobility,[29] an experience out of which there was formed for him an intuition of the new public, secure in its secularity, for which, some twenty years earlier in Rome, he had already decided that he wanted exclusively to write. *Elective Affinities* is intended for this public: the Silesian-Polish aristocracy, lords, emigrants, Prussian generals, who were then to be found in the Bohemian baths and around the Empress of Austria. This did not hinder the poet from critically illuminating their life relationships. For *Elective Affinities* sketches a thin but very sharp image of the decay of the family in the then-dominant class.[30] But the power to which this institution in its dissolution falls victim is not the bourgeoisie but, rather, feudal society restored to its original condition in the form of magical forces of fate. Words concerning the nobility that Goethe fifteen years earlier puts in the mouth of the Magister in his drama about the Revolution, *The Excited Ones*, are at bottom the magic-patriarchal motif of this novel: "This arrogant race still cannot break free from the secret shudder that drifts through all living forces of nature, cannot deny the connection in which word and effect, deed and consequence remain eternally linked."[31] It is the same mode of thinking that in *Wilhelm Meister's Years of Apprenticeship* leads even the most decisive attempts to shape the image of a fully developed bourgeoisie back to an afterimage of mystical, medieval associations—the secret Tower Society. Goethe was not able to imagine the development of the bourgeois world of culture, which he accomplished far more universally than any of his predecessors or successors, other than in the framework of an ennobled feudal state. And as the mismanagement of the German restoration, into which the last twenty years of his productivity fell, estranged Germany from him even more, this dreamed-up feudalism acquired patriarchal traits from the Orient. The Morning-Land Middle Ages of the *West-Eastern Divan* dawned.

Together with a new type of philosophical lyric of German and European literature, this book captured the greatest poetic embodiment of the love for antiquity. Not only political necessities referred Goethe to the Orient. The powerful [2:733] late blossoming that unfolded Goethe's erotic passion in his most advanced age allowed him to experience even old age as renewal, indeed as a costume that had to become united with the eastern one in which his encounter with Marianne von Willemer turned into a short, intoxicating celebration. *West-Eastern Divan* is its after-song. Goethe grasped history, the past, only insofar as he succeeded in engulfing them in his own existence. In the succession of his passions, Frau von Stein represents the embodiment of antiquity, Marianne von Willemer that of the Orient, Ulrike von Levetzow, his last love, the unification of these phenomena with the images of German girls from his youth. This is what "Marienbad Elegy," his very last love poetry, teaches. Goethe underscored the didactic turn of this last volume of poems through his notes on the *Divan* in which, supported by Hammer-Purgstall and Diez, he presents his Oriental studies to the public. In the wide latitude of the Oriental Middle Ages, under princes and viziers, in the presence of splendid imperial courts, Goethe dons the mask of the undemanding, wandering, drinking Hatem and thereby confesses poetically to that hidden trait of his being that he once confided to Eckermann: "Magnificent buildings and chambers are for princes and empires. Living in them, one feels calmed . . . and desires nothing more. That is fully contrary to my nature. In a magnificent apartment such as I had in Karlsbad I am immediately lazy and inactive. But a modest apartment like this poor room we are in, a little bit disorderly-orderly, a little gypsylike, is the right thing for me; it leaves my inner nature complete freedom to be active and to create out of myself."[32] In the figure of Hatem, reconciled with the experience of his virile years, Goethe lets the restlessness, the wildness of his youth come to expression one more time. In many of these songs, employing his mighty means, the poet bestowed upon the wisdom of beggars, tavern dwellers, and vagrants the highest form they ever found.

Wilhelm Meister's Journeyman Years brings out most starkly the didactic trait of the late writing. The novel, which lay at rest for a long time and was then hastily ended, [2:734] is rich in inconsistencies and contradictions and was in the end treated by the poet like a repository in which he had Ecker-mann enter the content of his notebooks. The countless short stories and episodes out of which the work emerged are only loosely connected. The most important of them is the "Pedagogical Province," an extremely strange hybrid-construct in which one glimpses Goethe's confrontation with the great socialist works of Sismondi, Fourier, Saint-Simon, Owen, Bentham. Their influence hardly emerged from unmediated reading but was strong enough among his contemporaries to convince Goethe to undertake the experiment of connecting the feudal with the bourgeois-practical direction that came to fruition so decisively in these writings. The classicistic ideal of culture defrays the costs of this synthesis. It recedes all along the battle line. Very character-istically, agriculture shows up as obligatory, while not a sound is heard about instruction in dead languages. The "humanists" from the *Years of Appren-ticeship* have all become artisans: Wilhelm a surgeon, Jarno a miner, Philine a seamstress. Goethe took over the idea of professional education from Pestalozzi. The praise of the trades, which Goethe struck up in "Werther's Letters from Switzerland," reappears here. That was rather a reactionary stance in these years, when the problems of industry began to occupy the national economists. Incidentally, the social-economic thoughts for which Goethe here advocates correspond to the ideology of bourgeois philanthropy in its most utopian development. An inscription on the uncle's model proper-ties announces "Ownership and Common Property." Another motto: "From the Useful through the True to the Beautiful."[33] The same syncretism is char-acteristically expressed in religious instruction as well. If, on the one hand, Goethe is an enemy of Christianity who denied this enmity, on the other hand, he honors in religion the strongest guarantor of every hierarchical form of society. Indeed, here he even reconciles with the image of the Passion of Christ that, for decades, aroused his most passionate revulsion. The ordering of society in the Goethean sense, that is, through patriarchal and cosmic norms, came to expression most purely in the character of Makarie. The experiences of his [2:735] practical, political activities were not able to influence these fundamental convictions of his, despite contradicting them often enough. The attempt to unify those experiences with these convictions and to express this in the totality of a literary work had to remain as fragmentary as the structure of this novel shows it to be. And even in the poet himself there arise lingering reservations when he seeks the happier, more harmonious future of his characters in America. The end of his novel has them emigrating there. This has been called an "organized communistic escape."[34]

If Goethe, during his mature creative years often swerved away from the literary in order to devote himself more freely to his moods and inclinations in theoretical investigations or administrative affairs, still the great phenomenon of his last years as well as the immeasurable circle of his continuing natural-philosophical, mythological, literary, artistic, philological studies; of his earlier engagement with mining, finance, theater, freemasonry, diplomacy—all of this concentrically consolidates into one last powerful literary work: *Faust, Part Two*. According to his own report, Goethe labored on both parts of the work for over sixty years. In 1775, he brought to Weimar the first fragment, the "Urfaust." It already contains some of the main traits of the later work: the figure of Gretchen, who is the naive counterimage of the self-reflective primal man, Faust,[35] but also the child of the proletariat, the unwed mother, the child murderer who is condemned and for whom the blazing social critique of the Sturm und Drang crowd had nourished itself in poems and dramas for a long time; the figure of Mephisto, then already much less the devil of Christian doctrine than the earth-spirit of magical kabbalistic traditions; finally, in Faust, already the titanic primal man, the twin brother of a Moses planned in Goethe's early years, who, like Moses, was meant to attempt the feat of snatching the secret of Creation from divine nature. In 1790, the *Faust* fragment appeared. In 1808, Goethe presented the completed first part for the first edition of his works with the publisher Cotta. Here, for the first time, the plot comes forth in sharp strokes. It is constructed on the basis of the "Prologue in Heaven," which presents the wager between the Lord God and Mephisto about Faust's soul. God grants [2:736] the devil free play with Faust. But Faust makes this pact with the subservient devil: his soul must succumb to the devil only if he should ever say to the moment: "Yet stay a while! You are so beautiful! / Then, you may put me in chains / Then, I will gladly expire! / Then, may the death knell sound / Then, you are free from your service."[36] The fulcrum of the poem is, however: Faust's wild, restless striving for the absolute ruins Mephisto's art of seduction, the circle of sensuous pleasures is quickly gauged, without chaining Faust. "So I stagger from desire to enjoyment / And in enjoyment I languish for desire."[37] The longer Faust's longing pushes onward into the limitless, the more decisive it is. The first part of the drama comes to an end in Gretchen's dungeon amid cries of woe. This first part, viewed in itself, is one of Goethe's gloomiest creations. And it has been possible to say of it that the Faust saga—in the sixteenth century as a world-legend and in the eighteenth century as a world-tragedy of the German bourgeoisie—succeeded in expressing how this class had lost its wager in both cases. With the first part, Faust's bourgeois existence comes to an end. The political scenarios of the second part are imperial courts and ancient palaces. The contours of Goethe's Germany, which still shines through the Romantic Middle Ages of the first part, have disappeared in the second part, and the whole prodigious movement of thought into which this second part leads is in the last instance bound to the image of the German Baroque through the medium of which the poet also sees antiquity. Goethe, who precisely had tried his whole life long to bring classical antiquity before his eyes in a non-historical manner and, as it were, in a vacuum, projects now in the classical-Romantic phantasmagoria "Helen" the first great image of antiquity as seen through the past of Germanness itself. The remaining parts of the poem are constructed around this work, later the third act of the second part. It can scarcely be stressed decisively enough how much of this later part, especially in the scenes that take place at the emperor's court and in the encampment, is a political apologia, a political return on Goethe's erstwhile work at court. If the poet [2:737] had to conclude his ministerial activity in deepest resignation with a capitulation to the intrigues of a princely mistress, at the end of his life he outlines an ideal Germany of the Baroque era by raising all the possibilities of the statesman's reign to the greatest level, and yet also intensifying all the unattainabilities of such reigning to the point of the grotesque. Mercantilism, ancient and mystical experimentation with nature, completion of the state through a monetary system, completion of art through antiquity, completion of nature through the experiment—these are the signature of the epoch Goethe invokes: the European Baroque. And it is finally not a dubious aesthetic but, rather, an innermost political necessity of this work that at the end of the fifth act the Catholic heaven opens up, with Gretchen as one of the penitents. Goethe saw too deeply to be able to quiet himself amid his utopian regression to absolutism in the Protestant princedom of the eighteenth century. Soret said these deep words about the poet: "Goethe is liberal in the abstract sense, but in praxis he tends towards the most reactionary principles."[38] In the condition that crowns Faust's life Goethe lets the spirit of his praxis come to expression: to win land from the sea, an action that prescribes to nature a history that inscribes itself in nature—that was Goethe's concept of historical efficacity, and all political forms were to him at bottom only good for protecting, for guaranteeing this kind of efficacity. In a secret utopian intertwining play of agrarian-technical action and artistry with the political apparatus of absolutism, Goethe saw the magic formula by the power of which the reality of social conflicts was supposed to evaporate into nothing. Feudal dominion over farmed lands managed by the bourgeoisie—that is the conflicting image in which Faust's supreme happiness in life finds expression.

Shortly after the completion of the work, Goethe died on the 22 of March 1832. At his death, the tempo of Europe's industrialization was undergoing rapid growth. Goethe foresaw the development. In an 1825 letter to Zelter, there is this: "Wealth and speed are what the world admires and what everyone strives for. Railroads, express post, steamships, and all sorts of facilitations of communication are [2:738] what matters to the educated world, to overeducate and thus to remain in mediocrity. And it is, indeed, also a result of universality that a mediocre culture becomes common: that is what the Bible societies, the Lancaster method of instruction, and whatnot, all strive for. Actually, it is the century for competent heads, for lighthearted, practical people who, equipped with a certain skillfulness, feel their superiority over the crowd, even if they are not themselves gifted for the highest. Let us, as much as possible, hold onto the state of mind at which we arrived; we, along with perhaps only a few, will become the last ones of an epoch that will not soon return."[39] Goethe knew that his immediate legacy would be weak, and the bourgeoisie, in whom the hope of establishing German democracy again came alive, did in fact latch onto Schiller. The first important protests in literary form came from the vicinity of Young Germany. Thus Börne: "Goethe always flattered only selfishness, lovelessness; that's why the loveless love him. He taught the cultured people how one could be cultured, openminded, and without prejudices, yet still be an egomaniac; how one can have all the vices without their crudeness, all the weaknesses without their ridiculousness; how to keep the spirit pure from the dirt of the heart, how to sin respectably, and how to ennoble the material of any worthless thing through a beautiful art form. And because he teaches them this, the educated people worship him."[40] Goethe's hundredth birthday in 1849 passed silently in comparison with Schiller's ten years later, which took the shape of a large demonstration of the German bourgeoisie. The apparition of Goethe first came into the foreground in the [eighteen] seventies, after the foundation of the empire, when Germany was on the look-out for monumental representatives of its national prestige. Major dates: founding of the Goethe Society under the patronage of German princes; the Sophien-edition of the works, under princely influence; stamping of the imperialistic Goethe image in the German institutes of higher education. Despite the endless literature that Goethe philology brought forth, however, the bourgeoisie was able to make only very imperfect use of this forceful spirit for its own purposes, to say nothing of the question of how far it was able to penetrate into his intentions. His [2:739] whole creativity is full of reservations about this class. And if he penned a lofty literature into it, he did so with his face turned away. He therefore did not, to the remotest degree, have the effect that corresponded to his genius; indeed, he freely renounced such an effect. And thus he proceeded—so as to give form to the subject-matters that fulfilled him, a form that has withstood to this very day its dissolution by the bourgeoisie because it could remain ineffectual but could not be falsified or trivialized. This intransigence of the poet against the average bourgeois way of thinking became topical with the reaction to naturalism and a new side of his production thereby became topical as well. Neo-Romanticism (Stefan George, Hugo von Hofmannsthal, Rudolf Borchardt), in which high-level bourgeois poets made an effort, under the patronage of the weakened feudal authorities, for the last time to rescue the front line (at least in cultural terms) of the bourgeois class, gave Goethe philology (Konrad Burdach, Georg Simmel, Friedrich Gundolf) a scientifically significant stimulus. This direction disclosed, above all, a style and some works of Goethe's late years that one left unattended in the nineteenth century.

20

GOETHE'S POLITICS AND VIEW OF NATURE

[2:1475] *Our collaborator, Walter Benjamin, received from the Russian state a commission to write the article on "Goethe" for the* Great Soviet Encyclopedia *currently in preparation. The task, of course, is supposed to be accomplished in* [2:1476] *a Marxist-materialist manner. The difficulties of doing so are prodigious.—We are publishing here a few particularly important parts from the Benjaminian draft, ones that will be all the more interesting to our readers, since the comprehensive work will not be published in German but, rather, in Russian. What's more: in our view, this work presents the most ingenious and thorough analyses that we've ever read concerning this important circle of problems, one that is decisive for German intellectual history—and it does this in a highly concentrated form. With this publication we will not, admittedly, redress the radical stupidity of "not wanting to know anything more about Goethe."*

*

Goethe and the Revolution

It is beyond doubt that Goethe experienced the enlightened despotism of the eighteenth century as problematic long before the irruption of the French Revolution, after his experiences as a Weimar legation counselor. He was unable to reconcile himself to the Revolution not only as a consequence of his inner connections with the feudal regime and not only as a consequence of his fundamental rejection of all violent disruptions of public life but above all because it went against his grain; indeed, it was impossible for him to reach any fundamental views in matters of state life. If he never expressed himself about the "limits of the effectiveness of the state" as clearly as, for example, Wilhelm von Humboldt, it was because his political nihilism went too far for him to dare do more than hint at it. Suffice it to say that, later on, Napoleon's program to destroy the German people at its roots had nothing monstrous about it for Goethe, who precisely in such explosions glimpsed the external appearance of a community in which great individuals could draw their circles of activity—circles of activity in which they could patriarchally switch on and send out to each other their spiritual signals over centuries and across state borders. It has been said correctly that the Germany of Napoleon was the epitome of Romanesque-French inflected Franconia—for him, the most fitting place to maneuver. But the prodigious sensitivity, the pathological shattering into which the great political events of his time transposed him also worked its way into his relationship to the Revolution. This shattering, in which the poet was struck by certain episodes of the French Revolution as though they were personal blows of fate, made it impossible for him to regulate in general the world of the political purely on the basis of principles, just as it was completely impossible to make this possible for the private existence of the individual human being.

In light of the class contradictions of Germany of that time, the situation can be represented in this way: Goethe felt himself to be not, like Lessing, a champion of the bourgeois classes, but much more their deputy, their ambassador to German feudalism and princedom. His permanent wavering can be explained by the conflicts of this representative position. Still, the greatest representative of classical bourgeois literature—which formed the only unassailable claim of the German people to its reputation as a modern nation of culture—could not conceive of bourgeois culture in any framework other than an ennobled feudal state. If Goethe rejected the French Revolution, this occurred not only in the feudal sense—out of the patriarchal idea that any culture, including one that is bourgeois, could flourish only under the protection and in the shadow of absolutism—but just as much in the sense of the petty bourgeoisie, that is, the private man who anxiously seeks to shore up his existence against the political disruptions all around him. Neither in the spirit of feudalism nor in the spirit of the petty bourgeoisie was, however, this rejection univocal and total. That is why not a single one of the literary works, in which for an entire decade, he tried to sort out and come to terms with the Revolution, could capture a central place in the total context of his oeuvre.

*

Goethe's Natural-Scientific Studies

The political problems that burdened Goethe's production in the nineties were the reason he tried to withdraw from this production in manifold ways.

His great asylum was the study of nature.[1] Schiller recognized the escapist character that inhabited the natural-scientific occupations of these years. In 1787 he writes to Körner: "Goethe's spirit has molded all the people who count themselves among his circle. A proud philosophical contempt for all speculation and investigation, with an attachment to nature driven to affectation and a resignation to the five senses; in short, a certain childlike simplicity of reason characterizes him and his whole present sect. There, one would rather look for herbs or practice biology than be caught up in empty demonstrations. The idea can be completely healthy and good, but one can also exaggerate a great deal."[2] This natural-scientific study made Goethe only more aloof from political events. He conceived of history only as natural history, grasped it only insofar as it remained bound to the creature. That is why the pedagogy that he later developed in [*Wilhelm Meister's*] *Journeyman Years* was the most advanced post that he was able to attain in the world of the historical. This natural-scientific direction went against politics, but it went against theology, too. In the poet's Spinozism, hostile to the church, it found its most fruitful formation. While he goes against the pietistic writings of his friend Jacobi, because the latter puts forth the thesis that nature conceals God, the most important thing about Spinoza, for Goethe, is that nature as well as spirit are a revealed aspect of the divine. That is what is meant when Goethe writes to Jacobi: "God has punished you with metaphysics ... but me he has blessed with physics."

The concept under which Goethe represents his revelations of the physical world is the "urphenomenon." It was originally formed in the context of his botanical and anatomical studies. In 1784 Goethe discovers the morphological formation of the skull bones out of modified bones of the spinal column, one year later *The Metamorphosis of Plants*. Under this designation he understood the circumstance that all organs of the plant, from the roots to the stamen, are only modified forms of the leaf. He thus arrived at the concept of the "urplant," which Schiller declared to be an "idea" in his first famous conversation with the poet but which Goethe would not allow to stand without attributing to it a certain sensuous intuitability. Goethe's natural-scientific studies occupy the position in the context of his works often taken up by aesthetics among lesser artists. One can understand precisely this side of Goethe's creativity only by realizing that he, in contrast to almost all the intellectuals of this epoch, never made peace with "beautiful semblance." Not aesthetics but rather the intuition of nature reconciled poetry and politics for him. For this very reason, however, it cannot be denied how refractory the poet was toward certain innovations even in these natural-scientific studies—in the sphere of the technical as well as the political. On the threshold of the natural-scientific age, which would broaden the acuity and the sphere of sensuous perceptions so prodigiously, he leads back again to the old forms of exploring nature and writes: "The human being in himself, insofar as he uses his healthy senses, is the greatest and most accurate physical apparatus that can exist, and it is precisely the greatest harm of the new physics that the experiments have become divided off, as it were, from the human being and . . . one is only willing to recognize nature in what is shown by artificial instruments." Science, as he conceives it, has as its foremost natural task to sort and clean up the human being in his activity and his thinking. The alteration of the world through technology was not really his concern, even though in his old age he gave an astonishingly clear account of its unavoidable significance. The highest usefulness of knowledge about nature, for him, was determined in the form that it gives to a life. He developed this intuition into a rigorous pragmatism: "Only what is fruitful is true."

Goethe belongs to the family of those great spirits for whom there is at bottom no art in the stripped-down sense. For him, the doctrine of the urphenomenon as natural science was at the same time the true doctrine of art, just as, for Dante, it was scholastic philosophy and, for Dürer, the technical arts. Only the discoveries of his botany were pathbreaking for science in the strictest sense. The osteological writings are also important and recognized: the reference to the human intermaxillary bone, though it was not really a discovery. Largely ignored remained the *Meteorology*, sharply contested the *Theory of Colors*, which, for Goethe, crowned his natural-scientific work; indeed, according to certain statements one might think it crowned his lifework in general. The discussion of this most comprehensive document of Goethean natural science has for some time now been renewed. The *Theory of Colors* stands in sharp opposition to Newtonian optics. The fundamental opposition, from which Goethe's sometimes extremely bitter and decades-long polemic takes its point of departure, is this: Newton explains white light to be a compositum of colored lights; Goethe, by contrast, as the simplest, most indivisible, most homogenous thing we know. "It is not composed, ... least of all, of colored lights." The *Theory of Colors* takes colors to be metamorphoses of light, phenomena that form themselves in the struggle of light with darkness. Alongside the thought of metamorphosis, that of polarity, which runs through all of his research, is decisive for Goethe. Dark is not a mere absence of light—for then it would not be noticeable—but, rather, a positive counterlight. In his later years the thought occurs to him in this context that animal and plant perhaps developed out of the primal condition through light or darkness respectively. It is a peculiar trait of these natural-scientific studies that in them Goethe accommodates the spirit of the Romantic school just as much as he opposes its spirit in his aesthetics.—Goethe's philosophical orientation is understood much less from his poetic than from his natural-scientific writings. From the time of his youthful epiphany, which is recorded in the famous fragment "Nature," Spinoza remained, for him, the patron of his morphological studies. Later, these made it possible for him to engage in a confrontation with Kant. While Goethe had no relation to the major critical work—the *Critique of Pure Reason*—and equally the *Critique of Practical Reason*—the ethics—he had the highest admiration for the *Critique of Judgment*. This is because in the latter work Kant discarded the teleological explanation of nature that was a pillar of Enlightenment philosophy, of Deism. Goethe had to agree with him on this point, for his own anatomical and botanical researches represented far more advanced positions in the attack of bourgeois natural science against teleological natural science. Kant's definition of the organic as a purposiveness whose purpose lies not outside but inside of the purposive creature itself corresponded to Goethe's concepts. The unity of whatever is beautiful, including whatever is naturally beautiful, is always independent of purposes—in this, Kant and Goethe are in unison.

Goethe and Napoleon

In 1795 Goethe wrote, "We don't want the radical upheavals that could prepare for classical works in Germany." This radical change—it is the emancipation of the bourgeoisie that occurred in 1848, too late to still bring forth any classical works. A German essence, a German spirit of language, these were, to be sure, the strings on which Goethe played his powerful melody; but the sounding board of this instrument was not Germany but, rather, Napoleon's Europe. The same thing hung before Goethe and Napoleon's eyes: the social emancipation of the bourgeoisie under the political form of despotism. This emancipation was the "impossible," the "incommensurate," the "unattainable," which sat in them as the deepest thorn. It wrecked Napoleon. In contrast, one can say about Goethe that, the older he became, the more he formed his life according to this political idea, consciously stamping it as the incommensurate, the unattainable, and elevating it into the microarchetype of his political idea. Assuming that fully distinct lines could be drawn, poesy could represent the bourgeois freedom of this state, while the regime completely corresponded to the despotism characteristic of his private affairs. At bottom, however, the intertwining effect of these incompatible strivings can be pursued just as much in his life and in his writing: in his life, as the freedom of erotic breakthrough and as the most rigid regime of "renunciation," in the writing nowhere so much as in the second part of *Faust* whose political dialectic gives the key to Goethe's position. Only in this context can it be understood how in his last thirty years Goethe was able to subordinate his life completely to the bureaucratic categories of balance, mediation, postponement. It is senseless to judge his actions and his gestures according to an abstract standard of morality. The absurdity of the attacks that Börne directed at Goethe in the name of Young Germany lies in this abstraction. Precisely in his maxims and in the most remarkable peculiarities shown by the regime of his life, Goethe can be understood only from the political position that he created for himself and in which he immersed himself. Its hidden yet all the deeper affinity with Napoleon's position is so decisive that the post-Napoleonic era, the power that brought down Napoleon, could no longer understand it. The son of bourgeois parents ascends, leaves everything behind, becomes the heir of a revolution before whose power everything in his hands trembles (French Revolution, Sturm und Drang), and at the moment when he has most profoundly shaken the rule of the surviving forces, founds via a coup d'état his own rule in the same old, the very same feudal forms (Empire, Weimar).

21
WEIMAR

I.

[4:353] In small German cities, it is impossible to imagine the rooms without windowsills. But rarely have I seen such wide ones as on the Weimar Market Square, in the "Elefanten" [Hotel]. There, they make the room into a loggia that became, for me, the view onto a ballet such as even the stages of Neuschwanstein and Herrenchiemsee could not offer to Ludwig II.[1] For it was a ballet of early morning. Around 6:30, tuning began: resonant basses, shadowing violin umbrellas, flower flutes, and fruit timpani. The stage still almost empty; market women, no buyers. I fell asleep again. Toward nine o'clock, when I awoke, it was an orgy: markets are the orgy of the morning hours, and hunger, as Jean Paul would have said, ushers in the day as love ushers it out.[2] Syncopating, coins came in, and slowly girls pushed and shoved with net shopping bags that, swelling on all sides, gave an invitation to enjoy their curves. Scarcely, though, did I find myself dressed and on solid ground, wanting to step onto the stage, but the sparkle and freshness were gone. I understood that all gifts of the morning, like sunrise, want to be received at their zenith. And was not that which still shone on the delicately checked plaster a mercantile dawn? Now it lay buried beneath paper and garbage. Instead of dance and music, only exchange and business. Nothing can have vanished so irreversibly as a morning.

II.

In the Goethe-Schiller Archive, staircases, rooms, exhibition cases, libraries are white. The eye meets no custom house where it could rest. Like sick people in hospitals, the manuscripts lie embedded there. But the longer one exposes oneself to this harsh light, the more one thinks one recognizes a capacity of reasoning at the foundation of these institutions of which they are themselves unconscious. Just as a long period of lying in a sickbed makes the stricken person's countenance spacious and calm, allowing it to become a mirror of emotions that a healthy body expresses through resolute decisions, through reaching out in a thousand ways, by issuing commands [4:354]—in short, just as lying in a sickbed transforms the human being back into the sphere of sheer facial expression, it is not for nothing that these pages, like those who suffer from sickness, lie on their repositories. The fact that everything that today consciously and sturdily confronts us as Goethe's "Works" in countless book-like shapes once consisted in this single, most fragile shape, which is that of script; and the fact that what emerged from this script can have been only the rigorous, purifying element that, for the few who are close to them, reigns over the recovering and the dying—we don't like to think about all of this. But didn't these pages also stand in a crisis? Didn't a shudder pass over them, and no one knew whether it was from proximity to annihilation or proximity to posthumous fame? And aren't these pages the loneliness of literature? And the bed on which it came around? And among its pages are there not some whose unnamable text rises only as a glimpse or a breath out of the mute, shaken strokes?

III.

One knows how primitive Goethe's study was. It is low, has no carpet, no double windows. The furniture is plain. He could easily have had it otherwise. There were leather armchairs and upholstery back then, too. This room in no way stands in advance of its time. A volition held figure and forms in limits; no one should have to be ashamed of the candlelight by which the old man in a nightshirt, arms spread on a discolored cushion, sat at the medium-sized table and studied. To think that, today, the quiet of such hours only gathers again in deepest night. But if one were allowed to eavesdrop on them, one would understand the way of leading a life, with determination and creativity, one would know how to harvest the never-recurring grace, the ripest yield of these last decades in which even someone who was rich had to feel the hardness of life on his own body. Here, the old man celebrated the monstrous nights with Care, Guilt, Need, before the hellish dawn of bourgeois comfort shone in through the window.[3] We are still waiting for a philology that would open before us this nearest, most defining environment—the veritable antiquity of the poet. This study was the cella of the small building that Goethe [4:355] had destined exclusively for two things: sleep and labor. One cannot even begin to measure out the meaning of the neighborhood of the tiny bedroom and this study, so secluded from a bed chamber. Only the threshold separated him, like a step, during labor, from the bed in state. And when he slept, his work waited for him next door to win him back every night from the dead. Those allowed by a happy coincidence to collect themselves in this space experience in the ordering of the four rooms where Goethe slept, read, dictated, and wrote the forces that summoned a world to give him an answer whenever he struck up its innermost element. But we have to make a world resound in order to allow the weak overtone of an inward element to ring out.

22

TWO DREAMS OF GOETHE'S HOUSE

525. In a dream, I saw myself in Goethe's study. It had no similarity to the one in Weimar. Above all, it was very small and had only one window. The desk abutted the opposite wall with its narrow side. Before it, there sat the extremely aged poet. I stood to the side as he interrupted himself and gave me as a gift a small vase, an ancient vessel. I turned it about in my hands. A prodigious heat prevailed in the room. Goethe got up and walked with me into the next room, where a long banquet table was set for my relatives [*Verwandtschaft*]. But it seemed calculated for far more people than they would amount to. It was probably set for ancestors [*Ahnen*] as well. At the right end, I took a seat next to Goethe. When the meal was over, he got up with difficulty, and with a gesture I asked for permission to support him. When I touched his elbow, I began to cry from emotion.

526. Visit in the Goethe House.[1] I can't remember having seen rooms in the dream. It was a line of whitewashed corridors like in a school. Two English lady visitors and a curator are the dream supernumeraries. The curator exhorts us to sign the visitors' book that lay open on a desk on a windowsill at the far end of a hallway. As I step up to it, thumbing through it, I find my name already entered in a large, awkward child's handwriting.

23

GOETHE'S THEORY OF COLORS

[3:148] *Goethe's Theory of Colors*. Edited and introduced by Hans Wohlbold. Eugen Diederichs, Jena[1]

Last winter, the Berlin Bibliophile Evening distributed a facsimile edition of Goethe's *Contributions to Optics* to its members as a commemorative gift.[2] It might have occurred to some of those who received the gift—such as the onlooker who signed up—that this work, as the enfant terrible among Goethe's brainchildren, might not be particularly suitable to be cited in a closed society.[3] Has it not been said that the freedom of this roundtable should be brought to consciousness in the most flattering way? Those who have been looking forward to it would be especially pleased that, in the meantime, a publisher and an editor have quite publicly and explicitly declared their support for it, and they have not spared the cost and effort to dispatch it to the kind of people who are a little bit quaint, but neatly dressed, and above all, equipped with all kinds of multicolored playthings.

As difficult as the matter may seem for every layperson, every physicist, and every Goethe researcher, it soon becomes obvious that it can be approached with benefit from several sides. And this is also indeed so, if one leaves aside the most proximate question: Newton or Goethe—who was right? For, first of all, as is well known, there are various chapters in the *Theory of Colors* that have nothing to do with mathematical physics. Among them, people have always particularly liked the last section of "The Sensual-Moral

Effect of Color." It leads to the inexhaustible region of color symbolism, where [3:149] people entrusted the poet and his readers with countless pleasures for themselves. Unfortunately, this custom has also not been suspended in this case. People cannot here seek interesting comparisons that may have been suggested, for example, between Goethe's interpretation of color and the extraordinary one in Kandinsky's work, *On the Spiritual in Art*.[4] All the more important are hints that the editor has given in another direction. Just as it is quite certain that in accordance with the matter of truth in physics the *Theory of Colors* is relevant beyond the context of Goethe-related research, so is it equally certain that, with regard to the matter of philosophy, the former belongs to the latter's center.[5] And in a quite excellent manner Wohlbold understood how to present the *Theory of Colors* as a counterpart to *The Metamorphosis of Plants*. "Just as the primal plant as an idea seeks to form itself into a sensible plant in the material world, light wants to create an expression for itself in darkness. Therefore, just as in the former case, so in the latter we can speak of a metamorphosis." Goethe's theory "does not pretend to develop colors from light; rather, it tries to convince us that color is produced simultaneously by light and what opposes it." This is the meaning of the famous words: "Colors are the deeds and sufferings of light."[6]

It is a pity, such a pity, that the editor wants to have these truths seen in the most adequate way through the distorting mirror of Rudolf Steiner's world picture. The puny, erratic temper that runs through the products of this school has also smudged an important section of his well-designed manuscript. For, in the hundred-year debate about Goethean optics, there is a definite, decisive question that may no longer, and never again be covered up: does Goethe's physical theory of color stand apart from Newton's; that is, can it possibly be maintained independently from Newtonian theory? Or is it the contrary—that is, if one of them is true, must the other be false, and vice versa? And if Newton's theory is not really an argument against Goethe's, and if it is supposed to be true that physics is "not at all entitled to make a judgment on Goethe's *Theory of Colors*" and is "not competent on this question," then [3:150] exactness requires that this be emphasized: Goethe himself, known as he was for speaking about Newton in the most drastic terms (he calls him the "chief of the Cossacks"), was altogether unclear about this situation. One thing, though, should nevertheless be certain, namely, that the matter cannot by any means be treated as the editor dreams. He explains: "It does not depend, after all, on calculations and external proofs. There is a feeling, one could almost say, an instinct, for what is a right way and a wrong way. Proofs lie, like the fate of stars, in one's own breast. What is decisive in the end is the inner gain. If contemplation of nature is to have any value, it can ultimately lie only in an elevation of humanity, in an intensification of lived experience, an inner shaping and transformation." Now this is indeed the language of a "guardian of the threshold." It is worrisome enough that the editor wrote the catalog for the optical collection of the physical cabinet in the Goethe House.[*]

The altercation between Goetheans and physicists has remained a matter of positional warfare for a century.[7] The author is undeniably at home in Goethe's positions. Goethe's convictions are his own: that the purely natural, physical-psychic endowment of humanity delivers images of existence to humanity that are the most important for humanity and that optics has nothing to gain by "tormenting spectra through many narrow gaps and glasses."[8] Simmel, however, already took a deep look into these presuppositions of the Goethean stance.[9] Certainly, one can only gain something if, for immanent connections in Goethean optics, one abides by both Simmel and Wohlbold. But one must then not forget what one of the most brilliant interpreters of the *Theory of Colors*, S. Friedländer, wrote about the most important question, the question concerning the altercation [between Goethe and Newton] and the decision: "True enlightenment will be able to take place only through a mathematically educated Goethean; and a Goethean mathematics is not so much a wooden iron as a wooden horse, with the assistance of which Goethe's Greeks will eventually conquer the barbaric Troy of optics and [3:151] finally win back the Helen of color-beauty, she who was taken from them."[10]

---

[*]   Incidentally, it bears no further relation to the Goethe-National Museum.

24

AGAINST A MASTERPIECE
On Max Kommerell, *The Poet as Führer in German Classicism*

[3:252] If there ever were a German conservatism that held itself upright, it would have to regard this book as its Magna Carta.[1] For the last eighty years, there has been no such thing. And so we are presumably not far from the truth with the assumption that Kommerell has scarcely found a more comprehensive critique than what follows here, encountering him from a different side. This book delivers one of those rare moments, which is thought-provoking for the critic, since no one asks questions about the work's quality, its stylistic form, or its author's qualifications. None of these matters can be doubted in the least. Rarely has the history of poetry been written in this way: its many-sided elaborations, the sharp-edged, impenetrable surface of that symmetrical, diamantine certainty that we have long known as the George school's black stone of Kaaba. From the praise of blood, the contempt for music, and the hatred of the masses down to the love of boys, there is not a single motif that would not report for duty in response to a loud or whispered appeal and not one that has failed to grow since we last encountered it. The critical maxims, the yardsticks of value that Gundolf's writings still handled in such a rattling, mastersinger manner, have here been [3:253] thrown on the scrap heap, or rather have melted down in the embers of an experience that could forgo the hieratic division of work and life, for in both cases, it verifies the physiognomic mode of seeing, which is in a strictest sense unpsychological.[2] For this reason, almost everything one finds here about the individual poets—even more so about their friendships, feuds, encounters, and separations than about their person—is marked by a gaze of singular precision and daring. The wealth of true anthropological insights, as so often in horoscopes, in chiromantic, and in esoteric writings in general, is astounding. George's doctrine of the hero must be counted, after all, among these occult disciplines. Here, in alternating manner, it throws light on a mantic, a Pan-like, a satyr-like, even a centaur-like side of the figures at the Weimar court of the muses. One senses just how often the classics found themselves on horseback.

How did this motility come over figures that so readily freeze in the poses of their monuments? The author did not hold himself to the past alone: he also discovers what did not occur. Let it be understood: he does not invent this—as though it were something like a fantasy—but simply and clearly discovers it, that is, discovers something that in accordance with truth did not happen. His image of history emerges out of the background of the possible, against which the relief of the real casts its shadows. It is in keeping with this that nothing is composed for effects or spotlights and that the far-flung and dark parts seem to be the most thoroughly formed ones. In this work, the great antagonisms—Jacobi against the young Goethe, Herder against the Weimar Goethe, Schiller against the Schlegels, Klopstock against the king—are shaped for the first time, and only in the interplay with them do the friendships of the classical period gain their firm arrangement. One will neither expect nor desire that the presentation of these antagonisms be nonpartisan. Where the accents fall is, however, characteristic of the work and its secret intention. Nothing is random in this regard; but few things are more revealing than the annihilation of the two Schlegels in a confrontation with Schiller. It would be absurd to seek "historical justice" here. Something else is at stake. Romanticism stands at the origin of the rejuvenation of German lyric poetry, which George completed. It also stands at the origin of the philosophical and critical development that today rises up [3:254] against this work.[3] Seen strategically, pushing Romanticism into the background is not a futile endeavor, but it is even less an unsuspicious one. With the origins of its own stance, it denies the forces that outgrow these origins from their center. The classicism about which we hear in this book is a late and very statesmanlike discovery of the George circle. It is no accident that a student of Wolters undertakes this discovery.[4] Every dialectical examination of George's poetry will posit Romanticism at the center; every heroizing, orthodox one can do nothing cleverer than show Romanticism to be something as close as possible to nothing.

In fact: the book founds an esoteric history of German poetry with a radicalism unattained by any of its predecessors in the George circle. This is a literary history only for the profanum vulgus; in truth, a salvation history of the Germans. Unfolding in encounters, alliances, testaments, and instructions, it is a history that at every moment threatens to veer into the apocryphal, the unsayable, and the suspect. A doctrine of true Germanness and the inscrutable paths of German ascendency, pregnant with the future, circles around the affinity [Verwandtschaft] between German and Greek ingenium.[5] The German is heir to the Greek mission; Greece's mission is the birth of the hero. It goes without saying that this Greekness appears as a mythological forcefield detached from all contexts. It is also no accident when a famous passage about Greek and German spirit that appears in one of Hölderlin's letters can be heard resonating, albeit softly, when it is demanded of patriotic poetry that it be most intensely permeated by the ways of the tribe, while at the same time, however, keeping the greatest inner distance from it, and when shame is named as poetry's surest seal of authentication.[6] Words that let one intimate the significant culture setting forces into motion, forces that here poetize a Germanic twilight of the gods. For rune, divination, eon, blood, fate—they now stand, after the setting of Lechter's sun, which used to bathe them in its glow, as so many thunderclouds in the sky.[7] It is they who give us lightning bolts as the signposts according to which, as Florens Christian Rang, the deepest critic of Germanness since Nietzsche, says: "Night suffocates us only more darkly: the dreadful worldview of world-death instead of world-life."[8] How [3:255] feeble, though, and how long-winded is the phraseological thunder that follows them. The latter indeed booms in all books of the [George] circle. It does not exactly win anyone over for their teachings; it is not convincing when one feels how the speakers there are nowhere out of breath. "That all preachers and recruiters—even if they recruited for the purest cause and preached nothing but love—leave one empty-handed, for they take even the richest human being only as material for their purposes"—something of this experience, which Goethe was destined to have with Lavater, and that was so masterfully formulated by Kommerell, is also transmitted to the reader of Kommerell's own book. The more one reads it, the more the image of Hellas, too, dissolves in the dazzling light of a morning "when the youth feel the birth of a new fatherland in glowing unification and in the clanking of previously all-too-deeply buried weapons." "Our word 'hero,'" another passage reads, "has not yet gone through this reality. . . . But something not yet real wafts about this word: whereas the neighboring peoples borrow their naming of the hero from the Greeks, *we* possess the self-grown stem of the word and, with it, the claim to the thing that it names. But if under this stem and through this claim the hero turns into a demigod: who, then, would still shy away from the hardest hammer and the hottest forge of our future fate?"[9]

Flowery imagery? Oh, no; this is the clanking of steel runes, the dangerous anachronism of sectarian language. One can altogether understand this book only from a basic consideration of the relationship that sects have to history. For them, history is never a subject of study, always an object of their claims. They seek to award themselves that which was as a title of origin or as a paradigm. In this way, classicism here becomes the model. It is the great concern of the author to construct from classicism the first canonical case of a German insurrection against time, of a holy war of the Germans against the [twentieth] century, as George later proclaimed it. It would be one thing to establish grounds for this thesis; a second thing, to investigate whether this fight ended up victorious; and a third thing, to verify whether the fight was truly an exemplary one. For the author, the first implies the second; but the third occupies the first rung. So much so that he sees the fight as a paradigm; for this reason, he declares it victorious and does not in the end lose any sleep over his object [3:256], [that is,] the stance of the factions. Indeed, where did the factions stand? Is it feasible to reduce this complex process, whose very complexity—Goethe demonstrates this—makes it so oppressive, to the back-and-forth play between the heroic and the banal? There is heroism enough in the men of classicism: classicism itself was anything but a heroic spiritual stance; it was a stance of resignation. And no one but the singular Goethe was able, without shattering, to maintain this stance until the very end. Schiller and Herder were destroyed by it. And those who remained outside of Weimar, Hölderlin not least among them, hid their heads from this "movement." Goethe, however—his opposition to the age was that of a restorative domineering nature. Its sources did not flow from some past antiquity but from the primordial rocks of the oldest power—indeed, from the oldest relations of nature themselves. Schiller, by contrast, constructed the opposition in a historical manner. His restorationist stance was an ethos and far from anything original. Kommerell knows all of this as well as anyone. But it has no validity for him. It is as if, for him, antiquity and thereby history in general ended with Napoleon, with the last hero.

The greatness of this work is, of course, entirely bound up with such anachronisms. For it reprises the great Plutarchian line of biography. In this way, its distance from the more recent, fashionable biographical style of a Ludwig is even greater than from Gundolf's history of poets. Plutarch presents the hero pictorially, often as a model but always as completely external to the reader. Ludwig seeks to render the hero internal to the reader but especially to himself, the author. He incorporates the hero; he soaks him up; nothing remains. The success of such works lies in this: they furnish one and all with a little "inner Napoleon," an "inner Goethe." It has been remarked wittily but correctly that there are only a few people who have not missed out on becoming a millionaire by a hair's breadth at some point in their lives; similarly, one can say of most people that they have not lacked the opportunity to become great men. Ludwig's skill lies in leading his readers on slippery paths back to those turning points and staging for their benefit their washed-out and worn-out existence as the great design of a heroic life. When [3:257] Kommerell calls forth the image of a Goethe, not for a moment does it share the reader's air, much less his mood. In its development of Goethe's youth—in the chapter "The Wanderer and His Companions"—it can thus happen that the work here and there has the dignity of a commentary on *Poetry and Truth*. To place Goethe's youth under the concept of an altercation with the contemporaneous forms of leadership [*Führertum*] is more than insightful. Here lies the basis for his presentation of the poet's relationship with Carl August, which he recognizes as the exemplary case of education and human formation in Goethe's life and which he suggestively finds reflected in Goethe's relationships to Napoleon and Byron—a section that belongs among the few inspired ones that have been written about Goethe's life. Here, one cannot fairly expect that the relationship "prince and poet" would be grasped historically, not just timelessly mythologically, and that its peculiarity in the German states around 1780 would come to light. This remains enough. For instance, there is the tone in which Schelling addresses the old Goethe in his letters, so breathtaking in its reverence from which death has not yet taken away any of its burden. In such passages "divination" has reversed, and at the height of its daring and its success, it becomes a simple, objective, infallible reading. Like a great collector of antiques, the author takes lived hours into his hands. It is not that he talks about them; one sees them because he turns them around in his hand in such a knowing, inquiring, reverent, touched, appraising, and questioning manner, looking at them from all sides, and giving them not the false life of empathy but the true one of tradition. This is ever so closely related to the author's peculiar kind of obstinacy: a collecting one. For, if, among systematizers, the positive and the negative always lie thoroughly separated and worlds apart, then in this book both of these—preference and repudiation—narrowly collide with each other. One poem is singled out from a cycle of songs, one moment from an existence, and the author sharply distinguishes persons and thoughts that in terms of their disposition seem very closely related.

Just how little he can dare to undertake at bottom a "rescuing" of classicism is best proven by the chapter, [3:258] "Legislation." Not for nothing does it show how completely alienated we are from what brought Goethe to the revelation of ancient art during his Italian journey; it shows how much rococo is concealed even in his work and how unacceptable are, if not the maxims, then the models of his art critique. Kommerell's image of classicism, insofar as it is lasting, lives off the claim to dominion that he recognizes in classicism. The impotence of this claim, however, belongs as much to its image as to his title. "To this day," writes the author, "the average cultured person has not fully grasped the alpha and omega of Weimar culture, and covers over a shameful nakedness with the theological, philosophical, musical badge of a beggar's pride: to stand beyond semblance." If this is true—and it is true—then a forceful misconception, indeed an ambiguity, must have been at the very basis of Weimar culture. It was susceptible to being misunderstood to such a frightening degree that, when around the middle of the [nineteenth] century, philistines resolutely turned their backs on the noblest inheritance of the people, they did so in the name of Schiller, and it required a Nietzsche to raise doubts about the reconcilability of the spirit of Weimar and [the Battle of] Sedan.

It directly follows that the author's conclusion concerning classicism is condemned to remain, in turn, a wisdom of stars and fate. "Thus, for us, as for no other people, a destiny that is difficult to interpret is ripening: the division of dominion and a twofold moment, one open and one secret. Hölderlin being overwhelmed by the spirit of the times—even though it falls under the same calendrical date—belongs to a different eon: his moment is no less true but points to a different central point than the moment of Goethe, and Jean Paul's dream figures seem bloodless only until their terrestrial brothers stride across our soil. All this stirred in enigmatic fullness within the German perimeter of two decades, and in our spiritual heavens there stood the sun, a dawn, and the eternal stars all at the same time." That is true, beautiful, and significant. Precisely in the face of such a florally open, florally flaming vision, we, however, must profess our allegiance to the unsightly truth, to the laconism of seed and fecundity—thereby, however, to theory, which leaves behind the spellbinding circle of show [*Schau*].[10] If there are timeless images, there are certainly no timeless theories. Tradition [3:259] cannot make a decision about them, only originality. The genuine image may be old, but the genuine thought is new. It is of today. Granted, this today may be paltry. But whatever shape it may take, one must seize it firmly by the horns so as to gain the capacity to query the past. It is the bull whose blood must fill up the pit if the spirits of the departed ones shall appear at its edge.[11] It is this deadly thrust of thought that is lacking in the works of the George circle. Instead of sacrificing the today, they avoid it. A martial element must live in every critique; it, too, knows the daemon. A critique that is nothing but show loses itself, cheats poetry of the interpretation it owes to it, and stunts its growth. It should not be forgotten that critique must unconditionally affirm itself for it to accomplish anything. Indeed, perhaps it must—one reflects on the theories of the brothers Schlegel—accord itself the highest rank. The author is very far removed from this. According to his image, the thinker is "forever expelled from the creative innocence of the artist." The fact that innocence never safeguards creativity, whereas creativity constantly fabricates innocence—it is this untroubled truth that the student of Stefan George cannot admit.

A chapter on Hölderlin concludes this salvation history of the Germans. The image of the man that it therein unfolds is a fragment of a new *vita sanctorum* and can no longer be assimilated by any history. Hölderlin's almost unbearably dazzling outline lacks the shadowing that here, above all, theory would have granted. This, though, was not the intention. A warning memorial of the German future was supposed to be erected. Overnight, ghostly hands will thereupon paint a great "Too Late." Hölderlin was not of the stamp of those who are resurrected, and the country whose seers' visions appear above corpses is not his. No sooner than purified can this earth become Germany again, and not in the name of Germany can it be purified, let alone in the name of a secret Germany, which is ultimately nothing other than official Germany's arsenal wherein the magic cloak of invisibility hangs alongside the steel helmet.

25

ONE HUNDRED YEARS OF WRITING ON GOETHE

[3:326] The following bibliography of a few important or characteristic writings on Goethe neither makes nor fulfills any claim to be scientific or scholarly. Rather, the selection had to be arbitrary by necessity. This would perhaps be unforgiveable if its intention were to familiarize the reader with Goethe and his oeuvre, no matter the detour. This, though, is in no way the case; rather, the only intention here was to give a sense of the wealth of literary repercussions of this poetic life and work, a perspicuous overview of which is no longer obtainable either in terms of individual details or by individual persons. Hence, Goethe's works, letters, and conversations were to be left aside; also such writing by those closest to him as well as "classical writers" in general; by contrast, in addition to certain standard works that either aim to render Goethe present to the reader or are concerned with the scholarly investigation of his work, certain peripheral works, above all, were taken into consideration. If the layperson may not get his money's worth with respect to many of the following titles, the Goethe scholar or the historian of culture will here and there have occasion to take some notice of this or that book.

> "For this fact cannot in Germany be denied: the more written about an author, the less he infiltrates the consciousness of the crowd."
>
> Ludwig Geiger, "The Cult of Goethe." *German Revue*, September 1910

From the Apparatus of the Goethe Scholar

On Goethe: Literary and Artistic Notices. Edited by A. Nicolovius. Leipzig, 1828.

> First attempt at a Goethe bibliography with a compendium of the most important judgments about Goethe. With respect to such judgments, [3:327] it builds on Varnhagen von Ense's *Goethe in the Testimonies of His Contemporaries on August 28th*. Berlin, 1823.

Goethe in the Judgment of His Contemporaries: Newspaper Critiques, Reports, Notes on Goethe and His Works. Collected and published by Julius W. Braun. A supplement to all editions of Goethe's works. 3 vols. Berlin, 1883–85.

> Foundational sourcebook for the study of Goethe's influence on the Germany of his time, generally overestimated in terms of its depth.

Concerning the Knowledge of the Goethe Manuscripts, by Dr. Phil. Carl Burkhardt, Privy Council, Director of the Archive and Archivist of the Grand Duke of Saxony. Vienna, 1899.

> Contains facsimiles of the handwriting of fifty persons whom Goethe employed as clerks. Important work for the chronology of the manuscripts.

Catalog of the Kippenberg Collection. 3 vols. Leipzig, 1928.

> The collection constitutes the richest fund of manuscripts by Goethe and his circle as well as drawings and sculptures of all kinds that exist outside of the Weimar Archive. The magnificently illustrated catalog is a certain kind of cultural history of those who belonged to the upper ten thousand in Germany around the turn of the eighteenth century.[1]

Goethe as a Patron of the Weimar Library. A list of all works borrowed by him. Edited by Elise von Keudell. Published with a Preface by Professor Dr. Werner Deetjen. Weimar, 1931.

> No work compares to this title index when it comes to giving an idea of the highly qualified apparatus that became an ever more necessary condition for Goethe's poetic works the longer he continued to write.

Chronicle of Goethe's Life. Compiled by Baron Flodoard v. Biedermann. Leipzig.[2]

> Attempts at producing chronological tables of Goethe's life were already undertaken before Biedermann, Saupe's, in particular. The contemporary reader will feel closest to this book published by Insel. No other [3:328] work on Goethe has more to suggest to the reader's imagination than this plain compilation of names and dates.

Concerning Goethe's Physiognomy

Elegy, September 1823. Goethe's Fair Copy with Ulrike v. Levetzow's Letter to Goethe and a Portrait from Her Youth. Published by Bernhard Suphan, Weimar. Publishing House of the Goethe Society, 1900. Writings of the Goethe Society, Vol. 15.

> The manuscripts, from which the Goethe Gesellschaft made available, among others, the Marienbad Elegy and the *West-Eastern Divan* in the form of complete replicas (*Facsimile of the "Divan" Manuscript*, published by Burdach, Vienna 1911, Writings of the Goethe Gesellschaft, vol. 26), are the only testimonies of Goethe's expressive movement that have reached us.

Goethe's Outer Appearance: Literary and Artistic Documents by His Contemporaries. Published by Emil Schäffer. Leipzig, 1914.

> The iconographic part of the book is less extensive than Schulte-Strathaus's. The work has nevertheless retained its value due to the rich selection of literary descriptions of Goethe's appearance.

Goethe's Biographic Schema in Faithful Reproduction of His Manuscripts. Published by George Witkowski. Leipzig, 1922.

> Facsimile reproduction of the octavo notebook in which, on October 11, 1809, Goethe began to note down keywords concerning *Poetry and Truth* on individual sheets titled by the dates of various years. The book gives insight into the tricks of the trade that one encounters elsewhere in Goethe. For instance, how the poet, so as to spur himself to the completion of a gap in his *Faust*, incorporated into the Faust manuscript a bundle of empty paper corresponding to the length of the missing part.

Goethe's Portraits. Published by Ernst Schulte-Strathaus. Munich (Propyläen Edition of Goethe's Complete Work. First supplement. Goethe's Portraits).

> Complete iconography of all portraits that Goethe himself [3:329] sat for, based on the preliminary work by Rollett and Zarncke.

Earliest Reflections on Goethe

Goethe Presented from the Viewpoint of a Close Personal Association. A posthumous work by Johannes Falk. Leipzig, 1832.

> Contains loose characterizations of Goethe's mother, Goethe's humor, etc., also conversations or, rather, interviews with the poet.

Goethe's Character and Private Life: First and Second Report. In: Library of the First Knowledge of the World. Published by H. Malten. Vol. 3, 7th to 9th part. Aarau, 1833.

> Translation of an essay in the *Edinburgh Revue*. Lively, impartial, and detailed presentation with a first-rate characterization of the imperial posture of Goethe's life's last period. Looking down from a sublime peak, "he saw the waves of a thousand different opinions follow upon and battle each other at his feet; he saw multiple dynasties of poets dethroned one after the other; he saw twenty philosophical systems seize hold of public opinion and collapse back into nothingness. He laughed at their impotence, which could not unsettle him, because he, the patriarch, had not taken any daring steps that would have exposed him to the blows that most reputations succumb to."

Conversations Concerning the Portrayal of the Goethean Manner of Poetry and Thought. A Memorial by Carl Friedrich Göschel. 3 vols. Schleusingen, 1834–38.

> Göschel was a religiously attuned Hegelian, and the book constitutes a more or less loose stringing together of edifying and aesthetic reflections that share the tendency to reconcile Goethe with faith.

On the Goethean Correspondence. G. G. Gervinus. Leipzig, 1836.

> In this text, the author makes clear for the first time the reserve with which he, as a representative of the sturdiest [3:330] German liberalism, confronts Goethe. It became the foundation of his very critical presentation of Goethe in the fifth volume of the "History of German Poetry."[3] It was precisely out of his reservations about Goethe's later Weimar period that Gervinus became the first to perceive the phenomenon of Goethe's late poetry.

Goethe at the Turning Point of Two Centuries. By Karl Gutzkow. Berlin, 1836.

> The text was called forth by Wolfgang Menzel's invectives against Goethe.[4] It prepares, with various political caveats, the apologia of the poet from the viewpoint of genius that would later issue in a platitude. "When the young generation formed itself through his work, it could not have found another means that divided the fog of the moment in such a sunny manner, no other vehicle that led them so safely over the heaving tides of stubborn attacks. The time can begin when one is clear about this talent."

Goethe, for a Closer Understanding of Him. By C. G. Carus. With the addition of a series of previously unpublished letters from Goethe to the editor. Leipzig, 1843.

> Finds access to Goethe via the Romantic philosophy of nature and thus stands closest, among the older texts, to certain Goethe interpretations of the present, especially the most recent results of *Faust* research. A subterranean tradition runs from Carus via Bachofen that, along with Klages's attempts mentioned below, led back, in turn, to the interpretation of Goethe in a significant way.

Goethe from the Human Standpoint. Carl Grün. Darmstadt, 1846.

> The first attempt at a critical response to Goethe's humanism. "The Goethean praxis of humanism . . . remains stuck in theory. The praxis is aesthetically idealized; it is not practically enacted; it cannot be practically enacted." [3:331]

A Few Monographs

Göthe's Wilhelm Meister Developed in Its Socialist Elements, by Ferdinand Gregorovius. Königsberg, 1849.

> Lively and independent studies that critically examine Goethe's political stance under the influence of the 1848 movement. "Göthe's political indifference misleads him . . . to the most fantastical illusion and the most adventurous endeavor, namely wanting to realize his social democracy under any form of state whatsoever, even an absolutist one. . . . The poet forgot here that the organism of the state only forms itself out of the moral and ideal elements of society and that the state can never rest on a principle opposed to that of society, which it joins together as the highest unity."

Goethe as Statesman. In: Prussian Yearbooks, vol. 10. Berlin, 1862.

> To this day, an extensive, foundational study whose author, Adolf Schöll, is the publisher of Goethe's correspondence with Frau von Stein.

Goethe's Directorship of the Weimar Theater, presented in episodes and documents by Ernst Pasqué. 2 vols. Leipzig, 1863.

> Very rich presentation of the relationships of the most important actors or theatergoers in Weimar to the court theater and Goethe.

Goethe as Secretary of War, by Adolf Stern. In: *Die Grenzboten,* 57. 1898.

> Superb monograph that presents Goethe's tenacious diplomatic efforts, eventually crowned by success, to reduce Weimar's military budget.

Fernand Baldensperger. *Goethe en France*. Paris, 1904.

> One of the foundational works for the field of comparative literary studies established by Baldensperger. The effects of the Goethean works are traced, with special reference to *Werther* and *Faust*, throughout [3:332] the nineteenth century in the various Romantic, naturalist, and Parnassian circles of poets.

Goethe as Researcher of the Soul, by Ludwig Klages. In: *Jahrbuch des Freien Deutschen Hochstifts*, 1928, edited by Ernst Beutler on behalf of the Hochstift's administration. Frankfurt am Main.

> Attempt to render the author's doctrine of the difference between the world of appearances and the world of facts productive for the interpretation of the Goethean mode of thinking, particularly in his scientific research. Goethe is presented as the first "researcher of appearance [*Erscheinungsforscher*]." This essay provides in one of its notes a highly significant perspective on the theory of colors.

Concerning Goethe's Language

Goethe's Language and Its Spirit. By Dr. E. [*sic*] Joh. Aug. O. L. Lehmann. Berlin, 1852.

> Stylistic analysis of the Goethean language based on a precise inventory of its grammatical peculiarities.

Concerning the Language of the Old Goethe: An Essay on the Language of the Individual, by Ernst Lewy. Berlin, 1913.

> As the author relates in the Preface, a rejected "habilitation thesis." In any case, a significant work of the comparative science of writing, whose principles are applied here to the language of the old Goethe, so that the latter's affinity with the various foreign language types comes to light.[5] The author can rather frequently base himself on the important study *Word and Meaning in Goethe's Language*, by Ewald A. Boucke, Berlin, 1901.

Goethe's Vocabulary: A Linguistic-Historical Dictionary for Goethe's Entire Works, by Prof. Paul Fischer, Privy Student Council. Leipzig, 1929.

> Standard work in two parts. Part 1, German dictionary, part 2, dictionary of loanwords. Gives precise insight into Goethe's overwhelmingly large vocabulary. [3:333]

Goethe Cult

Thoughts on Goethe, by Viktor Hehn. Berlin, 1887.

The Goethe worship of Gregorovius's Romanophile circle. The outstanding reputation of this book withstands a critical verification only in a few chapters, least so in the extensive chapter "Goethe and the Public: A Literary History in Brief." This first attempt at a history of Goethe literature, which may well have been the most serious desideratum of this anniversary year, is disfigured by the ressentiment that breaks through, especially in the treatment of Börne.[6]

Rudolph Huch, *More Goethe*. Leipzig and Berlin, 1899.

Journalistic variant of the Goethe cult, simultaneously a document of the Art Nouveau style in literature. In view of a perspective on the future of "the only still existing school for merchants and soldiers," the author believes himself able to lead the German people back to Goethe.

Goethe Calendar for the Year 1906. Published on Christmas 1905 by Otto Julius Bierbaum. Leipzig, 1905.

With this calendar there begins a series of publications that fritter away Goethe's work and milieu more or less tastefully, allowing the hurried aesthete to cover his need of quotations and edifying sayings. It is the spirit of these calendars to which the well-known Goethe portraits by Carl Bauer constitute the counterpart in the monumental style.

Dante and Goethe. Dialogues by Daniel Stern (Marie Duchess d'Agoult). Translated by her Granddaughter, Daniela Thode. Heidelberg, 1911.

As evinced by the title, this volume leads into the multibranched circle of German enthusiasts for Italy and Goethe around Liszt and Wagner. The dialogues that are led between ideal partners in a pale, solemn language borrow from the imagistic world of a Feuerbach. The strongly worded reflections, in which the bitter fate of the author's life still resonates, are all the more surprising in this context.

[3:334] *The Book about Goethe's Succession*. Berlin, 1911.

The author is Eugen Guglia.—The work is a latecomer of the "rays of light" or "harmonies" type as they were compiled from the classics during the Biedermeier period.

Goethe Antagonism

Goethe as Human Being and Writer. Edited from the English and annotated by Friedrich Glover. Braunschweig, 1823.

> The book was published anonymously. The specification "from the English" is fictitious. The author is C. H. G. Köchy. In its first part, the work contains inter alia the apocryphal dissertation about fleas. The second part contains thirty-eight sections of anecdotes from Goethe's life, permeated by sneering and obscene allusions. The motto is characteristic: "Nasty human being, how you frighten me."

Faust: The Third Part of the Tragedy in Three Acts. In faithfulness to the spirit of the Second Part of the Goethean *Faust*, composed by Interpretobal Symbolizetti Allegoriovic Mystifizinsky. Tübingen, 1862.

> The author, Friedrich Theodor Vischer, here executes in the form of parody the verdict against *Faust* that he had pronounced in theoretical form in his *Critical Remark on the First Part of Goethe's "Faust," That Is, the "Prologue in Heaven."* By Fr. Vischer. Zurich, 1857. He closes with the Chorus Mysticus: "The most tasteless / Here is tasted / The very trickiest / Here was aimed for / The unforgivable / Here may be forgiven / The eternally boring / Carries us along."[7]

Goethe and No End in Sight. Inaugural speech upon assuming the rectorate of the Royal Friedrich Wilhelm University on October 15, 1892, given by Emil Du Bois-Reymond, Berlin.

> Reaction of the mechanistic-materialist school against the attempt by von Helmholtz to bring to bear Goethe's scientific point of view during the general assembly of the Goethe Gesellschaft in Weimar 1892.[8] "Goethe would have turned away with a shudder from Darwinism . . . from the emergence of the human being [3:335] out of chaos, out of the eternity-to-eternity mathematically determined play of atoms, and from the icy end of the world—from these images that our generation contemplates so unfeelingly, just as it got used to the horrors of taking the train— from all these he would have turned away."

Goethe. By P. J. Möbius. 2 vols. Leipzig, 1903.

> Applies the stencil "genius and madness" to Goethe, with the author not being discriminating when it comes to the choice of examples. The book receives its peculiar accent from Möbius's declared belief in the methods of Gall.[9]

From the Camp of Goethe's Opponents. With an appendix. Unpublished letters to Börne. By Dr. Michael Holzmann. Berlin, 1904.

> The most important source work for knowing the attacks directed against Goethe. Contains notes on, and excerpts from, Spaun, Spann, Pustkuchen, Grabbe, Müllner, Glover, Schütz, Menzel, Hengstenberg, Knapp, Görres, Börne. Compare Julian Hirsch, *The Genesis of Fame*, and the content-rich but unserious book, *The Untalented Goethe: Anti-Goethe Criticism in the Goethezeit.* Vienna, n.d.

Occult Books

Faust's Bequest: The World of Spirits, Souls, and Bodies. Popular Promotion of General Culture, Love of Humanity, and Tolerance. Karlsruhe, 1892.

> Mystic-theurgist compendium in the style of Blavatsky. The author is Friedrich Behrends, whose picture is placed opposite the title: a dignified gentleman with a full beard in a velvet jacket, a bowler hat on his head, sitting on a plush armchair in front of a southern landscape.

Goethe's Bequest. Else Frucht. 2 vols. Munich and Leipzig.

> Following the cabbalistic interpretation of *Faust* by Ferdinand August Louvier, the author attempts to prove that the key to this Goethean work was buried in his garden by the Ilm, where the garden house constitutes the temple under which the key is supposed to be located. [3:336] The author discovers allusions to this factual situation in countless passages of the second volume of *Faust*.

Theodor Hammacher, *Of the Mysteries: Fantasies, Songs, and Sayings, with Prophecies of Bakis, the Witch's One-Times-One, and the Golden Wedding of Oberon.*

> The popular taste for secrets has here interwoven Goethe's lines with little verses of its own provenance. The pastime of a dilettante who, as he says, "in the presence of and associating with the gods, dared to taste the nectar from their table."

Curiosities

Novel of a Poet's Life. First through third section. Goethe's youth. Goethe's adulthood. Goethe's old age. By K. Zianitzka.[10] 3 vols. Leipzig, 1863.

> The first of the novels about Goethe, later followed by others, such as Klara Hofer's *Spring of a German: The Story of the Young Goethe*, Leipzig, or Albert Trentini's *Goethe, the Novel of His Awakening*, Munich, 1926.

"Goethe as Firefighter." In *For the Fire Brigades of Ludwig Jung, Chairman of the Bavarian State Committee on Firefighting,* no. 6. Munich and Leipzig, 1886.

> Goethe's participation in the firefighting operations on the occasion of a Weimar fire, based on official documents.

Goethe Memorial Book: Florilegium from the Works of the Poet by Arthur v. Wyl, containing blank pages for the recording of favorite passages chosen by oneself or a friend. Nuremberg, n.d.

> Around 1900. Unleashes all the horrors of the poetry album and intensifies them with the help of illustrations of Goethe's poetry as well as color-picture postcards. Among the illustrators: Wold, Friedrich, W. v. Kaulbach, and others.

Quid boni periculosive habeat Goethianus liber qui affinizitates electivae inscribitur proponebat Henricus Schoen. Lutetiae Parisiorum, MDCCCII.[11]

> Moral-philosophical treatise, essentially a compilation [3:337] of the various judgments about *Elective Affinities* found in the secondary literature. With a chapter on the French translation of the work: "Goethiis et Interpretum decend genus."

Goethe Sermons. By Julius Burggraf, formerly first pastor at St. Ansgari in Bremen. Ed. and pub. by Carl Rösener, Pastor at St. Andreas in Erfurt. Gießen, 1913.

> Here the culture-philistine's shapeless ideal of Goethe marries the pulpit's eloquence sunk to its lowest level. "Come hither, then, you two most forceful Goethean figures, Faust and Mephistopheles, followed upon by Iphigenia and Orestes! The spirit of your poet has a right to our pulpit!"

"Biogenetic Analysis of 'Faust.'" In Adrien Turel, *The Rebirth of Power from Capacity.* Munich, 1921.

> Interpretations of *Faust* produced by a "working group on biogenetic psychology," based on a Freudian foundation and in the form of the feuilleton.

Intermezzi Scandalosi from Goethe's Life. Berlin, 1925. (Private printing.)

> Contains Goethe's petitions to the local authorities and police pertaining to his domestic staff. The problematic circumstances under consideration here are further illuminated by Anton Kippenberg's *Stadelmann's Happiness and End,* private printing by the Stadelmann Gesellschaft. Stadelmann was one of Goethe's servants.

The Popular Goethe Image

Goethe's Life and Writings. By G. H. Lewes. Translated by Dr. Julius Frese. 2 vols. Berlin, 1857.

> The first wide-ranging biography of Goethe, which at the time responded in fact to a real need, since the author could rightfully say: "Books on Goethe are countless, but there is not a single one among them that would give the desired insight into the outer circumstances in which Goethe moved." Plain, without any understanding of Goethe's late poetry.

[3:338] *Lessing, Schiller, Goethe, Jean Paul: Four Commemorative Speeches on German Poets.* By Moritz Carrière. Gießen, 1862.

> Fixes the stencil according to which Goethe's life became a component of culture [*Bildung*], just as the *Collected Works* became a component of the bookcase and Stieler's portrait of the parlor.

Goethe: His Life and Works. By Alexander Baumgartner, SJ. 3 vols. 2nd enlarged and improved ed. Freiburg im Breisgau, 1885–86.

> In coarse language that is not weighed down by any euphemisms at all, the author takes issue with what from the standpoint of his denomination and his [ecclesiastical] order appears as Goethe's sensual paganism. Additionally, a compendium of Weimar gossip from Goethe's time.

Goethe: His Life and Works. By Dr. Albert Bielschowski. 2 vols. Munich, 1896.

> "It is . . . the mild, tastefully sublimated psychologism of this point of view that sympathetically accommodated the zeitgeist of 1895 and still of 1910—this is what earned this book its great success," writes Rudolf Unger in his "Transformations of the Goethe Image in Literature over the Last Hundred Years."[12]

Goethe: The Man and the Work. By Eduard Engel. With thirty-two portraits, eight illustrations, and twelve manuscripts. 2nd ed. Berlin, 1912.

> Marks the low point of popular Goethe literature. Here is that type of "independence" in judgment that best distinguishes the philistine.

Goethe: History of a Human Being. By Emil Ludwig. Edition for the people in one volume. Stuttgart and Berlin, 1924.

> As is known, this work satisfied the needs of the broadest audience. It allowed the reader to find, if not his way in Goethe's work, then surely at least a small Goethe in himself.[13] [3:339]

The Philosophical Goethe Image

Goethe and His Works. By Carl Rosenkranz. 2nd improved and enlarged ed. Königsberg, 1856.

> Rosenkranz was the first to set himself the task of drawing up an overall spiritual image of Goethe. His book consists of retrospective transcriptions of improvised lectures, and though it is based on the guiding principles of Hegelian philosophy, it is lively and impulsive. Superior to the mass of successors simply on the basis of the following principle: "Never separate the assessment of the form from the development of the content." And in this way the contents not only of Goethe's poetry but also of contemporaneous historiography (Niebuhr's), philosophy of religion (Strauß's), and journalism (Gutzkow's) flow into his work.

Hermann Grimm, *Goethe Lectures at the Royal University.* 2 vols. Berlin, 1877.

> After Rosenkranz, the first general presentation of significance, lingering for the most part on the highpoints of Goethean creation. Grimm employs a language rich in imagery that is at once precise and original. As the last of the Goethe works, it still participates in a lively tradition. It was Grimm in whom an old Marianne von Willemer first confided the secret of her coauthorship of the *Divan*.

Houston Stewart Chamberlain, *Goethe.* Munich, 1912.

> The most remarkable among the presentations that deal with Goethe as a model. In Goethe, "the nature common to us all deliberately ascends to a higher rung and lays there lasting foundations; here we all can and should build, so that we may come to stand higher."[14]

Goethe. By Georg Simmel. Leipzig, 1913.

> The most enthralling and, for the thinker, most stimulating presentation that Goethe has ever found. If Franz Mehring was the first to gather the sociological material for a future presentation of Goethe, then one finds the most valuable indications of the latter's dialectical structure in Simmel.

[3:340] Max Kommerell, *The Poet as Führer in German Classicism.* Berlin, 1928.

> One of the most original and most daring presentations of Goethe's person, with special consideration of his relationships of friendship and antagonism with his contemporaries. Sketches, in the sense of Stefan George, an image of the Weimar court of the muses lacking women altogether.[15]

Franz Mehring, *Concerning Literary History from Calderon to Heine*. Published by Eduard Fuchs. With an introduction by August Thalheimer. Berlin, 1929.

> Contains the first attempts at a presentation of Goethe from the standpoint of historical materialism with a wealth of valuable reflections on the societal structure of the German bourgeoisie at that time. Walter Benjamin has continued Mehring's attempts in differing fashion in his contribution "Goethe" to the *Great Soviet Encyclopedia*.[16]

26

FAUST IN THE SAMPLE CASE

[3:340] There exists a kind of sanctimoniousness in the Goethe cult that is not driven by those who produce something but by real philistines, vulgar laity. Every conversation is dominated by the consecrated name, every new publication about Goethe is applauded—yet he himself is no longer read, which is why his works are no longer known, and knowledge about him no longer advances. This affair partly melts into sheer stupidity; partly it serves like religious sanctimoniousness as a cover in which all kinds of humanness are hidden, so that it not be noticed. The great universality of the name precisely serves all of this.

—Gottfried Keller in the year 1884[1]

Nothing can be so tasteless and impudent that someone instructed in history cannot connect it with a phenomenon that in its time represents something upstanding and honest. In Goethe's youth, the "beautiful sciences" dominated the [3:341] professorial lectern. What now stands before our eyes as clear and distinct—moral philosophy, aesthetics, sociology, history of literature—could all at that time come under discussion in the very same lecture. If this seems antiquated and superficial, it was then probably a prerequisite for an impartial confrontation with the thoughts that were dominant in England and Holland through the works of Shaftesbury and Hemsterhuis. If one finds the resonance of this intellectual movement in [*The Sorrows of Young*] *Werther*, it was in any case concluded for Goethe with this work. And the older he became, the more clearly Goethe showed not only the most decisive aversion to the cult of bel esprit but also a mode of production that removed his works once and for all from every sentimental point of view, especially a rhetorical one. The later works in which Goethe deliberately inserted into the course of his fantasy certain barriers and dams made from the hardest of realia—such as the *West-Eastern Divan*, *Wilhelm Meister's Journeyman Years*, and *Faust, Part Two*—thus add such great difficulties to the traditional eclectic mode of view, which was directed toward enjoyment instead of productive appropriation, that the first twenty-five years of Goethe literature left them by the wayside. And this is not the only instructive fact that would have been gained by examining earlier Goethe literature, most especially *Faust* literature. The reader of Eugen Kühnemann's new *Faust* commentary[*] is thus confronted with the first curiosity of this, in every sense monstrous book, not least its length: with more than a thousand pages, this book has not a single discussion of the results of *Faust* research—no references in its index to Fischer, to Witkowski or Burdach. This, in fact, is how things get simplified. Accordingly, it actually says so: "Part Two [of *Faust*], which is divided in the clearest way into five acts and is thus closer to a regular play than Part One, presents itself from the outset far more like the work of a continuous thought and plan carried out in the clearest consciousness, in comparison to the Part One. Each of the five acts is a small world unto itself; but they all still [3:342] belong together as a true planetary system with a single sun. The sun is the poetic thought of Faust."

In 1919, a slender volume was published. Kühnemann could easily have seen it, since it was written by one of his close colleagues, a professor of classical philology at the University of Breslau, Konrat Ziegler. In the book entitled *Thoughts on Faust, Part Two*,[†] the author maps out the fragile and arbitrary composition of this drama—how Goethe repeatedly deviated from the underlying plan under the influence of heterogeneous moods and business matters and how little the traditional assessment of this book could be maintained. The author, as previously mentioned, is a philologist, and he "who thinks according to a philological method," as Kühnemann condescendingly puts it, "remains a philologist, even if he treats subjects that are conventionally considered as philosophy." It is therefore doubtful that Kühnemann

---

[*] Eugen Kühnemann, *Goethe*. Zwei Bände. Leipzig: Insel-Verlag, 1930.

[†] *Gedanken über Faust II*. Von Konrat Ziegler. Stuttgart: J. B. Metzleresche Verlagsbuchhandlung, 1919.

would declare his colleague worthy of those "professorial chairs of German spirit" that are "invested by full-fledged philosophers who are not only men of reliable artistic understanding but also artistic figures in their own right," for the author of this awkward, skeptical work can claim nothing for himself beyond the fact that he read through *Faust, Part Two* very attentively and thoughtfully. Be that as it may, Ziegler has drawn attention to a number of things that only promote insight into the greatness of the poetry. We follow him all the more gladly as he shows us the way to grasp the predominance of Kühnemann's speech battalions with their chattering regiments and false columns, with fluttering phrases at their heads and brass bands at the tip of their back.

One of Ziegler's main concerns is related to the preparation of the Helen act.[2] Based on the drafts, he demonstrates the amount of time Goethe entertained the idea of having Faust "in the hollow foot of Olympus" ask Persephone to release Helen from the dead and how in the end, giving up, he abandoned the attempt to give shape to this plan, thus exposing his work to the greatest dramaturgical inconsistency.[3] This Zieglerian problem is the pivotal point [3:343] of the most recent Faust research itself. If the highly significant work,[*] which we are about to discuss, was published later than Kühnemann's concoction, this fact says very little, for its author, Gottfried Wilhelm Hertz, only picked up the thread—with rare luck, admittedly—where others left off. In a nutshell, where Kühnemann sees "the work of a continuous thought and plan carried out in the clearest consciousness," there stands a prodigious struggle within late Goethe.[4] And just as in the way of a proper philologist (even though Kühnemann, like G. W. Hertz, holds office at the Supreme Fiscal Court), he develops the most breathtaking occurrence from two verses:

> In your name, Mothers, who, your throne
> In boundlessness, eternally dwell alone
> And yet together! Around your head
> Images of life actively hover, yet without life.
> What once was, in all luster and shine,
> Still stirs here, for it wants to be eternal.

---

[*]   *Nature and Spirit in Goethe's Faust.* By Gottfried Wilhelm Hertz, 1931. Verlag Moritz Diesterweg. Frankfurt am Main.

> And you distribute it, almighty powers,
>
> To the tent of the day, to the vault of the nights.
>
> The sweet course of life grasps some,
>
> The bold magician seeks out the others.[5]

The last two lines, which are decisive, had a variant that reads:

> The sweet course of life grasps some,
>
> The poet confidently seeks out the others.[6]

What lies between these two versions is not only a part of the Faust poem's fate but also a portion of the history of Faust research. The spiritualist interpretation of the poem, as represented by Kuno Fisher and Witkowski, was also unable to measure the relation of tension that exists here. Needed for this is the most intimate connection of *Faust* to Goethe's natural-scientific studies. Goethe belongs to the family of great minds for whom there is in principle no art in the isolated sense; for him, the doctrine of the urphenomena of nature—like, for Dante, the philosophy of [3:344] scholasticism and, for Dürer, the theory of perspectivism—was at the same time the true theory of art.[7] What, in Goethe, comes into conflict with these two verses was the aesthetic-spiritualist semblance-essence of Helen. On the one hand, there is her real being, on the other hand, her appearance—thus she stood, in Goethe's mind, for a long time in discord. Her real being triumphed. While she was originally supposed to be "received alive in the house of Menelaus," she appears henceforth, as Goethe himself writes, "truly alive" or as the "true." Petitioning the underworld for her release could not now, however, procure for her such a life. What took its place—like the incorporation of the homunculus into the living ocean and thus into the ocean of the living—"modeled the natural process by which a spirit acquires a human body," so that spectators now had to say to themselves "that they no longer, as formerly in the imperial court, had the unreal specter of the Greek queen before their eyes but had, instead, the queen herself in her full ancient reality," as one may glean from Hertz. And one will unconditionally agree with Hertz when he explains why Goethe did not therefore want the life of Helen in Act III to be indebted to either the magician or the poet. "In the interim, between the original conception of the motif in the winter of 1827/28 and the new beginning of the work in the late summer of 1829, the poet of *Faust* was again enthralled by his old penchant for natural philosophy, and so he could no longer be content with the aesthetic image; precisely then, he consciously held himself to the region where metaphysics and natural history overlap, therefore where the serious, faithful researcher loves to linger." Lingering, however, is no less the attitude of the real philologist, who, as Goethe said apropos of the natural scientist, "makes himself intensely identical" to phenomena.[8] And what an astonishing find nestles into the hands of the philologist in this way; as a final example, here is the interpretation that Hertz finds for the famous verses of the Mothers, in which he addresses them as urphenomena:

> Some sitting, others stand and walk,
> Howsoever it goes. Forming, transforming,
> Eternal entertainment of the eternal mind.[9]

[3:345] "The setting of the stone, the mobility of the animal kingdom, the upward striving of the plant world that is bound to the soil"—in this way "the inhabitants of the Mothers' world are here divided into three large groups—in conspicuous agreement with the objects of the three kingdoms of nature: the kingdom of mobility, belonging to the animal capable of changing its place; the kingdom of the plants, clinging to its place, to be sure, but standing upright on the surface of the ground; the kingdom of the stones, whose existence or place language prefers to designate as its seat."

Now, however, as announced, in order to catch our bragging chatterbox from behind, one need only resolve to let him speak. What does he know about the Mothers? "In the shaping, self-transforming change of the formations, the eternal meaning of truth always fulfills itself as the same . . . toward the Mothers." So it is said of Faust, "he must penetrate—the essential roots of Being, the eternal meaning-giving forces and forms of ultimate truth, whose appearances are the objects of reality. He who grasps the deepest may conjure beauty anew in its purest appearance as the highest figure of these entities, Greek beauty in its highest form." Instead of going back to clarify the confusion of these last sentences in their purest appearance, we move forward to the interpretation of Helen, listening to "what Goethe has done with his Helen tragedy": "He grasps antiquity in the Germanic soul, that is, in the shape of the Germanic soul, which became possible only through the culture of Christianity, and which seeks the deepest and final point of the soul. . . . Nature and the spirit of human life have come together and become perfect beauty. The task of form arises here for the artist in its highest sense: the spiritual sense of human life enters from its ultimate depth. The spirit of the Helen poem is thus designated in the most precise way."

Reading this gives one the courage to dare to designate the spirit of this interpretation in the most precise way: it consists in the innermost conviction that the differences between Goethe and Kühnemann are of no consequence. This is because the basis for the human sciences that the [3:346] author claims to have established is so very broad: "The highest would be attained if such a book constituted within itself a proficient piece of life, even if one would otherwise know nothing about who Herder, Kant, Schiller, Goethe were." We, however, know something about this life. We also want to reveal it. For years, Kühnemann visited universities around the world as a visiting professor. At the end of his preface, one learns a few names: New York, Los Angeles, St. Louis, Riga. Now that he is back from his grand tour, we get to know (through the mediation of the publisher, which produced the best editions of Goethe's works in Germany)[10] the suitcase from which the author, while abroad, presented samples of Herder, Kant, Schiller, and Goethe. Every merchant entertains the dream of a monopoly. It is self-evident that Kühnemann calmly envisages such an order of things, since his books make superfluous any knowledge of "who Herder, Kant, Schiller, and Goethe were." The German soldier, it was said, carried his *Faust* in his backpack. The traveler has stripped it from him. Kühnemann is familiar with the international market. Let us hope that the priceless realia that form the publisher's collection of Goethe do not end up where the author offered German idealism for sale.

27

BOOKS ON GOETHE—BUT WELCOME ONES

[3:352] Every word not spent on speaking about Goethe this year is a blessing, and so nothing is more welcome than laconic anniversary books. Two of this kind, unequal in worth but both praiseworthy, will be introduced here. They are written by Goethe specialists. Both, however, have justified this not always commendable origin through a spirited conception and a conscientious execution. One of them thus reaches far beyond specialization [3:353] and attains the breadth of popularity, while the other reaches through compact facticity and attains philosophical depth. We speak of *Goethe, a Picture Book* by Rudolf Payer-Thurn (Leipzig: G. Schulz) and *Chronicle of Goethe's Life* by Flodoard von Biedermann (Leipzig: Insel-Verlag). Both books further share meticulousness combined with a lack of grounding principles. This is a productive combination. Just as the chronicle, perspicuously rubricated through the individual dates of the years, comprehends the most varied facts about epochal encounters or works—and does so down to the most far-fetched curiosities—so the picture book has also variously emancipated itself from the portrait and the picturesque so as to include manuscripts, books read or written by Goethe, sketches from Italy and Germany, illustrations of his works, the obituary of his granddaughter, the commemorative print with which he expressed his appreciation for the congratulations he received on the fiftieth anniversary of his service, even his travel carriage. While, among these images, many will be familiar to those who are knowledgeable, the pretty, colorful plates enclosed in the volume still have the merit of guiding uninformed readers, and since an orderly apparatus explains the plates, they are able to acquire far more pleasant and more solid instruction from this work than from the clichéd literary histories produced for the German home. To return, however, to Biedermann's *Chronicle*: no one in the world can be so knowledgeable that there could be no profit in returning to this book again and again. On the contrary, the more readers know of Goethe, the deeper this compilation, which exclusively keeps to names and dates, will move their fantasy. Until now, something comparable has perhaps existed only in the edition of Goethe's poems that H. G. Gräf prepared in chronological order.[1] Readers for whom one or another episode in Goethe's life became pictorial through the mere configuration of verses that therein emerged—one need think only of the prodigious sequence through which the poem dedicated "To the Full Moon Rising" arose in Dornburg after the death of Karl August or the lines from the *Divan*, "No Longer on a Page of Silk"[2]—such readers are well prepared to study this chronicle.

28

NEW LITERATURE ABOUT GOETHE

By Detlev Holz[1]

[3:418] Joseph A. von Bradish, *Goethe's Elevation to the Nobility of the Empire and the Baronial Nobility of His Grandsons*. Leipzig, 1933. Alfred Lorentz Publisher (Publications of the Association of German Writers and Friends of Literature in New York, vol. 1).

This publication provides an unusually valuable collection of documents. While it is published as a postscript to the Goethe anniversary year, its significance elevates it decisively above the great mass of anniversary publications. It comprises two cycles of documents, each opened by a short, pertinent introduction. The first consists of the dossier that issues into Goethe's elevation to the nobility by Joseph II, German emperor; the second, the documents concerning the elevation of his grandsons seventy-eight years later to the rank of Baron in Saxe-Weimar as well as the later documents that secured Wolfgang von Goethe the recognition of this rank in Prussia. Whereas the documents of the first collection remain within the frame of a year, the ones of the second stretch over five. Saying which of the two is more revealing would prove an embarrassment. The first still breathes the air of the Holy Roman Empire of the German Nation in its attitude and language; the business concluded between Vienna and Weimar has a completely different face than the cautious negotiations whose scene remained restricted to the Grand Duchy of Saxe-Weimar. And it is further telling how eagerly engaged the grandson conducts himself and how extraordinarily measured Goethe, by contrast, follows from afar the process that concerns him. There are not many episodes in Goethe's life that could give the observer a higher sense of Goethe's art of living and his prudence or a more dignified sense of the difficult circumstances that marked his entrance into Weimar. While it was not the intention of the author to contribute to Goethe's social physiognomy, it nevertheless comes to light in the excerpts that introduce the document collection. And the brighter this light, the more enigmatic this physiognomy. The physiognomy of his grandsons, by contrast, is less enigmatic. Their five-year-long battle for the "recognition" [3:419] of the alleged Goethean baronial title has a tragicomic tinge. The two brothers remained the last ones of the lineage whose hereditary dignity they had endeavored to raise above that of the poet.

Georg Keferstein, *Bürgertum and Bourgeois Character in Goethe*. Weimar, 1933. Publishing House of Hermann Böhlau's Successors.

The title of this work promises much; the work itself delivers little.[2] One may hold its unfortunate point of departure responsible for this. It consists in the opposition between the life of the artist and bourgeois existence, an opposition for which the author—he is not silent about this—owes a debt to Thomas Mann's works and essays. Now Mann has in fact—especially in his study *Goethe and Tolstoy*—occasionally resorted to such categories, but not without the deployment of his entire cautiousness as a writer. All of Mann's novels deal with the appearance of the artist as an interesting yet, from the perspective of society, worrisome variant of the bourgeois type, whose confrontation with other variants of the same type presents, so to speak, an altercation within the bourgeoisie. It goes without saying that Goethe's historical position elevates him high above such a quarrel. Even without any further investigation into this position, the following may be ascertained: Goethe's shape—in its bourgeois as well as its nonbourgeois traits—can appear only with respect to the historical circumstances that surrounded the living man in a life-sized way. The altercation between feudality and bourgeoisie whose fiery glow fell on Germany from the West is pivotal for the determination of Goethe's social significance. The author, who seeks to project Goethe's giant realm onto the grid of common sense, does not promote this significance. A vulgar psychology of the bourgeois, unclouded by any historical reflection, is the foundation of his thoughts. Unclear oppositions—for instance, between "philistine" and "capitalist bourgeois"—alternate with half-truths, such as: "Drama always goes for the extraordinary"; "The craftsman embodies the

[3:420] essence of the bourgeois in its purest form"; "Classicism's rigorous form-bestowal" stands "closer to the bourgeoisie . . . than formless Romanticism." That the bourgeoisie in question consisted of scholars and cattle traders, lawyers and court tutors, pastors and factory owners, public servants and craftsmen, farmers and merchants; that at the turn of the [eighteenth] century it knew trends and crises of the most varied nature; that Goethe pondered them all in manifold ways—[Keferstein's] writing imparts little or nothing about all of this. Psychological and social categories as well as normative and historical categories become confused, such that the tensile force requisite for cognition is slain. The root of the evil may admittedly lie deeper: in an apologetic intention, to whose purposes—honorable as they may be—one reluctantly sees the shape of the poet made subservient.[3]

29

POPULARITY AS A PROBLEM
On Hermann Schneider, *Schiller's Work and Legacy*

[3:450] In order scientifically to approach "the widest possible circles of readers"—as Hermann Schneider's *Schiller* intends to do—more is needed than knowledge.[1] The great popularizers of modern physics teach us best about this. They bring the reader into the game and give him the certainty that he is being propelled forward. This certainty need not in any way attach to the material—no reader will have any practical use for the theory of relativity.[2] But something else benefits him: with knowledge he comes to adopt a thinking that is not just new to him. For once in his life, even for a short time, he takes up the standpoint on which the avant-garde [3:451] of today's science stands. That's what is decisive.

One can say that all labor in service of popularization that is unable to produce such a feeling of the laity with the vanguard is lost labor. It is precisely today that physics has the most brilliant popularizers—like Eddington—because it finds itself in a revolution, and the slogans of the avant-garde are being heard throughout its entire field.[3] On the other hand, this means that not every object of knowledge can be popularized at all times. It is not factual difficulty but, rather, the absence of a historical constellation that forms the real obstacle. About that, of course, even anniversaries can change nothing.

Hermann Schneider, who, in his solid and readable studies *From Wallenstein to Demetrius*, published in 1933 (see the literary section of the *Frankfurter Zeitung*, 29 July 1934),[4] admitted that he received the impetus for his investigations from the peculiar "feeling of alienation" that affects today's reader before Schiller, and this time, on the occasion of Schiller's 175th birthday, intends to lay down "the fundamentally thin partition of this feeling" (Stuttgart and Berlin: J. G. Cotta Publishing House, 1934). He thereby does not want to make it easy for himself. "For five quarter centuries we have been bored by ceremonial speakers, schoolmasters, and family booklets with the perfect, sky-blue, pale Schiller," he opines. But this summary judgment demonstrates with a certain recklessness—which is undoubtedly a condition of popular presentation—that the productive and interesting thing about the Schiller-problem can at the moment be made present only with difficulty. The one hundred and twenty-five years in question was precisely the era that would require special attention in a Schiller-discussion today: therein falls the great Schiller anniversary of 1859, in which the features of the Schiller image were for the first time detached from the background of courtly Weimar and set into the light of German bourgeois life. At that time, Schiller was more popular than ever: the avant-garde of the bourgeoisie had taken its slogans from him, and that was precisely why bourgeois science was able to present him to a broad audience.

If the author glosses over [3:452] this era, underestimating it, if he leaves aside the history of Schiller's fame, which, according to the interesting hints in Julian Hirsch's *Genesis of Fame*, still remains a desideratum of science, this is certainly understandable, for, if he had not done so, the immediacy of his text would have been jeopardized.[5] It's only that, unfortunately, this leads nowhere. And that is particularly palpable where the work is on its firmest ground— for example, in the chapter on Schiller's dramatic style. The external imperative to arrive at popular statements about a "Schiller-style" is, of course, not the appropriate way to gain insight into the theatrical history of Schiller's individual dramas, which the author knows intimately.

Thus, in conclusion, the wish is not to be entirely dismissed that the press had published the text about Schiller and Cotta for its own anniversary celebration, which coincided with Schiller's anniversary, for an, albeit more limited, circle of readers.[6] One would hope that the publishing house makes up for this.

DETLEV HOLZ

30

LETTERS ABOUT, TO, AND FROM GOETHE

[4:954] In this section [of the *Frankfurter Zeitung*], we intend to publish in what follows a series of letters of significant Germans, letters that, without claiming a historical or thematic connection with one another, nevertheless have *one thing* in common. They bring to mind an attitude that is designated as humanistic in a German sense and that seems all the more appropriate to reinvoke at this moment, [4:955] the more one-sidedly those who, often with seriousness and complete consciousness of their responsibility, when referencing works of art and literature, call German humanism into question. Announced in these letters is that force, that expression in the shaping of *private* life, which this epoch of German humanism made its own. The following letter is, as it were, the first stroke of the bell that would ring out this epoch. With it, Zelter responds to the news of Goethe's death that had been given to him by Chancellor von Müller.

[4:152]   **Karl Friedrich Zelter to Chancellor von Müller**

Berlin, 31 March 1832

Only today, most honored Sir, can I thank you for the friendliest sympathy, whatever this time the occasion may be.

What was to be expected, to be feared, has indeed necessarily come to pass. The hour has struck. The sage stands still, as the sun did for Gideon, for lo and behold, the man lies stretched out on his back, the one who strode the universe on pillars of Heracles, while below him the powers of the earth agitated for the dust around their feet.

What can I say of myself? What can I say to you? To all of you there? And everywhere?—As he passed on, going away from me, so I now move closer to him day by day, and will catch up with him, so as to eternalize the lovely peace that for so many years brightened and animated the space of thirty-six miles between us.

I now have one request: do not cease to honor me with your friendly communications. You will fathom what I should know, since the relationship that never suffered a disturbance, one between two intimate acquaintances, in essence always united, even if, in terms of content, they were far from each other—this you know. I am like a widow who lost her husband, her lord and provider! And yet I am not allowed to mourn; I am supposed to be astonished at the wealth he brought to me. Such treasure is for me to preserve and to make the interest into my capital.

Forgive me, noble friend! I should not lament, and yet my old eyes do not want to obey and hold themselves dry. Once, though, I saw him cry; that must justify me.

Zelter

[...]

[4:202] Before crossing his threshold after arriving in Weimar, the seventy-five-year-old Zelter sent the following letter to the seventy-eight-year-old Goethe. It has often been remarked that in our literature splendor and glory cling to the young, to those first starting out, and most of all, to those who are precocious.[1] Every new engagement with Lessing reaffirms how seldom in this literature there is an appearance of the manly. Here is a friendship that bursts out of the familiar space of the German cultural world, a friendship in which two old men, with an almost Chinese consciousness of the dignity of old age and its desirability, spend the waning days of their lives with each other, making the astonishing toasts we possess in Goethe's correspondence with Zelter, the most perfect of which may be the following:

Karl Friedrich Zelter to Goethe

You are so agreeably at home in the womb of nature, and I hear you speak so fondly of the primal forces that work through the universe, unseen by generations of humanity, that I have the presentiment of something similar; indeed, I mean to understand you at the deepest level, and nevertheless am too old and too far behind to begin a study of nature.

Whenever I now go on a lonely trip over summits and mountaintops, through gorges and valleys, for me, your words turn into thoughts that I would like to call *mine*. This, though, fails at every locale, and only my own small talent can save me from sinking.

Since, after all, we're now together as we are, I would think—for I so gladly understand you—that you would deign to lay my cornerstone so as to fortify my innermost longing: how nature and art, spirit and body are everywhere connected, but their separation—this is death.

So, by having traversed, like a winding thread, the Thuringian mountain range from Coburg to here, I painfully thought again of Werther: I cannot everywhere feel or see with the fingers of thoughts what's under and what's nearest to me; but what so naturally appears to me as a body and a soul are One Being.

[4:203] To be sure, our long-term correspondence has not been lacking in material; you have so sincerely taken part in my fragmentary knowledge of musical things, where we, like the rest, still always muddle about—who, then, should have been able to tell us?[2]

But still, in front of others, I would not at all like to appear too beggarly with regard to others. Call it pride—this pride would be my pleasure. Ever since my youth I've felt myself drawn, even compelled toward those who know more, those who know the best, and courageously, indeed merrily I fought and bore whatever displeased me about them—I certainly knew what I wanted, even if I did not know what I experienced. You were the only one who sustained and sustains me; I could let go of myself, but not let go of you.

Tell me when I should visit you. I expect our professor, but I don't know when he can come.

Weimar, Thursday, 16 October 1827
[. . .]

[4:209] Little is to be said in advance about this letter from Goethe; a short commentary will follow it. In fact, philological interpretation seems the humblest way to proceed in relation to so great a document, especially when there is nothing in brief that can be added to what Gervinus said about the general character of Goethe's last letters in his text *On Goethe's Correspondence*.[3] On the other hand, the data for the outward comprehension of these lines

LETTERS ABOUT, TO, AND FROM GOETHE 243

are fully at hand. Thomas Seebeck, the discoverer of entoptic colors, died on December 10, 1831. Entoptic colors are color images that become visible through a certain moderate light stimulus in translucent bodies. Goethe saw in them a principal experimental proof of his theory of color in its opposition to Newton's; he therefore took the strongest interest in their discovery, and from 1802 to 1810 he had a close relationship with their Jena-based author. When Seebeck later worked in Berlin and became a member of the [Royal-Prussian] Academy of the Sciences, this relationship with Goethe slackened. Goethe became suspicious of Seebeck for not consistently promoting the *Theory of Colors* from such a visible position. So much for the presuppositions of the following piece of writing. It represents the response to a letter in which Moritz Seebeck, the son of the researcher, while giving Goethe the news of his father's passing, assured him of the admiration that the deceased man felt for him to the very end, an admiration that "had a firmer ground than a merely personal inclination."

Goethe to Moritz Seebeck

3 January 1832

To your very valuable writing, my dearest one, I must most truly reply: that the untimely parting of your excellent father be a great personal loss for me. I think all too gladly of the valiant men who, in full activity, are concurrently striving to increase knowledge and expand insights. When once a silence slips between friends who have grown distant, thereupon resulting in a muting and thereby generating a rift baselessly and needlessly, so we must [4:210] unfortunately discover therein a kind of helplessness that can stand out in benevolent, good characters and that, like other errors, we ought to overcome and seek to set aside in a conscious manner. In my eventful and compendious life I have often been guilty of such neglect and in the present case do not want to reject from myself altogether the reproach against me.[4] This much, though, can I say for certain: for the one who departed too early, I never once lacked inclination as a friend, nor sympathy and admiration as a researcher; indeed, I often thought of bringing something important to the inquiry through which then all the evil spirits would have been scared off at once. Nevertheless, life, which rushes by, has among its marvels this one, too: that so eager in activity, so desirous for enjoyment, we seldom know how to treasure and keep hold of the specifics of the moment. And so in the most advanced age there remains a duty left over to recognize at least in its peculiarities the human, which never left us, and to calm ourselves through reflection on the lack, the liability for which is not entirely to be averted. Sincerely commending you and your dear family with my best wishes,

J. W. von Goethe[5]

This letter is one of the last that Goethe wrote. Its language, like he himself, stands at a boundary. The Goethean speech of old age expands German in an imperial sense that has not the slightest touch of imperialism. In a little-known yet, for this reason, all the more significant study, *On the Language of Late Goethe*, Ernst Lewy showed how the tranquil, contemplative nature of the poet in advanced old age yields in him certain characteristic grammatical and syntactical constructions. Lewy points out the predominance of compounds, the loss of articles, the emphasis on abstractions, and many other features that, working together, result in giving "every word as much a semantic content as possible"[6] and match the whole structure of subordinating languages like the Turkic family as well as assimilative languages like the Greenlandic family. Without directly adopting this linguistic thought, the following remarks [4:211] seek to elucidate how far off this language lies from the customary one:

"be a great personal loss [*ein großer persönlicher Verlust sei*]"

—The indicative would at the very least be possible here; the subjunctive at this point betrays the fact that the feeling dominating the writer no longer craves on its own a path to writing, to expression; Goethe, as chancellor of his own interiority, announces this feeling.

"in full activity [*in voller Tätigkeit*]"

—The words stand in contrast to: dead; a euphemism that is felt in a truly ancient way.

"a kind of helplessness [*eine Art von Unbehilflichkeit*]"

—The writer chooses for the comportment of old age an expression that would sooner be appropriate for an infant, and he does this so as to be able to posit something physical in place of something spiritual and thereby simplify the offense, though it be done by force.

> "do not [want] to reject from myself altogether [*nicht ganz von mir ablehnen*]"

—Goethe could certainly have written "do not [want] to reject altogether." He writes "do not [want] to reject from myself altogether . . . against me" and thereby offers himself, his very own body, in support of the reproach, according to an inclination that favors abstraction when expressing sensible things, which lets them, for their part, suddenly reverse into a paradoxical visibility when expressing spiritual things.

> "life, which rushes by [*das vorüberrauschende Leben*]"

—In another passage, this life is called troubled and pressed: epithets that make it excessively clear that the writer himself, when in contemplation [*betrachtend*], withdraws to its banks in the spirit, if not in the image, of that other old man's saying with which Walt Whitman differs: "Now I will set myself in front of the door and contemplate life."[7]

> "specifics of the moment [*Einzelheiten des Augenblicks*]"

—"To this moment I would like to say: Linger yet, you are so beautiful."[8] Beauty is the fulfilling moment; but the lingering moment is sublime, like the moment that is scarcely advancing any longer, at the end of life, which these epistolary lines hold on to.

> "the human in its peculiarities [*das Menschliche . . . in seinen Eigenheiten*]"

—Such are the ultimate points toward which the great humanist withdraws as into an asylum: the idiosyncrasies that govern the last periods of life, even these he places under the patronage of humanity. Just as weak plants, the mosses, ultimately break through the stone masonry of an imperturbable, deserted building, so here does feeling penetrate, bursting the joints of an imperturbable posture.

31

MYTHIC ANXIETY IN GOETHE

It is known that the works of Walter Benjamin, the eminent German philologist and critic, have had a profound echo in the academic and literary milieux of the avant-garde, in particular those works on the origins of German drama ("Ursprung des Deutschen Trauerspiels") and on the Notion of Art-Criticism in German Romanticism ("Der Begriff der Kunst-Kritik in der Deutschen Romantik"). The following pages are excerpts from a long study of Goethe's Elective Affinities, *published in its entirety in the* Neue Deutsche Beiträge *by Hugo von Hofmannsthal, who saw in this study "an unprecedented penetration into the Goethean mystery" ("ein beispielloses Eindringen ins Geheimnis"). The change of political regime in Germany does not allow for proceeding with the project of a book publication. Walter Benjamin, who has written the article on Goethe in the Great Soviet Encyclopedia, has placed the most rigorous philological methods in the service of a literary investigation that is as far removed from all aesthetic formalism as from all historical positivism. The reader will be able to form an idea of the author's dialectical procedure based on the following fragment.*

Mythic humanity pays with its anxiety for its dealings with daemonic forces.[1] Anxiety has often manifested itself in Goethe's existence as well. Its symptoms, which the biographers have only mentioned in an anecdotal manner and not without a certain repugnance, would have to be brought entirely to light by an examination that would show us with formidable precision the force exerted by archaic authorities in the life of a man who, without them, would perhaps never have become the greatest poet of his people. Anxiety about death includes all other anxieties; it is the most intense one. For it is death that threatens most forcefully the shapeless anarchy of natural life that constitutes the forbidden circle of myth. The poet's aversion to death and to all that evokes death has the character of a supreme superstition. It is known that no one dared to speak of death in his presence. Less known is the fact that he avoided being at his dying wife's bedside. His correspondence reveals the same state of mind at the moment of his son's death. Nothing is more significant than the letter that announces this loss to Zelter in passing and closes with the truly daemonic words: "And thus, beyond the graves, onwards!" And it is in this sense that one should equally understand the words ascribed to the dying poet. In them, mythic life opposes its impotent desire for light to the nearby darkness. Finally, it is into this anxiety that, toward the end of his life, the extraordinary cult of the self sunk its roots. *Poetry and Truth*, the diaries, the publication of the correspondence with Schiller, the care dedicated to the sorting of the correspondence with Zelter: these are all so many efforts to elude death. Even more clearly in everything he says about the afterlife is expressed an apprehension that, instead of concealing within itself the idea of immortality as hope, demands immortality as a guarantee of *future* activity. And just as the idea of immortality in myth appears, according to a recent interpretation, to be nothing but a *not being able to die*, so it is neither, in Goethean thought, the soul's return to its native land but rather a flight—from the Unlimited into the Unlimited. According to the comments that he made the morning after Wieland's death, and reported to us by Falk, he wants a natural immortality and, as if to stress what is inhuman in immortality, he wants to know that it is exclusively reserved for great minds.

No feeling is richer in variations than anxiety. Anxiety about death is joined by anxiety about living, like a keynote is joined by its innumerable overtones. Yet the traditional interpretation neglects and even silences the Baroque play of the anxiety of living. And because this interpretation seeks to find a norm in Goethe, it is rather far from suspecting the struggle of forms of life that occurs in him. Goethe himself has concealed this struggle too deeply. Whence the moments of solitude in his life and his now painful, now haughty silences. In his work on *The Correspondence of Goethe*, Gervinus has shown how this isolation established itself during the first Weimar period. Gervinus was the first to draw attention to these phenomena in Goethe: he was perhaps the only one to sense their importance, no matter how erroneous his manner of judging them may have been. Thus, neither the taciturn folding back onto himself in the last period, nor taking interest in the contents of his own existence, an interest-taking that was eventually pushed to paradox, has escaped him. In these two behaviors one indeed recognizes the anxiety of living; in communing with himself, the anxiety about the immensity and force of life; in the gesture of pulling together his own existence, the anxiety about the flight from life. Gervinus believes he can determine exactly the turning point that separates the production of the late Goethe from that of the first periods; it is, he tells us, the moment when Goethe plans his journey to Italy in 1797. In a letter to Schiller dating from this period, Goethe speaks of objects that, without being "absolutely poetic," awaken in him a certain poetic state. And he says: "So I have attentively considered the objects that produce such an effect, and to my great surprise I noticed their essentially symbolic character." And further on: "If in the future, as the journey progresses, one wanted to direct one's attention less to the particular aspects than to the profound strangeness of things, one would thus bring back a beautiful harvest for oneself as well as for others. I will first try to pick up on the symbolic character of everything that surrounds me here, in anticipation of practicing later in places that I see for the first time. If I could succeed, then there is every chance that without letting myself go adrift in this type of exercise, but deepening it everywhere, in every type, every instance, to the extent that the occasion would offer itself, I would return with rather considerable spoils, even from countries that I already know." "It is allowed to state," Gervinus observes, "that this attitude was constantly present in his later poetic productions; the experiences that he had previously presented in all their concrete complexity, as art demands it, he now measures according to a certain criterion of spiritual profundity, which often leads him to lose himself in the unfathomable. Schiller penetrates with great perspicacity this new experience that is so mysteriously veiled. . . . 'A poetic demand, without poetic disposition nor object,' this appeared to him to be Goethe's case." In fact, the object would matter much less than the fixed intention to deepen its signification. (And nothing is more characteristic of classicism than the effort to seize the symbol and to diminish its objective import by the same token.) According to Schiller, it would be the intention that would mark the limit, and here as elsewhere, the banal and the spiritual would not be in the choice of the subject-matter but only in the manner of treating it. The way such places looked to Goethe, he claims, each street, each bridge, etc., would have seized him in a moment of exaltation. If Schiller could have sensed the uncertain consequences for

Goethe of this new manner of seeing, he would not have encouraged him to abandon himself to it without reserve, since this manner of considering objects ends up giving universal importance to the smallest details. . . . The immediate consequence of all this is in fact that Goethe begins accumulating files and travel journals into which he inserts everything he can collect from newspapers and other periodicals: excerpts from sermons, bulletins, theater bills, ordinances, price lists, etc.; he adds observations, confronts these with public opinion, underlines his personal opinion, takes note of the teaching that emerges from this, thus hoping to obtain materials for future use. This already announces clearly that gravity pushed to ridiculousness with which he will classify his travel notes and consider the most minute thing with an air of the initiated. It is thus that each medal that he receives, each piece of granite that he gives away takes on special importance in his eyes. And when he finds the rock salt that Friedrich the Great, despite all his orders, had been unable to find, he sees in it I know not what kind of miracle and sends a "symbolic" sample of it to his friend Zelter in Berlin. Nothing more characteristic of this state of mind as it developed more and more during the years of old age than the will, so to speak, to make it a principle for himself to assiduously contradict the old adage *nil admirari*, to, on the contrary, admire everything, to judge all things "significant, strange, incommensurable!"

An element of enthusiasm but also and always of anxiety doubtless enters into this conduct, which Gervinus paints in such a measured and magisterial manner. The poet freezes in the chaos of symbols; he loses the freedom of the modern human being and, as a result, approaches the ancients. Taking action, he goes astray in the middle of signs and oracles. There was no shortage of these in Goethe's life. It was such a sign that indicated to him the way to Weimar. Indeed, in *Poetry and Truth*, he recounts how during a walk, while meditating on his future and still hesitating to choose between poetry and painting, he consulted an "oracle." Anxiety about responsibility was without a doubt the most spiritualized one for him. It is this anxiety that lies at the origin of the conservative mentality that he evinced in political and social matters. And it was this anxiety that constituted the cause of his tragic evasions in his erotic life. Certainly, this anxiety equally determined his own interpretation of *Elective Affinities*. In fact, this very work brings to light such depths of his life that, because they had never been revealed by Goethe's confessions, remained equally inaccessible to the traditional interpretation that refers exclusively to his own words.

There was in Goethe's existence a relentless struggle to free himself from the grip of mythic powers, a struggle to which the *Affinities* novel testifies, all the while giving an account of the reign of these powers. Affected by the profound and formidable experience that he had of them—the experience that these powers remain irreconcilable without repeated sacrifice—Goethe rose up against them. Originally, the tendency that he had struggled to follow with an iron will, in spite of an inmost discouragement, had been to submit himself to the mythic powers wherever they still reigned, going so far as to lend himself to the consolidation of their reign as only a servant of this world's powers can. Now, the day after the last and most difficult of these submissions that he thought he could demand from himself, the real capitulation at the end of a thirty-year struggle against marriage, marriage being the menacing symbol, in his eyes, of the mythic spell—at that point, this solidarity with the mythic forces faded. And one year after his marriage imposed itself on him in those days of tormented destiny, by beginning *Elective Affinities*, he raised his complaint against this world with which he had made a pact in the prime of his life, a complaint whose vigor would become even more pronounced in the later works. *Elective Affinities* thus mark a turning point in his work.[2] With them the last series of creations begins, from which he can no longer detach himself absolutely; their pulse would remain alive within him until the end. Thus, the note in his diary from 1820 does not fail to be moving: "began reading the *Elective Affinities*"—and the following scene, reported by Heinrich Laube, is of an unspeakable irony: "A lady says to Goethe what she thought of *Elective Affinities*: I cannot in the slightest approve of this book, Monsieur von Goethe; it is truly immoral and I would never recommend it to a young woman. After that, Goethe very gravely kept silent for a good moment and then responded in an almost pious tone: I regret that, nevertheless, it is my best book." This last series of his work testifies to a purification that could no longer be liberatory. It was perhaps because in his youth he had too often taken flight to the fields of poetic art that old age, with a terribly vengeful irony, shut him up definitively in poesy. Goethe subordinated his life to the authorities that prescribed to him those *circumstances* susceptible to giving rise to poetic creations. That is why the look he casts on the data of his own existence acquires an expiatory sense. *Poetry and Truth*, the *Oriental Divan*, and *Faust, Part Two* were to mark the three stations of that hidden penance. The task of historizing his life as it fell to *Poetry and Truth* consisted in *verifying* and in *poeticizing* the materials and the autobiographical circumstances destined to form the canonical life of the Poet.

Furthermore, the old Goethe had sufficiently penetrated the essence of poetry that he could not but behold with horror the absence of all poetic circumstances in his milieu. It was this bitter experience that he had to share with the early Romantics. But to convert or to join a national community was the kind of solution that Goethe had abhorred in some of them. Yet the same problems that the early Romantics tried to solve with more or less haphazard means were to lead Goethe to take his greatest flight. He substituted poetic authorities for those of myth. From this came to him the power to impose a poetic regime on his life. From this, too, the necessity to forgo all community. From this, finally, the capacity to exclude from poetry the contingencies of his life. The completion of *Faust, Part Two* was to be the supreme manifestation of such a regime, which imposed a law on life to the point of prolonging its duration. And if myth still seemed to exercise its anxiety-inducing empire on *Elective Affinities*, this first work of the years of old age already brings with it the message of a purer world.

Translated from the German by Pierre Klossowski

32

TWO NOTES FROM THE *ARCADES PROJECT*

[5:577] In studying Simmel's presentation of Goethe's concept of truth, it became very clear to me that my concept of origin in the *Trauerspiel* book is a rigorous and obligatory transposition of this basic Goethean concept from the realm of nature to that of history. Origin—it is the concept of urphenomenon transferred from the pagan nexus of nature into the Jewish nexuses of history.[1] Now, in my work on the arcades I am equally concerned with fathoming an origin. To be specific, I pursue the origin of the forms and mutations of the Paris arcades from their beginning to their demise, and I locate this origin in the economic facts. Seen from the standpoint of causality, however (and that means considered as causes), these facts would not be urphenomena; they become such only by letting the whole series of the arcade's concrete historical forms emerge from themselves in their own, self-appropriating development—"unfolding" might be a better term—just as the leaf unfolds from itself all the riches of the empirical world of plants[2] (N2a,4).

. . .

[5:592] The dialectical image is that form of the historical object which satisfies Goethe's requirements for the object of an analysis: to exhibit a genuine synthesis.[3] It is the urphenomenon of history (N9a,4).

Books by and about Goethe in "Registry of Readings"

481) Schiller and Goethe: *Correspondence*

552) Goethe, *Pandora*

559) Goethe, *Maxims and Reflections* [see 287n19]

565) *Goethe and Romanticism*, vol. 1. (Correspondence with the early Romantics)

575) Goethe. *The Metamorphosis of Plants* (and much else from *Morphology*, vol. 1)

580) Friedrich Schlegel, "Goethe" <[review of] *Works*, vols. 1–4> [From *Characteristics and Critiques*, vol. 2, 1802–29]

603) Goethe, *Faust, Part Two*

612) Goethe, "Gods, Heroes, and Wieland"

638) *Correspondence between Goethe and Reinhard*

646) Goethe, "Meteorology: Attempt at a Theory of Weather"

647) Goethe, "The Collector and His People"

677) Adolph Hansen, *Goethe's Metamorphosis of Plants*

732) Goethe, *Correspondence with Marianne von Willemer*

752) *Goethe's Lili* [Anna Elisabeth Türckheim] *in Her Letters*

782) Goethe, *Elective Affinities*

788) *Correspondence between Goethe and Göttling*

795) Alfred Peltzer, *The Aesthetic Significance of Goethe's Theory of Colors* (trash)

801) Goethe, "The Roman Carnival"

842) François-Poncet, *Les affinités électives de Goethe* [Goethe's Elective Affinities] (looked through)

897) Goethe, *The Natural Daughter*

1080) Karl Gutzkow, *On Goethe at the Turning Point of Two Centuries*

1083) Goethe, *Stella*

From "Verzeichnis der gelesenen Schriften," 7:437–60; WBA 397; trans. PF. Parentheses are Benjamin's own; brackets are editorial interpolations; angle brackets derive from GS. No attempt is made here to identify the books and editions Benjamin read or the dates when he read them, though it can be presumed that he read the first book around 1916–17 and the last around 1927–28. It could be further noted that the first book, namely, the volume of correspondence between Goethe and Schiller, is the only appearance of Schiller's name in the extant pages of the Registry; the last book, the comedy *Stella*, comes under discussion in the 1930 radio broadcast "Prescription for Comedy Writers: A Conversation between Wilhelm Speyer and Walter Benjamin" (7:614; RB 280). As noted in the Introduction (14), Benjamin also drew up a small list of mostly obscure books and articles that are directly concerned with Goethe's *Elective Affinities*, WBA 511; it will be published in the fourth volume of WuN.

Further Readings

Benjamin-Goethe

This brief guide is divided into English- and German-language discussions of Benjamin's relation to Goethe.

Two essays in *Walter Benjamin and Romanticism*, ed. Andrew Benjamin and Beatrice Hanssen (London: Continuum, 2002), are especially helpful in relation to the first of the two major texts in this volume: David Ferris's "Benjamin's Affinity: Goethe, the Romantics, and the Pure Problem of Criticism" (180–96) and Sigrid Weigel's "The Artwork as Breach of Beyond: On the Dialectic of Divine and Human Order in Walter Benjamin's 'Goethe's Elective Affinities'" (197–206). To view Benjamin's relation to Goethe under the optic of polar-opposite perspectives, see Richard Block, "Selective Affinities: Walter Benjamin and Ludwig Klages," *Arcadia* 35.1 (2000): 117–36; and Rochelle Tobias, "Irreconcilable: Ethics and Aesthetics for Hermann Cohen and Walter Benjamin," *MLN* 127.3 (2012): 665–80. For two views concerning the question of marriage in "Goethe's Elective Affinities," see Will Bishop, "The Marriage Translation and the Contexts of Common Life: From the Pacs to Benjamin and Beyond," *Diacritics* 35.4 (Winter 2005): 59–80; and Marcus Bullock, "Goethe versus Benjamin: Elective Affinities and Marriage Equality," *Monatshefte* 112.1 (Spring 2020): 76–101. And for help in understanding the part of "Goethe's Elective Affinities" that Benjamin himself considered close to impenetrable (the first paragraph of the third section, 79–81 and

134–35), see Paul North, "Apparent Critique: Inferences from a Benjaminian Sketch," *Diacritics* 40.1 (2010): 70–97; and Eli Friedlander, "The Appearance of the Ideal of Philosophical Questioning in the Work of Art," *Yearbook of Comparative Literature* 57 (2011): 103–16.

A variety of other approaches to the theme of Benjamin-Goethe can be found in the following essays: Stanley Corngold, "Genuine Obscurity Shadows the Semblance Whose Obliteration Promises Redemption: Reflections on Benjamin's 'Goethe's Elective Affinities,'" in *Benjamin's Ghosts: Interventions in Contemporary Literary and Cultural Theory*, ed. Gerhard Richter (Stanford: Stanford University Press, 2002), 154–68; N. K. Leacock, "Character, Silence, and the Novel: Walter Benjamin on Goethe's *Elective Affinities*," *Narrative* 10.3 (2002): 277–306; and Sigrid Weigel, "Fidelity, Love, Eros: Benjamin's Bireferential Concept of Life as Developed in 'Goethe's *Elective Affinities*,'" in *Walter Benjamin and Theology*, ed. Colby Dickenson and Stéphane Symons (New York: Fordham University Press, 2016), 56–74.

For books with substantial discussions of Benjamin's reception of Goethe, see Stéphane Mosès, *The Angel of History: Rosenzweig, Benjamin, Scholem*, trans. Barbara Harshav (Stanford: Stanford University Press, 2009); John McCole, *Walter Benjamin and the Antinomies of Tradition* (Ithaca, N.Y.: Cornell University Press, 1993); Beatrice Hanssen, *Walter Benjamin's Other History of Stones, Animals, Human Beings, and Angels* (Berkeley: University of California Press, 1998); Astrida Orle Tantillo, *Goethe's "Elective Affinities" and the Critics* (Rochester, N.Y.: Camden House, 2001); Alison Ross, *Walter Benjamin's Concept of the Image* (London: Routledge, 2015); Matthew Charles, *Modernism between Goethe and Benjamin* (London: Bloomsbury Academic, 2019); Márton Dornbach, *The Saving Line: Benjamin, Adorno, and the Caesuras of Hope* (Evanston: Northwestern University Press, 2021); and Kevin McLaughlin, *The Philology of Life: Walter Benjamin's Critical Program* (New York: Fordham University Press, 2023).

Among the more numerous studies of Benjamin-Goethe in German, the following are a selection of especially helpful ones: Uwe Steiner, "'Zarte Empirie': Überlegungen zum Verhältnis von Urphänomen und Ursprung im Früh- und Spätwerk Walter Benjamins," in *Antike und Moderne: Zu Walter Benjamins "Passagen"* (Würzburg: Königshausen & Neumann, 1989), 20–40; Uwe Steiner, "'Das Höchste wäre: zu begreifen, daß alles Factische schon Theorie ist': Walter Benjamin liest Goethe," *Zeitschrift für Deutsche Philologie* 121.2 (2002): 265–84; Burkhardt Lindner, "Goethes Wahlverwandtschaften," in *Benjamin-Handbuch: Leben-Werk-Wirkung*, ed. Burkhardt Lindner, Thomas Küpper, and Timo Skandies (Stuttgart: Metzler, 2011), 472–93; and Ursula Marx and Alexandra Richter, "Philosophische Alchemie," in *Entwendungen: Walter Benjamin und seine Quelle*, ed. Jessica Nitsche and Nadine Werner (Stuttgart: Fink, 2019), 97–124.

A variety of approaches to Benjamin's work on Goethe can be found in *Benjamins Wahlverwandtschaften. Zur Kritik einer programmatischen Interpretation*, ed. Helmut Hühn, Uwe Steiner, and Jan Urbich (Frankfurt am Main: Suhrkamp, 2015). On the relation of Benjamin to Simmel in the context of their Goethe studies, see Eva Geulen, "Nachlese: Simmels Goethe-Buch und Benjamins *Wahlverwandtschaften*-Aufsatz," in *Morphologie und Moderne: Goethes "anschauliches Denken" in den Geistes- und Kulturwissenschaften seit 1800*, ed. Jonas Matsch (Berlin: De Gruyter, 2014), 195–218. Finally, for an illuminating discussion of how "Goethe's Elective Affinities" has been effectively ignored, overlooked, and misunderstood in the sphere of German literary studies, see Vivian Liska, "Die Mortifikation Der Kritik: Zum Nachleben von Walter Benjamins Wahlverwandtschaften-Essay," in *Walter Benjamin und die Romantische Moderne*, ed. Heinz Brüggemann, Günter Oesterle, Alexander von Bormann, et al. (Würzburg: Königshausen & Neumann, 2009), 247–62.

Translations of *Elective Affinities* and Goethe's Scientific Writings
Three relatively recent translations of *Elective Affinities* (which are united in their choice of this as their title) are: Goethe, *Elective Affinities: A Novel*, trans. David Constantine (Oxford: Oxford University Press, 2008); *The Sorrows of Young Werther—Elective Affinities—Novella*, trans. Judith Ryan (Princeton: Princeton University Press, 1995); *Elective Affinities*, trans. R. H. Hollingdale (Harmondsworth: Penguin, 1978). Translations of several of the central texts on nature and scientific method to which Benjamin refers throughout the volume can be found in Goethe, *Scientific Studies*, ed. and trans. Douglas Miller (Princeton: Princeton University Press, 1995).

Guide to Names

Abeken, Bernhard Rudolf (1780–1866), German literary historian and philologist best known for editing the collected works of the German jurist and writer Justus Möser; also published studies on Goethe, Cicero, and Dante.

Adorno, Theodor (1903–69), German sociologist, philosopher, composer, founding member of the Frankfurt School of Social Research, and friend of Benjamin, who generally referred to him by his paternal surname, Wiesengrund.

Adorno-Karplus, Margarete (Gretel) (1902–93), German chemist, friend of Benjamin, and wife of Theodor Adorno.

Arnim, Bettina von (1785–1859), German Romantic writer who is best known for her salon and social circle, which included writers such as Goethe and composers such as Liszt and Beethoven; married to Achim von Arnim, sister of Clemens Brentano.

Arnim, Ludwig "Achim" von (1781–1831), German Romantic novelist and poet best known for his work *Des Knaben Wunderhorn*, cowritten with Clemens Brentano; married to Bettina von Arnim.

Ashley-Cooper, Anthony (1671–1713), British writer, philosopher, and the third Earl of Shaftesbury, who is best known for his book on aesthetics and the sublime entitled *Characteristics of Men, Manners, Opinions, Times*.

D'Aurevilly, Jules Barbey (1808–89), French poet, philosopher, and critic best known for his collection of short stories, *The She-Devils*.

Bachofen, Johann Jakob (1815–87), Swiss anthropologist and historian known for his voluminous and influential work on matriarchy.

260 GUIDE TO NAMES

Baechtold, Jakob (1848–97), Swiss literary scholar, best known for his biography of Gottfried Keller and *History of German Literature in Switzerland*.

Baldensperger, Fernand (1871–1958), French academic and literary historian who founded the *Revue de littérature comparée*.

Ballard, Jean (1893–1973), French poet, writer, and coeditor of *Cahiers du Sud*.

Bamberg, Felix (1820–93), German writer, diplomat, editor, and publicist.

Basedow, Johann Bernhard (1724–90), German pedagogue, writer, and educational reformer, best known for his *Elementarwerk* and the founding of the Philanthropinum school.

Bauer, Karl (1868–1942), German painter and writer, best known for his portraits of Goethe, George, and Beethoven.

Baumgartner, Alexander (1841–1910), Swiss literary scholar and writer, best known for his work on Goethe as well as his multivolume study *Geschichte der Weltliteratur*.

Béguin, Albert (1901–57), Swiss translator, editor, and scholar, best known for his study of dreams in the era of German Romanticism.

Beheim, Michel (ca. 1420–ca. 1470), medieval German poet.

Benjamin-Kellner, Dora (1890–1964), journalist, educational theorist, and author of the novel *Gas gegen Gas*; married Benjamin in 1917, divorced in 1929; daughter of the translator Anna Kellner and the Zionist leader Leon Kellner.

Bentham, Jeremy (1748–1832), British jurist and philosopher; founder of modern utilitarianism.

Bernoulli, Carl Albrecht (1868–1937), Swiss writer and Evangelical theologian, best known for his writings on Johann Jakob Bachofen and Friedrich Nietzsche.

Bertuch, Friedrich Justin (1747–1822), German publisher, editor, and philanthropist.

Beutler, Ernst (1885–1960), German literary historian and director of the Freies Deutsches Hochstift.

Biedermann, Flodoard von (1858–1934), German literary historian; son of Woldemar von Biedermann.

Biedermann, Woldemar von (1817–1903), German literary historian and jurist who published several volumes of conversations with Goethe; father of Flodoard von Biedermann.

Bielschowsky, Albert (1847–1902), German literary historian who specialized in Goethe's work.

Bierbaum, Otto Julius (1865–1910), German writer, editor, and poet best known for his novel *Stilpe* and poetry collection *Irrgarten der Liebe*.

Blaß, Ernst (1890–1939), German Expressionist poet, critic, and journalist.

Blavatsky, Helena (1831–91), Russian author and occultist; founder of the Theosophical Society.

Bloch, Ernst (1885–1977), German philosopher; acquaintance of Benjamin's, best known for his *Spirit of Utopia* and *Principle of Hope*.

Böhlendorff, Casimir (1775–1825), German poet and writer, mostly remembered for his correspondence with Friedrich Hölderlin.

Bois-Reymond, Emil du (1818–96), German physiologist and philosopher of science.

Boisserée, Sulpiz (1783–1854), German art historian and collector who helped construct the Cologne Cathedral.

Boll, Franz (1867–1924), German scholar; best known for his work on the ancient astronomer Ptolemy and his history of astrology, *Sternglaube und Sterndeutung*.

Borchardt, Rudolf (1877–1945), German writer and translator, friend of Hugo von Hofmannsthal's and frequent contributor to *Neue Deutsche Beiträge*.

Börne, Ludwig (1786–1837), German Jewish journalist and author; cofounder of the Young Germany movement.

Boucke, Ewald A. (1871–1943), German literary scholar; author of *Wort und Bedeutung in Goethes Sprache*.

Brentano, Clemens (1778–1842), German Romantic poet and novelist; brother of Bettina von Arnim; best known for *Des Knaben Wunderhorn*, a collection of folk songs cowritten with Achim von Arnim.

Brion, Marcel (1895–1984), French writer, critic, biographer, historian, and editor.

Buff, Charlotte (1753–1828), one of Goethe's early amorous interests; often seen as the inspiration for Lotte in *The Sorrows of Young Werther*.

Burdach, Konrad (1859–1936), professor of German in Halle and Berlin, whose expertise included medieval and Renaissance literature as well as Goethe scholarship.

Bürger, Gottfried August (1747–94), German writer associated with the Sturm und Drang movement, best known for his ballads.

Burggraf, Julius (1853–1912), German literary scholar and Evangelical pastor.

Burkhardt, Carl August Hugo (1830–1910), German historian and archive director in Weimar who wrote numerous studies of literature.

Carrière, Moriz (1817–95), German historian, best known for his works *Die philosophische Weltanschauung der Reformationszeit*.

Carus, Carl Gustav (1789–1869), German painter who worked as a naturalist, researcher, gynecologist, and anatomist.

Cassou, Jean (1897–1986), French writer, poet, and editor; an active member of the French Resistance and after the Second World War became the director of the Musée National d'Art Moderne.

262 GUIDE TO NAMES

Chamberlain, Houston Stewart (1855–1927), British German writer whose *Foundations of the Nineteenth Century* was prized by Hitler and other eliminationist anti-Semites.

Claudius, Matthias (1740–1815), German lyric poet, journalist, and editor of *The Wandsbeck Messenger*.

Cohen, Hermann (1842–1918), German Jewish philosopher; cofounder of the Marburg school of neo-Kantianism.

Cohn, Alfred (1892–1954), Benjamin's classmate and lifelong friend; brother of Jula Cohn; businessman in Berlin, Mannheim, Barcelona, and Paris.

Cohn, Jula (1894–1981), German sculptor; sister of Alfred Cohn who married Fritz Radt in 1925.

Cotta, Johann Friedrich (1764–1832), German founder of the publishing house bearing his name.

Deetjen, Werner (1877–1939), German librarian, worked in the ducal library in Weimar.

Diederichs, Eugen (1867–1930), influential German publisher.

Diez, Heinrich Friedrich von (1751–1817), German orientalist scholar who also served as a diplomat to the Ottoman Empire.

Dilthey, Wilhelm (1833–1911), German philosopher and historian, influential in the vitalist movement.

Dürer, Albrecht (1471–1528), German artist and painter.

Eckermann, Johann Peter (1792–1854), German writer and poet, best known for his friendship with Goethe as expressed in *Conversations with Goethe*, a book Benjamin greatly admired.

Eddington, Arthur Stanley (1882–1944), British astrophysicist, who is most famous for confirming the general theory of relativity during a 1919 eclipse.

Engel, Eduard (1851–1938), German literary scholar, novelist, and linguist.

Ermatinger, Emil (1873–1953), Swiss literary scholar, best known for *Das dichterische Kunstwerk*.

Eybenberg, Marianne von (ca. 1770–1812), German Jewish friend of Goethe who, together with her sister Sara Meyer, participated in the Berlin salons hosted by, among others, Rahel Levin and Henriette Herz.

Falk, Johannes Daniel (1768–1826), German poet and publisher known primarily for his Evangelical poetry and hymns.

Feuerbach, Ludwig (1804–72), German philosopher and inspiration for the Young Hegelians, best known for *The Essence of Christianity*.

Fischer, Kuno (1824–1907), German philosopher and literary scholar; author of an eight-volume history of philosophy.

GUIDE TO NAMES 263

Fischer, Paul (1854–1937), German literary critic, writer, and theologian, best known for his work on Dostoevsky.

Fourier, Charles (1772–1837), French writer who helped found what would later be called utopian socialism.

François-Poncet, André (1887–1978), French diplomat and ambassador to Germany from 1931 to 1938; High Commissioner to West Germany, 1949–55; author of a book on *Elective Affinities*.

Friedländer, Salomo (1871–1946), German Jewish writer and philosopher, best known for *Creative Indifference*.

Fritsch, Jakob Friedrich von (1731–1814), German politician based in Weimar.

Frommann, Carl Friedrich Ernst (1765–1837), German publisher and foster father of Minna Herzlieb.

Frommann, Johanna (1765–1830), wife of Carl Friedrich Ernst Frommann.

Fuchs, Eduard (1870–1940), Marxist cultural historian and art collector, best known for his multivolume study *Illustrierte Sittengeschichte vom Mittelalter bis zur Gegenwart*.

Gall, Franz Joseph (1758–1828), founder of phrenology.

Geiger, Ludwig (1848–1919), German literary scholar and important figure in Reform Judaism alongside his father, Abraham Geiger; related to Moritz Geiger, a philosopher who was among the few professors whose classes Benjamin did not consider useless or comical.

George, Stefan (1868–1933), German poet and translator whose "circle" included many (exclusively male) poets and scholars of the period.

Gervinus, Georg Gottfried (1805–71), German literary scholar and political historian, best known for a history of German poetry.

Giotto (ca. 1267–1337), Italian architect, mosaicist, and painter.

Glover, Friedrich. See entry for Christian Heinrich Gottlieb Köchy.

Goethe, Cornelia (1750–77), sister of Goethe; married to Johann Georg Schlosser.

Goethe, Johann Caspar (1710–82), German Imperial Councilor, jurist, husband of Catharina Textor, and father of Johann Wolfgang von Goethe.

Goldberg, Oskar (1885–1953), German Jewish philosopher, religious thinker, and founder of a circle of associates who was interested in the intersection of mysticism and biology.

Görres, Joseph von (1776–1848), German philosopher, writer, and mystic; founder of the *Rheinischer Merkur*.

Göschel, Carl Friedrich (1784–1861), German lawyer and scholar who discussed such topics as Goethe, Hegel, and Christianity.

264 GUIDE TO NAMES

Göschen, Georg Joachim (1752–1828), German publisher and Leipzig bookseller, who from 1787 to 1790 published the first complete edition of Goethe's writings.

Grabbe, Christian Dietrich (1801–36), German dramatist, best known for his play *Don Juan und Faust*.

Gräf, Hans Gerhard (1864–1942), German editor and writer who specialized in research on Goethe.

Gregorovius, Ferdinand (1821–91), German historian and medievalist, best known for his account of the history of Rome in the medieval period.

Gries, Johann Diedrich (1775–1842), German translator of Torquato Tasso and Calderón, affiliated with the Jena Romantics.

Grimm, Hermann (1828–1901), German professor of art history at the University of Berlin; son of Wilhelm Grimm and husband of Gisela von Arnim.

Grimm, Jacob (1785–1863), German folklorist and linguist who, together with his brother Wilhelm Grimm, collected (or wrote) *Grimms' Fairy Tales* and initiated the massive German dictionary associated with their names.

Grimm, Wilhelm (1786–1859), German folklorist and linguist who, together with his brother, Jacob, collected (or wrote) *Grimms' Fairy Tales* and initiated a massive dictionary of the German language; father of Hermann Grimm.

Grisebach, Eduard (1845–1906), German diplomat and poet.

Grün, Karl (1817–87), German journalist and politician associated with early socialist movements; spent much of his life in exile.

Grünewald, Matthias (ca. 1470–1528), German painter.

Guglia, Eugen (1857–1919), Austrian writer, historian, and editor-in-chief of *Wiener Zeitung*.

Gundolf, Friedrich (1880–1931), German Jewish scholar, literary historian, poet, and member of the George circle, best known for his works on Shakespeare and Goethe.

Günther, Johann Christian (1695–1723), German lyric poet who served as an important source of inspiration to Goethe; best known for his "Leonore" poetry cycle.

Gutzkow, Karl (1811–78), German dramatist, journalist, and writer affiliated with the Young Germany literary movement.

Hafez (ca. 1325–ca. 1390), Persian mystic and lyric poet whose poetry collection *Divan* served as inspiration for Goethe's *West-Eastern Divan*.

Hamacher, Theodor (1825–65), German painter known for his portraits.

Hamann, Johann Georg (1730–88), German theologian and writer, friend of Kant's and critic of Enlightenment thought.

GUIDE TO NAMES 265

Hammer-Purgstall, Joseph Freiherr von (1774–1856), Austrian orientalist scholar; translator of Hafez's *Divan*.

Hebbel, Christian Friedrich (1813–63), German novelist, poet, and dramatist.

Hebel, Johann Peter (1760–1826), German Lutheran theologian and poet primarily known for his collection of poems written in the Alemannic dialect and stories he published in his almanac *Der Rheinländische Hausfreund*.

Hehn, Victor (1813–90), German cultural historian and academic, best known for his studies of Italy and Goethe.

Heilborn, Ernst (1867–1942), German Jewish editor, journalist, and writer who worked at *Das Literarische Echo* and the *Frankfurter Zeitung*.

Heine, Heinrich (1797–1856), German Jewish Romantic poet, essayist, and journalist; related to Benjamin on his mother's side.

Heinle, Christoph Friedrich (Fritz) (1894–1914), German poet, a close friend of Benjamin's, who together formed a plan to edit a journal in July 1914; a month later, at the beginning of the war, he killed himself.

Helmholtz, Hermann von (1821–94), German physicist and philosopher of science.

Hemsterhuis, François (1721–90), Dutch Enlightenment author.

Hengstenberg, Ernst Wilhelm (1802–69), German Protestant theologian, and author of various works on the Hebrew Bible, including *Christology of the Old Testament*.

Herbertz, Richard (1878–1959), German Swiss professor of philosophy; director of Benjamin's doctoral dissertation.

Herder, Johann Gottfried von (1744–1803), German writer, poet, and philosopher; friend of Goethe's, but their friendship was later broken off; associated with the Enlightenment, the Counter-Enlightenment, Weimar classicism, and Romanticism.

Hertz, Gottfried Wilhelm (1874–1951), German jurist and author of *Natur und Geist in Goethes Faust*, which Benjamin admired.

Herzlieb, Minna (1789–1865), foster daughter of Carl Friedrich Ernst Fromman who is said to have inspired several of Goethe's works; often seen as the prototype for the character of Ottilie in *Elective Affinities*.

Hirsch, Julian (1883–1951), German literary scholar, author of *The Genesis of Fame* and *The Religion of Genius*.

Hofer, Klara (1875–1955), pseudonym of the German novelist and short story writer Klara Höffner, author of *Goethes Ehe*.

Hofmannsthal, Hugo von (1874–1929), Austrian poet, writer, editor, and librettist.

D'Holbach, Baron (1723–89), French German Enlightenment philosopher, best known for his *System of Nature*.

266   GUIDE TO NAMES

Holtei, Karl von (1798–1880), German dramatist, actor, and theater producer, who produced vaudeville-like "Lustspiele."

Hölty, Ludwig Christoph Heinrich (1748–76), German poet and member of the Grove League of Göttingen.

Holzmann, Michael (1860–1930), Austrian librarian, best known for his studies of Ludwig Börne.

Horkheimer, Max (1895–1973), German Jewish sociologist and philosopher, founding member of the Frankfurt School of Social Research.

Huch, Rudolf (1862–1943), German Brazilian writer, best known for his satirical works.

Humboldt, Wilhelm von (1767–1835), German linguist and educational reformer; conceived and helped found the University of Berlin.

Husserl, Edmund (1859–1938), Austrian German philosopher; founder of the phenomenological movement.

Iffland, August Wilhelm (1759–1814), German dramatist, actor, and director of the National Theater in Berlin.

Jacobi, Friedrich Heinrich (1743–1819), German writer who spearheaded the movement against Enlightenment thought.

John, Johann August Friedrich (1794–1854), one of Goethe's valets who transcribed some of his work.

Kandinsky, Wassily (1866–1944), Russian painter and writer associated with the Blue Rider group.

Karl August, Grand Duke (1757–1828), Grand Duke of Saxe-Weimar who befriended Goethe and brought him to Weimar.

Kaulbach, Wilhelm von (1805–74), German painter and illustrator whose clients ranged from Ludwig I to Johann Friedrich Cotta.

Keller, Gottfried (1819–90), Swiss politician and writer; author of *Green Henry*, among many other works.

Keudell, Elise von (1867–1952), German educator who worked at the ducal library in Weimar.

Kippenberg, Anton (1874–1950), German writer who founded Insel-Verlag.

Klages, Ludwig (1872–1956), German writer and psychologist, best known for his promotion of vitalism and contributions to graphology.

Klauer, Martin Gottlieb (1742–1801), German sculptor and teacher; affiliated with the Weimar Free-Drawing School.

Kleist, Heinrich von (1777–1811), German poet, writer, and dramatist, whose outstanding comedy, *The Broken Jug*, Goethe poorly staged at the Weimar-court theater.

Klinger, Friedrich Maximilian von (1752–1831), German dramatist and novelist whose play, *Sturm und Drang*, lent its name to the artistic and cultural movement.

Klopstock, Friedrich Gottlieb (1724–1803), a major figure in German letters, widely credited with expanding the range of German poetry.

Kluckhohn, Paul (1886–1957), German literary scholar and historian in Münster, Danzig (Gdańska), Vienna, and Tübingen; one of the original editors of the *Deutsche Vierteljahrsschrift für Literaturwissenschaft und Geistesgeschichte*.

Knapp, Albert (1798–1864), German theologian and poet; founder of the first German animal welfare organization.

Köchy, Christian Heinrich Gottlieb (1769–1828), German legal scholar and lawyer; author of *Goethe as Human Being and Writer* under the pseudonym Friedrich Glover.

Kommerell, Max (1902–44), German literary scholar and translator, critic; associated with the George circle.

Köppen, Karl Friedrich (1808–63), German journalist and pedagogue affiliated with the Young Hegelians.

Körner, Theodor (1791–1813), German poet, soldier, and member of the Lützow Free Corps during the Napoleonic Wars.

Kräuter, Theodor (1790–1856), German librarian in Weimar who served as one of Goethe's secretaries.

Kühnemann, Eugen (1868–1946), German literary historian, visiting professor at several US universities.

Kurella, Alfred (1895–1975), German political activist and writer, who became a Soviet citizen in 1937 and then a member of the East German government.

Lācis, Anna (Asja) (1891–1979), Latvian actor, dramaturge, and author of *Revolutionär im Beruf*: amorous interest of Benjamin's, to whom he dedicated *One-Way Street* and with whom he cowrote an essay on the city of Naples.

Laube, Heinrich (1806–44), German novelist, dramatist, and director of the Burgtheater in Vienna.

Lavater, Johann Kasper (1741–1801), Swiss writer and pastor, best known for his multivolume *Physiognomische Fragmente*.

Lechter, Melchior (1865–1937), German painter and designer, best known for his book illustrations.

Lederer, Emil (1882–1939), German sociologist and economist, professor at the University of Heidelberg until forced into exile by the Nazi regime.

Lehmann, Johann August (1802–83), German educator who authored studies of Goethe, Klopstock, and Lessing.

Leisewitz, Johann Anton (1752–1806), German writer and dramatist; associated with the Sturm und Drang movement as well as the Grove League of Göttingen.

Lenz, Jakob Michael Reinhold (1751–92), German writer who was a principal representative of the Sturm und Drang movement.

Lessing, Gotthold Ephraim (1729–81), German Enlightenment philosopher, writer, and dramaturg; friend of Moses Mendelssohn and author of *Nathan the Wise*.

Levetzow, Ulrike von (1804–99), amorous interest of Goethe's who is said to have inspired some of his late poetry.

Lewes, George Henry (1817–78), British writer and author of an influential biography of Goethe; married (out of official wedlock) to George Eliot.

Lewy, Ernst (1881–1966), German Irish Jewish linguist; author of *Der Bau der europäischen Sprachen* as well as an unorthodox study of Goethe's late style that Benjamin admired.

Liszt, Franz (1811–86), Hungarian pianist and composer.

Louvier, Ferdinand August (1830–1900), German scholar whose work focused primarily on Goethe.

Luden, Heinrich (1778–1847), German historian who taught at the University of Jena; author of a twelve-volume history of the German people.

Ludwig, Emil (1881–1948), German Swiss writer, best known for his biographical studies of Goethe and Napoleon.

Mann, Thomas (1875–1955), Nobel Prize–winning novelist, essayist, and short story writer.

Manzoni, Alessandro (1785–1873), Italian novelist and poet, best known for *The Betrothed*.

Masaccio (1401–28), Italian painter and influential figure of the Renaissance.

Mehring, Franz (1846–1919), Marxist historian and literary scholar; author of an authoritative biography of Marx and a participant in the German Revolution.

Menzel, Wolfgang (1798–1873), German literary historian and writer, best known for his antagonism with reform-minded writers of the Vormärz period.

Merck, Johann Heinrich (1741–91), German literary critic, author, and naturalist who developed a close relationship with Goethe.

Meyer, Johann Heinrich (1760–1832), Swiss painter and critic who served as an advisor to Goethe on matters related to the visual arts.

Meyer, Richard Moritz (1860–1914), German literary scholar, best known for his works on Goethe, Nietzsche, and world literature.

GUIDE TO NAMES   269

Mézières, Alfred (1826–1915), French literary scholar and politician whose work on German, Italian, and English literature earned him entrance into the Académie Française.

Miller, Johann Martin (1750–1814), German writer, theologian, and member of the Grove League of Göttingen.

Möbius, Paul Julius (1853–1907), German neurologist known for his psychological studies of figures such as Goethe, Schopenhauer, and Nietzsche.

Mörike, Eduard (1804–75), German Romantic poet, writer, and Protestant pastor.

Müller, Friedrich (1749–1825), also called "Painter Müller," German painter and poet known for his *Faust's Life Dramatized* and his drama *Golo and Genovefa*.

Müller, Friedrich von (1779–1849), German politician, lawyer, and civil servant in Weimar whose conversations with Goethe were recorded in a like-named volume.

Müllner, Adolph (1774–1829), German dramatist and stage director, best known for his play *Die Schuld*.

Nicolai, Friedrich (1733–1811), German writer, historian, satirist, bookseller, and editor of the journal *Allgemeine deutsche Bibliothek*.

Nicolovius, Alfred (1806–90), German academic and author who specialized in legal studies.

Niebuhr, Carsten (1733–1815), German explorer who famously led the Danish-Arabia expedition, of which he was the sole survivor.

Noeggerath, Felix (1885–1960), German writer, scholar, and translator whom Benjamin befriended at the University of Munich in 1915; very little of his work was published.

Novalis (1772–1801), pseudonym of Georg Philipp Friedrich Freiherr von Hardenberg, German poet and philosopher who, along with Friedrich Schlegel, played a decisive role in early German Romanticism.

Owen, Robert (1771–1858), Welsh social reformer and businessman widely considered to be the founder of the cooperative movement and an architect of utopian socialism.

Pasqué, Ernst (1821–92), German librettist and opera singer who also worked as a director and writer.

Paul, Jean (1763–1825), pseudonym of Johann Paul Friedrich Richter, German writer whose largely comic works cannot be identified with any of the usual designations for the cultural movement of the period.

Payer-Thurn, Rudolf (1867–1932), Austrian historian and founder of the Goethe Society in Vienna.

Pestalozzi, Johann Heinrich (1746–1827), Swiss education reform activist whose theory of education was widely influential.

Pustkuchen, Friedrich (1793–1834), German theologian and writer, best known for his work on Evangelism and pedagogy; author of a multivolume sequel to Goethe's *Wilhelm Meister's Apprenticeship.*

Radek, Karl (1885–1939), Polish Lithuanian Russian revolutionary, associate of Lenin, who helped establish the German Communist Party; became a member of the executive committee of the Communist International, but fell out of favor under Stalin's rule, accused of treason, and died in a labor camp.

Radt, Fritz (1893–1978), childhood friend of Benjamin's; married Jula Cohn in 1925; a chemist who specialized in organic compounds.

Radt, Grete (1891–1979), participant in the Free Student Association, sister of Fritz Radt, and friend of Benjamin's.

Raich, Johann Michael (1832–1907), German publicist, editor, and Catholic theologian.

Rang, Florens Christian (1864–1924), German writer, Protestant theologian, and friend of Benjamin's during the years when he wrote "Goethe's Elective Affinities."

Reich, Bernard (1894–1972), dramaturg in Germany, the Soviet Union, and after WWII especially Latvia, partner (then husband) of Asja Lācis.

Reichard, Heinrich August Ottakar (1751–1828), German writer, librarian, and theater director in Gotha.

Reinhard, Karl Friedrich Graf von (1761–1837), French diplomat and writer who held a variety of governmental positions during the French Revolution and the July Monarchy.

Rickert, Heinrich (1863–1936), neo-Kantian philosopher whose classes and seminars Benjamin attended at the University of Freiburg im Breisgau.

Riemer, Friedrich Wilhelm (1774–1845), Goethe's secretary and tutor to his son, August; chief Weimar librarian.

Rollett, Hermann (1819–1904), Austrian poet and writer, best known for his work *Frühlingsboten aus Österreich.*

Rosenkranz, Karl (1805–79), German philosopher and writer who befriended Hegel and Schleiermacher.

Rothacker, Erich (1888–1965), German philosopher, one of the original editors of the *Deutsche Vierteljahrsschrift für Literaturwissenschaft und Geistesgeschichte.*

Rotten, Elisabeth (1882–1964), Swiss peace activist and educational reformer who cofounded the International Women's League for Peace and Freedom.

Sachsen, Sophie von (1845–67), Dutch princess who became Grand Duchess of Saxe-Weimar-Eisenach.

Saint-Simon, Henri de (1760–1825), French theorist and early proponent of utopian socialism.

Salomon-Delatour, Gottfried (1892–1964), privatdozent in sociology at the University of Frankfurt when he became acquainted with Benjamin, later professor in Frankfurt; forced to flee Nazi Germany, he became a professor of sociology at the New School and Columbia.

Saupe, Julius (1809–71), German literary historian, best known for works on Goethe and Shakespeare.

Schäffer, Emil (1874–1944), Austrian Jewish playwright and art historian.

Schelling, Friedrich (1775–1854), philosopher, associated with early German Romanticism, and, while in Jena, a friend of Goethe's.

Schlegel, August (1767–1845), German translator, literary critic, and professor of Indology; important figure of Jena Romanticism; brother of Friedrich Schlegel.

Schlegel, Dorothea (1764–1839), German poet and writer, author of the novel *Florentin*; daughter of Moses Mendelssohn and wife of Friedrich Schlegel.

Schlegel, Friedrich (1772–1829), German scholar, writer, and philosopher; along with Novalis, the decisive figure in early German Romanticism; brother of August von Schlegel; husband of Dorothea Schlegel.

Schmidt, Julian (1818–86), German literary historian who authored studies of Romanticism as well as nineteenth-century German literature.

Schneider, Hermann (1886–1961), German literary historian.

Schoen, Ernst (1894–1960), German composer; childhood friend of Benjamin's.

Scholem, Arthur (1863–1925), publisher and father of Gerhard-Gershom Scholem.

Scholem, Gershom-Gerhard (1897–1982), German Jewish Israeli scholar; longtime friend of Benjamin's, best known for his many contributions to the study of medieval and early modern Jewish mysticism.

Schöll, Adolf (1805–82), German writer, art historian, archaeologist, and chief Weimar librarian.

Schönemann, Lili (1758–1817), wife of Bernhard Friedrich von Türckheim and amorous interest of Goethe's.

Schubart, Christian Friedrich Daniel (1739–91), German poet, journalist, and composer.

Schulte-Strathaus, Ernst (1881–1968), German literary historian and antiquarian who became affiliated with the Nazi Party.

Schultz, Franz (1877–1950), professor of German at the University of Frankfurt am Main; supported Benjamin in his effort to be "habilitated" but withdrew his support in the final phase of the process.

Schuster, Julius (1886–1949), German botanist and historian who specialized in paleobotany.

Schütz, Alfred (1899–1959), Austrian American scholar whose work concerned the intersection of phenomenology and sociology.

Seebeck, Moritz (1805–84), German educator and state councilor in Weimar; son of Thomas Seebeck.

Seebeck, Thomas (1770–1831), German physicist whose work centered on heat, electricity, and color; father of Mortiz Seebeck.

Seidel, Alfred (1895–1924), German sociologist, who wrote a dissertation in Heidelberg on historical materialism; committed suicide.

Seligson, Carla (1892–1956), a student of medicine and participant in the Youth Movement during the years she was close to Benjamin.

Seligson, Friederike (Rika) (1891–1914), sister of Carla, friend of Fritz Heinle; Heinle and Rika Seligson together committed suicide on 9 August 1914; Gertrude (Traute) Seligson (b. 1895) committed suicide a year later.

Simmel, Georg (1858–1918), German Jewish scholar who was one of the founders of modern sociology, author of a book on Goethe that Benjamin admired.

Sismondi, Jean Charles Léonard de (1773–1842), Swiss political economist and historian.

Solger, Karl Wilhelm Ferdinand (1780–1819), German philologist, associated with both Romanticism and German idealism; wrote studies of tragedy and irony that Benjamin disparaged.

Soret, Frédéric (1795–1865), Swiss scholar and numismatist who developed a close relationship with Goethe in Weimar.

Span, Martin (1757–1840), Austrian high-school teacher and author of books on Shakespeare and Goethe.

Spaun, Franz von (1753–1826), German mathematician who also wrote works on culture and literature, most notably *Der sarmatische Lykurg oder über die Gleichstellung der Juden und den Einfluß der Volksfeste*.

Stadelmann, Carl Wilhelm (1782–1844), German servant and secretary to Goethe.

Staël-Holstein, Anne Louise Germaine de (1766–1817), generally known simply as Madame de Staël; French Swiss aristocrat, influential author, and salonnière whose work includes *On Germany* and the epistolary novel *Delphine*.

Stein, Charlotte von (1742–1827), German playwright, lady-in-waiting at the court of Weimar, and friend of Goethe who is said to have inspired many of his works.

Steinbach, Erwin von (ca. 1244–1318), German architect who helped build the Strasbourg Cathedral.

GUIDE TO NAMES 273

Steiner, Rudolf (1861–1925), Austrian writer, pedagogue, and occultist; founder of the anthroposophical society and the Waldorf educational movement.

Stern, Adolf (1835–1907), German editor, literary historian, and author of the novel *Camoëns*.

Stern, Daniel (1805–76), pseudonym of Marie d'Agoult, French novelist and historian, best known for her history of the Revolution of 1848.

Stieler, Joseph Karl (1781–1858), German portraitist who worked as a Bavarian court painter.

Stifter, Adalbert (1805–68), German realist writer; author of, among many other works, *Der Nachsommer*.

Stolberg, Christian (1748–1821), German Count of Stolberg-Stolberg, brother of Count Fritz Stolberg; poet and translator.

Stolberg, Fritz (Friedrich Leopold) von (1750–1819), German Count of Stolberg-Stolberg, brother of Count Christian Stolberg; writer and translator associated with the Sturm und Drang movement.

Strauß, David (1808–74), German Protestant theologian, best known for his *Life of Jesus*.

Suphan, Bernhard Ludwig (1845–1911), German philologist and the original director of the Goethe and Schiller Archive in Weimar.

Textor, Catharina Elisabeth (1731–1808), daughter of Johann Wolfgang Textor, wife of Johann Caspar Goethe, and mother of Johann Wolfgang von Goethe.

Textor, Johann Wolfgang (1693–1771), German Imperial Councilor in Frankfurt, father of Catharina Elisabeth Textor and thus Goethe's grandfather.

Thalheimer, August (1884–1948), German political activist, Marxist theorist, and member of the Social Democratic Party.

Tieck, Ludwig (1773–1853), German poet, translator, and writer closely associated with Jena Romanticism.

Tobler, Georg Christoph (1757–1812), Swiss writer, priest, and translator.

Trentini, Albert von (1878–1933), Austrian playwright and writer; author of a novel titled *Goethe*.

Trippel, Alexander (1744–93), Swiss sculptor, best known for his portrait busts, including two of Goethe.

Türckheim, Anna ("Lili") Elisabeth (1758–1817), daughter of a wealthy banker, engaged in an intense erotic engagement with Goethe in 1775, whom she later credited with her moral education.

Turel, Adrien (1890–1957), Swiss writer and poet.

GUIDE TO NAMES

Unger, Erich (1887–1950), German Jewish philosopher, associated with Oskar Goldberg; aspects of his work were important to Benjamin in the early 1920s and perhaps later as well.

Unger, Rudolf (1876–1942), German literary historian, associated with German-nationalist vitalism.

Varnhagen, Karl August von Ense (1785–1858), German biographer and soldier in the Austrian army; married to Rahel Varnhagen.

Varnhagen, Rahel (née Levin; 1771–1833), German Jewish writer who established one of the famous salons in Berlin, married to Karl August Varnhagen.

Vischer, Friedrich Theodor (1807–87), German writer and philosopher.

Vogel, Carl (1798–1864), German physician who served as the personal doctor to Goethe as well as the Grand Duke of Weimar.

Voß, Heinrich Johann (1751–1826), German academic and writer affiliated with the Grove League of Göttingen; widely read translator of Homer.

Vulpius, Christiane (1765–1816), Goethe's wife and mother of their son August.

Walter, Julius (1841–1922), German scholar, best known for a history of aesthetics in Greco-Roman antiquity.

Weber, Marianne (1870–1964), German sociologist and activist for women's rights.

Weber, Max (1864–1920), German sociologist, whose work was foundational for the discipline.

Weißbach, Richard (1882–1950), German publisher, located in Heidelberg, published several of Benjamin's early writings, including his translation of Baudelaire's *Tableaux parisiens*.

Werner, Zacharias (1768–1823), German dramatist, poet, and priest; onetime friend of Goethe's.

Wieland, Christoph Martin (1733–1813), German Enlightenment poet, translator, and editor; friend of Goethe's and principal figure in Weimar classicism.

Willemer, Marianne von (1784–1860), Austrian singer and dancer who is said to have inspired much of Goethe's poetry in *West-Eastern Divan* and was revealed in the late nineteenth century to have been the author of some of its most cherished poems; married to Johann Jakob Willemer.

Winckelmann, Johann Joachim (1717–68), German archaeologist and art historian, best known for his *History of Art in Antiquity*.

Witkowski, Georg (1863–1939), German Jewish literary historian, best known for his studies on Goethe.

Wohlbold, Hans (1877–1949), German anthroposophist, disciple of Rudolf Steiner's, who wrote a study of the latter's "lifework."

GUIDE TO NAMES 275

Wolf, Friedrich August (1759–1824), German philologist who produced a discipline-founding study of Homer's epics.

Wolters, Friedrich (1876–1930), German translator, poet, and historian; prominent member of the George circle.

Zarncke, Friedrich (1825–91), German philologist, best known for his works on both Goethe and medieval literature.

Zelter, Carl Friedrich (1758–1832), German composer, musician, and pedagogue who had a particularly close friendship with Goethe in their later years.

Zianitzka, Kathinka (1801–77), pseudonym of Kathinka Zitz-Halein, German poet, political activist, and writer.

Ziegler, Konrat (1884–1974), German philologist.

Glossary

Parentheses refer to the page(s) where the translation is discussed in the endnotes or Introduction.

ablösen: to release
Ahnen: ancestors
ahnen, Ahnung: to intimate, intimation
Allheit: totality
angoisse: anxiety
Angst: fear
Anschaulichkeit: visibility, intuitability
Anschauung: intuition, vision
Aufgabe: task
aufprägen: to imprint
Augenblick: instant, moment
Augenfälligkeit: conspicuousness
Ausdruck: expression
ausdruckslos, das Ausdrucklose: expressionless, the expressionless
Ausgang: ending
Ausgleich: balancing
Ausprägung: stamp
Äußerung: outward expression, statements (321n50)
aussöhnen: to conciliate

278 GLOSSARY

Bangigkeit: anxiety

Bannkreis: spell

Bedeutung: meaning, significance

Befreiung: liberation

Begierde: desire

beleben: to enliven

Beschwörung: conjuration

Bestand: existence

bestehen: to persist, to exist

Bestreben: endeavor

Betrachtung: approach, consideration, reflection (300n1 and 333n180)

Bewandtnis: mobilization

Beziehung: relation, reference

Bildlichkeit: imagistic quality

Bildner: image-maker

Bildung: education, culture

Bund: covenant

dämonisch: daemonic

Darstellung: presentation, depiction, preparation

Dasein: existence

Denkmal: memorial

Dichtung: literary work, literature, poetry

Doppelsinn: double meaning

durchwalten: to pervade, to permeate

Eindeutigkeit: univocity

Einlösung: release

Einspruch: protest

Einstellung: attitude

Entblößung: laying bare

Entkräftung: debilitation

Entsagung: renunciation

Entscheidung: decision

Entschluß: resolution

Entsprungenes: [something] sprung forth

Entsühnung: de-expiation (321n42)

erfragen: to inquire [into]

Erinnerung: recollection

erkennbar: cognizable

Erkenntnis: cognition, recognition

Erlebnis: lived experience

erlogen: mendacious

Erlösung: redemption

Erscheinung: appearance

Erschütterung: to be shaken, to be shattered

erstarren: to freeze

Ewigkeit: eternity

Formulierbarkeit: formulability

forterben: to pass [itself] on

Fügung: joining

furchtbar: fearful

gebannt: spellbound

Gebilde: formation

Geborgenheit: security

Gedächtnis: memory

Gedichtete: the poetized, that which has been poetized

Gehalt: matter, content (302n1 and 313n4)

Geist: spirit, mind

Geistigkeit: intellectuality, spirituality

gelegen: occasional

Gelegenheit: occasion

Gemüt: mind

Geschehene: the occurrence, that which has occurred

Geschick: destiny

Gesinnung: ethos, character, disposition

Gesittung: mores

Gestalt: shape

Gewalt: violence, force

Haltung: stance

Hülle: cover

Inbegriff: sum total (298n6)

Inhalt: content

ins Wort fällt: stops in midphrase (306n6)

Kommentar: commentary

Körper: corporeal body

Kraft: force

Kritik: critique, criticism

GLOSSARY

Kunstkritik: art critique
Läuterung: purification
Lebenden: living beings
Lebendige: what is alive
Lebendigkeit: vitality
Lehre: doctrine, theory
Leib: living body
Leidenschaft: passion
Lösung: separation
Macht: power
Mächtigkeit: cardinality (308n1)
Mannesalter: manhood
Mehrheit: plurality
moralisch: in a moral manner
musische: muse-related (300n2)
Nachbild: afterimage
Neigung: inclination (332n161)
Nichtige: nullity
Offenbarung: revelation
Poesie: poesy
Prägnanz: pithiness
Recht: law, right, justification
retten: to rescue
Rettung: salvation, rescue
Rührung: being touched
Sache: thing, fact
Sachgehalt: subject-matter (313–14n4)
sachlich: matter-of-fact
Sachverhalt: state of affairs
Schaffen: formation, creation
Schaffende: creative artist
Schau: show, view (35 and 294n69)
Schein: semblance, appearance
scheinhaft: semblant
Scheme: shadow
schicklich: appropriate
Schöpfer: Creator

Schöpfung: Creation

Schuld: guilt, fault, blame

Sinn: meaning, sense, mind

Sinnbild: emblem

Sitte: morals, customs

sittlich: moral, mores, ethical

Sittliche: what is right

Sittlichkeit: morality

Steigerung: elevation, intensification

Stellvertreter: representative

Stetigkeit: continuity

Stimmung: mood, atmosphere

Stoff: material

Sühne: expiation

Symbol: symbol

Symbolik: [the] symbolic, symbolism,

Teilnahme: sympathy

Todessymbolik: symbolism of death

Trieb: drive

trüb, Trübung: turbid, turbidity

Übermensch: superhuman

überweltlich: beyond this world

Unberührbarkeit: inviolability, untouchability

Unfaßlichen: incomprehensible

Ungeheuere: the prodigious, monstrous

Ungluck: bad luck

Unheil: misfortune

Untergang: decline, demise

untergehen: to decline

Urbild: archetype

Urphänomen: urphenomenon (284n9 and 299n1)

Ursache: cause

Urschuld: primal guilt

Ursprung: origin

Verantwortung: responsibility, answering-for

Verblendeten: one who is bedazzled

Verblendung: bedazzlement

Verfall: decay
verfallen: to decay
Verfallensein: fallenness
Verhalten: comportment
Verhältnis: relationship
Verhängnis: disaster
Verheissung: promise
Verlogenheit: mendacity
Versäumnis: neglection
Versäumte: something neglected
verschlossen: closed off
Verschlossenheit: reticence
verschulden: to inculpate
versöhnen: to reconcile
Verstand: intellect
Verstummen: muting
Verwandtschaft: relationship, affinity, relatives, kin (316n6)
Vielheit: multeity
Volk: people, nation
Volksgemeinschaft: national community
vollenden: to complete, to consummate
Vollendung: completion, consummation
Vollkommenheit: perfection
Vorbild: model
Vorstellung: representation, notion
vorweltlich: primeval
Wahl: choice
Wahrheitsgehalt: truth-of-the-matter (313n4)
Wahrnehmung: perception
Wesen: essence, being
wirklich: actual, real
Wissen: knowing, knowledge
zerfallen: to collapse
Zerrissenheit: turmoil
zweideutig, Zweideutigkeit: ambiguous, ambiguity

Notes

Introduction

1. Hannah Arendt, *Men in Dark Times* (New York: Harcourt Brace, 1968), 167.
2. Walter Benjamin, *Understanding Brecht* (London: Verso, 1973).
3. Arendt, *Men in Dark Times*, 167. It is worth noting that when Arendt makes this claim, she is implicitly not making a seemingly similar claim that can be found in her scathing portrait of Stefan Zweig, written shortly after his suicide, which was itself shortly after Benjamin's: "There is no better document of the Jewish situation in this period than the opening chapters of Zweig's [*World of Yesterday*]: They provide the most impressive evidence of how fame and the will to fame motivated the youth of his generation. Their ideal was the genius that seemed incarnate in Goethe" (Arendt, *Reflections on Literature and Culture*, ed. Susannah Gottlieb [Stanford: Stanford University Press, 2007], 62). And it should not be forgotten that it was Benjamin who encouraged Arendt to publish her book on Rahel Varnhagen, who was not an insignificant agent in the establishment of the cult of Goethe.
4. See Hannah Arendt and Walter Benjamin, *Arendt und Benjamin: Texte, Briefe, Dokumente*, ed. Detlev Schötter and Erdmut Wizisla (Frankfurt am Main: Suhrkamp, 2006), 163, 165, and 167.
5. This quotation is slightly modified: *Dichter* is here translated as "author" rather than as "poet."
6. Gershom Scholem, *Walter Benjamin: The Story of a Friendship*, trans. Harry Zohn (New York: Schocken, 1981), 94.
7. See Charlotte Wolff, *On the Way to Myself* (London: Methuen, 1969), 193–222.

284 NOTES TO PAGES 4–5

Here is one index of Wolff's unreliability with regards to the Benjamins: she claims that Walter went to Danzig to argue with her parents about the direction of her career; see 194. This was supposed to have happened during the time he was writing his essay on *Elective Affinities*. It is not impossible, to be sure; but it is highly unlikely. On the friendship between the Benjamins and Wolff, see Samuel Dolbear and Esther Leslie, *Dissonant Waves: Ernst Schoen and Experimental Sound in the 20th Century* (Cambridge, Mass.: MIT Press, 2023), 142. An early and influential example of presenting "Goethe's Elective Affinities" in terms of the Benjamin-Kellner marriage can be found in Berndt Witte, *Der Intellektuelle als Kritiker* (Stuttgart: Metzler, 1976), esp. 61–63.

8. See especially the following radio broadcast: "The Gypsies," especially its concluding remarks (7:165; RB 102–3); "Dr. Faust" (7:180–88; RB 119–26); a portion of "Cagliostro" (7:192–93; RB 130–31); and "What the Germans Were Reading While Their Classical Authors Were Writing" (4:641–70; RB 304–35), which was developed for the commemoration of the one hundredth anniversary of Goethe's death (see 35–38).

9. Two of Benjamin's notes from the late 1910s are excluded from this collection for this reason, though in contrary ways. The first is titled "On Shame" (6:69–71), which includes several quotations from Goethe's *Theory of Colors*; its argument, however, does not converge with "Goethe's Elective Affinities." For, even as Benjamin discusses nakedness in the essay (156), and indeed "Laying Bare" is the heading of its penultimate paragraph (156–59), nowhere is there a reflection on shame—or its absence. (The word appears only once, in passing, 146.) Benjamin seems to have purposively excluded the phenomenon from consideration, and the final aphorisms with which he concludes "On Shame" are similarly absent or excluded from the argument of the essay: "An expressionlessly signifying appearance [*ausdrucklos bedeutende Erscheinung*] is the color of fantasy. An expressionlessly signifying appearance of elapsing [*Vergehen*] is the blushing of shame" (6:71). The other missing fragment is "Theory of Cognition," which neither mentions Goethe nor draws attention to his theory of science; but it does work with an important Goethean neologism, namely, urphenomenon, and concludes with the implicit equation of urphenomena with what Benjamin calls "symbolic concepts" (6:46; SW 1:276–77). One further text should be noted in this context of missing items: a fragment of a story Benjamin wrote under the title "Schiller and Goethe: A Layman's Fantasy" (7:635–36; Walter Benjamin, *The Storyteller: Tales Out of Loneliness*, ed. and trans. Sam Dolbear, Esther Leslie, and Sebastian Truskolaski [New York: Verso, 2016], 5–10). Even though his name is in the title, Goethe does not enter the story.

10. This is an immense topic of reflection and scholarship, so much so that it

forms a theme of the research program at the Simon Dubnow-Leibniz Institute for Jewish History under the title "The Jewish Goethe, History of an Elective Affinity," the results of which can be accessed at https://www.dubnow.de/en/research-project/dr-berg-the-jewish-goethe. By naming the project after Goethe's novel, *Elective Affinities*, the directors of the program take their cue from Max Weber, as discussed later in the Introduction; see 15. For a variety of perspectives on this putative "elective affinity," see *Goethe in German-Jewish Culture*, ed. Klaus Berghahn and Jost Hermand (Rochester, N.Y.: Camden House, 2001); for a judicious treatment of Goethe's relation to Judaism, see Karin Schutjer, *Goethe and Judaism: The Troubled Inheritance of Modern Literature* (Evanston: Northwestern University Press, 2015). The Introduction does not specifically treat this theme, for it is nowhere directly addressed in Benjamin's extant writings on Goethe; but this in itself could be taken as a central feature of what Benjamin is doing with Goethe, early and late. Thus, for instance, the two major readings of *Elective Affinities* that Benjamin confronts in "Goethe's Elective Affinities"—in opposing ways—were written by Jews, one of whom (Friedrich Gundolf, whose last name was originally Gundelfinger) departed from Jewish traditions, whereas the other (Hermann Cohen, who was a leader of the Jewish community for much of his life) publicly and privately embraced them. Benjamin severely criticizes the former (see 123–27) while presenting the insight of the latter as of paramount importance (see 99 and 152). As is evident from several of the notes and fragments in the first part of the volume, especially the "Categories of Aesthetics," the concept of creation that traverses the writings in the first part of this volume derives from certain interpretations of the opening chapters of the Hebrew Bible. And it is likewise evident that the pairing of Houston Stewart Chamberlain and Georg Simmel near the end of his "One Hundred Years of Writing on Goethe" is an indirect response to the question raised by "the Jewish Goethe," with Simmel's book implicitly refuting Chamberlain's; see 225. It is also noteworthy that Benjamin's Jewishness (paired with Cohen's) is an element of Erich Rothacker's response to "Goethe's Elective Affinities," although it does not seem to be a factor in the negative decision of the journal he coedited; see 20.

11. For a discussion of Benjamin's Abitur-essay in the context of an inquiry into his relation to Goethe, see especially Ursula Marx and Alexandra Richter, "Philosophische Alchemie," in *Entwendungen: Walter Benjamin und seine Quelle*, ed. Jessica Nitsche and Nadine Werner (Stuttgart: Fink, 2019), esp. 109–10.

12. Benjamin alludes to the famous line in which Goethe says of his literary works that they are "only fragments of a great confession" (WA I, 27:110; *Poetry and Truth*, part 2).

286   NOTES TO PAGES 7–9

13. For Goethe's use of the term "solidity," see WA I, 30:213: *Italian Journey* ("Whoever, having eyes with which to see, looks around in earnest must become solid; he must grasp a concept of solidity, one that never before became, for him, so lively").

14. The distinction between *Genie* and *Genius* is also of importance to the argument pursued in "Goethe's Elective Affinities" (129), where it is repeated in reference to a passage from the second of the poems that Benjamin examines in "Two Poems of Friedrich Hölderlin," namely, "Blödigkeit" (Timidity). Once Benjamin began to distinguish *Genie* from *Genius*, he also started to associate this distinction—one might say, Nietzsche-wise, as though it is akin to the opposition between Apollo and Dionysus—with various others. This is most evident in "The Metaphysics of Youth" (2:91–94; SW 1:6–17) and Socrates (2:129–32; SW 1:52–54), where the two terms for "genius" are associated with both sexual and "spiritual" identities. In many (though not all) later writings, this is less so—not least because he adds a third term, *ingenium*, which is closer to *Genius* than *Genie*, yet without a similar set of sexual-spiritual associations; see, for example, "Against a Masterpiece" in this volume, 209, or (for an earlier version) "Schemata for the Psychophysical Problem," 6:78; TCV 98. A study of the distinction in Benjamin's early writings can be found in Johannes Streizinger, *Revolte, Eros und Sprache: Walter Benjamins "Metaphysik der Jugend"* (Berlin: Kadmos, 2013), 142–52. The source of the distinction can be traced to his early reflections on the "genius-related" (*geniushaft*) character of "paganism" in contrast to Judaism: "Paganism emerges in the sphere of the daemonic and the genius-related" (6:90). Finally, for an illuminating example of Benjamin's later treatment of genius qua *Genie*, see "Goethe," 170 and especially 173.

15. See Friedrich Hölderlin, "Gesang des Deutschen/Song of the German," a translation of which can be found in Hölderlin, *Poems and Fragments*, trans. Michael Hamburger (Cambridge: Cambridge University Press, 1980), 610–15.

16. For a discussion of the term *Gehalt* and its translation as "matter," see 302–3 and 312. Goethe's introduction of the term "poetized" can be found in Goethe, WA IV, 21:153; letter to Carl Friedrich Graf von Reinhard, 31 December 1809. Benjamin alludes to this letter in "Goethe's Elective Affinities" (111).

17. See Felix Noeggerath, *Synthesis und Systembegriff in der Philosophie*, ed. Hartwig Wiedebach and Peter Fenves (New York: Peter Lang, 2023), 10. The Afterword to this volume (113–36), which includes the first publication of Noeggerath's dissertation, traces the interplay between synthesis and diathesis in the intertwined work of Noeggerath and Benjamin, which began in Munich in 1915–16 and resumed in Ibiza in the early 1930s; for Benjamin's notes on their later conversations, see 6:191–92 and 752.

NOTES TO PAGES 10–13   287

18. Elisabeth Rotten, *Goethes Urphänomen und die platonische Idee* (Gießen: Töpelmann, 1913).

19. Benjamin lists Goethe's *Maxims and Reflections* as 559 on his "Registry of Readings" (7:441; see 253). This indicates that he probably acquired in the summer or fall of 1918 the 1909 edition of the posthumous collection printed in Weimar (which begins, oddly enough, with Ottilie's diaries, extracted from *Elective Affinities*, as though her maxims and reflections, which are joined together by the "red thread" of her love for Eduard, were Goethe's own). In this letter from February 1918, however, he refers to a volume of the Weimar *Sophien*-Ausgabe, probably section II, volume 11, *Zur Naturwissenschaft: Allgemeine Naturlehre: I. Theil* (Böhlau, Weimar, 1893). This is also the volume Benjamin cites at the beginning of his dissertation (1:10; SW 1:116), even though in general, he did not use or cite the Weimar Ausgabe. For his later assessment of its significance in relation to Goethe's afterlife, see 193.

20. Scholem, *Walter Benjamin*, 63.

21. Gershom Scholem, *Tagebücher, nebst Aufsätzen und Entwürfen bis 1923*, ed. Karlfried Gründer, Herbert Kopp-Oberstebrink, and Friedrich Niewöhner (Frankfurt am Main: Jüdischer Verlag, 1995–2000), 1:157; see also 1:49 and 1:38. A week or so after Scholem receives Benjamin's letter, he experiences what he calls a "miracle": "For the first time in my life I have a desire to read Goethe" (*Tagebücher*, 2:150). Desire, of course, is the opposite of renunciation, and the desire to read Goethe, whose work he had previously found undesirable, is thus a form of renunciation, induced by Benjamin's letter. Scholem, however, immediately implies that this is not so: "This [desire] is a consequence of Grete's letter"—not, in other words, Walter's.

22. Scholem, *Tagebücher*, 2:149.

23. See Scholem, *Walter Benjamin*, 63; see also 311–12.

24. See Søren Kierkegaard, *Stages on Life's Way*, trans. Howard and Edna Hong (Princeton: Princeton University Press, 1988), 148–57.

25. Friedrich Gundolf, *Goethe* (Berlin: Bondi, 1916). As one measure of the book's immediate success, Wolfgang Hüppner identifies sixty-five reviews that were published between 1916 and 1922; see his essay "Zur Kontroverse um Friedrich Gundolfs 'Goethe,'" in *Kontroversen in der Literaturtheorie/Literartheorie in der Kontroverse*, ed. Ralf Klausnitzer and Carlos Spoerhase (Bern: Peter Lang, 2007), 183–205.

26. See especially a letter Benjamin wrote to Ernst Schoen, GB 1:457; May 1918; and "Notes on 'Objective Mendacity' I" (6:60; TCV 93). Benjamin makes a similar, though more elusive claim in a passage of "Goethe's Elective Affinities" that he cut from the published version because Borchardt was a close friend

NOTES TO PAGES 13–14

of Hofmannsthal and a frequent contributor to the *Neue Deutsche Beiträge*; see 143–44.

27. For a discussion of how the title of the novel, *Die Wahlverwandtschaften*, can be translated, see 316n6.

28. Benjamin sent a set of his writings that included "Toward the Critique of Violence" (published) and "Goethe's Elective Affinities" (manuscript) to a privatdozent in sociology at the University of Frankfurt, Gottfried Salomon (later, Salomon-Delatour, to distinguish him from Albert Salomon, whom Benjamin also knew; see 37). Salomon(-Delatour) then passed this dossier onto Franz Schultz, a senior colleague in the aesthetics department of the university; see GB 2:311; 1 February 1923, as well as the discussion in GS 1:818–19. Benjamin later wrote a habilitation thesis on German Baroque drama and submitted it to Schultz, who, apparently shocked by what he read, asked Benjamin to withdraw it from consideration as a habilitation thesis. For a concentrated presentation of the relevant documents in this imbroglio, see Burkhardt Lindner, "Habilitationsakte Benjamin," in *Benjamin im Kontext*, ed. Burkhardt Lindner, 2nd ed. (Frankfurt am Main: Athenäum, 1978), 324–41; for a concise description of its last stages, see Howard Eiland and Michael Jennings, *Walter Benjamin: A Critical Life* (Cambridge, Mass.: Harvard University Press, 2014), 222–25.

29. The text of *Gesammelte Schriften* reads as follows: "778) Alfred Seidel: Die Metaphysik der Produktionskräfte <recte: Produktionskräfte und Klassenkampf [Productive Forces and Class Conflict], Dissertation, Heidelberg 1922>" (7:449). There is no reason to make this correction, which obscures the date on which Benjamin read Seidel's work. This is one of many erroneous corrections on the list. Another, which similarly obscures accurate dating, can be found in the following entry 785, which misidentifies the date of the book in question, a translation of an adventure novel by the Swedish writer Frank van Heller; it first appeared in 1918 and was reprinted in 1921, but GS misidentifies its date of publication as 1923 (7:449). Still another error, which is directly relevant to Benjamin's interactions with those associated with the University of Heidelberg, appears in the dating of an essay by Karl Mannheim, which appeared in a Vienna-based journal in 1921 but which GS misidentifies as a text published in 1923 (7:450).

30. For an account of Seidel's academic career, see the introduction to the posthumous publication of his work; Alfred Seidel, *Bewußtsein als Verhängnis*, ed. Hans Prinzhorn (Bonn: Cohen, 1927), esp. 14–21. For an informative discussion of Seidel, see especially Christian Voller, "Alfred Seidel and the Nihilisation of Nihilism: A Contribution to the Pre-history of the Frankfurt School," in *The SAGE Handbook of Frankfurt School Critical Theory*, ed. Beverly Best, Werner

Bonefeld, and Chris O'Kane (Los Angeles: SAGE, 2008). See also Wolf Lepenies, *Between Literature and Science: The Rise of Sociology*, trans. R. J. Hollingdale (Cambridge: Cambridge University Press, 1988), 208–9. It is possible, incidentally, that Benjamin lent Seidel a copy of the manuscript of "Goethe's Elective Affinities," specifically the Heidelberg-located one he mentions in a letter to Rang (GB 2:366; 8 November 1923).

31. For a discussion of the *Archiv für Sozialwissenschaft und Sozialpolitik* and Emil Lederer in the context of Benjamin's publication of "Toward the Critique of Violence," see TCV 7–9; for a brief account of Benjamin's visit to Heidelberg in the summer of 1921, see TCV 264–65.

32. The appendix to Prinzhorn's posthumous edition of Seidel's later book includes an abstract of his dissertation that may be much closer to the spirit of the text Benjamin read than the dissertation itself, since it centers around the theme of metaphysics; see *Bewußtsein als Verhängnis*, 209–11; for the dissertation, see Alfred Seidel, "Produktivität und Klassenkampf: Ein Beitrag zur Interpretation des historischen Materialismus von Karl Marx und Friedrich Engels," *Archiv für die Geschichte des Widerstandes und der Arbeit* 18 (2008): 185–234.

33. Max Weber, "Die protestantische Ethik und der 'Geist' des Kapitalismus," *Archiv für Sozialwissenschaft und Sozialpolitik* 2 (1905): 54; reprinted in *Gesammelte Aufsätze zur Religionssoziologie* (Tübingen: Mohr, 1920), 83; see also 256–57 for further use of the term "elective affinities." (Talcott Parsons's translation of the treatise not only masks *Wahlverwandtschaften* under the word "correlations" but also drops the quotation marks; see Weber, *The Protestant Ethic and the Spirit of Capitalism*, trans. Talcott Parsons [London: Routledge, 2005], 49.) The concept of elective affinities has occasionally become a point of discussion among sociologists and historians of sociology; see, for instance, R. H. Howe, "Weber's Elective Affinities: Sociology within the Bounds of Pure Reason," *American Journal of Sociology* 84.2 (1978): 366–87; and J. J. R. Thomas, "Ideology and Elective Affinity" *Sociology* 19.1 (1985): 39–54. See also Micheal Löwy, *Redemption and Utopia: Jewish Libertarian Thought in Central Europe: A Study in Elective Affinity* (Stanford: Stanford University Press, 1992).

34. In reflecting on the circumstances surrounding Ottilie's death, especially the fact that it was precipitated by the death of a child whom she bore—that is, held in her arms—Benjamin may also have seen a way to advance the line of argument that he briefly proposed around the figure of Niobe near the end of "Toward the Critique of Violence" (2:199–200; TCV 57–58). The "Politics" project from which the latter emerges (see GB 2:119; 29 December 1920), which includes "Toward the Critique of Violence" as one of its elements, resonates with "Goethe's Elective Affinities" in many other ways, none of which

will be mentioned in this Introduction except for the following: both essays are concerned with peace, more exactly, with the difference between peace and the semblance of peace, which consists at best in a perpetual preparation for war. Benjamin emphasizes Kant's concept of eternal peace in the earlier essay (2:185–86; TCV 44–45); in the later one, he examines a configuration of characters that appears peaceable, despite their erotic conflicts; but this appearance requires nothing less than mythic—muted, ambiguous, obscure, quasi-sacral—sacrifice for its maintenance. This, however, does not mean that the appearance of reconciliation should not be pursued; on the contrary, "Goethe's Elective Affinities" thus complicates the uncompromising condemnation of compromise that Benjamin adopts from Erich Unger in the earlier essay (see 2:190–91; TCV 49–50).

35. For Benjamin's draft of the "Announcement of the Journal: Angelus Novus," dated 19 December 1921, see 2:241–46; SW 1:292–96.

36. It is here worth noting that, just before Benjamin names his own contribution to the initial issue of *Angelus Novus*, he indicates that he is hoping to include a contribution from the Dutch diplomat and sinologist Henri Borel that would concern "the spirit of the Chinese language" (GB 2:191; 15 September 1921), congruent with intention of the journal "to go beyond the perimeters of our language, indeed of the West, and direct itself toward other religions" (2:245; SW 1:295).

37. The editors of the *Gesammelte Briefe* are unable to identify the author of the novella whose title Benjamin cites, "The Death of the Lovers," but they suggest that it may be the work of Wolf Heinle, Fritz Heinle's brother; GB 2:221. Could this have been a novella about the double suicide (Fritz Heinle, Rika Seligson)? It is, of course, impossible to say; but the title of the novella suggests a certain proximity with the novella internal to *Elective Affinities*, "The Queer Childhood Neighbors," which is concerned with the life, or rebirth, of the lovers.

38. In their lucid biography, Eiland and Jennings make a similar suggestion, though they do not consider the possibility that Benjamin asked Paul Cassirer whether he would be interested in supporting a new journal; see *Walter Benjamin: A Critical Life*, 182–83. Eiland and Jennings's presentation of the *Angelus Novus* project is helpful in elucidating many aspects of Benjamin's life and work of this period (see esp. 150–57); but it does not indicate that "Goethe's Elective Affinities" (under the title "critique of the Goethean elective affinities") was to be Benjamin's contribution to the initial issue of the journal and, though it outgrew this function, was still to be published there, perhaps in installments, until Weißbach scuttled the whole project.

39. Quoted in Holger Dainat, "Benjamin, Rothacker und die *Deutsche Vierteljahrsschrift*," *Mitteilungen: Marbacher Arbeitskreis für Geschichte der Germanistik* 2 (1991): 23. On Schultz's possession of the manuscript, which he received from Gottfried Salomon-Delatour, see 288n28.

40. Quoted in Andrea Albrecht, Holger Dainat, and Hans-Harald Müller, "Dokumentenanhang zur Geschichte der DVjs (1914–1949)," *Deutsche Vierteljahrsschrift für Literaturwissenschaft und Geistesgeschichte* 97 (2023): 834. For an extensive discussion of this incident, see Dainat, "Benjamin, Rothacker und die *Deutsche Vierteljahrsschrift*," 23–27.

41. Albrecht, Dainat, and Müller, "Dokumentenanhang zur Geschichte der DVjs," 834; cf. 827.

42. The letter from Rothacker to Benjamin, dated 26 April 1923, is reproduced in GB 2:331–32; 14 April 1923.

43. Benjamin's intention of adding something on *Pandora* is repeated in one of the *curriculum vitae* he wrote in 1928 (see 6:219 and 37). Benjamin, incidentally, did not think highly of the work whereby Rothacker obtained his "license to teach," namely, *Einleitung in die Geisteswissenschaften* (Introduction to the Human Sciences, 1st ed., 1920); see GB 2:291; 6 December 1922. Benjamin and Rothacker had another, apparently friendly meeting in Capri; see GB 2:479; 29 August 1924.

44. For the full documentation of the Heidegger-Rothacker interaction, see Joachim Storck and Theodore Kisiel, "Martin Heidegger und die Anfänge der *Deutsche Vierteljahrsschrift für Literaturwissenschaft und Geistesgeschichte*," *Dilthey-Jahrbuch für Philosophie und Geschichte der Geisteswissenschaften* 8 (1992–93): 181–225.

45. For a discussion of this never-written essay, see Theodore Kisiel, *The Genesis of Heidegger's "Being and Time"* (Berkeley: University of California Press, 1993), 270.

46. For a brief account of the courses that Benjamin and Heidegger took together in Freiburg, see Peter Fenves, "Entanglement—of Benjamin with Heidegger," in *Sparks Will Fly: Heidegger and Benjamin*, ed. Andrew Benjamin and Dimitris Vardoulakis (Albany, N.Y.: SUNY Press, 2015), 6–10.

47. The essay to which Heidegger refers (the first published by the journal) is Konrad Burdach, "Faust und die Sorge," *Deutsche Vierteljahrsschrift für Literaturwissenschaft und Geistesgeschichte* 1 (1923): 1–60; see Heidegger, *Sein und Zeit*, 11th ed. (Tübingen: Niemeyer, 1967), 197. Burdach's essay is concerned with the opening of *Faust, Part Two*, specifically the "four grey women" (for Benjamin's invocation of these figures, see 338n3); Rickert's essay is concerned with the end of *Faust, Part Two*, under the title "Fausts Tod und Verklärung," *Deutsche Vierteljahrsschrift für Literaturwissenschaft und Geistesgeschichte* 3 (1925): 1–74.

NOTES TO PAGES 22–27

48. For the discussion around Rickert's contribution, about which Rothacker seemed less than impressed, see Storck and Kisiel, "Martin Heidegger und die Anfänge der *Deutsche Vierteljahrsschrift*," 211–17, including the following note from one of Rothacker's letters to Kluckhohn: "Volume 1, starting with Heidegger, if not Rickert" (211). Heidegger, for his part, thought that it would be "grotesque" (218) to have his work published in conjunction with Rickert's.

49. See Heidegger's letter to Rothacker, 4 January 1924, printed (with editorial interpolations) in Storck and Kisiel, "Martin Heidegger und die Anfänge der *Deutsche Vierteljahrsschrift*," 203.

50. Hugo von Hofmannsthal and Florens Christian Rang, "Briefwechsel: 1905–1924," *Die Neue Rundschau* 70 (1959): 439.

51. Hofmannsthal and Rang, "Briefwechsel," 440.

52. These remarks are taken from a letter Hofmannsthal writes for Benjamin (in English) in conjunction with a possible (though unlikely) appointment of the latter to the recently opened Hebrew University in Jerusalem; see 313n4.

53. For further information about this situation, see Scholem, *Walter Benjamin*, 143–56.

54. WBA 511; among the reasons to suppose that the list of bibliographical items on this page postdates the completion of the published text is that it does not so much as allude to any of them, much less cite them as sources. All of the cited texts, incidentally, are rather obscure contributions to Goethe scholarship.

55. See also Walter Benjamin, *Ursprung des deutschen Trauerspiels* (Berlin: Rowohlt, 1928), n.p. = 263. An image of this page (along with those of the entire book) is accessible via the digital portal of the University of Hamburg's library: https://digitalisate.sub.uni-hamburg.de/.

56. Lācis and Reich were officially married in 1957; for an informative description of their relationship, see Līga Ulberte, "Anna Lācis and Bernhard Reich: Life and Love in the Theatre," *Canadian Review of Comparative Literature / Revue Canadienne de Littérature Comparée* 45.1 (March 2018): 51–68. On Benjamin's relation to Lācis, see also Heinrich Kaulen, "Walter Benjamin und Asja Lacis. Eine biographische Konstellation und ihre Folgen," *Deutsche Vierteljahrsschrift für Literaturwissenschaft und Geistesgeschichte* 69 (1995): 92–122.

57. See Asja Lācis, *Revolutionär im Beruf: Bericht über proletarisches Theater; über Meyerhold, Brecht, Benjamin und Piscator*, ed. Hildegard Brenner (Munich: Rogner & Bernhard, 1971), 55. The error, as noted by the editors of GS (2:1472), concerns the number of names associated with "Goethe" in the *Soviet Encyclopedia*.

58. For a discussion of the experimental character of "Goethe," see Stephan Pabst, "Der sowjetische Goethe: Benjamins *Enzyklopädie*-Artikel 'Goethe' im Verhältnis

zu seinem *Wahlverwandtschaften*-Aufsatz," in *Benjamins Wahlverwandtschaften. Zur Kritik einer programmatischen Interpretation,* ed. Helmut Hühn, Jan Urbich, and Uwe Steiner (Frankfurt am Main: Suhrkamp, 2015), esp. 372–73.

59. As noted earlier, this passage serves as the first epigraph in Noeggerath's 1916 dissertation; see *Synthesis und Systembegriff,* 10.

60. For a brief account of Radek's public satire of Stalin's "Socialism in One Country" as equivalent to a Russian aristocrat in the nineteenth century, buried deep in the hinterlands and reading about England's economy, declaring "Liberalism in One Country," see Adam Ulam, *Stalin: The Man and His Era* (Boston: Beacon Press, 1989), 266. It is as though, upon meeting Benjamin, Radek was practicing the wit he would soon direct against Stalin.

61. The lost radio broadcast on "Young Russian Writers" is related to an essay he wrote under the title "New Literature in Russia" (2:755–62) for the first issue of the *Internationale Revue* (1927), which included abstracts in Dutch, French, and English. For reports of what Benjamin discussed under "Young Russian Writers," see WuN 9.2:780–82; see also Sabine Schiller-Lerg, *Walter Benjamin und der Rundfunk: Programmarbeit zwischen Theorie und Praxis* (Munich: Sauer, 1984), 530.

62. See especially "Two Types of Popularization" (4:671–73; RB 369–71) and "Popularity as a Problem" (238–39). In these reflections on the popularization of science/scholarship, Benjamin presents the theory of relativity as a test case; this is true, too, in relation to "Goethe," as indicated in some remarks he makes in the *Moscow Diary* immediately prior to his description of his first visit to the offices of the *Soviet Encyclopedia* (6:320–21; MD 38).

63. See Большая советская энциклопедия, ed. Soviet-Encyclopedia Committee (Moscow: Soviet-Encyclopedia Publisher, 1926–81), vol. 16 (1929), 530–60.

64. The headings other than those used for "Goethe's Politics and View of Nature" (194–99) are "Goethe-Schiller" (2:1479) and "Goethe's Court, *Elective Affinities, Divan, Faust*" (2:1480).

65. For Benjamin's remarks about his first trip to Weimar, see GB 1:21; 31 July 1910; and for his description of what he expects to experience at the student-association conference there, see GB 1:230; 23 May 1914.

66. See Salomo Friedländer, *Schöpferische Indifferenz* (Munich: Georg Müller, 1918), 313–14.

67. For a comparison of "Goethe" with the review of Kommerell that proceeds in a different direction than the one sketched here, see Adrian Brauneis, "Walter Benjamins 'Goethe'-Typoskript (1928), Eine Untersuchung seiner polemischen Konzeption," *Text & Kontext: Zeitschrift Für Germanistische Literaturforschung in Skandinavien* 39 (2017): 135–73; see also Gabriele Guerra, "Zur Literaturkritik

294 NOTES TO PAGES 34–38

des Konservativen: Walter Benjamin liest Max Kommerell," in *Literaturkritik Heute: Tendenzen, Traditionen, Vermittlung*, ed. Heinrich Kaulen and Christina Gansel (Göttingen: V & R Academic, 2015), 239–51.

68. This difference is further emphasized by Benjamin's blistering attack on Gundolf's attempt at a "magisterial" treatment of the Baroque German dramatist Andreas Gryphius; see 3:86–88.

69. Once it is pointed out, it becomes apparent that the word *Schau* in Kommerell's book is something like a writerly tick; see, for an example (one of dozens), his description of the *Schau* Goethe was granted, or achieved, during his wanderings in forestial terrains: "we cannot know" this *Schau*; but "we can know the force that flowed from it" (Kommerell, *Der Dichter als Führer in der deutschen Klassik* [Berlin: Bondi, 1928], 147).

70. The version in GS (4:641–70) derives the text of the radio play published in a 1932 issue of a radio-oriented journal *Rufer und Hörer*; for a transcript of the play, see WuN 9.1:7–50, which forms the basis of the translation in RB 304–35.

71. See Gottfried Wilhelm Hertz, *Natur und Geist in Goethes Faust* (Frankfurt am Main: Diesterweg, 1931); Albert Salomon, "Goethe," *Die Gesellschaft* 9 (1932): 233–59.

72. As noted earlier, Benjamin told Rothacker that he was considering adding a section on *Pandora*, where he would presumably expand the theme of hope (and also perhaps that of marriage); the play-fragment—which Goethe wrote just before *Elective Affinities* and seems to have abandoned so as to pursue the latter—appears in Benjamin's "Registry of Readings" under number 552 (7:441; 253). With respect to Goethe's story of reduction qua miniaturization, "The New Melusine," see "Goethe's Elective Affinities," 134. For many years Benjamin expressed the intention of writing something on this story. Its initial stages can be found in a set of notes he wrote on "Logic and Language" that refer at a certain point to another note (6:23; SW 1:272) that he himself misplaced; in the same context, he recommends that Scholem read the story outside the context of its publication in *Wilhelm Meister's Journeyman Years* (GB 2:137–38; 14 February 1921). The last reference to this project can be found in a passage of a letter he wrote to Gretel Adorno-Karplus (in French) that touches on the theme of "reduction (Verkleinerung)" as it appears in Adorno's forthcoming book on Wagner: "This passage [in Adorno's manuscript] recalls to me one of my oldest projects about which you perhaps remember having heard me speak: I meant to produce a commentary on Goethe's 'New Melusine'" (6:385; 17 January 1940).

73. The University of Muri—named after a village near Bern where Benjamin and Scholem lived in proximity for a short time while waiting out the First World

War—is a (confabulated) institution of higher education that the two of them created for the purpose of satirizing those with which they were all too familiar.

74. For further discussion of the failure of Benjamin's plan to publish a Goethe book with Insel-Verlag, see Uwe Steiner, "'Das Höchste wäre: zu begreifen, daß alles Factische schon Theorie ist': Walter Benjamin liest Goethe," *Zeitschrift für Deutsche Philologie* 121.2 (2002): 265–84, esp. 265–66; see also Marx and Richter, "Philosophische Alchemie," 109–10.

75. Concerning the city of Frankfurt am Main awarding Kippenberg its Goethe-Plakette, see Hanna Leitgeb, *Der ausgezeichnete Autor: Städtische Literaturpreise und Kulturpolitik in Deutschland 1926–1971* (Berlin: De Gruyter, 2017), 157–58. With respect to Insel-Verlag eventually publishing a book by Benjamin, see *Goethes Wahlverwandtschaften* (Frankfurt am Main: Insel, 1955); reprinted 1964.

76. See Hainer Michalske, "Öffentliche Stimme der 'Inneren Emigration'? Über die Funktion der 'Frankfurter Zeitung' im System nationalsozialistischer Propaganda," *Jahrbuch für Kommunikationsgeschichte* 3 (2001): 170–93.

77. For informative discussions of the "German physics" movement that are important points of departure for contemporary debates concerning its emergence in the early 1920s and status under the Nazi regime, see Alan Beyerchen, *Scientists under Hitler: Politics and the Physics Community in the Third Reich* (New Haven, Conn.: Yale University Press, 1977); and Philip Ball, *Serving the Reich: The Struggle for the Soul of Physics under Hitler* (Chicago: University of Chicago Press, 2014). The year 1935 is often said to be the pinnacle of "German physics" because it was the last full year in which one of its principal proponents, Johannes Stark (who won a Nobel Prize in 1919), presided over the Deutsche Forschungsgemeinschaft.

78. Hirsch introduces his study of the "genesis of fame" or "glory"—*Ruhm* means both—by emphasizing the basic difference between a claim that "Goethe is a German poet" and a claim that "Goethe is a genial poet" (Julian Hirsch, *Die Genesis des Ruhmes: Ein Beitrag zur Methodenlehre der Geschichte* [Leipzig: Barth, 1914], 8). The use of Goethe as a prime example is no accident, for it signals to the genesis of Hirsch's own scholarly project: "Hirsch distanced himself from pro-genius writings of some of his university teachers in Wroclaw and Berlin, like Erich Schmidt and Gustav Roethe, who were both also Friedrich Gundolf's professors. . . . Shortly before Hirsch's publication of *Die Genesis des Ruhmes* (1914), Gundolf had published his habilitation thesis in 1911 on Shakespeare (*Shakespeare und der deutsche Geist*), and in 1912 the genius-affirming essay 'Vorbilder' (Role models) which appeared in *Jahrbuch für die geistige Bewegung* (Yearbook for the intellectual movement). In its preface, Gundolf and Friedrich Wolters . . . praised 'the greatest works of the spirit,' the 'great feat' of the 'great men' of history" (Julia Köhne, "Insufficient Recognition:

296 NOTES TO PAGES 42–44

Comparing Julian Hirsch's and Edgar Zilsel's Analyses of the Glorification of Personalities," in *Edgar Zilsel: Philosopher, Historian, Sociologist*, ed. Donata Romizi, Monika Wulz, and Elisabeth Nemeth [Berlin: Springer, 2022], 227).

79. Benjamin first mentions a lecture at the Sorbonne in a letter to Max Horkheimer (GB 5:179; 16 October 1935), above all, because he wants to emphasize the degree to which he remains hard at work despite "the hardships of [his] current existence" (GB 5:180). Soon thereafter Benjamin tells Werner Kraft about the lecture, adding that he made a "tour" of the faculty members of the Institut des Études germaniques. Among those he met, he found Henri Lichtenberger, its founder, to be "the worst" (GB 5:193; 28 October 1935). For a discussion of Lichtenberger's role, see Hans Manfred Brock, "Henri Lichtenberger, père fondateur de la germanistique française et médiateur entre la France at l'Allemagne," in *Les Études germaniques en France (1900–1970)*, ed. Michel Espagne and Michael Werner (Paris: CNRS Éditions, 1994), 155–69.

80. Marcel Brion, "Une traduction de Baudelaire par Walter Benjamin," *Cahiers du Sud* 12 (1926): 399. Benjamin returned the favor, so to speak, by publishing a report in the journal for *Die Literarische Welt* (see 4:483–85). The Marseilles-based journal also published a translation of (appropriately enough) "Hashish in Marseilles" (4:409–16; SW 6:673–79); see *Les Cahiers du Sud* 22 (1935): 26–33. On the long-standing relation between Benjamin and Brion, see Sofia Cumming, "Berlin—Paris—Marseille: Walter Benjamin and *Les Cahiers du Sud*," *Monatshefte* 113 (2023): 257–71.

81. Albert Béguin, *L'âme romantique et le rêve; essai sur la romantisme allemande et la poésie française* (Marseilles: Editions des Cahiers du Sud, 1937).

82. The two notes from the *Arcades Project* that close this book have generated a lively debate concerning Benjamin's use of the concept of urphenomenon; see "Further Readings" for a variety of perspectives on this convergence.

83. The Introduction could not have been written without the constant assistance of the coeditors of this volume, Kevin McLaughlin and Susan Bernstein. I also want to thank Zakir Paul for an instantaneous response to my query about Benjamin's plan to give a lecture at the Sorbonne. Ursula Marx kindly sent me a facsimile of the list of books and essays on *Elective Affinities* that Benjamin compiled (see 24 and 54; it will be published as part of the critical edition that she and her colleagues are currently preparing). Finally, this Introduction greatly benefited from the comments of Susannah Young-Ah Gottlieb.

1. A Remark on Gundolf: Goethe

"Bemerkung über Gundolf: Goethe," Scholem collection; ca. 1916–17; trans. JC. Benjamin had given Scholem a copy of this protoreview and later described it

NOTES TO PAGES 47–48   297

as follows: "About Goethe—as you can imagine from my scathing review of Gundolf's book—I have *much* to say. I await what you'll find there" (GB 1:44; 30 March 1918).

1. The book in question is Friedrich Gundolf, *Goethe* (Berlin: Bondi, 1916); see also "Goethe's Elective Affinities," 122–25.
2. Gundolf introduces three categories: work, letter, conversation. He further proposes that letters are "more reliable testimony for Goethe's essence" than the conversations and draws a fundamental distinction between work, on the one hand, and both letters and recorded conversations, on the other: "Three main zones of Goethe's outward expressions encircle concentrically from outside to the inside the middle of his essence, in different densities of composition: his conversations, his letters and his works. . . . The conversations and letters only have meaning for us in relation to Goethe's work. Without the works, they would be of no value to anyone" (*Goethe*, 9–11).
3. A considerable number of Benjamin's early writings are concerned with lying, ranging from the ancient Cretan liar's paradox (6:57–59; SW 1:210–12) to a more recent phenomenon he calls "objective mendacity" in a variety of letters and fragments, beginning perhaps with this protoreview of Gundolf's presentation of Goethe as hero. In a letter to Ernst Schoen, Benjamin gives perhaps his most succinct explanation of what is meant by the phrase: "In [Rudolf Borchardt] there can be found the 'reversal of an idea,' which Mr. Scholem specified in his most recent letter to me as characteristic of modern books; it is what I call objective falsehood. In [Borchardt's] case, it is directed toward history, and it is based on an inversion that seems to have become canonical for our time—namely, the falsification of the medium into the organ. He turns history, the medium of the creative artist, into its organ" (GB 1:457–58; May 1918). For a brief discussion of Borchardt, whom Benjamin criticized in a passage of "Goethe's Elective Affinities" that was excised from its original publication, see 330n150; for Benjamin's more extensive presentations of objective mendacity, see 6:60–63; TCV 93–97.
4. For Benjamin's notes on pragmatic history, see 6:93; TCV 76–77.
5. To give an impression of what Benjamin means by this remark, it is helpful to have the table of contents of Gundolf's book in mind:

> First Part: Being and Becoming:
> Beginnings, First Educational Powers, Leipzig, Strassburg, Herder, Shakespeare, New Lyric Poetry, Titanism, Faust, Humor and Satire, Werther, Egmont, Lili, Sociality and Friendship, Physiognomics, Weimar, Society, Landscape

298   NOTE TO PAGE 48

Second Part: Education/Culture:

Preliminary Stages and Transitions to Italy, Karl August, Beginnings of Science, Charlotte von Stein, Summative Poetry, Humanity, Iphigenia, Elpenor, Tasso, Wilhelm Meister's Theatrical Mission, Italy, Nature, Culture [*Kultur*], Art, Adventure and Acquaintances, Poetry, History and Politics, Mathematics, Return, Christiane, Elegies, Epigrams and Epistles, Classicism and Rationalism, Theater, The Revolution, Schiller, Critique of Society, Theory and Creativity, Hermann and Dorothea, The Great Ballads, Wilhelm Meister's Years of Apprenticeship

Third Part: Renunciation and Completion:

The Old Goethe, Napoleon, Bettina, Beethoven, Elective Affinities, Sonnets, Pandora, Poetry and Truth, Historical and Biographical Works, West-Eastern Divan, Lyric Poetry of Old Age, World Literature, Marienbad Elegies, Wilhelm Meister's Journeyman Years, Novelle, Eckermann, Faust II

6. The word translated here (and throughout the volume) as "sum total" is *Inbegriff*. It is a crucial term in several fragments in the first part of this volume, culminating in the opening paragraph of the third section of "Goethe's Elective Affinities" (134–35). *Inbegriff* can simply mean "collection," but its connection with *Begriff* (concept) suggests that the designated collection is conceived or comprehended under some category. In the *Critique of Pure Reason* Kant used *Inbegriff* to designate a certain kind of totality; see, for example, A 155; B 194. In the late nineteenth century, it was adopted by the mathematician Georg Cantor in two ways: on the one hand, it was one of the terms like "aggregate," "manifold," and "set" that designates an object of study; and, on the other, it helps illuminate what terms like "manifold" and "aggregate" mean. Thus, for example, he defines "set" (*Menge*) as "every 'many' that can be thought of as one, that is, every *Inbegriff* of determinate elements that can be combined into a whole by a law" (Cantor, *Gesammelte Abhandlungen*, ed. Ernesto Zermelo [Hildesheim: Olms, 1962], 1:204). It is often translated in mathematical contexts as "aggregate," but to retain the mathematical resonance of the term, it is here translated as "sum total." (Benjamin became familiar with set-theoretical terms through several friends who studied mathematics at an advanced level, including Scholem, and through his interactions with his maternal great-uncle, Arthur Schönfliess, whose work in the first decade of the twentieth century was largely concerned with advancing Cantorian set theory.)

7. Benjamin is alluding to one of Friedrich Schlegel's "Athenaeum Fragments" ("The historian is the backward-looking prophet," no. 80) as well as to the title of Goethe's most widely read novel, *The Sorrows* (Leiden) *of Young Werther*.

2. On a Lost Conclusion to the Note on the Symbolic in Cognition

"Zum verlornen Abschluss der Notiz über die Symbolic in der Erkenntnis," WBA 496; ca. 1919; trans. PF. The basis for the translation is the transcription in WuN 3:143–44.

1. "Urphenomenon" (*Urphänomen*) is a Goethean neologism that he first developed in conjunction with his studies of nature. For an accessible and informative discussion of the emergence and function of the term, see Sebastian Meixner, "Urphänomen (Original/Primordial Phenomenon)," *Goethe-Lexicon of Philosophical Concepts*, 2.1 (December 2022), https://goethe-lexicon.pitt.edu/GL/article/view/46 (accessed September 2023). As is evident in this volume, Benjamin continually returns to the idea of the urphenomenon, sometimes criticizing Goethe's application of the term (see, for example, 112), sometimes adopting it for his own purposes (see, for example, 252).

2. Benjamin's discussion of the distinction between idea and ideal derives from two principal sources. First, Kant establishes this distinction in the opening part of the section of the *Critique of Pure Reason* titled "The Ideal of Pure Reason" (A 567–71; B 595–79). Second, in their initial meeting, Goethe and Schiller spoke about the former's work on the metamorphosis of plants. For the sake of illustration, Goethe made a sketch, prompting "a symbolic plant to spring up before [Schiller's] eyes," whereupon Schiller said, much to Goethe's annoyance, "this is not an experience, this is an idea" (WA I, 36:251; *Poetry and Truth*, "First Encounter with Schiller"); see also Benjamin's discussion of this encounter in "Goethe," 177.

3. This sentence requires a small commentary on its translation: "[A]lle Erkenntnisse müssen durch ihren latenten symbolischen Gehalt Träger einer gewaltigen symbolischen Intention sein, welche sie unter dem Namen der Ontologie dem System selbst einordnet, dessen entscheidende Kategorie Lehre, auch Wahrheit, nicht Erkenntnis ist." Three terms—specifically *Gehalt, gewaltig,* and *Lehre*—are of central importance to several of the texts in this volume. *Lehre*, here translated as "doctrine," can also mean "teaching" and in scholarly-disciplinary contexts "theory." For Benjamin's conception of *Lehre*, see "On the Program of the Coming Philosophy" (2:166–69; SW 1:106–70) and GB 1:389–90; 22 October 1917. The adjective/adverb *gewaltig* derives from *Gewalt*, which can be translated in several ways, including "force," "power" (in the sense

of the Latin juridical term *potestas*), and "violence." In this volume, with few exceptions, *gewaltig* is translated as "forceful/forcefully/forcibly," while *Gewalt* is most often translated as "force." It should not be forgotten, however, that concurrently with some of the writings that resulted in "Goethe's Elective Affinities," Benjamin wrote a series of political reviews and essays, including his 1921 essay "Toward the Critique of Violence [*Gewalt*]." For discussions of the translation of *Gehalt* as "matter," see 302n1 and 313n4.

3. Supplements To: On the Symbolic in Cognition

"Nachträge zu: Über die Symbolik in der Erkenntnis," WBA 497; ca. 1919–20; trans. PF. The basis for the translation is the transcription in WuN 3:145.

1. The word "approach" here and elsewhere in the volume (with a notable exception, 156) translates *Betrachtung*. Although the German word became associated with the sense of sight and is therefore often translated as "contemplation," it derives, like the verb *trachten* ("strive," "aspire"), from the Latin word *tractare* ("draw," "handle," "manage," "treat"), which also yields such terms as *tractate* and *treatise*. In the opening paragraph of his *Origin of the German Trauerspiel*, under the heading "A Concept of the Tractate" (1:207–9; O 1–3), Benjamin reconnects the terms. *Betrachtung* is thus best captured in formal contexts by a term that suggests a roundabout and hence methodical treatment—in other words, an "approach" in the sense that the word often carries in scholarly contexts.

2. The word "muse-related" translates *musische*, which Benjamin here contrasts with "artistic" in other contexts, including a fragment that GS dates to 1915 or 1916:

Art	—Symbolic cognition-level of truth
	— Symbol of the existence of holiness
The muse-related:	The perfection of the beauty that is accidental (6:90)

3. Beyond the general reference to Jean Paul (Johann Paul Friedrich Richter), Benjamin is probably referring to *Maximes & pensées de H. de Balzac* (Paris: Plon, 1852); see his note on Balzac from this period (2:602). Benjamin often refers to Wilhelm von Humboldt's writings on language; see, for instance, "Reflections on Humboldt" (6:26; SW 1:424–25). In conjunction with his "altercation with expressionism" (GB 2:68; 13 January 1920), which included his lost review of Ernst Bloch's *Spirit of Utopia* (for a discussion, see TCV 17–18), Benjamin read Wassily Kandinsky's *Concerning the Spiritual in Art* in translation around 1920; see "The Medium through which Artworks Continue to Influence

Later Ages" (6:126–27; SW 1:235) as well as some brief remarks in "Goethe's Theory of Colors" (205).

4. Early Romantic Theory of Art and Goethe

"Die frühromantische Kunsttheorie und Goethe," appendix to: Dr. Walter Benjamin, *Der Begriff der Kunstkritik in der deutschen Romantik* [The Concept of Art Critique in German Romanticism] (Bern: Francke, 1920), 121–31; WBA 429; trans. KM. Benjamin submitted his doctoral dissertation (without the appendix) to the University of Bern on 27 June 1919. It was published in its entirety as the fifth in a series of volumes edited by Benjamin's dissertation director, Richard Herbertz. It was printed in Berlin by the press of Arthur Scholem, who was Gershom's father; for a description of the circumstances of its publication, see Uwe Steiner's discussion in WuN 3:186–88. The first edition and all subsequent editions of Benjamin's dissertation, *The Concept of Art Critique in German Romanticism*, include a "contents" page with topics that correspond to paragraphs in each section of the text. The appendix consists of seven paragraphs: an introductory paragraph on "Early Romantic Theory of Art and Goethe" followed by six paragraphs that correspond to the six topics listed in the respective section of the "contents" page. Here these topics are provided in footnotes marked with asterisks at the beginning of the paragraphs to which they refer.

In a letter to his friend Ernst Schoen, Benjamin says the following about his recently completed dissertation: "I've written for it an esoteric afterword in which I would have communicated it as *my* work" (GB 2:26; 14 May 1919). The importance of the appendix to Benjamin's overall intention is confirmed by the first paragraph of the two-paragraph notice of its publication that Benjamin posted in *Kant-Studien* 26 (1921): 219. Here is the paragraph in full:

> The object of the work is the Romantic concept of art critique, presented in light of a metahistorical problem, that is, one posed in an absolute manner. This problem runs: what cognitive value for the theory of art does, on the one hand, the concept of its idea, on the other hand, its ideal possess? "The *a priori* of a method in this context is understood under the term 'idea'; there corresponds to it the ideal as the *a priori* of the coordinated matter" [see 54]. The said-problem cannot actually be itself discussed in the present work; it surfaces, rather, in the final chapter. In a comparison of the Goethean concept of the ideal (or urphenomenon) with the Romantic concept of the idea, this chapter seeks to clarify the purest meaning of the philosophy-historical process in reference to the metahistorically posed problem. "The question of the relationship between the Goethean and the Romantic theory of art coincides with the question concerning the

302 NOTE TO PAGE 54

relationship between the pure content and the pure (and, as such, rigorous) form. The question concerning the relationship between form and content, which is often erroneously posed with a view toward the individual work and is never precisely solvable in such a context, arises in this sphere. For form and content are not substrates in the empirical formation but, rather, *relative* distinctions in it, encountered due to necessary, *pure* art-philosophical distinctions. The idea of art is the idea of its form, just as its ideal is the ideal of its content. The fundamental systematic question of the philosophy of art can therefore also be formulated as the question concerning the relationship between the idea and the ideal of art [see 60]." (1:707; WuN 3:160)

1. The phrase at the end of the sentence is "zugeordneten Gehalts." Benjamin here introduces *Gehalt* as a technical term for the ensuing analysis. As is immediately clear, *Gehalt* is somehow to be distinguished from *Inhalt*, which can be translated as "content" without further comment. The translation of *Gehalt*, by contrast, poses a problem not only here but in every subsequent reference to Goethe's work. Benjamin signals as much in the programmatic essay he wrote around 1915 under the title "Two Poems of Friedrich Hölderlin": "it is here proposed that an aesthetic commentary will be attempted, and this intention demands some preliminary remarks on method. The inner form, which Goethe calls *Gehalt*, is to be demonstrated in these poems" (2:105; EW 171). It would be a mistake to suppose that Benjamin is alluding to any passage in Goethe's work where he says something like "By *Gehalt*, I mean, first, something different than *Inhalt*, and second, 'inner form.'" The point of this clause is not to alert readers to a distinction that is to be found ready-made in Goethe's reflections, such that it would require a citation; it is, in reverse, to propose that Goethe's use of the term *Gehalt* should be seen as an equivalent of what will here be called, first, "inner form," then "poetic task," and above all, "the poetized" (*das Gedichtete*), which is indeed a term Goethe occasionally uses (see, for example, WA IV, 21:153; letter to Carl Friedrich Graf von Reinhard, 31 December 1809; and 323n69).

The distinction between *Inhalt* and *Gehalt* is one of the appendix's esoteric dimensions, which corresponds to the emergence of Goethe as an object of study. This, however, only further indicates how difficult it is to translate *Gehalt*, such that it is not confused with *Inhalt*. A note Benjamin probably wrote in preparation for his dissertation is helpful in this regard. The note proposes a concept of *Urgehalt* that is presumably modeled on the Goethean concept of urphenomenon. The term *Urgehalt* is applicable, above all, to mythology—not, however, because it is supposed that myths are the content of art but, rather,

NOTES TO PAGE 55   303

as a designation of the formative "matter" that is metamorphosed into the individual myths that lie at the basis of significant works of art: "*Urgehalt*: mythology / (Material/Common [*Stoff/Gemeiner*] *Gehalt*, intensified through irony) becomes particular *Gehalt*" (7:731; WuN 3:142; cf. 6:125). Only one passage in Benjamin's dissertation directly results from this line of thought, a footnote near the end in which Benjamin briefly explains what is meant by Friedrich Schlegel's notion of "the poetization of the material [*Poetizierung des Stoffes*]" (1:103; SW 1:175): "This theory . . . comprises two moments: first, the annihilation of the material in subjective, playful irony; second, its elevation and ennoblement in mythological *Gehalt*" (1:103; SW 1:197). *Gehalt*, in short, can be seen as the "material" that gives an artwork the kind of transsubjective significance that is expressed by the term "myth." It is for this reason that *Gehalt* is translated here as "matter": it is the basis of a work that, as such, makes it repeatedly matter. (For a discussion of Benjamin's diversification of *Gehalt* into *Sachgehalt* and *Wahrheitsgehalt* in the opening paragraph of "Goethe's Elective Affinities," see 91–92.)

2. Gershom Scholem records a similar remark that he attributes to Benjamin in a diary entry from June 1919; see Scholem, *Tagebücher, nebst Aufsätzen und Entwürfen bis 1923*, ed. Karlfried Gründer, Herbert Kopp-Oberstebrink, Friedrich Niewöhner, and Karl Grözinger, 2 vols. (Frankfurt am Main: Jüdischer Verlag, 1995–2000), 2:449.

3. Benjamin is here distinguishing *Vernehmen* from *Wahrnehmen* (perception); the former is associated with the sense of hearing, on the one hand, and the establishment of a tribunal-like "hearing"—hence, a formal interrogation—on the other. It is because of its association with interrogation that *Vernehmen* forms the root of *Vernunft*, that is, "reason," understood as a faculty or capacity that consists in making inquiries concerning reasons qua "grounds." *Wahrnehmen*, by contrast, is associated with all modes of sensuous receptivity; see Benjamin's contemporaneous fragments on perception (6:32–38; SW 1:92–96). In his preface to his *Origin of the German Trauerspiel*, Benjamin introduces the notion of an *Urvernehmen* or "primal hearing" (1:216–17; O 13).

4. Apropos of the double sense of the term "completed," Benjamin attended Heinrich Rickert's fall-semester lectures on "the philosophy of completed life" at the University in Freiburg in 1913; see his description in GB 1:112; 7 June 1913. Regardless of how unimpressed (unimpressed? yes) he may have been by Rickert's attempt to rescue philosophy from the then-popular currents of vitalism, Benjamin adopts his former professor's concern with completion and perfection in his writings of the 1910s and early 1920s.

5. For a brief discussion of Goethe's concept of urphenomenon, see 299n1.

6. The following several sentences, starting with "The concept of 'that which is

304 NOTES TO PAGES 56–66

presented'" and concluding with "where the relationship between work and archetype is treated)," derive from Benjamin's marginal notes in his copy of the printed text. This note, like the following one (see endnote 9 below), may stem from an effort on Benjamin's part to produce a second edition of his study (see WuN 3:186).

7. Several items in this volume attest to the persistency of Benjamin's attempt to describe and circumscribe the strength and limitations of the Goethean concept of science; see especially 111–13 and 176–78.

8. This is an allusion to the account by Pliny the Elder in chapter 36 of his *Natural History* of the ancient Greek painter Zeuxis, whose painting of grapes is said to be so verisimilar that birds tried to eat them.

9. The sentences beginning with "Here, though, everything" until the end of the paragraph derive from Benjamin's marginal notes in his copy of the printed text; see endnote 7 above.

5. Life Built Up from the Elements

"Leben aus den Elementen aufgebaut," WBA 1313; "Historisch Mythisch," WBA 1156; ca. 1919–20; trans. PF.

1. The word is "Historisch," which suggests the record of events in contrast with "history" (*Geschichte*), understood as the events that occurred.

2. This is a reference to the group of poets, writers, and scholars who congregated around Stefan George, which includes Friedrich Gundolf, who moved from the inner circle to a peripheral position because of the academic positions he acquired.

6. Purity and Rigor Are Categories of the Work

"Reinheit und Strenge sind Kategorien des Werkes . . . ," WBA 1317; ca. 1919–20; trans. PF.

1. The right-side terms are all drawn from the Table of Judgment and the corresponding Table of Categories in Kant's *Critique of Pure Reason* (A 70; B 95; A 80; B 106): universal and singular are quantities of judgment; totality is a quantitative category that corresponds to singular judgment, while limitation is a qualitative category that corresponds to infinite judgment. It is also possible that Benjamin is attempting to distinguish categories of the work from those of art in accordance with Kant's distinction between mathematical (homogeneous) and dynamical (heterogeneous) synthesis (see A 529–30; B 557–58).

7. Notes toward a Work on the Idea of Beauty

"Zu einer Arbeit über die Idee der Schönheit," WBA 1203; ca. 1919–21; trans. PF.

1. The term *Völkerwanderung* (sometimes translated as "migration period" or, to use an earlier locution, "barbarian invasion") refers to the movement of Germanic ("Gothic") peoples during the final stages of the Western Roman Empire. More broadly speaking, Benjamin appears here to be adopting a motif that was developed by a group of scholars associated with the circle around Oskar Goldberg, especially Erich Unger. In a series of sketches that Benjamin wrote under the title "Capitalism as Religion," he specifically refers to page 44 of Unger's book, *Politics and Metaphysics* (6:102; TCV 92), where the following promotion of a renewed *Völkerwanderung*—away from the space of capitalism—can be found: "There is a logical either-or: either frictionless commerce or a wandering of peoples; that is, either the transport of goods contributing to physiological existence or the search for such goods. . . . The assault on the 'capitalist system' must remain forever futile in the place where it reigns supreme. Capitalism is the most powerful and most profound of all systems, and it can integrate every objection raised against its existence in the region where it remains in force. In order to organize anything against capitalism in general, the following is indispensable: to step away from its effective area" (Unger, *Politik und Metaphysik* [1921], repr. ed. Manfred Voigts [Würzburg: Königshausen & Neumann, 1989], 48).

2. Here, too, Benjamin is alluding to the thought of Erich Unger. While discussing the figure of the tragic hero in the *Origin of the German Trauerspiel*, Benjamin refers to Unger's notion of the "violence of the framework [*Gewalt des Rahmens*]" (1:294; O 111).

8. Categories of Aesthetics

"Kategorien der Ästhetik," WBA 1314; ca. 1920; trans. PF. The manuscript page also includes the draft of a letter to Ernst Blass.

1. See Mörike's widely known poem "Auf eine Lampe" (Upon a Lamp), the last line of which Benjamin here quotes, interpolating an exclamation mark: "Was aber schön ist, selig scheint es in ihm selbst" (Eduard Mörike, *Sämtliche Werke* [Berlin and Leipzig: Tempel, 1918], 80).

2. Benjamin may be referring to any number of images associated with the Temptation of St. Anthony, but the most likely one is that of the Isenheim Altarpiece painted by Matthias Grünewald, whose work he elsewhere mentions; see, for example, "Socrates" (2:130; SW 1:52).

306   NOTES TO PAGES 69–72

3. Goethe, WA I, 42.2:139: Beauty.

4. The phrase "moral act" here translates "moralischer Akt." The use of the term *moralisch* indicates that Benjamin is probably conceiving of the act in terms of Kantian moral theory in which goodness is understood as a function of the will under the axiom that goodness is what the pure will wants.

5. This is, of course, an allusion to the opening chapter of Genesis, as Benjamin notes in the final sentence of the fragment, and the notion of "release" here may be understood as an interpretation of the completion of Creation on the sixth day, leaving time for a day of rest. As for the possible sources of the representation of this release as a moral action, whereby Creation is freed, to a degree, from its Creator, this is far from clear. It can be attributed to a variety of commentators; but it may be Benjamin's own reading of the opening chapter of Genesis, which derives from a backward expansion of his commentary on the second and third chapters of Genesis in his 1916 treatise "On Language as Such and on Human Language" (esp. 2:148–50; SW 1:67–69).

6. This paragraph is crossed out.

9. On "Semblance"

"Über 'Schein,'" WBA 1183; ca. 1920–21; trans. PF.

1. Christian Friedrich Hebbel, *Tagebücher*, ed. Felix Baumberg (Berlin: Grote, 1887), 2:360; diary entry for 25 December 1851.

2. See Michel Beheim, "Ain beispel von ainem weib, was vorn schan und hinden schraglich" (An exemplary tale of a woman who, from the front, was beautiful and, from the rear, horrible); *Die Gedichte des Michel Beheim*, ed. Hans Gille and Ingeborg Spriewald (Berlin: Akademie, 1968–72), §279.

3. Edmund Husserl introduced the idea of the "eidetic sciences" in the opening sections of *Ideas for a Pure Phenomenology and Phenomenological Philosophy* (1913), especially §9. Another attempt on Benjamin's part to conduct an eidetic experiment can be found in "Eidos and Concept" (6:29–31).

4. For the original edition of the text, see Jules Barbey D'Aurevilly, *Memorandum* (Caen: Hardel, 1856), 91.

5. Benjamin is probably referring to the opening passage of *The Birth of Tragedy*, where Nietzsche begins an inquiry into "the beautiful semblance of the dream world," associated with Apollo and presented as the "presupposition of all visual art" (§1).

6. "Was diesem Schein Einhalt gebietet, das Leben bannt und der Harmonia ins Wort fällt ist das Ausdruckslose." The phrase "ins Wort fällt" means "interrupt," not as in the interruption of a conversation with another voice but, rather, an

NOTES TO PAGES 74–76   307

interruption that stops a speech in midsentence. The speech in this case is a "harmony," and the phrase is translated accordingly: "stops harmonia in mid-phrase," implicitly suggesting a silence that is different from tragic silence and moral muteness. Benjamin uses the phrase "ins Wort fällt" in "The More Power-fully the Expressionless Comes Forth in Poetry" (82), and much of this para-graph, including the phrase in question, is slightly modified for a passage in the third section of "Goethe's Elective Affinities" (142).

10. Beauty

"Schönheit," WBA 1315; ca. 1920–21; trans. PF.

1. This paragraph revolves around the German term *Mitteilung*, which is here translated as "communication" but, as *Mit-teilung*, means "im-" or, more accu-rately, "coparting." The last, epigram-like sentence of the paragraph runs: "Die Kunst teilt von der Schönheit nur mit."
2. The remaining remarks are found on the reverse side of the fragment, which GS places in the editorial notes.
3. Friedrich Gottlieb Klopstock, "Die Grazien," in *Sämtliche Werke* (Leipzig: Göschen, 1839), 4:302; ll. 6–7; see "Goethe's Elective Affinities," 91.
4. On "de-expiation" (*Entsühnung*), see 321n42. Here, perhaps more than any-where else in his extant work, Benjamin distinguishes "de-expiation" from "expiation" (*Sühne*) by emphasizing that the former consists in a relation to others, whereas the latter consists in an action that alters one's own status, spe-cifically from guilty to restored innocence.

11. Beauty and Semblance

"Schönheit und Schein," WBA 1316; ca. 1920–21; trans. PF. The manuscript also includes a copy of Hölderlin's poem "Blödigkeit" (Timidity) in someone else's handwriting.

1. The text of GS includes two interpolations: "I. Alle<s> Lebendige" and "II. Alle<s> Kunstartige." The latter term suggests whatever is of the order of art, hence "artificial."

12. Truth and Truths / Cognition and Cognitions

"Wahrheit und Wahrheiten / Erkenntnis und Erkenntnisse," WBA 516; ca. 1919–20; trans. PF. A complementary line of thought, probably written around the same time, can be found in "Theory of Cognition," which identifies urphenomena with "symbolic concepts" (6:46; SW 1:276–77).

308 NOTES TO PAGES 78–80

1. Goethe, WA II, 3:121; Reflections on the Theory of Colors and Handling of Color in Antiquity. Benjamin uses this as the same passage from the *Theory of Colors* for the epigraph with which he begins the "Cognition-Critical Preface" he added to his habilitation thesis, *Origin of the German Trauerspiel* (1:207; O 1).

2. Goethe, WA II, 3:121.

3. See Goethe, *Sämmtliche Werke*, ed. Karl Goedeke (Stuttgart: Cotta, 1875); contrariwise, for the epigraph to the "Cognition-Critical Preface" (see 1:410), he cites the so-called Jubilee-edition, *Goethes Sämtliche Werke*, ed. Konrad Burdach, Eduard von der Hellen, et al. (Stuttgart and Berlin: Cotta, 1902–7), 40:140–41.

13. Theory of Art Critique

"Theorie der Kunstkritik," WBA 0400/30–31; ca. 1920–21; trans. PF. This became a draft of the opening paragraph of the third part of "Goethe's Elective Affinities" (134–35), which Benjamin himself considered perhaps too difficult, as he indicates to Hofmannsthal (GB 2:410; 13 January 1924).

1. The term *Mächtigkeit* derives from the word "power" (*Macht*) and can be used in various contexts to indicate both a high degree of power and a certain degree of resistance to power, hence "thickness." In the late nineteenth century, Gregor Cantor adopted it for the development of set theory; it is now generally replaced by *Kardinalität* ("cardinality"). It is so translated because of its close connection to the set-theoretical term *Inbegriff* (see 298n6) and the problem of infinitude, as expressed in the idea of the "infinite task" (see below).

2. The term "infinite task" is closely associated with the methods and aims of the Marburg school of neo-Kantianism, initiated by Hermann Cohen, which transformed the Kantian concept of the thing-in-itself into that of an infinite task. Adopting this perspective while also seeking to transform it so that "infinite" would not be understood in terms of an endlessly progressive timeline, Benjamin considered writing a dissertation on this idea and produced some notes that indicate the direction his dissertation would have taken (see 6:51–52).

3. Benjamin may have come across a logical-grammatical notion of virtuality while undertaking research in the thought of Duns Scotus as the locus of a possible habilitation thesis (see 6:22; SW 1:228).

4. Kant spoke of his major philosophical initiative as a "critical business" (see, for example, the conclusion to the Preface to the *Critique of Judgment*, Aka 5:170).

14. The More Powerfully the Expressionless Comes Forth in Poetry

"... kann sein [...] Je mächtiger in der Dichtung das Ausdrucklose hervortritt," WBA 344; ca. 1921–22; trans. PF. This set of reflections is on verso of "Baudelaire, II III" (6:133–35; SW 1:361–62), which Benjamin drafted in preparation for a talk he gave at the Reuß and Pollak bookstore in Berlin on 15 March 1922 in conjunction with the forthcoming publication of his translation of Baudelaire's *Tableaux parisiens*.

1. It is not clear whether this parenthetic remark refers to the preceding (lost) pages or is preparation for those that follow. If it refers to the extant notes, the title could be reformulated as "The Linguistic Side to the Moral Nature of the Expressionless."
2. For similar formulations of this sentence, see "On 'Semblance'" (72) and "Goethe's Elective Affinities" (142).
3. This is an allusion to the fact that Hölderlin's life was split in half; in its first part, the poet was lucid, whereas in the second he was—to use a term often applied to his post-1806 condition—"benighted."

15. The Sacramental Also Turns into the Mythic

"Ins Mythische wandelt sich auch das Sakramentale," WBA 1325; ca. 1923–25; trans. PF. This set of notes was placed in Benjamin's offprint of "Goethe's Elective Affinities" between pages 165 and 166, which corresponds to 154 (1:194). GS suggests that this placement was an error and that the notes belong elsewhere in the essay (1:837).

1. Benjamin is here working with the double meaning of the verb *verraten* as "betraying" and "revealing," the latter translated as "giving away," since the exposure of the grammatical subject ("Satan") cannot be mistaken for a revelation. For Nietzsche's most prominent depiction of the "spirit of gravity" (*Geist der Schwere*), see the section in part 3 of *Thus Spoke Zarathustra* under this title.

16. With Reference to François-Poncet

"Erwähnung von François-Poncet," WBA 1325; ca. 1923–25; trans. JC. This set of notes was inserted into Benjamin's offprint of "Goethe's Elective Affinities" (WBA 1324; see 311) between pages 144 and 145, which corresponds to 138 (1:176). It may have been conceived in conjunction with his plans to expand the essay into a book; see 24–25.

310 NOTES TO PAGES 86–88

1 The book under examination is André François-Poncet, *Les affinités électives de Goethe: Essai de commentaire critique* (Paris: Alcan, 1910). The book is numbered 842 in Benjamin's "Registry of Readings" (probably read in 1921), where he adds "looked through" (7:451) in parentheses, indicating that, unlike most of the books in the registry, he did not read it cover to cover. These notes may respond to a second, more thorough reading.

2 François-Poncet concludes the analysis to which Benjamin refers in the following way: "At no point did it seem that the Captain retained the memory of the strange adventure that is supposed to have happened to him; furthermore, in the novella, we leave the pseudo-Captain in the arms of his former enemy, and we find him alone in the novel, without the slightest explanation for the new drama that caused his happiness to be shattered. This lacuna would suggest that Goethe conceived the idea of associating the Captain with the hero of 'The Queer Tale' only after he had already completed the novel; hence the evident lack of coherence and the artificial nature of the connection" (187). Benjamin's final question refers to an element in the general "queerness" of the story, in which it is uncertain as to whether in the "real" events from which the story is said to be generated, the young man who would later became a captain (and then a major) rescued his one-time enemy, now lover, or, in reverse, was rescued by her; see the narrator's remarks at the beginning of part 2, chap. 11; WA I, 20:336; *Elective Affinities*.

3 The editors of GS suggest that "character" (*Artung*) can also be read as "respiration" (*Atmung*).

4 The source of this note is WBA 1325, verso. It is printed in GS separately from the notes directed at François-Poncet's book; but as noted below, Benjamin's reflections on Ottilie's status as an orphan respond to a passage in *Les affinités électives de Goethe*.

5 See Goethe, WA I, 20:369; *Elective Affinities*, part 2, chapter 14. François-Poncet discusses this scene through the notion of Ottilie's putative "mutual independence of soul and body" (80).

17. Concerning Elective Affinities

"Zu den Wahlverwandtschaften," WBA 1317; ca. 1922–23; trans. KM. The verso of the manuscript contains corrections of, and questions about, the typescript for "Goethe's Elective Affinities." The headings, with one exception, are marked in one of the manuscripts, designated by GS as M^1 (see 311; see also 313n2 for a discussion of their exclusion from the published version).

1. Benjamin often produced at least one "outline" (*Disposition*) for his longer projects. This was a long-standing practice, begun during his high-school years

NOTE TO PAGE 91   311

when he was required to outline his work, including his Abitur-essay on Grill-parzer and Goethe (see 6–7). In "Teaching and Evaluation," he mocks this requirement, outlining a canto of Goethe's *Hermann and Dorothea* as a demonstration of its dubious educational value (2:36; EW 91–92).

18. Goethe's Elective Affinities

"Goethes Wahlverwandtschaften," *Neue Deutsche Beiträge* 2.1 (April 1924): 83–138 [Parts I and II]; *Neue Deutsche Beiträge* 2.2 (January 1925): 134–68 [Part III]; Akademie der Künste, Berlin, Walter Benjamin Archive 1320/1321 [Parts I and II]; WBA 1322/1323 [Part III]; trans. KM. A small number of offprints of the complete essay were produced under the title *Goethes Wahlverwandtschaften von Walter Benjamin* (Munich: Verlag der Bremer Presse, 1925), pagination running from 83 to 174, with several empty pages in front and back; WBA 1324. A copy of the offprint is housed in the Herzogin Anna Amalia Bibliothek and can be viewed through its digital portal: https://haab-digital.klassik-stiftung.de/viewer/index/. There are three extant manuscripts: first, a typewritten version, originally in the possession of Jula Cohn, which GS designates as M¹ (National Library of Israel, Walter Benjamin Collection, ARC. 4° 1598/04/85; WBA 1319); second, a handwritten version, designated as M² in GS (ARC. 4° 1598/04/85); and third, an outline, "Concerning Elective Affinities," designated as M³ (see 88–90). M¹ is much closer to a fair copy than M², but the typescript that served as the basis for the published text has been lost. The fourth volume of WuN is currently being produced by Martin Kölbel and Ursula Marx under the editorial directorship of Christoph Gödde, Henri Lonitz, and Thomas Rahn; it will include transcriptions of all surviving manuscripts.

The translation here departs in several places from the text as it is reconstructed in GS. We are not in a position to account for the many textual variants (most of which are very slight); but variants that appear significant are described in the endnotes using the following abbreviations: NDB (the essay published in the *Neue Deutsche Beiträge*); WBA 1324 (Benjamin's copy of the offprint); M¹ ("Jula-Cohn manuscript"); and M².

1. All footnotes derive from M¹, including the dedication to Jula Cohn, which can also be found in M². The dedication does not appear in NDB. According to Gershom Scholem, this is because Hugo von Hofmannsthal did not allow dedications in his journal. The editors of GS decided to add the dedication to their edition of the essay in accordance with Scholem's directive, as expressed in the following letter from May 1973: "The dedication to Jula Cohn in my view belongs in the text itself. . . . [Benjamin's] intention was

definitely to dedicate the work to her publicly" (1:846). Scholem's words indicate, however, a degree of hesitation about the dedication: it is only his "view," on the one hand, and yet nevertheless "definite," on the other. Even if Benjamin did intend to dedicate the essay or the planned book (see 24–25) to Jula Cohn, there is reason to suppose that he would have framed the dedication, as he did the dedication to his wife, Dora Kellner-Benjamin, in the *Origin of the German Trauerspiel* and the dedication to Asja Lācis in *One-Way Street*. Each of these frames provides an optic through which the direction of the dedication can be discerned. By insisting that the essay be dedicated to Jula Cohn *simpliciter*, Scholem adds his own frame—and also, oddly enough, presumes that Benjamin would have dedicated it to her using only her "maiden name," even as he prepared for a book publication after her marriage to a childhood friend, Fritz Radt, also the brother of another friend of his, Grete Radt (see 10). As briefly noted in the Introduction, Scholem proposed in the 1970s that the relation between Benjamin and his wife developed into "a situation which, to the extent that I was able to understand it, corresponded to the one in Goethe's *Elective Affinities*" (Scholem, *Walter Benjamin: The Story of a Friendship*, trans. Harry Zohn [New York: Schocken, 1981], 94). This, of course, cannot be taken as a literal statement, for, though Dora had been previously married (like Charlotte in the novel), Walter had not—and was therefore ill-suited for the role of Eduard; furthermore, neither Walter nor Dora were members of the lower nobility who had the financial means and the unnerving desire to cut themselves off from the rest of the world except for a few figures who would help them beautify their estate. What Scholem obviously meant was that the Benjamins' marriage was in trouble, as Walter found himself attracted to Jula Radt (in 1925, Radt-Cohn), while Dora was drawn toward another mutual friend, Ernst Schoen. However this may be, Radt-Cohn gave Scholem a manuscript containing a short series of sonnets that Benjamin had dedicated to her; 7:64–67; see Walter Benjamin, *Sonnets*, trans. Carl Skoggard (Louisville, Canada: Pilot Editions, 2014), 368–79. One of these, "Sonett in der Nacht" (Sonnet in the Night), which invokes the name Jula, includes some of the same images that can be found in the final paragraphs of "Goethe's Elective Affinities." It should be noted, finally, that Scholem delighted in uncovering the real-life persons whom he sees lying hidden in Benjamin's critical writing. This began in November 1917, when, after obtaining a manuscript of Benjamin's reflections on Dostoevsky's novel *The Idiot* (see 2:237–41; SW 1:78–81), he was seized by the "shattering" realization that it was really about Friedrich (Fritz) Heinle, whose suicide Benjamin was able to survive, as Scholem surmises, only by giving up his youth, so that it could be retained as an "idea" (Scholem, *Tagebücher, nebst Aufsätzen und Entwürfen bis 1923*, ed. Karlfried Gründer, Herbert Kopp-Oberstebrink, and Friedrich Niewöhner [Frankfurt am Main: Jüdischer Verlag, 1995–2000], 2:82).

2. Like the dedication, the headings derive from M¹. All but one (see 134) correspond to the "outline" (*Disposition*); see "Concerning Elective Affinities," 88–90. At the end of a letter he wrote to Hofmannsthal, Benjamin indicates that the headings should not be published (GB 2:411; 13 January 1924). This suggests that Hofmannsthal was in possession of a fair copy that included them. Benjamin may have indicated that they should not be published because he knew that Hofmannsthal did not include paragraph headings in NDB essays and saw no reason to ask for a suspension of this practice. (Correspondingly, it seems evident that the copy in Hofmannsthal's hands did not contain a dedication.) For the expansion of the essay into a book (see 24–25 and 37–38), the paragraph headings would probably have been both expanded (in terms of content) and contracted (in terms of their alphanumeric designations).

3. Friedrich Gottlieb Klopstock, "Die Grazien," in *Sämtliche Werke* (Leipzig: Göschen, 1839), 4:302; ll. 6–7.

4. "Truth-of-the-matter" here and henceforth translates *Wahrheitsgehalt*, "subject-matter" *Sachgehalt*. In a letter of recommendation Hofmannsthal wrote for Benjamin in April 1928 in conjunction with the prospect of the latter's appointment at the newly founded Hebrew University of Jerusalem, Hofmannsthal—writing in English with which he was thoroughly familiar, even if his spelling was imperfect—begins his evaluation as follows: "His strength of penetration in treating a literary subject is extraordinary. He does not try to make you *see* his object, but he instantly throws you into the depths [*sic*] of the matter (depths [*sic*] scarcely attainable to the spirit of an ordinary scholar) and from there he makes you feel the relationship, yea the unity of things which on the surface seem far from having to do with one another" (7:878). "Instantly" clearly refers to the opening paragraph of "Goethe's Elective Affinities," which Hofmannsthal assiduously studied; see the letter he wrote to Florens Christian Rang upon first looking at the essay, reproduced in Hofmannsthal and Rang, "Briefwechsel: 1905–1924," *Die Neue Rundschau* 70 (1959): 439. And the term "matter" here is just as clearly Hofmannsthal's translation of *Gehalt*. For this reason—along with those described in the editorial remarks on the opening paragraph "Early Romantic Theory of Art and Goethe" (53–54), which reprises the opening paragraph of "Two Poems of Friedrich Hölderlin" (2:105; EW 171)—*Gehalt* is here translated as "matter" in Benjamin's contrasting constructions: *Sachgehalt* ("subject-matter") and *Wahrheitsgehalt* ("truth-of-the-matter").

314   NOTE TO PAGE 91

By 1921, when Benjamin began working on an essay around Goethe's novel, both *Sachgehalt* and *Wahrheitsgehalt* had been circulating in academic writings, though the latter was far more prevalent than the former. Rudolf Eucken, for example, published a widely read book under the title *Der Wahrheitsgehalt der Religion* a few years after he won the 1908 Nobel Prize for Literature. Benjamin's innovation consists in coordinating the two terms, such that they acquire a function akin to the Kantian distinction between noumenon and phenomenon. *Sachgehalt*, for its part, resembles another term that became a key element of academic philosophy in the period, namely, *Sachverhalt*, which was translated as "atomic fact" by the initial translator of a treatise Ludwig Wittgenstein published around the same time as Benjamin was drafting "Goethe's Elective Affinities" (see Wittgenstein, *Tractatus Logico-Philosophicus*, trans. C. K. Ogden [London: Kegan Paul, 1922], 25). Subsequent translators of the *Tractatus* replaced "atomic fact" with "state of affairs," which may be more appropriate in general but misses Wittgenstein's close association of *Sachverhalt* with *Tatsache*, which is generally translated as "fact," for it, too, derives from the act of making something happen (*Tat-Sache* is equivalent to *factum*, which derives from *facere*, "to make" or "to do," as does *Tun* in German). With respect to the *Sach(e)* element of both terms, *Sachgehalt* and *Sachverhalt*, it is broadly equivalent to the Latin word *res* as well as the Germanic word *ding*, both of which originally derive from the juridical resolution of something in dispute. Like *res* and *ding* qua *thing*, *Sach(e)* was eventually generalized to mean anything whatsoever—that is, anything that transcends "subjective" perspectives and interests. As with the Latin *causa* from which the French word *chose* (= "thing") derives, *Sache* forms the root of *Ursache*, that is, "cause," beginning with the cause of a conflict that requires expiation, viz. juridical redress. Whereas the *Verhalt-* element in *Sachverhalt* suggests a condition that "holds" something in relation to something else, the *Gehalt-* element in *Sachgehalt* indicates not so much the thing being contained as the conditions that solicit containment, which can be understood as the underlying or a priori "matter." As is well known, the Latin term from which the English term *subject* derives, namely, *subjectum*, was conceived among medieval-scholastic philosophers as a translation of the Aristotelian term for *hupokeimenon* ("that which lies below"). "Subject" in this context is closer to "object" than it is to "the subject," understood as the seat of consciousness. This semantic shift did not affect all uses of the term *subject*, and this includes the first term in the phrase "subject-matter." While drafting "Goethe's Elective Affinities," Benjamin was in the process of testing out the possibility of producing a habilitation thesis on scholastic speculative grammar (see 6:22–23; SW 1:228) and was thus concerned with fields

NOTE TO PAGE 92   315

of reference where "subject" had not undergone the aforementioned semantic shift. The "subject" in "subject-matter" specifies the "thing" around which a dispute forms and commentary sets out to resolve, and so "subject" serves as the translation of *Sache* whenever its use derives from its separation from *Gehalt*.

With respect to *Wahrheitsgehalt*, its translation is relatively simple, for it goes without saying that its initial component, *Wahrheit*, should be translated as "truth." There is a degree of truth to this standard translation; but it should not be forgotten that "Goethe's Elective Affinities" contains an altercation with traditional concepts of truth that is as wide ranging, subtle, and consequential as the one Wittgenstein undertakes in his contemporaneous treatise. *Wahrheitsgehalt* is here translated as "truth-of-the-matter," which preserves the genitive construction while adding a definite article as an index of the enigmatic instant—if this is the right temporal term—in which, as Benjamin emphasizes, "the truth-of-the-matter proves itself such [viz. true] as that of the subject-matter" (94).

In only two contexts does Benjamin return to the pair of "matter"-terms in his later writings. In both cases, moreover, his reflections are schematic and probably not intended for publication. The first context, from the late 1920s, concerns the issue of criticizability, uncriticizability, and "false critique" (see 6:169 and 6:178–79). The second probably arises in the late 1930s in response to Theodor Adorno's invocation of "truth-of-the-matter" in his critique of Benjamin's work on the *Arcades Project*. "The duration of the effect of a literary work"—Benjamin writes in the collection of aphorisms titled "Central Park"—"stands in inverse relation to the conspicuousness of its subject-matter. (Truth-of-the-matter? See *Elective Affinities* essay)" (1:689; SW 4:190; see also GB 6:186; 9–12 December 1938). And another note similarly reprises the opening paragraphs of "Goethe's Elective Affinities," which, as Hofmannsthal notes, "instantly" throws the reader into the "depths of the matter": "The truth-of-the-matter is bound up with the subject-matter; the more various parts of the latter fade, the clearer various parts of the former become" (7:765).

5. Nowhere else in the essay does Benjamin refer to either the figure of the alchemist or that of the chemist. The point of doing so here is doubtless related to the title of the essay, which refers, of course, to the title of Goethe's novel (see the following endnote), itself borrowed from contemporaneous chemistry. As for alchemy, this scarcely ever comes under discussion in Goethe's works and only a few times in Benjamin's; see the brief remarks in a fragment "On the Middle Ages" (2:132–33; EW 239) as well as similarly brief remarks in one of the final paragraphs of the *Origin of the German Trauerspiel* (1:403; O 251). Even if Benjamin rarely discusses either the figure of the alchemist or the practice

316   NOTE TO PAGE 93

of alchemy, there are nevertheless two places in writings prior to "Goethe's Elective Affinities" where he seeks to capture a concept of critique through an appeal to a chemistry-laden distinction. The first of these can be found in a letter dated from around the winter of 1916 when Benjamin describes his horror at reading Thomas Mann's promilitarist "Gedanken im Krieg" (Thoughts during War, 1914). How, Benjamin asks, can one undertake a critique of what he calls "the night" when critique, derived from the ancient Greek word *krinein*, consists in separation, and during the night, no separation can be seen? Without invoking such alchemical terms as "the philosopher's stone" or "the elixir of life"—both of which are implied in his reference to the figure of the alchemist in the opening paragraph of "Goethe's Elective Affinities"—Benjamin proposes a "supra-chemical material" that operates in an enigmatically "diathetic" (rather than synthetic) manner: "True critique does not go against its object: it is like a chemical material that attacks another only in the sense that it reveals its inner nature by decomposing it, not by destroying it. The supra-chemical material that attacks *spiritual* things in such a manner (diathetically) is light. This does not appear in language" (GB 1:349; end of 1916). Benjamin's doctoral dissertation culminates in a claim that can be understood as the consequence of this formulation of "true critique": "Critique is the preparation of the prosaic core of every work. The concept of 'preparation' is thereby understood in the sense used in chemistry, as the production of the material through a specific process to which others are submitted" (1:109; SW 1:178). "Goethe's Elective Affinities" takes flight, as it were, from these complementary conceptions of critique.

6. The word "approach" translates the German *Betrachtung* when it is used—as is often the case—in a methodological sense; for an explanation, see 300n1, where it is noted also that there is an important exception, specifically a passage in this essay where Benjamin quotes a sentence from the novella, 156. The final phrase in this sentence translates *einer der strengsten und sachlichsten Ausprägungen menschlichen Lebensgehalts.* In both NDB and the manuscripts, the essay's title does not mark typographically "elective affinities" as the title of Goethe's novel. This could be seen as a matter of a convention. Gundolf's *Goethe* (see 122–27) is similar to Benjamin's essay in this regard; so, too, is Cohen's *Aesthetics of Pure Feeling* (see 99). Even so, the lack of diacritical marks is significant. After appearing with no diacritical marking in the title of the essay, the word *Wahlverwandtschaften* occurs for the first time on page 83 of NDB (91), also unmarked, and it remains so. This stands in contrast with, for example, Kant's *Metaphysics of Morals*, which Benjamin places in quotation marks. The practice of leaving "Wahlverwandtschaften" and "die Wahlverwandtschfaten" unmarked introduces a consistent ambiguity: the terms refer at once to Goethe's novel as

well as to the affinities (or relationships) that he chose, to the extent that it is possible to do so. The translation of the title retains this suggestion, but in order to avoid confusion, "die Wahlverwandtschaften" (without diacritical marks) is almost always translated as *Elective Affinities* rather than "the elective affinities." It should be further noted that, though the translation of *Die Wahlverwandtschaften* as *Elective Affinities* is a time-honored tradition—with the alternative translation, "Kindred by Choice," rarely coming into favor—both terms in the German title are key elements of Benjamin's argument. *Wahl* means "choice" and is associated with an "election" (hence also the act of "voting") among a finite range of options. *Verwandtschaft* derives, of course, from *verwandt*, which means "relation" or "relationship" in the genealogical sense, hence both "kindred" and (especially in the singular) "kin." Goethe ultimately (though probably indirectly) drew the title of his novel from a treatise by the Swedish chemist Tobern Bergman, *Disputatio de attractionibus electivis* (1775), which was translated into German as *Wahlverwandtschaft*. On the chemistry that gives rise to the novel, see Georg Schwerdt, *Goethe als Chemiker* (Berlin: Springer, 1998), esp. 319–30. Probably before Benjamin turned his attention to Goethe's novel, he wrote a series of reflections on the relation between *Verwandtschaft* and analogy. Scholem's archive of Benjamin's writings includes one of the early stages of his reflection on this topic; see "Analogy and Affinity [*Verwandtschaft*]" (6:43–45; SW 1:207–9). Though much of this note is tentative, it is emphatic about one point, which runs counter to the chemical analogy that gives Goethe the title of his novel: *Verwandtschaft*, according to Benjamin, has nothing in principle to do with causality. This means, among other things, that, though there may be a difference between a "relationship by choice" (*Wahlverwandtschaft*) and a "relationship by blood" (*Blutverwandtschaft*), it is not fundamental or categorial. Analogy and *Verwandtschaft*, by contrast, are also distinguished from each other: analogy is based on reason qua "ratio," whereas the "essence" of *Verwandtschaft*, removed from all *rationes*, including the calculation of causes, remains "enigmatic" (6:43; SW 1:207). Although marriage is often viewed as the paradigmatic form of a "relationship by choice"—in contrast to consanguinity—Benjamin's inquiry into "Goethe's Elective Affinities" positively avoids any suggestion along these lines. This, ultimately, is the best reason to translate *Die Wahlverwandtschaften* as *Elective Affinities* in the context of Benjamin's inquiries: *affinity* is not associated with unidirectional causality.

7. Kant, Aka 6:278.

8. GS reads *des Siegelns* (sealing) based on M¹ and M²; but both NDB and WBA 1324 read *des Siegels* (imprint), which is what is translated here.

9. Kant, Aka 6:277.

318   NOTES TO PAGES 95–101

10. See Hermann Cohen, *Die dramatische Idee in Mozarts Operntexten* (Berlin: Cassirer, 1915), 105–15.

11. Goethe, WA I, 20:107; *Elective Affinities*, part 1, chapter 9.

12. Goethe, WA I, 20:108; *Elective Affinities*, part 1, chapter 9.

13. Kant, Aka 6:409: *Metaphysics of Morals*, Doctrine of Right.

14. The phrase "justification in law" translates "im Recht die Rechtfertigung." Instead of "persistence" (*Bestehen*), M¹ has "eternity" (*Ewigkeit*).

15. This sentence alludes to the final one in "Toward the Critique of Violence" (2:203; TCV 60).

16. The word "action" in this sentence translates *Handlung*, which can also mean "plot."

17. Goethe, WA II, 1: *Theory of Colors*, preface.

18. B., "Ueber Goethes Wahlverwandtschaften," *Zeitung für die elegante Welt* (2 January 1810); cited in Julius Braun, *Goethe im Urtheile seiner Zeitgenossen. Zeitungskritiken, Berichte, Notizen, Goethe und seine Werke betreffend* (Leipzig: Schlicke, 1885), 3:234. Benjamin slightly modifies his source (which GS corrects); the translation follows NDB.

19. In M¹ this sentence reads: "Water is the chaotic primal element of life: here, however, not in the rough wave that brings about the doom of human beings."

20. In WBA 1324 Benjamin added "something primeval."

21. Anonymous, "Ueber Goethes Wahlverwandtschaften," *Evangelische Kirchen-Zeitung* [Reform-Church newspaper] 5.59 (23 July 1831): 468; the review appeared over the course of five issues in the summer of 1831. Benjamin modifies his source (which GS corrects); the translation follows NDB. The satirical remark refers to WA I, 20:362; *Elective Affinities*, part 2, chapter 13.

22. Wilhelm Ferdinand Solger, "Über die Wahlverwandtschaften" (1809), *Nachgelassene Schriften und Briefwechsel*, ed. Ludwig Tieck und Friedrich von Raumer (Leipzig: Brockhaus, 1826), 1:175–85; Albert Bielschowsky, *Goethe. Sein Leben und seine Werke*, 11th ed. (Munich: Beck, 1907), 2:256–94.

23. Hermann Cohen, *Aesthetik des reinen Gefühls* (Berlin: Cassirer, 1912), 2:131.

24. Benjamin is alluding to one of the remarks in Ottilie's diary, WA I, 20:260; *Elective Affinities*, part 2, chapter 5.

25. For the sentence in the quotation, see Hans Gerhard Gräf, *Goethe ueber seine Dichtungen. Versuch einer Sammlung aller Aeußerungen des Dichters ueber seine poetischen Werke* (Frankfurt am Main: Rütten & Loening, 1901), 1:436 (no. 868); this is one of the conversations recorded under the heading "1810, *Elective Affinities*." With respect to the unusual parenthetical aside, the translation includes a remark about Johann Peter Hebel that Benjamin added in M¹. The phrase in question, "zu bösern Häusern," can be found in several of Hebel's stories, including two

involving his favorite rogues: "The Three Thieves" and "How Zundelfrieder and His Brother Once Played a Prank on Red-Haired Dieter." And certain editions of Grimm's dictionary do take note of the phrase, citing Hebel as one of the sources; see Jacob Grimm and Wilhelm Grimm, *Deutsches Wörterbuch*, ed. Moriz Heyne (Leipzig: Hirzel, 1877), 4.2:648–49. The source of the images of "houses" is said to be not astrological houses but rather economics. "Bad houses" are those where business declines. "Fiasco," which seems to come from the image of broken flasks, may be the closest word in English.

26. Goethe, WA G, 6:167; conversation with Eckermann, 21 July 1827. To this are added these remarks: "This latter sentiment is aroused in us when we see a moral evil approaching actors or agents and spreading over them, as, for example, in *Elective Affinities*. Fear [*Angst*], on the other hand, emerges in the reader or spectator when actors or agents are threatened by a physical danger."

27. Goethe, WA G, 3:254; conversation with Sulpiz Boisserée, 5 October 1815.

28. "Masonic-inflected" derives from WBA 1324.

29. WA I, 20:97; *Elective Affinities*, part 1, chapter 9.

30. K. f. d., "Die Wahlverwandtschaften: Ein Roman von Goethe 1809," *Jenaische Allgemeine Literatur-Zeitung* (18–19 January 1810); cited in Julius Braun, *Goethe im Urtheile seiner Zeitgenossen*, 3:241.

31. Latin phrase: "Of the dead nothing but good is to be said."

32. Goethe, WA I, 20:207; *Elective Affinities*, part 2, chapter 1.

33. Benjamin is alluding to an incident in the novel involving Luciane and the Architect; see Goethe, WA I, 20:232–33; *Elective Affinities*, part 2, chapter 4.

34. Goethe, WA I, 20:210; *Elective Affinities*, part 2, chapter 2.

35. Richard Moritz Meyer, *Goethe* (Berlin: Hoffmann, 1898), 1:316–17: "[Goethe and Schiller] converge in the recognition of the ideal types as the invincible foundation of poetry. Of all the catchphrases that have been used to contrast Goethe and Schiller, the most frequently used observation is that Goethe proceeds inductively, Schiller deductively: the latter goes from the general to the particular, Goethe from the particular to the general. This is not entirely true; but it indicates a very important point. Yet if they came from different sides and went to different destinations, they were still moving along the same path and had to meet in the middle. And this center is formed by the types. They contain enough individual elements to represent the particular, enough general elements to be able to represent the general. 'Every character, however peculiar, and everything to be represented, from the stone up to the human being, has universality; because everything repeats itself, and there is not a thing in the world that only exists once'; so says Goethe himself. And now art emphasizes those cases in which this generality emerges particularly clearly, those cases,

320 NOTES TO PAGES 103–104

those objects that Goethe calls 'symbolic': 'eminent cases,' which in a character-istic multiplicity as representatives consists of many others and because these typical cases and objects mediate between 'nature,' that is, the abundance of individual things, and the 'idea,' that is, the spiritual concentration of what belongs together, they become Goethe's supreme concept, 'nature,' and Schiller's highest concept, the 'idea,' at the same time."

36. Though the phrase "eternal return/recurrence of the same" is, of course, associated with Nietzsche, Benjamin does not name him here—or anywhere else in the essay. And it is perhaps not insignificant that he uses a variant of the phrase, "eternal return/recurrence of *all* the same" (*ewigen Wiederkehr **alles** Gleichen*), that Nietzsche never once uses.

37. Goethe, WA I, 20:344–45; *Elective Affinities*, part 2, chapter 9.

38. Friedrich Gundolf, *Goethe* (Berlin: Bondi, 1916), 554; see also his "A Remark on Gundolf: Goethe" (47–49). The source of Benjamin's polemical relation to Gundolf is by no means clear, but it is consistent; see his critique of the book Gundolf wrote on the Baroque poet and dramatist Andreas Gryphius, 3:86–88. He attended at least one of Gundolf's lectures during a visit to Heidelberg in the summer of 1921 and found him "enormously puny and harmless in his personal effect, entirely different than in his books" (GB 2:171; 20 July 1921).

39. The discussion of fate and character in these—and subsequent—paragraphs of the essay represents a recapitulation of the argument Benjamin developed in a more abstract form in an essay published in the journal *Die Argonauten* under the title "Fate and Character" (2:171–79; SW 1:201–6). In a letter to Hof-mannsthal, Benjamin indicated that he no longer wished to engage in a "frontal assault" (*Frontalangriff*) on concepts (*Begriffe*), as he had sought to do in "Fate and Character" (GB 2:410; 13 January 1924).

40. Friedrich Wilhelm Riemer, *Briefwechsel zwischen Goethe und Zelter in den Jahren 1796 bis 1832* (Berlin: Duncker & Humblot, 1833–34), 3:474; attachment to a letter to Goethe, 10 December 1810. Zelter may be alluding to a passage in the novel where Ottilie says of herself that she "stepped out of her path" (WA I, 2:370; part 2, chapter 14; see also 87). *The Accomplices* (1768–69) is one of Goethe's comedies. Alcest (played by Goethe in the first performance on 9 January 1777) has had a love affair with Sophie, now married unhappily to Söller. While staying at the inn of Sophie's father, Alcest's money is stolen from his room during the night. Because the guilty party remains a mystery until the end, the characters come to share in the guilt and thus are "partners in guilt" (*Mitschuldigen*).

41. See Bielschowsky, *Goethe*, 2:276. The adjective "natural-philosophical-ethical" translates the German *naturphilosophisch-ethisch*, which refers to a mode of

NOTES TO PAGES 104–106   321

research and reflection that is distinct from "natural philosophy," as it was conducted in western European countries and often therefore retains its German name, *Naturphilosophie*. Especially important for Goethe in this context was the work of Friedrich Schelling, whom Goethe brought to the University of Jena in light of the latter's treatise *Von der Weltseele* (On the World Soul, 1798).

42. The word "de-expiation" in this sentence translates *Entsühnung*. In ordinary contexts—if such is possible for a word like *Entsühnung*—there is little semantic difference between it and its root term, *Sühne*, "expiation." The same is true of the corresponding terms in Latin, *piare* and *expiare*; see the entry under "Entsühnen," written by Jacob Grimm, in Jacob and Wilhelm Grimm, *Deutsches Wörterbuch* (Leipzig: Hirzel, 1862), 3:637–38. For Benjamin, however, here and in several of his early writings, especially "Toward the Critique of Violence," the two terms function as antonyms, such that "ent-" (like the Latin "ex-") indicates not the completion of a process but, rather, its undoing. It is not out of the question, however, that the semantic proximity of *Sühne* and *Entsühnung* in "ordinary" contexts suggests that undoing is completion and completion correspondingly requires undoing. For this reason, an alternative translation of *Entsühnung* would be "ex-piation" (see TCV 31–34).

43. In M¹ "bad luck" (*Unglück*) is to be found instead of "fatum."

44. Gundolf, *Goethe*, 562–63: "[E]ach and everything appears in one place as a stage prop, a setting, a landscape, at others as a daemonic link of doom, and so, like the people and the events, the things in this novel also have the aspect of freedom and of necessity . . . or rather we are imperceptibly led by the master, who knows in advance, through a graceful labyrinth of persons, events, landscapes, objects, with the feeling of his and our freedom, until we realize that we are spellbound, that everything is enchanted and that from every harmless corner disaster looks at us, one whose inescapable circle has closed tightly around us. But this is precisely the pathos of this work, no less tragically sublime and moving than that from which Sophocles's *Oedipus* stems."

45. Goethe, WA I, 46:33; Winckelmann, section 1, Catholicism.

46. In M¹ Benjamin adds above the citation: "Something like a non-moralistic sense of 'sacrifice' to be indicated here?"

47. Benjamin inserts the word "lebenden" (= *vivant*) in brackets.

48. Abeken, "Ueber Goethes Wahlverwandtschaften (Fragmente aus einem Briefe)," reprinted in Gräf, *Goethe ueber seine Dichtungen*, 1:443 (no. 869); Abeken is referring to a passage in part 2, chapter 6; WA I, 20:270–71.

49. Solger, *Nachgelassene Schriften und Briefwechsel* (Leipzig: Brockhaus, 1826), 1:182; see note 46 above.

50. The word "statements" here translates *Äußerungen*. It occurs again below where

322   NOTES TO PAGES 106–109

it has a broader signification and is translated as "outward expressions" (97). For an earlier version of the reflections contained in this passage, see "A Remark on Gundolf: Goethe," 47–48.

51. Goethe, WA IV, 43:179; letter to Zelter, 21 November 1827; cf. WA IV, 43:189, letter to Kaspar Graf Sternber, 27 November 1827.

52. Madame la Baronne de Staël-Holstein, *Œuvres complètes* (Paris: Didot, 1861), 2:150: "One cannot deny that there is in this book a profound knowledge of the human heart; but it is a discouraging knowledge; life is represented here as a rather indifferent thing, however one spends it; sad when one delves into it, pleasant enough when one dodges it, susceptible to moral illnesses which must be cured if one can and from which one must die if one cannot."

53. Christoph Martin Wieland, letter to Caroline Herder (though the addressee is uncertain), 15 November 1809; cited in Gräf, *Goethe ueber seine Dichtungen*, 1:423–24 (no. 855a).

54. Friedrich Heinrich Jacobi, letter to Friedrich Köppen, 12 January 1810; cited in Wilhelm Bode, *Goethe in vertraulichen Briefen seiner Zeitgenossen. Auch Lebensgeschichte* (Berlin: Mittler & Sohn, 1921–23), 2:233.

55. Though the review in question, "Ueber Goethes Wahlverwandtschaften," appeared anonymously (see 321n48), Benjamin is suggesting that Hengstenberg, as editor of the *Evangelische Kirchen-Zeitung*, was responsible for it.

56. For a discussion of these events, which was probably the source of Benjamin's remarks here, see Carl Schüddekopf and Oskar Walzel, *Goethe und die Romantik. Briefe mit Erläuterungen* (Weimar: Goethe Gesellschaft, 1899), 58–66. Werner's letter to Goethe is dated 23 April 1811. In sending the sonnet Benjamin cites in full, Werner describes *Elective Affinities* as "a book that is, for me, eternally remarkable" (62).

57. Friedrich Ludwig Zacharias Werner, *Sämmtliche Werke, Aus seinem handschriftlichen Nachlasse*, edited by his friends (Grimma: Comptoir, 1840), 2:24. Benjamin's version of the sonnet differs in small ways from the one printed in this then-rare volume.

58. As GS indicates, in the process of putting together the fair copy that was sent to Hofmannsthal, Benjamin mixed up "former" and "latter" with reference to the two reviews; the translation follows GS in correcting the error.

59. Wilhelm and Caroline von Humboldt, *Wilhelm und Caroline von Humboldt in ihren Briefe*, ed. Anna von Sydow (Berlin: Mittler & Sohn, 1909), 3:356; letter from Wilhelm to Caroline, 6 March 1810.

60. Goethe (following a practice that was common at the time) combines a word written in Greek letters with a suffix in Latin letters (or Fraktur), καρτεpirien. The source of the Greco-German term Goethe uses (and perhaps invents) is the

NOTES TO PAGES 109–112   323

ancient Greek word καρτερεῖν, which means "to stand steadfast," "to be patient," "to persevere," "to endure," etc.

61. Goethe, WA G, 2:286; conversation with Riemer, 6–10 December 1809.

62. Latin phrase: "the story teaches."

63. Alfred Mézières, *Goethe. Les Œuvres expliquées par la vie (1795–1832)*, 2nd ed. (Paris: Didier, 1874), 2:208.

64. Bettina von Arnim, *Goethes Briefwechsel mit einem Kinde*, 2:100. There has long been a lively scholarly discussion as to the authenticity of this putative "Correspondence with a Child." For Goethe's use of the term *Versäumnis*, here translated as "neglection," in his incontrovertibly authentic correspondence, see 243.

65. Goethe, WA G, 6:136; conversation with Eckermann, 5–6 May 1827: "The only product on a *larger* scale in which I am aware of having worked from the presentation of a comprehensive idea would be my *Elective Affinities*. The novel has thus become comprehensible to the intellect; but I don't want to say that this made it any better! Rather, I am of the opinion: the more incommensurable and incomprehensible to the mind a poetic production, the better."

66. Goethe, WA IV, 20:345–46; letter to Zelter, 1 June 1809.

67. Goethe, WA G, 7:9; conversation with Eckermann, 9 February 1829; Benjamin slightly modifies the quotation.

68. One fragment has been discovered, an outline of part 1 of the novel; for a transcription, see Goethe, *Die Leiden des jungen Werthers, Die Wahlverwandtschaften, Kleine Prosa Epen*, ed. Waltraub Wiethölter and Christoph Brecht (Frankfurt am Main: Suhrkamp, Deutscher Klassiker, 2006), 975–77.

69. See Goethe, WA IV, 21:153; letter to Carl Friedrich Graf von Reinhard, 31 December 1809. Benjamin cites the key phrase: "the poetized asserts its right as does that which has occurred." Benjamin adopted this term and made it central to his early essay on Hölderlin's poetry, in which he asserts that "the poetized" designates the "precondition" of the poem (2:105; SW 1:18).

70. Wilhelm and Caroline von Humboldt, *Wilhelm und Caroline von Humboldt in ihren Briefe*, 3:356; letter from Wilhelm to Caroline, 6 March 1810.

71. The epithet of "Olympian," applied to Zeus in Homer's *Iliad*, became associated with Goethe during his lifetime as part of the effort by the poet himself and those around him to identify him with a vision of classical antiquity as what the eighteenth-century German art historian Johann Joachim Winckelmann called "noble simplicity and quiet grandeur."

72. On the Goethean concept of urphenomenon, see 299n1. The sentence in M[1] is slightly different and perhaps clearer: "He sought to show the presence of 'true' nature as urphenomenon in [perceptible] appearances, as he presupposed them in artworks. He was never, however, able to attain the logical center

NOTES TO PAGES 112–113

of this highly productive relationship, since he never determined 'true' nature in a conceptual manner" (1:850). For Benjamin's later exposition of Goethe's theory of nature, see 178–79.

73. Goethe's advertisement for *Elective Affinities* appeared anonymously in the *Morgenblatt für gebildete Stände* on 4 September 1809; as noted below (332n164), it was reprinted in Julius Braun, *Goethe im Urtheile seiner Zeitgenossen*, 3:211.

74. Solger, *Nachgelassene Schriften und Briefwechsel*, 204; letter to Abeken, 28 October 1810.

75. *God and World* (1798–1827) includes "Entoptic Colors," "Metamorphosis of Plants," and "Primal Words. Orphic" to which Benjamin returns below.

76. Goethe, WA II, 1:x; preface.

77. The fragment in question, printed in WA under the title "Die Natur. Ein Fragment," was written—or, more accurately, transcribed from conversations with Goethe—by Johann Georg Christop Tobler and published in the *Tiefurt Journal* in 1783. Whether it belongs among Goethe's writings or conversations is a matter of dispute (or perhaps of semantics); it appears in any case at the beginning of the WA edition of his texts on natural science, specifically II, 11:5–9. Benjamin, for his part, does not describe Goethe as its author, only that he "remained faithful to [its] propositions . . . even in advanced old age." This is indisputably supported by his conversation with Friedrich von Müller, dated 24 May 1828, where Goethe emphasizes that the fragment did indeed "reflect" his view at the time and immediately proceeds to identify the only thing it lacks, namely, "completion" (*Erfüllung*) of this vision, which consists in an intuition of the "two great driving forces in all nature: the concept of *polarity* and that of *intensification* [Steigerung]" (WA II, 11:11; cf. WA III, 11:222; 24–30 May 1828).

78. Goethe, WA II, 11:9; "Nature. A Fragment."

79. Benjamin cites Goethe's work as *Poetry and Truth*, reversing the order of the title under which it first appeared starting in 1811 as *Aus meinem Leben: Dichtung und Wahrheit* (Tübingen: Cotta, 1811). Throughout this translation the title is given as cited by Benjamin. Riemer and Eckermann both report discussions with Goethe about the title of his work. According to Riemer, the proposal of the title *From My Life: Poetry and Truth* was "applauded" by Goethe "with the small transposition of poetry and truth, for euphonic reasons, because in that connection two identical letters collide and stick together" (Friedrich Wilhelm Riemer, *Mitteilungen über Goethe* [Leipzig: Insel, 1921], 188–89). In the quarto edition of Goethe's work that Riemer edited with Eckermann in 1837, the title *Poetry and Truth* was introduced and was used in many editions during the nineteenth century. Since the relevant volumes of the Weimar Ausgabe

(WA I, 26–29) appeared from 1887 to 1891, however, the preferred title has been *Poetry and Truth.* Here are Goethe's own comments on the title: "As for the somewhat paradoxical title of *Confidences from My Life, Poetry and Truth,* this was prompted by the experience that the audience always harbors some doubts about the veracity of such biographical attempts. In order to counter this, I committed myself to a kind of fiction [*Fiction*], so to speak without necessity, driven by a certain spirit of contradiction, because my most serious endeavor was to present as much as possible the actual basic truth that, insofar as I saw into it, had prevailed in my life and express it. But if such a thing is not possible in later years without allowing recollection and thus the imagination to work, and if one always finds oneself in the situation of exercising one's poetic ability, so to speak, then it is clear that it is more the results and how we think of the past now than the details as they occurred that will be put forward and emphasized. . . . I have understood everything that belongs to the narrator and the narrative here under the word 'poetry,' in order to be able to use for my purpose the true [*des Wahren*] of which I was myself conscious" (WA IV, 46:241–42; letter to Zelter, 15 February 1830).

80. Goethe, WA I, 29:173–74; *Poetry and Truth,* part 4, chapter 20.

81. On "Primal Words," which Goethe wrote in 1817 and twice published in 1820, see endnote 89 below.

82. The word "turbidity" (*Trübung*) alludes to Goethe's color theory, which revolves around his experiments with the effect and composition of light in turbid media.

83. Franz Boll, *Sternglaube und Sterndeutung. Die Geschichte und das Wesen der Astrologie* (Leipzig and Berlin: Teubner, 1918), 89. The last sentence refers to WA I, 14:57; *Faust, Part One,* ll. 1114–15. Benjamin also refers to Boll's work in the *Origin of the German Trauerspiel* in his discussion of *Hamlet;* see 1:334; O 163.

84. Goethe, WA IV, 48:129; letter to Zelter, 23 February 1831.

85. The source of this attribution of the last words to Goethe is Carl Vogel, his physician, who provided a detailed description of the poet's final days in the *Journal der praktischen Heilkunde* 76.2 (1833): 17: "'More light' is supposed to have been the last words—while I was out of the room—of the man who always hated darkness in every respect."

86. In NDB, "secret" (*heimlich*) replaces "heathen" (*heidnisch*), which is found in M¹.

87. See Goethe, WA G, 3:59–62; conversation with J. D. Falk, 25 January 1813.

88. See Georg Gottfried Gervinus, *Ueber den Göthischen Briefwechsel* (Leipzig: Englemann, 1836), 136.

89. Goethe, WA IV, 12:244; letter to Schiller, 16–17 August 1797.

NOTES TO PAGES 117–122

90. Gervinus, *Ueber den Göthischen Briefwechsel*, 140; *nil admirari* ("be astonished by nothing") derives from Horace, *Epistles*, I. 6.

91. Goethe, WA I, 28:175–76; *Poetry and Truth*, chapter 13.

92. Friedrich Hölderlin, "Patmos. Dem Landgrafen von Homburg," in *Sämtliche Werke* (Munich and Leipzig: Müller, 1916), 4:227; ll. 9–15.

93. Ancient Greek phrase that means "first" or "principal falsehood."

94. As noted in GS, this sentence is obscure. The following expansion is thus proposed: "The Orphic primal words apply to him: it is [neither] his daemon, the sun-like one; [nor] his Tyche, changing like the moon; [nor] his fate, ineluctable like the astral αναγκη. Not even Eros points beyond them [*sie*]—only Elpis does" (1:851). Even if this does clarify the sense, the sentence remains unchanged in NDB, M¹, and M², suggesting that Benjamin is not averse to a certain indeterminacy among these figures at this point. There is, however, a difference between, on the one hand, NDB, M¹, and M², and, on the other, M², where, instead of encountering the third-person plural "them" (*sie*), the reader finds the third-person singular masculine "him" (*ihn*): "It is his daemon that fleetingly shows itself sun-like, his Tyche that fleetingly shows itself changeable like the moon, his fate that fleetingly shows itself inescapable like astral anagke, his Eros that fleetingly shows itself in the solution of its *one single* task [*in der Lösung seiner einen Aufgabe*]—Elpis alone points beyond him" (1:851). GS proposes that "him" refers to "the redeemer."

What is less obscure is the next sentence, where Benjamin refers to the two versions of "Primal Words," first written in 1817 and twice published in close succession three years later. The first published version (in the otherwise natural-scientific volume *On Morphology*) consists in the five poems alone, "Δαιμον, Dämon," "Τυχη, das Zufällige," "Ερως, Liebe," "Αναγκη. Nöthigung," "Ελπις, Hoffnung" (WA I, 3:95–96); the second version (in *On Art and Antiquity*) adds a commentary on each of the first four poems but not the last one (WA I, 41:215–21). Here is why "Hope," according to Goethe, does not require him to add an explanation: "every fine mind will gladly take over the task of composing a commentary in a manner both ethical and religious" (WA I, 41:221).

95. The "schema" can be seen from the table of contents in Gundolf's *Goethe*, which is translated at 297n5.

96. This final remark is an allusion to the "Night" scene at the beginning of *Faust, Part One*, in which Faust stands before the "Earth Spirit" (*Erdgeist*) whom he conjures into existence and who calls him, sarcastically, "superhuman (*Übermensch*)" (WA I, 14:32; ll. 486–90). In the course of "Goethe's Elective Affinities," Benjamin implicitly distinguishes between the poet Stefan George and the "George school," one important member of which was Friedrich Gundolf.

NOTES TO PAGES 122–128   327

It would be a mistake, however, to treat Benjamin's polemic against Gundolf as a wholesale attack on every participant in the George circle: compare, in this regard, his treatment of Max Kommerell in "Against a Masterpiece," 207–13. See also the reflections on George that Benjamin wrote for *Die Literarische Welt* in 1928 on the occasion of the poet's sixtieth birthday (2:622–24). In a manuscript version of these reflections, Benjamin describes "J C" (= Jula Cohn) reading to him in her Munich studio (2:1432). A more comprehensive reflection on Goerge and his circle can be found in Benjamin's review of a coffee-table book dedicated to George that appeared in 1933; see 3:392–99; SW 2:706–11.

97. In M¹, instead of "people's community" or "national community" (*Volksgemein-schaft*), Benjamin wrote "national society" (*Volksgesellschaft*). The term *Volksge-meinschaft*, which was later appropriated by the Nazis as a political slogan, is also found in the *Origin of the German Trauerspiel* (1:285 and 287; O 100, 102).

98. Goethe, WA II, 1:ix; *Theory of Colors*, preface.

99. Gundolf, *Goethe*, 555.

100. The version of the central phrase in this sentence, as GS notes (1:852), is clearer in M¹ than in NBD: "it is not grasped with the great modesty of a true biography as the very archive of indecipherable documents" (without an "existence [*Dasein*]" that somehow complements but is different from "life").

101. See Alexander Baumgartner, *Göthe. Sein Leben und seine Werke*, 2nd ed. (Freiburg: Herder, 1885–86). See also "One Hundred Years of Writing on Goethe," 224.

102. See also "A Remark on Gundolf: Goethe," 47–49.

103. This is an allusion to Bettina von Arnim's sketches for a Goethe monument, which can be found in the last letter she sent to Goethe, reproduced in von Arnim, *Goethes Briefwechsel mit einem Kinde*, ed. Jonas Fränkel (Jena: Die-derichs, 1906), 2:207–11.

104. Benjamin is probably alluding to the following passage in the introduction to Gundolf's work: "For logos and eros are not necessary opposites; they are the same condition, only with different degrees of brightness" (Gundolf, *Goethe*, 13). Similar statements about the "unity of eros and logos" (688) are to be found throughout the book.

105. This sentence in M² is slightly yet significantly different: "For there is no *truth-fulness* [*Wahrhaftigkeit*] in things [*Sachen*] but, rather, only matter-of-factness [*Sachlichkeit*] in truth" (1:853).

106. Gundolf, *Goethe*, 566.

107. The following is added in M¹: "The question whether reconciliation is possible in the mythic world order was, for him, a vital question [*Lebensfrage*]" (1:853).

108. In October 1806 the Napoleonic troops, after their victory at the Battle of Jena and Auerstedt, arrived in Weimar and threatened to plunder Goethe's house.

328   NOTES TO PAGES 128–130

Christiane Vulpius succeeded in resisting the French soldiers and managed to preserve the house until Goethe was able to secure protection from the French authorities. Shortly thereafter (19 October 1806), Goethe and Vulpius were married. For a brief account of this episode, see Jeremy Adler, *Johann Wolfgang von Goethe* (London: Reaktion Books, 2020), 141–42.

109. Goethe, WA III, 7:26; 6 January 1820.

110. Goethe, WA G, 2:292; see also Heinrich Laube, *Neue Reisenovellen* (Mannheim: Hoff, 1837), 2:183.

111. Hölderlin, "Blödigkeit," in *Sämtliche Werke*, 4:68; ll. 1–5; for Benjamin's analysis of the poem, the title of which can be translated as "Diffidence" or "Timidity," see 2:116–17; SW 1:28–29.

112. See Goethe, WA I, 6:293; *West-Eastern Divan*, "No Longer on a Page of Silk." This poem was posthumously added to the collection; Benjamin uses one of its lines, "sketched in mobile dust," for a "novella" he read over the radio in December 1929; see GS 4:780–87; RB 260–66. Goethe's *West-Eastern Divan* is an 1819 cycle of poems translated from Persian on the basis of Joseph Freiherr von Hammer-Purgstall's 1812 German translation of Hafez's *Divan*; see *Der Diwan des Mohammed Schemsed-Din Hafis* (Stuttgart and Tübingen: Cotta, 1812–13). In "The Task of the Translator," Benjamin calls the "notes and essays" Goethe included in the *Divan* "the best comment on the theory of translation that has been published in Germany" (4:20; SW 1:261).

113. Goethe, WA I, 20:323–35; *Elective Affinities*, part 2, chapter 10. Benjamin emphasizes that the story, told by the companion of an English lord, includes a description of its status as novella. This is the last of the stories told by the companion, and it is different from the others, for, though, like the others, it concerns a "strange" [*sonderbar*] event, it is "gentler" [*sanfter*] and is therefore described as *wunderlich*, here translated as "queer." In the essay Benjamin does not discuss the relation of the novella to the life of the Captain; see, however, his commentary on François-Poncet's book, 86. It should not be assumed, moreover, that the Captain's role in the story is that of the young man who saves the young woman; it could be the reverse, or something altogether different, as the narrator suggests at the beginning of part 2, chapter 11.

114. See Goethe, WA III, 3:327: Diary 11 April 1808: "Schematizing short stories, especially 'Elective Affinities' and 'The Man of Fifty [included in *Wilhelm Meister's Journeyman Years*].'"

115. See Meyer, *Goethe*, 660: "Goethe's idea is dependent on Herder's theory of types. Every single thing belongs to a great type. The ideal of the species hovers, as it were, before every emerging essence; it thrives in it as 'inner creative power' and leads more and more the independent individual, the 'monade,' out

NOTES TO PAGES 131–139 329

of dynamic indefiniteness to classical development and perfection. The outer form is therefore only a reflection, only a symbol of the incomprehensible inner form."

116. George Simmel, *Goethe* (Leipzig: Klinkhardt & Biermann, 1913), 155–56.

117. Simmel, *Goethe*, 154.

118. See Goethe, 1, 20:336; *Elective Affinities*, part 2, chapter 11; see note 111 above.

119. The novella "The Foolish Pilgrim" is interpolated into the 1829 edition of *Wilhelm Meister's Journeyman Years*; WA I, 24:72–92; part 1, book 1, chapter 5.

120. The word *geschlossen* means "locked" as well as "closed."

121. This is an allusion to WA I, 20:331; *Elective Affinities*, part 2, chapter 10. The quoted phrase is not in Goethe's text.

122. In an earlier fragment, "Vivifying and Violence" (7:26; TCV 67), Benjamin reflects on the figure of the centaur in relation to biblical and ancient-Greek concepts of creation.

123. See Goethe, 1, 20:336; *Elective Affinities*, part 2, chapter 11; see note 111 above.

124. See Goethe, 1, 20:335; *Elective Affinities*, part 2, chapter 10: "and who could have denied them [the childhood neighbors] this [a blessing]?"

125. "The New Melusine" is a novella that Goethe included in *Wilhelm Meister's Journeyman Years*. Beginning in the early 1920s, Benjamin developed plans to write on this novella under the theme of "reduction (*Verkleinerung*)," as he writes many years later to Gretel Adorno-Karplus; GB 6:385; 17 January 1940 (for a brief discussion, see 294n72).

126. Stefan George, "Das Haus in Bonn," in *Der siebente Ring* (Berlin: Blaetter für die Kunst, 1907), 202.

127. This refers to the *tableaux vivants* in the novel; WA I, 20:269–75; *Elective Affinities*, part 2, chapter 6.

128. For a clarification of what Benjamin means by this term, see his earlier essay, "Fate and Character," esp. 2:176–79; SW 1:204–6.

129. See WA I, 20:370 and 394; *Elective Affinities*, part 2, chapters 14 and 17.

130. Gundolf, *Goethe*, 563.

131. See André François-Poncet, *Les affinités électives de Goethe: Essai de commentaire critique* (Paris: Alcan, 1910).

132. This is the spot in WBA 1324 where Benjamin inserted "With Reference to François-Poncet" (86–87).

133. The "event" in question is Ottilie's death by starvation.

134. Julian Schmidt, *Geschichte der deutschen Literatur seit Lessing's Tod*, 5th ed. (Leipzig: Grunow, 1866), 2:590.

135. The name *Herzlieb* (translatable as "heart love") echoes the word "heart" (*Herz*) in the preceding sentence.

330 NOTES TO PAGES 140–144

136. For Benjamin's early reflection on the literary form of the diary, see "Metaphysics of Youth" (2:96–103; SW 1:10–16).

137. Goethe, WA I, 4:97, which is an allusion to lines from a poem Goethe sent to Charlotte von Stein on 14 April 1776; WA I, 5.2:72; cf. WA IV, 3:282; letter to Wieland around the same time.

138. *Phaedrus* 251a and 254b; Benjamin cites the translation of Julius Walter, *Die Geschichte der Ästhetik im Altertum ihrer begrifflichen Entwicklung nach dargestellt* (Leipzig: Reisland, 1893), 286–87.

139. Schmidt, *Geschichte der deutschen Literatur seit Lessing's Tod*, 2:590.

140. Anonymous, "Die Wahlverwandtschaften: Ein Roman von Goethe," *Allgemeine Literatur-Zeitung* (1 January 1810); cited in *Goethe im Urtheile seiner Zeitgenossen*, 3:229. Mignon is a character in Goethe's novel, *Wilhelm Meister's Years of Apprenticeship*. Initially Wilhelm notes that this striking young woman's "forehead seemed to veil some secret" (WA I, 21:154; book 2, chapter 4). Wilhelm purchases Mignon from a troupe of traveling dancers and acrobats, and she is adopted by him.

141. See Homer, *Iliad*, book 3.

142. Helen is first conjured in Goethe, *Faust, Part Two*, Act 1; she disappears at the end of the act and reappears in the so-called "Helen," which Goethe repurposed as Act 3. At the beginning of this act, Helen appears on stage, certain that she will be sacrificed.

143. See Goethe, WA I, 15:213; "Helen," Classical-Romantic Interlude to Faust. On Goethe's abandonment of the plan to write the scene in question, see Benjamin's comments on Konrat Ziegler in "Faust in the Sample Case" (228–29).

144. See Homer, *Odyssey*, book 3.

145. In M¹, "the hint: Görres to Arnim, January 1810."

146. The translation of the phrase "Dies in ihm Wesende" by "this, which is becoming what it is in the work" is an approximation. It is notable that M¹ includes the relatively simple word *Lebende* in place of the enigmatic *Wesende*. The beginning of this sentence in M¹ can be translated as: "This, which lives in the work."

147. Friedrich Hölderlin, "Anmerkungen zum Ödipus," in *Sämtliche Werke* (Munich and Leipzig: Müller, 1913), 5:176.

148. Hölderlin, *Sämtliche Werke*, 5:315; letter to Casimir Böhlendorf, 4 December 1801; Benjamin discusses a later letter to Böhlendorf in *German Human Beings*, 4:171–72; SW 3:180–81.

149. Gerhard Scholem, "Lyrik der Kabbala?," *Der Jude* 6 (1921): 61.

150. These last two sentences were omitted from NDB; the basis of the translation, following GS, is WBA 1324 as well as M¹. Borchardt was a friend of Hofmannsthal's who made several contributions to NDB, including one that immediately

follows the first installment of Benjamin's essay. Despite expressing admiration for Borchardt's work, Benjamin associates him, like Gundolf (see 48–49), with "objective mendacity" (GB 1:457–58; letter to Ernst Schoen, May 1918). In a note written sometime in the late 1920s, perhaps around the time of Hofmannsthal's death in 1929, Benjamin seeks to capture the two writers' relation to Goethe: "One indicates a historical phenomenon of an astounding kind with the assertion that the Goethean conquest of a world of semblance had its frighteningly docile, frighteningly fixed Diadochi in Hofmannsthal and Rudolf Borchardt. In their case, this Goethean world—among those of the master, just one, for them the only one—in a hallucination of the temporal sense shunts the effective and evolving world; the Goethean world, meanwhile, is itself admittedly without reality and change, and for this reason not suited to be mistaken for a Greek primordial world, something Goethe, after all, never did. That neither Hofmannsthal nor Borchardt grant irony the slightest space with regard to this world likewise becomes revealing in this respect.... The claim to actual effect, however, which especially Borchardt makes ever more intransigently, as he imperialistically expands the dominion of semblance over the realm of science is itself a tell-tale sign. Because what can have an actual effect, *in the realm of forms and as form*, that means in the strictest sense of the word, unpolitically, is today only the thoroughly hidden, the inconspicuous, which seemingly and, to a certain extent, really is a renouncing of effect" (6:201–2; SW 2:286). These last remarks can be seen to connect Benjamin's own work, early or late, with the late-Goethean concept of renunciation, the "fable" (109) of which he elucidates in this essay; see also the reflections on renunciation in 183 and 186.

151. Goethe, WA IV, 20:366; letter to Marianne von Eybenberg, 16 June 1809.

152. Friedrich Wilhelm Riemer, *Briefwechsel zwischen Goethe und Zelter in den Jahren 1796 bis 1832* (Berlin: Duncker & Humblot, 1833), 1:373; letter from Zelter to Goethe, 1 October 1809.

153. Goethe, WA I, 1:169–70; "The Fisherman." A female figure emerges out of the parting waters in which a fisherman watches his line and listens to the tide that draws him into the depths, never to be seen again.

154. "Beautiful flow" translates *Schönfließ*, which is Benjamin's mother's maiden name.

155. Walter, *Die Geschichte der Ästhetik im Altertum*, 6.

156. Anonymous, "Ueber Goethes Wahlverwandtschaften," *Evangelische Kirchen-Zeitung* (16 July 1831): 452.

157. Werner, "Die Wahlverwandtschaften," in *Sämmtliche Werke, Aus seinem handschriftlichen Nachlasse*, 2:24.

332 NOTES TO PAGES 145–153

158. Von Arnim, *Goethes Briefwechsel mit einem Kinde*, 87; letter from Bettina to Goethe, 11 November 1809.

159. See Benjamin's notes on Stifter, which were included in a letter to Ernst Schoen, 17 June 1918 (GB 1:195–97; SW 1:111–13).

160. See Goethe, WA I, 28:79; part 3, book 11. In *Poetry and Truth* Goethe describes the deep impression made upon him by his visit in May 1771 to the Cloister of the Holy Ottilie on the Mont Sainte-Odile.

161. See Benjamin's notes on "inclination" (*Neigung*), 6:55; TCV 71. It should be noted that the word *Neigung* is of central importance in the dynamics of *Elective Affinities*; though often translated as "affection," its physical sense (consonant with a novel whose title refers to physical science) should not be elided.

162. This may be an allusion to Robert Musil's story "Die Vollendung der Liebe" (The Consummation/Perfection of Love); see *Vereinigungen* (Munich and Leipzig: Müller, 1911).

163. Bielschowsky, *Goethe*, 2:286.

164. As noted above (see 324n73), Goethe's advertisement for *Elective Affinities* appeared anonymously in the *Morgenblatt für gebildete Stände* on 4 September 1809 and was reproduced by Braun in *Goethe im Urtheile seiner Zeitgenossen*, 3:211; the term "simile" [*Gleichnis*] becomes an important element of the novel, captured in its title, in part 1, chapter 4; WA I, 20:47–57.

165. See Benjamin's fragment from 1919, "Analogy and Affinity [*Verwandtschaft*]" (6:43–45; SW 1:207–9); see also the discussion of *Verwandtschaft* and *verwandt* ("related") in endnote 6 above, 317.

166. Friedrich Hebbel, *Werke in zehn Teilen* (Berlin and Leipzig: Bong, 1910), 6:120.

167. Hebbel, *Werke*, 4:64.

168. Baumgartner, *Göthe*, 3:67.

169. Goethe, WA I, 3:27; l. 18; "Conciliation" (*Aussöhnung*), "Trilogy of Passion." Benjamin slightly modified the line from Goethe's poem.

170. Goethe, WA I, 3:382; the dedication of this poem is "To Madame Marie Szymanowska."

171. "Elegy" is the second poem in the cycle. "Trilogy of Passion" includes the following motto from Goethe's *Torquato Tasso*, ll. 3432–33; as noted in WA I, 3:381: "And if the human being becomes silent in his suffering / Grant me a God to whom I say that I suffer" (WA I, 3:21).

172. These three citations are from Goethe, "Conciliation," WA I, 3:27, ll. 6, 7, and 11, respectively.

173. Cohen, *Ästhetik des reinen Gefühls*, 2:125.

174. Carl Albrecht Bernoulli, *Johann Jakob Bachofen und das Natursymbol. Ein Würdigungsversuch* (Basel: Schwabe, 1924), 420.

NOTES TO PAGES 153-158   333

175. See Johann Jakob Bachofen, *Das Mutterrecht. Eine Untersuchung über die Gynaikokratie der alten Welt nach ihrer religiösen und rechtlichen Natur*, 2nd ed. (Basel: Schwabe, 1897), 330-31.

176. Goethe, WA I, 41.2:251; "Gleenings from Aristotle's Poetics." Benjamin slightly modifies the quotation.

177. See Simmel, *Goethe*, 63-65; see also Benjamin's later remarks concerning his rereading of Simmel's *Goethe*, which inform one of the two notes for the *Arcades Project* that conclude this volume, 252 and 348n1.

178. Without referring to his own essay, yet still placed in quotation marks, Benjamin cites this passage in a footnote to one of the later versions of "The Artwork in the Age of Its Technical Reproducibility": "Beautiful appearance as auratic reality altogether fulfills Goethean creativity. Mignon, Ottilie and Helen take part in this reality: 'The beautiful is neither the cover, nor the covered object but, rather, the object in its cover'—that is the quintessence of the Goethean as well as the ancient view of art. Its decay doubly suggests that a look be directed back at its origin. This lies in mimesis as the urphenomenon of all artistic actuation" (7:368; SW 3:127).

179. Kant's "Analytic of the Beautiful" in the first part of the *Critique of Judgment* proceeds in accordance with the table of categories, including the form of relation, understood in terms of judgments of taste, as "the purpose that is considered in them" (Aka 5:219).

180. The word "consider" (*betrachtet*) in the previous sentence could also be translated as "gaze at" or "contemplate," and Benjamin emphasizes the point by quoting a passage in the novella (WA I, 20:332; *Elective Affinities*, part 2, chapter 10), where *Betrachtung* connotes both (moral) consideration and (visual) glance or glare. This, incidentally, is Benjamin's only quotation from the novella.

181. By characterizing "sobriety" as "sacred," Benjamin alludes to Hölderlin's "Half of Life." See also "Two Poems of Friedrich Hölderlin," 2:125-26; SW 1:35. The word "wondrous" viz. "queer" refers to the neighbors in the novella in *Elective Affinities*.

182. Goethe, WA IV, 21:46; letter to Zelter, 26 August 1809.

183. Goethe, WA I, 23:159; book 8, chapter 2, ll. 4–11; *Wilhelm Meister's Years of Apprenticeship* (cf. WA I, 2:115).

184. Goethe, WA I, 15.1:239; *Faust, Part Two*, stage direction following l. 9944.

185. Goethe, WA I, 15.1:239; *Faust, Part Two*, Act 3, ll. 9945-50.

186. Goethe, WA I, 42.2:139; *Maxims and Reflections*, Beauty. As noted elsewhere (see 287n19), WA splits up *Maxims and Reflections* among ten volumes; Benjamin cites this passage from one of the several editions of this posthumously produced collection, which also can be found in his "Registry of Readings" (see 253).

334 NOTES TO PAGES 158–161

187. Goethe, WA I, 20:45; *Elective Affinities*, part 1, chapter 4.

188. Benjamin continues here his reflection on youth, which occupies many of his early writings and almost every one of his earliest publications, including those that touch on Goethe's work.

189. Von Arnim, *Goethes Briefwechsel mit einem Kinde*, 45–46; letter from Bettina to Goethe, 22 May 1809.

190. Goethe, WA I, 20:224; *Elective Affinities*, part 2, chapter 3.

191. Gundolf, *Goethe*, 569. "Subject-matter" is here the translation of *Gehalt* in accordance with the formal distinction between *Gehalt* and *Stoff* (material) that Gundolf makes in his Introduction, where he proposes the following "simile" [*Gleichnis*]: "The subject-matter is the living, radiating force [*Kraft*]; the material is the atmosphere that this irradiating force encounters in the course of its advance and that it consumes through its advancement, comprising the Goethean spheres of forces" (15). By citing Gundolf's use of *Gehalt* in the final paragraph of his essay, Benjamin implicitly returns to his opening paragraph, where he distinguishes between *Sachgehalt* and *Wahrheitsgehalt* and proposes a very different kind of simile—one that does not imply the notion of a "penetrating movement" that consists in total domination.

192. Goethe, WA G, 3:254; conversation with Sulpiz Boisserée, 5 October 1815.

193. In M¹, the phrase "beyond mere atmosphere [*über Stimmung*]" reads: "how very [above the line 'highly'] elevated beyond 'atmosphere' ['*Stimmung*']."

194. Goethe, WA I, 20:359; *Elective Affinities*, part 2, chapter 13.

195. The citation from *The Divine Comedy*, "als fiele eine Leiche," derives from George's translation; see Dante, *Die göttliche Komödie*, trans. Stefan George (Berlin: Bondi, 1912), 24. This seems to be the poem that "J C" (Jula Cohn) read to Benjamin in her Munich studio, as he recalls in a reflection on George written in 1928; see 2:1432.

196. On "Primal Words," see endnote 93.

197. In various notes and texts of the period, Benjamin reflects on theories of immortality; see, for example, "Death" (6:71; TCV 78) and, for a contrasting reflection, see his review of Dostoevsky's novel *The Idiot* (2:239–40; SW 1:80–81), which specifically refers to Goethe's *Conversations with Eckermann*. It would exceed the bounds of a note to describe the intensity with which Benjamin considered such matters as "afterlife" and "living-onward" (*Nachleben, Fortleben*).

198. In M¹ Benjamin writes "Catholic" rather than "Nazarene." He may have changed this so as to avoid offending Hofmannsthal.

199. See 329n126; the epigraph for the final section is drawn from the same poem, George's "Haus in Bonn."

19. Goethe

"Goethe," WBA 553 and WBA 554; trans. SB. Commissioned by the Soviet-Encyclopedia Committee in the spring of 1926, "schema" (GS 6:321; MD 39) and "exposé" (6:366; MD 81) written for, and perhaps during, Benjamin's trip to Moscow in the winter of 1926–27; the two extant typescripts written during the summer of 1928, completed in September–October. The text that Benjamin sent to the editors of the Большая советская энциклопедия (*Great Soviet Encyclopedia*) has been lost; an article under the title "Гёте (Goethe), Иоган Вольфганг" appeared in the 1929 published volume of the encyclopedia, where it was attributed to Benjamin along with five Soviet authors; for a more extensive discussion, see the Introduction, esp. 25–32. A translation of the negative assessment of Benjamin's article written by Anatoly Lunacharsky, People's Commissioner for Public Education, can be found in MD 130–32.

The extant typescripts appear to represent two different stages of composition as well as target audiences: WBA 554 was probably prepared for the purpose of producing German-language excerpts, including those that make up the article that appeared in *Die Literarische Welt* in the fall of 1928 (see 194–99). The translation of "Goethe" is based on the text as reconstructed in GS; the few variations are indicated in the endnotes. It should be noted that many of Benjamin's quotations of Goethe and others are slightly modified; none of these variations makes any difference in translation (be it English or Russian). The editors would like to thank Julia Bernhard (Walter Benjamin Archive, Akademie der Künste) for her generous help with the annotation of this article.

1. As noted in GS (2:1477), this is incorrect. Goethe visited Berlin for a few days in May 1778; for a brief description of his brief encounter in a long biography, see Nicholas Boyle, *Goethe: The Poet and the Age*, vol. 1, *The Poetry of Desire (1749–1790)* (Oxford: Oxford University Press, 1992), 300–301.

2. Goethe, WA I, 28:70; *Poetry and Truth*, part 3, book 11.

3. Karl Gutzkow, *Ueber Göthe im Wendepunkt zweier Jahrhunderte* (1835), ed. Madleen Podewski (Münster: Oktober, 2019), 12.

4. Goethe, WA I, 37:234; review of Wieland's novel, *Der goldne Spiegel oder die Könige von Scheschian* (1772).

5. Goethe, WA I, 19:17; *Sorrows of Young Werther*, book 1.

6. Goethe, WA I, 29:61; *Poetry and Truth*, part 4, book 17.

7. See Albert Bielschowsky, *Goethe. Sein Leben und seine Werke*, 17th ed. (Munich: Beck, 1909), 1:293; letter from Karl August to Minister von Fritsch, 10 May 1776.

8. Goethe, WA IV, 4:160; letter to Charlotte von Stein, 1–3 January 1780.

9. Goethe, WA IV, 5:149; letter to Lavater, 22 June 1781.

10. Goethe, WA IV, 6:97; letter to Knebel, 21 November 1782.

336 NOTES TO PAGES 173–186

11. An earlier, fragmentary version of this passage includes the following remark, which refers to the final scene in *Egmont*: "It's only that this image of the fearless man of the people (in a thoroughly ideal sense) remained hovering, all too superior in ultra-bright illumination, while the political realities received so much clearer expression in the mouths of Oranien and Alba" (2:1478).

12. Goethe, WA I, 8:303; *Egmont*, Act 5.

13. See Wilhelm von Humboldt, *Ideen zu einem Versuch, die Gränzen des Staats zu bestimmen*, written in 1792 (Breslau: Trewendt, 1851). For a translation, see *The Limits of State Action*, trans. J. W. Burrow (Cambridge: Cambridge University Press, 1969).

14. Benjamin is referring to the dramatic genre that received the name "Haupt- und Staatsaktion." Plays of this kind, which were written and performed from the end of the seventeenth to the middle of the eighteenth centuries, revolve around intrigues among princes and other high officials; for Benjamin's analysis of the genre, see *Origin of the German Trauerspiel*, 1:302–4; O 120–23.

15. Friedrich Schiller, *Briefe*, ed. Fritz Jonas (Stuttgart: Deutsche Verlags-Anstalt, 1892–96), 3:113–14.

16. Goethe, WA IV, 7:213; letter to Jacobi, 5 May 1786.

17. Goethe, WA IV, 20:90; letter to Zelter, 22 June 1808; see also WA II, 11.1:118; On Nature in General.

18. Goethe, WA I, 3:83, line 33; "Legacy [Vermächtnis]," 1829; cf. WA G, 9:130; conversation with Riemer 24 December 1806.

19. See Alexander Baumgartner, *Göthe. Sein Leben und seine Werke*, 2nd ed. (Freiburg: Herder, 1885–86), 2:432; letter to Jacobi, 15 July 1793.

20. Benjamin is probably alluding to Goethe's "Foreword" to a collection of his morphological writings from the late 1810s and early 1820s.

21. This paragraph is the beginning of an excerpt, like the three published in "Goethe's Politics and View of Nature" (194–99), that would have been titled "Goethe—Schiller; Goethe—Napoleon" (see 2:1479).

22. Gutzkow, *Ueber Göthe im Wendepunkt zweier Jahrhunderte*, 108.

23. Gutzkow, *Ueber Göthe im Wendepunkt zweier Jahrhunderte*, 45.

24. Goethe, WA I, 40:199; "Literary Sans-Culottism."

25. Benjamin is alluding to the "Chorus Mysticus" that concludes *Faust, Part Two*; WA I, 15:337; ll. 12104–11.

26. Gutzkow, "Der Stil Göthes," in *Handbuch der Deutschen Nationalliteratur*, ed. Heinrich Viehoff (Braunschweig: Westermann, 1882), 258.

27. This paragraph is the beginning of an excerpt that would have been titled "Goethe's Court; Elective Affinities; Divan; Faust" (2:1480).

28. Goethe, WA I, 4:125.

NOTES TO PAGES 187–196   337

29. In one of the typescripts, Benjamin writes "German" rather than "European" (2:1480).

30. Benjamin may be alluding to the subtitle of Thomas Mann's 1901 novel, *Buddenbrooks*, "The Decay of a Family."

31. Goethe, WA I, 18:56; *The Excited Ones* [*Die Aufgeregten*], Act 4, scene 2.

32. Goethe, WA G, 7:36; conversation with Eckermann, 23 March 1829.

33. Goethe, WA I, 24:94; *Wilhelm Meister's Journeyman Years*, part 1, book 1, chapter 6.

34. See Karl Grün, *Ueber Göthe vom menschlichen Standpunkte* (Darmstadt: Leske, 1846), 305; cf. 309. Grün speaks of a "communistic escape" but does not describe it as "organized."

35. Benjamin is alluding to Schiller's distinction between naive and sentimental poets in which he presents Goethe, like an ancient bard, as "naive," whereas modern poets like himself are "sentimental," that is, distant from their objects by virtue of their self-reflectivity; see Schiller, "On Naïve and Sentimental Poetry" (1795–96).

36. Goethe, WA I, 14:82; *Faust, Part One*, ll. 1700–1704.

37. Goethe, WA I, 14:164; *Faust, Part One*, ll. 3249–50.

38. See *Goethes Gespräche. Gesamtausgabe*, ed. Flodoard Freiherr von Biedermann (Leipzig: Biedermann, 1909–11), 4:298; 19 September 1830 (no. 2863).

39. Goethe, WA IV, 39:216; letter to Zelter, 6 June 1825; Benjamin also cites this passage in the "Foreword" to *German Human Beings*, 4:151; SW 3:167.

40. Ludwig Börne, Review of Bettina von Arnim's *Goethes Briefwechsel mit einem Kinde* (1835), reprinted in *Gesammelte Schriften* (Vienna: Tendler, 1868), 6:127.

20. Goethe's Politics and View of Nature

"Goethes Politik und Naturanschauung," *Die Literarische Welt* 4.49 (December 1928): 5–6; WBA 555; trans. SB. The text consists in excerpts from "Goethe" and contributes to its reconstruction; see the Introduction, 25–32. References in this article can be found in the endnotes to the corresponding passages in "Goethe."

1. The encyclopedia has "study of natural science" (176) rather than "study of nature."

2. The encyclopedia article quotes the penultimate sentence in the passage from Schiller's letter to Körner correctly: "There, one would rather look for herbs or practice mineralogy [not 'biology'] than be caught up in empty demonstrations" (176; for the reference see 336n15).

21. Weimar

"Weimar," *Neue Schweizer Rundschau* 21.10 (1 October 1928): 751–52; WBA 621; trans. SB. Reprinted in *Die Literarische Welt* 8.14 (1 April 1932): 3; WBA 622. The reprint appeared in a special issue titled "Goethe Day," commemorating the one hundredth anniversary of the poet's death. Several drafts of the essay can be found in WuN 8:242–47. Benjamin visited Weimar in the summer of 1928 in connection with his trip to Moscow. Apropos this short essay, he tells Scholem that it "represents in the loveliest manner the side of my Janus-head that turns away from the Soviet state" (GB 3:438; 14 February 1929). He says something slightly different to Hugo von Hofmannsthal: "'Weimar' is a byproduct of my 'Goethe' for the Russian encyclopedia. . . . I was in Weimar a year ago. The impression benefited in some places the essay for which the stay was intended. On these two pages, though, I sought to retain the essence, untroubled by the context of a presentation" (GB 3:472; 26 June 1929).

1. Neuschwanstein and Herrenchiemsee are two extravagant castles built at the behest of Ludwig II, King of Bavaria, for the sake of his own amusement.
2. Jean Paul (Johann Paul Friedrich Richter) often visited Weimar but, according to Schöttker, never stayed in the Elephanten Hotel; see WuN 8:438.
3. Benjamin is alluding to a scene near the end of *Faust, Part Two*, in which "four grey women" approach the door of Faust's palace, seeking entrance. They call themselves Lack (*Mangel*), Guilt (*Schuld*), Care (*Sorge*), and Need (*Not*); see WA I, 15:306–7; ll. 11384–97. Benjamin's ultra-abbreviated resetting of this scene under the guise of "bourgeois comfort" notably lacks Lack.

22. Two Dreams of Goethe's House

Ignaz Ježower, *Das Buch der Träume* (Berlin: Rowohlt, 1928), 271; trans. SB. These are two of the ten dreams published under the name "Walter Benjamin" in Ježower's massive collection. Benjamin reprinted them in reverse order as the second and third part of a section in *One-Way Street* titled "Nr. 113" (4:86–87). The heading of 525 is "Dining Room," that of 526 "Vestibule." "Nr. 113" refers to a basement of the Palais Royal in Paris that housed a casino in the late eighteenth and early nineteenth centuries; see WuN 8:352.

1. Besides Benjamin's trip to Weimar in 1928 (which predated the publication of Ježower's volume and could not therefore form the "residue" from which the dreams were constructed), he visited the city in the summer of 1910 (see GB 1:21; 31 July 1910) and in the spring of 1914 when he spoke at a meeting of the

NOTES TO PAGES 204–206   339

Independent Student Organization (see GB 1:226; 15 May 1914). He may have visited Weimar at other times as well.

23. Goethe's Theory of Colors

"Goethes Farbenlehre," *Die Literarische Welt* 4.46 (16 November 1928): 6; WBA 833; trans. JC. Complete documentation, including the page numbers for the passages cited in the review, can be found in WuN 13.2:167–70. In several of the drafts, Benjamin indicates that his primary concern revolves around the "polarity" (WuN 13.1:672) between Goethe's *Theory of Colors* and Newton's *Optics* and, more broadly, the difference between Newtonian and Goethean conceptions of how the natural sciences should be pursued and understood.

1. Johann Wolfgang von Goethe, *Goethes Farbenlehre*, ed. and introduction by Hans Wohlbold (Jena: Diederichs, 1928).
2. See Johann Wolfgang von Goethe, *Beyträge zur Optik*, with an afterword by Julius Schuster (Berlin: Funk, 1928).
3. Benjamin was himself one of the onlookers who visited the Berlin Bibliophile Evening Society; see GB 3:348 and 3:357; 11 and 26 March 1928.
4. For a brief account of Benjamin's interest in Kandinsky's *On the Spiritual in Art*, which he read in German translation around 1919, see the endnote to "Supplements To: On the Symbolic in Cognition" (300n3).
5. The phrase "the matter of truth in physics" translates "physikalischen Wahrheitsgehalt," while "the matter of philosophy" translates "philosophische Gehalt." On the translation of the word *Gehalt*, see 302n1. In the CVs that Benjamin began to produce around the time he wrote this review, he describes himself as having a long-standing "interest in the philosophical matter [*philosophischen Gehalt*] of literary writing and art forms" (6:216; see also 6:217–19).
6. Goethe, WA II, 1: ix; Didactic, preface: "Colors are the deeds of light, deeds and sufferings."
7. For a prominent version of this "battle," see Max von Laue's critique of Wohlbold's presentation of the superiority of Steiner's worldview, "Steiner und die Naturwissenschaften," *Deutscher Revue* 47 (1922): 41–49.
8. Georg Simmel, *Goethe* (Leipzig: Kleinkardt & Biermann, 1913), 64.
9. The passage from Simmel's *Goethe* to which Benjamin draws attention in the previous sentence is embedded in a broad reflection on Goethe's aesthetics, beginning with his admiration for Shaftesbury's identification of beauty with truth and his corresponding emphasis on unity; Simmel, *Goethe*, 63–67 (concerning Simmel, see also 155 and 225).
10. Salomo Friedländer, *Schöpferische Indifferenz* (Munich: Müller, 1918), 313–34.

340 NOTE TO PAGE 207

24. Against a Masterpiece

"Wider ein Meisterwerk. Zu Max Kommerell: Der Dichter als Führer in der deutschen Klassik," *Die Literarische Welt* 6.33–34 (15 August 1930): 9–11; WBA 871; trans. JR. Complete documentation can be found in WuN 13.2:267–71; for Heinrich Kaulen's account of Benjamin's "fascination" with Kommerell's book, see WuN 13.2:264–67.

The original draft of the review begins with a claim that may be characteristic of Benjamin but would doubtless have surprised the readership of *Die Litera-rische Welt*: "This book is a new and noteworthy demonstration as to how a view that derives from fullness by itself teaches something methodologically important. This presentation contributes more to a materialist history of litera-ture than many guild-oriented literary histories" (WuN 13.1:732). Many of the drafts are concerned with Kommerell's discussion of Hölderlin, but there is one intriguing passage about Goethe in contrast to Schiller: "Such is the great con-cern of this book: to construe classicism as a counter-movement against its age. The precision achieved here, however, should have been different from what the author's point of departure allowed for. Goethe, first of all, cannot be situated within this decisive element in the same way as Schiller. His opposition to the age was rooted in a restorative nature that went all the way down. The source of this nature did not, however, flow from some 'ancient' past but, rather, in the oldest foundation of existence and human nature itself" (WuN 13.2:737; for all of the extant drafts, see WuN 13.2:732–45).

In March 1934, using the pseudonym K. A. Stempflinger, Benjamin published in the *Frankfurter Zeitung* a review of Kommerell's book on Jean Paul under the title "The Dipped Magic-Wand" (2:409–17); for a discussion of why his work could appear in the *Frankfurter Zeitung* under the condition that it was attributed to a pseudonym, see 38. The first paragraph of this second review of a book by Kommerell emphasizes the degree to which the author can be counted among Stefan George's students only in a "mediated" manner. The next para-graph explains why this is so: "Two years ago, with a book on 'The Poet as Führer in German Classicism,' Kommerell already unmistakably indicated a distance that separates his work not only from that of like-minded friends but also from that of the [literary] guild. And however worrisome that early undertaking must have seemed, insofar as it represented an attempt to make the classics into a heroic age of the Germans, it has nevertheless afforded the author something that scarcely anyone among German literary historians had been able to claim for a long time: authority" (2:410). Benjamin also consid-ered reviewing Kommerell's essay on *Faust, Part Two*, which appeared in 1937 as part of a larger review of contemporary scholarship, but decided against doing so (see GB 5:634; 21 December 1937).

1. "This book" is Max Kommerell, *Der Dichter als Führer in der deutschen Klassik: Klopstock, Herder, Goethe, Schiller, Jean Paul, Hölderlin* (Berlin: Bondi, 1928).

2. For Benjamin's critique of Friedrich Gundolf's *Goethe*, see 47–49 and 122–27.

3. Like many of the remarks in the review, this one is self-referential insofar as the aim of Benjamin's dissertation on early German Romanticism, including its appendix on Goethe (53–62), is part of precisely what he here claims: a contribution to the philosophical and critical development that rises up against the George school.

4. For a discussion of Kommerell's relation to Friedrich Wolters, see Robert Norton, *Secret Germany: Stefan George and His Circle* (Ithaca, N.Y.: Cornell University Press, 2002), 705–7.

5. For an extensive reflection on the concept of ingenium, which is contrasted with genius, see "Schemata for the Psychophysical Problem" (6:78–79; TCV 98–99); see also the remarks in the Introduction on the distinction between *Genie* ("genius") and *Genius*, which of course also can be translated as "genius," 8–9.

6. The word "patriotic" translates *vaterländisch*, a technical term in Hölderlin's poetics; see, for example, Hölderlin's famous letters to Casimir Böhlendorff, the first dated 4 December 1801, the second 2 December 1802. Benjamin had access to them through the "critical-historical" edition of Hölderlin's *Sämtliche Werke und Briefe*, ed. Franz Zinkernagel (Leipzig: Insel, 1921), 4:530–34 and 4:538–40. In *German Human Beings* Benjamin reprints the second of these letters with a brief prefatory commentary, 4:171–73; SW 3:180–82.

7. Melchior Lechter was a book designer who was closely associated with the George circle.

8. Florens Christian Rang, *Deutsche Bauhütte: Ein Wort an uns Deutsche über mögliche Gerechtigkeit gegen Belgien und Frankreich und zur Philosophie der Politik* (Leipzig: Arnold, 1924), 51; see Benjamin's remarks, dated 23 December 1923, which were included in the appendix to the volume (reprinted in 4:791–92).

9. This is the final sentence of Kommerell's book (p. 488).

10. On Benjamin's adoption of the word *Schau*, here translated as "show," from Kommerell, who meant "view" or "intuition" (in German, *Anschauung*) but wanted to avoid a "philosophical" word, see the discussion in the Introduction, 34–35.

11. See Homer, *The Odyssey*, book 11 ("Nekuia").

342   NOTES TO PAGES 215–224

25. One Hundred Years of Writing on Goethe

"Hundert Jahre Schrifttum um Goethe," *Frankfurter Zeitung* 76.214 (20 March 1932): 6–7; WBA 895 and 896; trans. JR. This article, which was unsigned (though Benjamin cites himself in the last entry), appeared in a literary supplement commemorating the one hundredth anniversary of the poet's death. As Heinrich Kaulen notes, Benjamin makes several errors in citations as well as in bibliographical annotations. None of these is corrected in this translation; for complete documentation, see WuN 13.2:339–54.

1. This collection is named after Anton Kippenberg, founder and director of Insel-Verlag, who had recently rejected Benjamin's proposal to write a book on Goethe. Benjamin received the letter of rejection on 17 August 1931, whereupon he began a diary that was scheduled to continue "to the day of [his] death" (6:441); Benjamin also signals Kippenberg's presence in this contribution to the celebration of the Goethe centenary in his brief discussion of, not surprisingly, a book titled *Intermezzi Scandalosi from Goethe's Life*, 223.

2. See also "Books on Goethe—but Welcome Ones," 233–34.

3. See "Goethe's Elective Affinities" (116–17) and "Letters about, to, and from Goethe" (242).

4. Wolfgang Menzel, *Die deutsche Literatur*, 2 vols. (Stuttgart: Frankh Brothers, 1828).

5. See also "Letters about, to, and from Goethe" (244).

6. On Börne, see also "Goethe" (192).

7. These are a parody of the last lines of Goethe's *Faust, Part Two*, where "the eternal feminine" is said to "draw us onward." Vischer is one among many, including Nietzsche, who made fun of the poem that carries the title "Chorus Mysticus" and concludes one of Goethe's masterworks.

8. The actual date of Helmholtz's lecture was 1853; versions of the lecture were published many times thereafter.

9. Franz Joseph Gall invented the "science" of phrenology.

10. This is the pseudonym of Kathinka Zitz-Halein.

11. "What is good about Goethe's dangerous book, titled *Elective Affinities*, proposed by Henrich Schoen. Paris in Paris, 1802." The date is obviously wrong, and Benjamin mistranscribed one of the Latin words. This is a dissertation published in 1901.

12. Unger originally published this essay in 1921, and it was republished as the concluding item in *Aufsätze zur Literatur- und Geistesgeschichte* (Berlin: Junker und Dünnhaupt, 1929).

13. For more on Ludwig's book, see "Against a Masterpiece" (211).

NOTES TO PAGES 225–232   343

14. This is a peculiar remark inasmuch as Chamberlain's writings, including his representation of Goethe as a model of common humanity, are anti-Semitic from beginning to end. The next item, Simmel's *Goethe* (1913), is to be seen, however subtly, as the refutation of Chamberlain's *Goethe* (1912). (Simmel's father and mother were both of Jewish descent, though each of their families converted to Christianity, one to Catholicism, the other to Lutheranism.)
15. See "Against a Masterpiece," 207–13.
16. See "Goethe," 165–93.

26. Faust in the Sample Case

"Faust in Musterkoffer," *Frankfurter Zeitung* 76.214–15 (20 March 1932): Abendblatt 1, Morgenblatt, 9–10; WBA 897; trans. JC. As with the previous article, this one forms part of the newspaper's commemoration of the one hundredth anniversary of Goethe's death. For complete documentation, including page numbers for citations, see WuN 13.2:356–61.

1. Gottfried Keller, from a letter to Ludwig Geiger, which Benjamin probably cites from *Gottfried Kellers Leben, Briefe Tagebücher*, based on Jakob Baechtold's biography, edited by Emil Ermatinger (Stuttgart: Cotta, 1916), 3:460.
2. Benjamin is referring to Act 3 of *Faust, Part Two*, often called the "Helena," which was published independently from the yet-to-be-completed drama under the title "A Classico-Romantic Phantasmagoria."
3. On the (absence of) the figure Persephone, see the endnote to "Goethe's Elective Affinities," 141.
4. Benjamin also expresses his enthusiasm for Hertz's treatment of *Faust, Part Two* in his review of Georg Ellinger's *Geschichte der neulateinischen Lyrik in den Niederlanden*, 3:401; and in a letter to Albert Salomon, GB 4:81; 5 April 1932.
5. Goethe, WA I, 15:81, ll. 6427–36; *Faust, Part Two*, Act 1, Knight's Hall.
6. For the variant, see Hertz, *Natur und Geist in Goethes Faust*, 199.
7. See "Goethe," 178.
8. Benjamin cites the same passage in his dissertation; see 1:60; SW 1:192.
9. Goethe, WA I, 15:72, ll. 6286–88; *Faust, Part Two*, Act 1, Dark Gallery.
10. The publisher is Insel-Verlag, with which Benjamin apparently had a contract for a book on Goethe for the commemorative year; see 6:441, WuN 13.2:356. The fact that Insel would publish a one-thousand-page tome like Kühnemann's yet not publish anything of Benjamin's can be seen reflected in this parenthesis and, upon reflection, throughout the review; see 37–38.

344   NOTES TO PAGES 234–238

27. Books on Goethe—but Welcome Ones

"Goethebücher, aber willkommene," *Die Literarische Welt* 8.26 (24 June 1932): 5; WBA 900; trans. JR. For complete documentation, including page numbers of works cited, see WuN 13.2:368–69.

1. See Johann Wolfgang von Goethe, *Goethes Gedichte in zeitlicher Folge,* ed. Hans Gerhard Gräf, 2 vols. (Leipzig: Insel, 1917).
2. Benjamin uses a phrase from this poem, which was posthumously added to the *West-Eastern Divan,* for the title of the novella that was broadcast on 16 December 1929; see "Goethe's Elective Affinities," 129.

28. New Literature about Goethe

"Neue Literatur über Goethe," *Frankfurter Zeitung* 78.264 (27 May 1934): 6 (= Literaturblatt 67.21), WBA 935; trans. JR. The translation is based on WuN 13.1:449–50; for full bibliographic documentation, see WuN 13:2:437–41.

1. Benjamin had to use pseudonyms for publications in Germany during the Nazi era. Detlev Holz was the one he used most often. As noted in the Introduction (see 38), the *Frankfurter Zeitung* was allowed for a time to depart from the principle and procedures of *Gleichschaltung* ("synchronization," as it is often translated, though both terms are, of course, euphemisms).
2. Among the things that the title, *Bürgertum und Bürgerlichkeit,* promises—and very likely the point of this sentence—is a study of German bourgeoisie as well as a consideration of what it means to be a German "citizen" (*Bürger*) in 1934.
3. This is a strange remark, which can be read in several ways. Heinz Keferstein was a Nazi Party member, and he refers to the work of the Führer in stamping out the "Marxist spirit" in the preface to his work, originally a dissertation; for a brief discussion, see WuN 13.2:438–39.

29. Popularity as a Problem

"Volkstümlichkeit als Problem. Zu Hermann Schneider: *Schillers Werk und Erbe,*" *Frankfurter Zeitung* 79.321 (30 June 1935): 2 = *Literaturblatt* 68.26, WBA 961; trans. KM. The translation is based on WuN 13.1:467–69; for full bibliographic documentation, see WuN 13:2:472. This is Benjamin's last publication in Germany during his lifetime; see 39–40.

1. "Scientifically" translates *wissenschaftlich,* which could also be translated as "scholarly," since *Wissenschaft* has a much broader field of application than *science*; in the subsequent paragraphs of the review, which are concerned with

NOTES TO PAGES 238-239   345

literary studies, *Wissenschaft* would generally be translated as "scholarship," but this choice would blunt the force of Benjamin's argument. As for the term "knowledge," it translates *Wissen*, which, of course, is the root of *Wissenschaft* (just as the Latin word *scire*, "to know," is the root of *science*).

2. In referring to the theory of relativity, Benjamin is violating a ban on references to Jewish scientists, for, though Einstein is not mentioned, the theory of relativity is inextricably associated with his name. The year 1935 is often viewed in retrospect as the pinnacle of "German" or "Aryan physics," which not only rejected and suppressed the kind of "Jewish science" that, in Benjamin's terms, represents the "avant-garde" of contemporary physics (relativity and quantum theory) but also received governmental funding for a "German" replacement; for a brief discussion, see 295n77.

3. Benjamin read Eddington's Gifford lectures, *The Nature of the Physical World* (New York: Macmillan, 1928), in a German translation, the title of which better captures Eddington's overall intention, *Das Weltbild der Physik und ein Versuch seiner philosophischen Deutung* [The World-Image of Physics and an Attempt at Its Philosophical Interpretation], trans. Marie Freifrau Rausch von Traubenberg and H. Dieselhorst (Braunschweig: Vieweg & Sohn, 1931). Benjamin quotes a long passage from Eddington's book in a letter to Scholem concerning Kafka; see GB 6:111–12; 12 June 1938. In an unpublished part of his "Artwork in the Age of Its Technical Reproducibility" (1:1041), he singles out Lenin, Eddington, and Freud as successful popularizers.

4. Benjamin is referring to his own review of Schneider's earlier book, *From Wallenstein to Demetrius* (1933), which appeared in the *Frankfurter Zeitung* in July 1934 under the title "A Schiller Chapter," signed by Detlev Holz (3:420–21). The earlier review also begins with a discussion of the current "feeling of alienation" with respect to Schiller's dramatic works.

5. See Julian Hirsch, *Die Genesis des Ruhmes: Ein Beitrag zur Methodenlehre der Geschichte* [The Genesis of Fame-Glory: A Contribution to Historical Methodology] (Leipzig: Barth, 1914). Benjamin is probably referring to Hirsch's discussion of the one hundredth anniversary of Schiller's birth in 1859, when "Schiller's shape suddenly grew into gigantic proportions" (83). As Benjamin indicates, Schiller is only an incidental figure in Hirsch's study. Goethe and the Goethe cult, by contrast, are two of its central features—so much so that an entry in "One Hundred Years of Writing on Goethe" compares *The Genesis of Fame* with a collection titled *From the Camp of Goethe's Opponents* (222). Listed as 798 on the "Registry of Readings" (7:449), Benjamin read Hirsch's study while working on the first stages of "Goethe's Elective Affinities." After meeting Hirsch, he decided against asking him to participate in the *Angelus*

346 NOTES TO PAGES 239-241

Novus project; but his rationale, as expressed in a letter to Scholem, was entirely stylistic: "His book on *The Genesis of Fame* is filled with a considerable amount of monotony" (GB 2:204; 27 October 1921; this stylistic criticism is still discernible in the remarks Benjamin makes about *The Genesis of Fame* in his study of Eduard Fuchs, 2:469; SW 3:263). Nevertheless, as Benjamin probably recognized, *The Genesis of Fame* and "Goethe's Elective Affinities" share a common motivation in their rejection of Gundolf's brand of monumentalizing scholarship; for a brief discussion of Hirsch's relation to Gundolf, see 295n78.

6. The year 1934 was the 175th anniversary of Schiller's birth as well as the 275th anniversary of the Cotta Publishing House, which published many of Goethe's writings.

30. Letters about, to, and from Goethe

Walter Benjamin, "Briefe <I>," *Frankfurter Zeitung* 75.242–44 (1 April 1931): 13; WBA 383/1; *Deutsche Menschen: eine Folge von Briefen*, Auswahl und Einleitungen von Detlev Holz [pseudonym] (Lucerne: Vita Nova, 1936), 11, 71–72, 79–82; WBA 521; trans. PF. In the book that resulted from the newspaper articles, Benjamin replaced the brief remarks translated above (which initiate the series of letters he published in the *Frankfurter Zeitung*) with a page-long "Preface" that concludes with a quotation from a passage from late Goethe that Benjamin had earlier used for the then-unpublished article for the *Great Soviet Encyclopedia* (2:737–38; 192; see also "From Cosmopolitan to Metropolitan," 4:859). The brief remarks from the *Frankfurter Zeitung* are reprinted in WuN 10:107; an expanded version, different from the "Preface" to *German Human Beings*, can be found in WuN 10:15, and a translation of the "Preface" can be found in SW 3:167. Benjamin was advised to change the prefatory remarks so that, as the publisher of the volume Rudolf Roeßler notes in a letter to Karl Theme, "a prohibition [on distribution in Germany] cannot occur because of the *preface*" (WuN 10:387).

In addition to the letters about, to, and from Goethe, there is also one that concerns "how very much, by ordering and giving direction, the existence of this man [Goethe] had effects in far-lying circuits" (4:180; SW 3:186). This is the letter Johann Baptist Bertram wrote to Sulpiz Boisserée on 11 May 1811, when, as Benjamin proposes, Goethe decided that the second part of *Faust* was "capable of completion." And Goethe's adage that a certain irrationality is required in lyric poetry is mentioned in Benjamin's preface to his inclusion of a letter Gottfried Keller wrote to Theodor Storm (1:224; SW 3:215).

1. This alludes to the subtitle qua motto of *German Human Beings*: "Of honor without fame / of greatness without glory / of dignity without pay" (4:150;

NOTES TO PAGES 242–245   347

SW 3:167). For a discussion of why *Deutsche Menschen* is translated as "German Human Beings," see the Introduction, 41.

2. In speaking of his "fragmentary knowledge" of music, Zelter, as a (largely self-taught) musician, composer, conductor, and teacher of music, was being modest.

3. See Benjamin's extensive discussion of Gervinus's discussion of the late Goethe, 116–18 and 217.

4. On the word "neglection" (*Versaümniß*), see "Goethe's Elective Affinities," 110.

5. Goethe, WA IV, 49:190–91.

6. Ernst Lewy, *Zur Sprache des alten Goethe: ein Versuch über die Sprache des Einzel-nen* (Berlin: Cassirer, 1913), 25. Benjamin had long expressed interest in Lewy's book (see Gershom Scholem, *Walter Benjamin: The Story of a Friendship*, trans. Harry Zohn [New York: Schocken, 1981], 22 and 105–7); see also the brief discussion in "One Hundred Years of Writing on Goethe," 219.

7. See Brodersen's brief note about this unusual reference to Whitman in WuN 10:294.

8. Goethe, WA I, 14:82, l. 1700; *Faust, Part One*, Study. This is the crucial—and widely quoted—moment in which Faust establishes the terms of his wager with Mephistopheles.

31. Mythic Anxiety in Goethe

"L'Angoisse mythique chez Goethe," *Les Cahiers du Sud* 24 (1937): 342–48; WBA 1326; trans. JR. This is an excerpt from "Goethe's Elective Affinities," which stretches, with certain omissions (not marked in the translation), from 115 to 129. The excerpt appeared in a special issue of the Marseilles-based journal *Cahiers du Sud* that gathered essays on "Le Romantisme allemand" (see 42–43). References can be found in the corresponding passages in the translation of the full essay. It is not clear how many of the choices here—from the selection of the passages to the choice of French words and the precise syntactical formulations—are due to Klossowski or Benjamin. Klossowski also translated "The Artwork in the Age of Its Technical Reproducibility" for inclusion in a 1936 issue of the *Zeitschrift für Sozialforschung* (1:709–39).

In a public letter about Benjamin that appeared in a 1952 issue of *Mercure de France* in conjunction with the French translation of "The Storyteller," which he declined to translate, Klossowski describes his experience as a translator: "Benjamin, considering my initial version too free, had started translating it again with me. The result was going to be a text perfectly unreadable as a result of the fact that it was closely modeled on the slightest German expressions, for which Benjamin would accept no transposition. Often, the French syntax literally gave cramps to this irreducible logician. It made me think of this remark by

348 NOTES TO PAGES 246–252

Joseph de Maistre: 'He (Voltaire) delivers his imagination to the enthusiasm of hell, which lends him all its strength to drag him to the limits of evil,' and whose construction infuriated him" (Klossowski, "Lettre sur Walter Benjamin," reprinted in WuN 12:665–66).

1. The German word *Angst* in Benjamin's text is translated by the French word *angoisse* in Klossowski's translation. Klossowski's translation has been translated here as "anxiety" in light of his reading of Kierkegaard, as reflected in his publication of a commentary on the Danish philosopher in the journal *Acéphale* (edited by Georges Bataille) in 1937, coincident with the translation of this section of Benjamin's essay. The selection of this passage from Benjamin's essay suggests a context within which his work would have been received in France from the perspective of the group loosely described as the College of Sociology. In his "Letter on Walter Benjamin" (see above), Klossowski describes his participation in *Acéphale* without, however, referring to his translation of "Goethe's Elective Affinities."

2. The phrase "elective affinities" is translated by Klossowski as a plural noun, as in the German, while also being capitalized, indicating that it refers to the novel.

32. Two Notes from the *Arcades Project*

From "N [Erkenntnistheoretisches, Theorie des Fortschritts]," a folder of the *Arcades Project*; WBA 307, reproduced as WBA 476 (see 5:1262); ca. 1937–38; trans. KM.

1. See Georg Simmel, *Goethe* (Leipzig: Klinkhardt & Biermann, 1913), 20–29; as well as the pages noted below. This remark was first formulated in a set of notes Benjamin wrote under the title "Addenda to the *Trauerspiel* book," which may have been written in preparation for a second edition: "In studying Simmel's presentation of Goethe's concept of truth, in particular his excellent elucidation of the urphenomenon (p. 56/57ff., p. 60/61), it became irrefutably clear to me that my concept of 'origin' in the *Trauerspiel* book is a rigorous and obligatory translation of this basic Goethean concept from the realm of nature into that of history. 'Origin'—that is the theologically and historically different, theologically and historically living concept of urphenomenon, a concept fetched from pagan nexuses of nature into Jewish nexuses of history—that is 'origin' in the theological sense. Only for this reason can it fulfill the concept of genuineness" (1:953–54).

2. The phrase "self-appropriating development" translates "selbsteignen Entwicklung," while "unfolding" translates "Auswicklung." These terms clearly allude

NOTE TO PAGE 252 349

to Goethe's scientific work, including those marked under 575 in his "Registry of Readings": "*The Metamorphosis of Plants* (and much else from *Morphology*, vol. 1)" (253); see also an influential study of Goethe's morphological writings that appears in the Registry under 677, Adolph Hansen, *Goethes Metamorphose der Pflanzen: Geschichte einer botanischen Hypothese* (Gießen: Töpelmann, 1907).

3. See Goethe, WA II, 11.1:68–72, esp. 71–72; "Analysis and Synthesis." Benjamin draws the epigraph for *The Concept of Art Critique in German Romanticism* from this essay (see 1:10; SW 1:116), and he refers to the same passage of the essay in his critique of Albert Béguin's *L'âme romantique et le rêve* (see 3:559; SW 4:154).

Index of Goethe Citations (English-German)

Accomplices, The (Die Mitschuldige), 103,
320n40
"Analysis and Synthesis" (Analyse und Syn-
these), 9, 11, 28, 43–44, 349n3. See also
Maxims and Reflections

"Bride of Corinth, The" (Die Braut
von Corinth), 181

Campaign in France, The (Kampagne in
Frankreich), 184, 186
Clavigo, 171
"Collector and His People, The" (Der Sam-
mler und die Seinigen), 253
"Conciliation" (Aussöhnung), 152
Contributions to Optics (Beiträge zur Optik),
204. See also Theory of Colors
Conversations of German Emigrees (Unterhalt-
ungen deutscher Ausgewanderten), 176
Conversations with Eckermann (Gespräche
mit Goethe in den letzten Jahren seines
Lebens), 185, 188, 323n65, 329n26, 334n27

Daybooks and Yearbooks (Tag- und
Jahreshefte), 115, 186

Egmont, 114, 168, 173–74, 297n5, 336n11
Elective Affinities (Die Wahlver-
wandtschaften), 2–3, 13–16, 33, 86–161,
187, 246–51, 253–54, 257, 287n19, 310n2,
310n26, 312n1, 316n5, 323n65, 328n113,
332n161
Elpenor, 298n5
"Epilogue to Schiller's Bell" (Epilog zu
Schillers Glocke), 185
Epimenides' Awakening (Des Epimenides
Erwachen), 183
Excited Ones, The (Die Aufgeregten), 176,
187

Faust, 5, 6, 26, 36, 157, 171, 174, 216, 218, 219,
221, 222, 223, 227–32, 297n5, 326–27n96;
Faust, Part Two, 15, 16, 36–37, 50, 128, 129,
171, 182–83, 184, 190–92, 199, 228, 229, 250,
251, 253, 298n5, 330n142, 338n3, 340–41,
342n7, 343n2, 343n4, 346
"Fisherman, The" (Der Fischer), 144, 171,
331n153
"Foolish Pilgrim, The" (Die pilgernde
Törin), 131–32. See also Wilhelm Meister's
Journeyman Years

INDEX OF GOETHE CITATIONS

"God and the Bajadere, The" (Der Gott und die Bajadere), 181

God and World (Gott und Welt), 112, 324n75. See also "Primal Words. Orphic"

"Gods, Heroes, and Wieland" (Götter, Helden und Wieland), 253

Götz von Berlichingen, 167–68, 170

Grand Cophta, The (Der Gross-Cophta), 176

Hermann and Dorothea, 7, 176, 298n5, 311n1

Iphigenia in Tauris (Iphigenia auf Tauris), 171, 173, 176, 298n5

Italian Journey (Die Italienische Reise), 7, 186, 286n13

"Marienbad Elegy" (Marienbader Elegie), 152, 188, 216, 298n5, 333n171

Maxims and Reflections (Maximen und Reflexionen), 10–13, 141, 157–58, 253, 287n19. See also "Analysis and Synthesis"

"May Song" (Mailied), 167

Metamorphosis of Plants, The (Die Metamorphose der Pflanzen), 177, 196–97, 205, 253, 349n2

Meteorological Writings (Schriften zur Meteorologie), 178, 197, 253

"Mysteries, The" (Die Geheimnisse), 171

Natural Daughter, The (Die natürliche Tochter), 168, 176, 254

"Nature" (Die Natur. Ein Fragment), 113, 114, 178, 324n77

"New Melusine, The" (Die neue Melusine), 37, 134, 294n72, 322n125. See also *Wilhelm Meister's Journeyman Years*

"No Longer on a Page of Silk" (Nicht mehr auf Seidenblatt), 234, 328n112. See also *West-Eastern Divan*

"On German Manner and Art" (Von deutscher Art und Kunst), 167

"Only He Who Knows Yearning" (Nur wer die Sehnsucht kennt), 171

On Morphology (Zur Morphologie), 253, 326n94, 349n3

"Over All Peaks" (Über allen Gipfeln, Wandrers Nachtlied II), 171

Pandora, 19–20, 37, 253, 291n43, 294n72, 298n5

"Pedagogical Province" (Pädagogische Provinz), 189. See also *Wilhelm Meister's Journeyman Years*

Poetry and Truth (Dichtung und Wahrheit), 6, 113–14, 115, 118, 128, 185–86, 187, 211, 216, 247, 249, 250–51, 298n5, 324–25n79, 332n160

"Primal Words. Orphic" (Urworte. Orpisch), 114, 160, 326n94. See also *God and World*

"Roman Carnival, The" (Das Römische Carneval), 253

Roman Elegies (Römische Elegien), 174

"Rose on the Heath" (Heideröslein), 167

"Sorcerer's Apprentice, The" (Der Zauberlehrling), 181

Sorrows of Young Werther, The (Die Leiden des jungen Werthers), 5, 167, 168–69, 170, 219, 227, 297n5, 299n7

Stella, 171, 254

Theory of Colors (Farbenlehre), 5, 33, 78, 98, 112, 178, 197–98, 204–6, 243, 253, 284n9, 308n1, 339. See also *Contributions to Optics*

Torquato Tasso, 5, 6, 171, 298n5, 332n171

"To the Full Moon Rising" (Dem aufgehenden Vollmonde), 234

"To the Moon" (An den Mond), 171

"Treasure Hunter, The" (Der Schatzgräber), 181

"Trilogy of Passion" (Trilogie der Leidenschaft), 152, 333n171. See also "Conciliation"; "Marienbad Elegy"

Weimar Edition (Weimar- bzw. Sophienaus-
gabe), xi, 10, 193
"Welcome and Farewell" (Willkommen und
Abschied), 167
Werther's Letters from Switzerland (Briefe aus
der Schweiz), 171, 189
West-Eastern Divan (West–östlicher Divan),
93, 128–29, 167, 188, 216, 225, 228, 234,
250, 298n5, 328n112, 344n2. See also "No
Longer on a Page of Silk"
Wilhelm Meister's Journeyman Years (Wil-
helm Meisters Wanderjahre, oder Die
Entsagenden), 130–32, 174, 177, 189–90,
196, 228, 294n72, 298. See also "Foolish

Pilgrim, The"; "New Melusine, The";
"Pedagogical Province"
Wilhelm Meister's Theatrical Mission (Wil-
helm Meisters theatralische Sendung),
171, 298n5. See also *Wilhelm Meister's
Years of Apprenticeship*
Wilhelm Meister's Years of Apprenticeship
(Wilhelm Meisters Lehrjahre), 5, 184,
187, 189, 298n5, 330n140
"Winckelmann and His Century" (Winckel-
mann und sein Jahrhundert), 105
"Winter Journey in the Harz Mountains"
(Harzreise im Winter), 171
"With a Painted Ribbon" (Mit einem
gemalten Band), 167

Xenia (with Friedrich Schiller), 181

Name Index

Abeken, Bernhard Rudolf, 105, 108, 321n48

Adler, Jeremy, 238n108

Adorno, Theodor, 1, 294n72, 315n4

Adorno-Karplus, Gretel, 294n72, 329n125

Aeschylus, 6

Arendt, Hannah, 1, 4, 283n3

Aristotle, 153–54

Arnim, Bettina von, 110, 125, 141, 145, 158–59, 298n5

August, Karl (Grand Duke of Saxe-Weimar), 169–70, 172, 174, 183, 211, 234, 298n5

Bachofen, Johann Jakob, 153, 218

Baldensperger, Fernand, 219

Ball, Philip, 295n77

Ballard, Jean, 42–43

Balzac, Honoré de, 52, 300n3

Basedow, Johann Bernhard, 92–93

Bataille, Georges, 348n1

Baudelaire, Charles, xiii, 1, 17, 42, 44, 309

Bauer, Karl, 220

Baumgartner, Alexander, 12, 124, 151, 224

Beethoven, Ludwig van, 161, 298n5

Béguin, Albert, 43, 349n3

Beheim, Michel, 306n1

Behrens, Friedrich, 222

Benjamin, Walter, "Analogy and Affinity," 317n6; *Arcades Project*, 4, 44, 252, 296n82, 315n4, 333n177; "The Artwork in the Age of Its Technical Reproducibility," 42, 333n178, 345n3, 347; "Cagliostro," 283n8; "Capitalism as Religion," 15, 26, 305n1; *The Concept of Art Critique in German Romanticism*, 5, 9–10, 13, 16, 24, 28, 42, 53–61, 246, 301–2, 302n1, 308n2, 316n5, 341n3; "Death," 334n197; "Diary of the Seventeenth of August, Nineteen-Thirty, until the Day of My Death," 37, 38; "Dr. Faust," 283n8; "Eidos and Concept," 306n3; "Fate and Character," 16, 320n39; *German Human Beings*, 41–42, 337n39, 341n6; "Gypsies," 283n8; "Hashish in Marseilles," 296n80; "Logic and Language," 294n72; "Marseilles," 338; "The Medium through Which Artworks Continue to Influence Later Ages," 300n3; "Metaphysics of Youth," 286n14, 330n136; *Moscow Diary*, 27–28, 293n62; "Naples," 25; "New Literature in Russia," 293n61;

355

356 NAME INDEX

Benjamin, Walter (*continued*)
  One-Way Street, 19, 25, 33, 312n1, 338; "On Language as Such and on Human Language," 306n5; "On Shame," 284n9; "On the Image of Proust," xiii; "On the Middle Ages," 315n5; "On the Program of the Coming Philosophy," 299n3; *Origin of the German Trauerspiel*, 2, 24, 25, 28, 246, 252, 288n28, 300n1, 305n2, 308n1, 312n1, 315n5, 325n83, 327n97, 336n14, 348n1; "Prescription for Comedy Writers," 254; review of Albert Béguin, *L'âme romantique et le rêve*, 43, 349n3; "Revue or Theater," 25; "Schiller and Goethe: A Layman's Fantasy," 284n9; "Sleeping Beauty," 5; "Socrates," 286n14, 305n2; "Sonnet in the Night," 10; *Sonnets*, 312n1; "The Storyteller," 347; *Tableaux Parisiens* (translation of Baudelaire), 17, 42, 309; "The Task of the Translator," xiii, 17–18, 328n112; "Teaching and Evaluation," 7–8, 311n1; "Theory of Cognition," 284n9, 307n1; "Toward the Critique of Violence," 14, 288n28, 289n31, 289n34, 300n3, 318n15, 321n42; "Two Poems of Friedrich Hölderlin," 8, 286n14, 302n1, 313n4, 333n181; "Two Types of Popularization," 293n62; *Understanding Brecht*, 1; "Vivifying and Violence," 329n122; "What the Germans Were Reading While Their Classical Authors Were Writing," 35; "Young Russian Writers," 30–31, 283n8, 293n61
Benjamin-Kellner, Dora, 2, 312n1
Bentham, Jeremy, 189
Bergman, Torbern, 317n6
Bernhard, Julia, 335
Bernoulli, Carl Albrecht, 153
Bertram, Johann Baptist, 346
Bertuch, Friedrich Justin, 182
Beutler, Ernst, 219
Beyerchen, Alan, 295n77
Biedermann, Flodoard von, 215, 233–34
Bielschowsky, Albert, 99, 104, 148, 224

Bierbaum, Otto Julius, 220
Blass, Ernst, 16
Blavatsky, Helena, 222
Bloch, Ernst, 300n3
Boccaccio, Giovanni, 131
Böhlendorff, Casimir, 341n6
Bois-Reymond, Emil du, 221
Boisserée, Sulpiz, 159, 186, 346
Boll, Franz, 114–15, 325n83
Borchardt, Rudolf, 13, 143–44, 193, 287n26, 297n3, 330–31n150
Borel, Henri, 290n36
Börne, Ludwig, 183, 192, 199, 220, 222
Boucke, Ewald A., 219
Boyle, Nicholas, 335n1
Bradish, Joseph A. von, 235
Braun, Julius, 215
Brauneis, Adrian, 293n67
Brecht, Bertolt, 1
Brion, Marcel, 42, 296n80
Brock, Hans Manfred, 296n79
Büchner, Georg, 7
Buff, Charlotte, 168–69
Bukharin, Nikolai Ivanovich, 28
Burdach, Konrad, 193, 216, 228, 291n47
Bürger, Gottfried August, 166
Burggraf, Julius, 223
Burkhardt, Carl, 215
Byron, Baron ("Lord") George Gordon, 187, 211

Caesar, Julius, 174
Cantor, Georg, 298n6, 308n1
Carrière, Moriz, 224
Carus, Carl Gustav, 218
Cassirer, Paul, 19, 22, 290n38
Cassou, Jean, 42
Cervantes, Miguel de, 131
Chamberlain, Houston Stewart, 36, 225, 285n10, 343n14
Claudius, Matthias, 166
Cohen, Hermann, 9, 20, 95, 99, 152, 285n10, 308n2, 316n6

NAME INDEX 357

Cohn, Jula, 2–3, 10, 91, 311–12n1, 327n96, 334n195

Corngold, Stanley, xiv

Cotta, J. G., 180, 190

Croce, Benedetto, 24

Cumming, Sofia, 296n80

Dainat, Holger, 291nn39–41

Dante Alighieri, 160, 178, 197, 220, 230, 334n195

D'Aurevilly, Jules Barbey, 72

Deetjen, Werner, 215

D'Holbach, Paul-Henri Thiry (Baron), 166

Diderot, Denis, 166

Diederichs, Eugen, 204

Diez, Heinrich Friedrich von, 188

Dilthey, Wilhelm, 21

Dostoevsky, Fyodor, 16, 312n1, 334n197

Duns Scotus, John, 308n3

Dürer, Albrecht, 178, 197, 230

Eckermann, Johann Peter, 185, 188, 189, 298n5, 324n79

Eddington, Arthur Stanley, 40, 238, 345n3

Eiland, Howard, 288n28, 290n38

Einstein, Albert, 39–40, 345n2

Engel, Eduard, 224

Eucken, Rudolf, 314n4

Falk, Johannes, 115, 216, 247

Feuerbach, Ludwig, 220

Fischer, Kuno, 228

Fischer, Paul, 219

Fourier, Charles, 189

François-Poncet, André, 86–87, 138, 254, 310nn1–2, 310n5, 328n113

Friedländer, Salomo, 34, 206

Friedrich II of Prussia, 117, 249

Frucht, Else, 222

Fuchs, Eduard, 226, 346n5

Gall, Franz Joseph, 221, 342n9

Geiger, Ludwig, 214

George, Stefan, 134, 161, 193, 208, 210, 213, 225, 304n2, 326–27n96, 340

Gervinus, Georg Gottfried, 116–18, 217, 242, 247–49

Giotto, 140

Glover, Friedrich, 221, 222

Goethe, Cornelia, 166

Goethe, Johann Caspar, 165–66

Goldberg, Oskar, 305n1

Görres, Joseph von, 141, 222

Göschel, Carl Friedrich, 217

Göschen, Georg Joachim, 35

Göttling, Karl Wilhelm, 253

Grabbe, Christian Dietrich, 222

Gräf, Hans Gerhard, 234

Gregorovius, Ferdinand, 218

Grillparzer, Franz, 6–7, 311n1

Grimm, Hermann, 36, 225

Grimm, Jacob, 319n25, 321n42

Grimm, Wilhelm, 319n25, 321n42

Grün, Karl, 218

Grünewald, Matthias, 305n2

Gryphius, Andreas, 294n68, 320n38

Guerra, Gabriele, 293n67

Guglia, Eugen, 220

Gundolf, Friedrich, 9, 12, 13, 14, 18, 20, 34, 37, 47–49, 89, 103, 104, 121, 122–27, 138, 159, 193, 207, 211, 285n10, 287n25, 294n68, 295n78, 297nn1–5, 304n2, 316n6, 320n38, 321n44, 326–27n96, 327n104, 331n140, 334n191, 346n5

Günther, Johann Christian, 186

Gutzkow, Karl, 181, 217, 225, 254

Hafez, 328n112

Hamann, Johann Georg, 167

Hammacher, Theodor, 222

Hammer-Purgstall, Joseph Freiherr von, 188, 328n112

Hansen, Adolph, 253, 349n2

Hebbel, Christian Friedrich, 71, 150

Hebel, Johann Peter, 101, 318n25

Hehn, Victor, 220

NAME INDEX

Heidegger, Martin, 21–22, 40, 43, 291–92nn44–49

Heinle, Christoph Friedrich (Fritz), 16, 290n37, 312n1

Heinle, Wolf, 290n37

Heller, Frank von, 288n29

Helmholtz, Hermann von, 221

Hemsterhuis, François, 227

Hengstenberg, Ernst Wilhelm, 107, 145, 222

Herbertz, Richard, 301

Herder, Johann Gottfried von, 93, 167, 170, 185, 186, 208, 210, 232, 297n5, 328n115

Hertz, Gottfried Wilhelm, 37, 229, 230–31

Herzlieb, Minna, 110, 139

Hesiod, 144–45

Hiller, Kurt, 14

Hirsch, Julian, 40, 222, 239, 295n78, 345n5

Hofer, Klara, 222

Hofmannsthal, Hugo von, 22–23, 24, 27, 30, 32, 193, 246, 288n26, 311n1, 313n2, 313n4, 315n4, 320n39, 330–31n150, 334n198, 338

Hölderlin, Friedrich, 7, 8, 20, 60, 82, 118, 129, 143, 159, 187, 209, 210, 212, 213, 286n14, 302n1, 309n3, 323n69, 340, 341n6

Holtei, Karl von, 166

Holz, Detlev, 38–41, 235, 334n1

Holzmann, Michael, 222

Homer, 186, 323n71

Howe, Richard Herbert, 289n33

Huch, Rudolf, 216

Humboldt, Wilhelm von, 8, 52, 93, 108, 111, 175, 195, 300n3

Hüppner, Wolfgang, 287n25

Husserl, Edmond, 306n3

Ibsen, Henrik, 6

Iffland, August Wilhelm, 183

Jacobi, Friedrich Heinrich, 107, 177, 196, 208

Jennings, Michael, 288n28, 290n38

Ježower, Ignaz, 32–33, 338, 338–39n1

John, Johann August Friedrich, 185

Joseph II of Austria, 235

Kandinsky, Wassily, 52, 205, 300–301n3, 339n4

Kant, Immanuel, 10, 16, 51, 92–96, 156, 179, 198, 232, 290n34, 298n6, 299n2, 304n1, 308n4, 316n6, 333n179

Kasack, Wolfgang, 31–32

Kaulbach, Wilhelm von, 223

Kaulen, Heinrich, 292n56, 340, 342

Keferstein, Georg, 236–37

Keller, Gottfried, 37, 227, 346

Keudell, Elise von, 215

Kierkegaard, Soren, 12, 348n1

Kippenberg, Anton, 38, 223, 342n1

Kisiel, Theodor, 291nn44–45, 292nn48–49

Klages, Ludwig, 218–19

Kleist, Heinrich von, 140, 187

Klinger, Friedrich Maximilian von, 166

Klopstock, Friedrich Gottlieb, 91, 167, 170, 208

Klossowski, Pierre, xii, 42, 251, 347–48, 348n1, 348n2

Kluckhohn, Paul, 19–22

Knapp, Albert, 222

Köchy, Christian Heinrich Gottlieb, 221

Köhne, Julia, 295n78

Kommerell, Max, 34–35, 36, 40, 207–13, 225, 294n69, 327n96, 340–41

Körner, Theodor, 176, 196, 337n2

Kracauer, Siegfried, 30

Kraft, Werner, 296n79

Kräuter, Theodor, 185

Kühnemann, Eugen, 36–37, 40, 228–29, 232, 343n10

Kurella, Alfred, 43

Lācis, Asja, 25, 27, 29, 292n56, 312n1

Laube, Heinrich, 128, 250

Laue, Max von, 339n7

Lavater, Johann Kasper, 169, 209

Lechter, Melchior, 209, 341n7

Lederer, Emil, 14

Lehmann, Johann August, 219

Leisewitz, Johann Anton, 166

NAME INDEX

Leitgeb, Hanna, 295n75
Lenz, Jakob Michael Reinhold, 166, 168, 172, 186
Lepenies, Wolf, 289n30
Lessing, Gotthold Ephraim, 169, 175, 195, 224, 241
Levetzow, Ulrike von, 188
Lewes, George Henry, 224
Lewy, Ernst, 219, 244, 347n6
Lichtenberger, Henri, 296n79
Lindner, Burkhardt, 288n28
Liszt, Franz, 220
Louvier, Ferdinand August, 222
Löwy, Michael, 289n33
Luden, Heinrich, 174
Ludwig, Emil, 211, 224
Ludwig II (King of Bavaria), 200, 338n1
Lunacharsky, Anatoly, 335

Mann, Thomas, 43, 236, 316n5, 337n30
Manzoni, Alessandro, 187
Marx, Karl, 15, 30
Marx, Ursula, 285n11, 286n83, 295n74
Masaccio, 140
Mehring, Franz, 36, 225, 226
Meleager, 129
Menzel, Wolfgang, 217, 222
Merck, Johann Heinrich, 167, 186
Meyer, Johann Heinrich, 186
Meyer, Richard Moritz, 103, 130, 319n35
Mézières, Alfred, 110
Michalske, Hainer, 295n76
Möbius, Paul, 221
Mörike, Eduard, 69, 184, 305n1
Mozart, Wolfgang Amadeus, 95
Müller, Friedrich, 166
Müller, Friedrich von, 40, 185, 240–41, 324n77
Müllner, Adolph, 222
Musil, Robert, 332n162

Napoleon Bonaparte, 103, 174, 175, 182–84, 195, 198–99, 210, 211, 298n5

Newton, Isaac, 33–34, 178, 198, 204, 205–6, 243, 339
Nicolai, Friedrich, 181
Nicolovius, Alfred, 215
Niebuhr, Carsten, 225
Nietzsche, Friedrich, 63, 72, 85, 209, 212, 286n14, 306n5, 309n1, 320n36, 342n7
Noeggerath, Felix, 9–10, 44, 286n17
Norton, Robert, 341n4
Novalis, 16, 58, 61, 184

Owen, Robert, 189

Papst, Stephan, 292n58
Parsons, Talcott, 289n33
Pasqué, Ernst, 218
Paul, Jean, 52, 111, 187, 200, 212, 224, 300n3, 338n2, 340
Payer-Thurn, Rudolf, 233
Peltzer, Alfred, 253
Pestalozzi, Johann Heinrich, 189
Pindar, 92, 129
Plato, 9, 10, 51, 81, 140, 154–55, 160
Pliny the Elder, 304n8
Plutarch, 211
Proust, Marcel, xiii
Pustkuchen, Friedrich, 222

Radek, Karl, 28–30, 293n60
Radt, Fritz, 3, 8, 10, 312n1
Radt, Grete, 10, 312n1
Rang, Florens Christian, 19, 22–23, 209, 313n4
Reich, Bernard, 25, 27, 28–30, 292n56
Reinhard, Karl Friedrich Graf von, 253, 302n1
Richter, Alexandra, 285n11, 295n74
Rickert, Heinrich, 14, 21–22, 291n47, 292n48, 303n4
Riemer, Friedrich Wilhelm, 109, 171, 185, 324n79
Roeßler, Rudolf, 346
Roethe, Gustav, 295n78
Rollett, Hermann, 216

Rosenkranz, Karl, 36, 225
Rothacker, Erich, 19–22, 40, 285n10, 291n43, 294n72
Rotten, Elisabeth, 10, 13, 53
Rousseau, Jean-Jacques, 169

Saint-Simon, Henri de, 189
Salomon, Albert, 37, 288n28
Salomon-Delatour, Gottfried, 288n28, 291n39
Saupe, Julius, 215
Schäffer, Emil, 216
Schelling, Friedrich, 211, 321n41
Schiller, Friedrich, 5, 6, 30, 39–40, 93, 115, 116, 117, 166, 174, 176, 177, 180–82, 184–85, 186, 192, 196–97, 201, 208, 210, 212, 232, 238–39, 247, 248–49, 253, 254, 298n5, 299n2, 319n35, 337n35, 337n2, 340, 345nn4–5, 346n6
Schiller-Lerg, Sabine, 293n61
Schlegel, August, 208, 213
Schlegel, Friedrich, 16, 54, 57–58, 59, 62, 208, 213, 253, 299n7, 303n1
Schmidt, Eric, 295n78
Schmidt, Julius, 140
Schneider, Hermann, 238–39, 345n4
Schoen, Ernst, 2, 312n1
Scholem, Arthur, 301
Scholem, Gershom, 2, 10–11, 12, 16, 17, 26–27, 29, 30, 31, 32, 37–38, 42, 287n21, 294nn72–73, 297n3, 298n6, 301, 303n2, 311n1, 317n6
Schöll, Adolf, 218
Schönemann, Lili, 169
Schönfliess, Arthur, 298n6
Schubart, Christian Friedrich Daniel, 166
Schulte-Strathaus, Ernst, 216
Schultz, Franz, 19–20, 40, 288n28
Schutjer, Karin, 285n10
Schwerdt, Georg, 317n6
Scott, Walter, 187
Seebeck, Moritz, 243
Seebeck, Thomas, 243

Seidel, Alfred, 14, 288–89nn29–30, 289n32, 291n39
Seligson, Carla, 16
Seligson, Friederike (Rika), 16, 290n37
Shaftesbury, Lord, 227, 339n9
Shakespeare, William, 6, 174, 295n78, 297n5
Simmel, Georg, 36, 131, 155, 193, 206, 225, 252, 285n10, 339n9, 343n14, 348n1
Sismondi, Jean Charles Léonard de, 189
Solger, Karl Wilhem Ferdinand, 99, 105, 108, 112, 155
Sophocles, 138, 321n44
Soret, Frédéric, 185, 191
Span, Marin, 222
Spaun, Franz von, 222
Spinoza, Baruch, 177, 178, 196, 198
Spittler, Carl, 6
Stadelmann, Carl Wilhelm, 223
Stäel, Madame de, 107, 322n52
Stalin, Josef, 29, 293n60
Stark, Johannes, 296n77
Stein, Charlotte von, 171, 298n5
Steinbach, Erwin von, 167
Steiner, Rudolf, 33, 205
Steiner, Uwe, 295n74, 300
Stern, Adolf, 218
Stern, Daniel, 220
Stieler, Joseph Karl, 224
Stifter, Adalbert, 146, 332n159
Stolberg, Christian, 166, 169
Stolberg, Fritz, 166, 169
Storck, Joachim, 291n44, 292nn48–49
Storm, Theodor, 346
Strauss, David, 225
Streizinger, Johannes, 286n14
Suphan, Bernhard Ludwig, 216

Textor, Catharina Elisabeth, 166
Textor, Johann Wolfgang, 166
Thalheimer, August, 226
Theme, Karl, 346
Tieck, Ludwig, 184
Tobler, Georg Christoph, 324n77

Trentini, Albert von, 222
Türckheim, Anna Elisabeth, 253
Turel, Adrien, 223

Ulam, Adam, 293n60
Ulberte, Liga, 292n56
Unger, Erich, 290n34, 305nn1–2
Unger, Rudolf, 224

Varnhagen, Karl August von Ense, 215
Varnhagen, Rahel, 283n3
Vischer, Friedrich Theodor, 221, 342n7
Vogel, Carl, 325n85
Voller, Christian, 288n30
Voltaire, 166, 170, 174, 180, 348
Voß, Heinrich Johann, 166, 167
Vulpius, Christiane, 12, 179, 298n5, 328n108

Wagner, Richard, 220, 294n72
Walter, Julius, 145, 330n138
Walzel, Oskar, 322n56
Wartenburg, Paul Graf Yorck von, 21
Weber, Alfred, 14
Weber, Marianne, 14
Weber, Max, 14–15, 285n10

Weißbach, Richard, 16–19, 290n38
Werner, Zacharias, 107, 136, 145
Whitman, Walt, 245
Wieland, Christoph Martin, 107, 115, 169, 170, 172, 182, 247, 253
Willemer, Marianne von, 129, 188, 225, 253
Winckelmann, Johann Joachim, 105, 173, 323n71
Witkowski, Georg, 216, 228, 230
Witte, Bernd, 284n7
Wittgenstein, Ludwig, 314n4
Wohlbold, Hans, 33, 204, 205, 206
Wolf, Friedrich August, 186
Wolff, Charlotte, 2, 283n7
Wolters, Friedrich, 208, 295n78
Wyneken, Gustav, 14

Zarncke, Friedrich, 216
Zelter, Carl Friedrich, 40, 41, 103, 106, 111, 115, 117, 144, 157, 181, 185, 192, 240–42, 247, 249, 320n40, 347n2
Zeuxis, 303n8
Zianitzka, Kathinka, 222
Ziegler, Konrat, 228–29
Zweig, Stefan, 283n3

Note on the Translators

As explained in the "Note on Translation," the initial translator of each text in this volume is marked by his or her initials in the first (unnumbered) endnote.

Susan Bernstein

Professor of comparative literature and German studies at Brown University, Susan Bernstein is the author of *Virtuosity of the Nineteenth Century—Performing Music and Language in Heine, Liszt, and Baudelaire* (Stanford University Press, 1998); *Housing Problems—Writing and Architecture in Walpole, Goethe, Freud, and Heidegger* (Stanford University Press, 2008); and *The Other Synaesthesia* (SUNY Press, 2023). She has also published on topics such as the Uncanny, Nietzsche, Kant, and Poe. She has translated works by Werner Hamacher.

Jan Cao

Assistant professor in the Department of Literature and junior researcher at Si-Mian Institute for Advanced Studies at East China Normal University, Shanghai, Jan Cao received her PhD in German literature and critical thought from Northwestern University, where she completed a dissertation on the botanical poetics of Paul Celan and Tawada Yoko. Her essays can be found in the *Germanic Review, German Quarterly, Games and Cultures*, the *Journal for Cultural Research*, and *CHI Conference on Human Factors in Computing Systems*. Her current book project is tentatively titled *Portals: An Aesthetic Theory of Video Games*.

Peter Fenves

The Joan and Serapta Professor of Literature at Northwestern University, Peter Fenves is a professor of German, comparative literary studies, and Jewish studies. He is the author of *A Peculiar Fate: World-History and Metaphysics in Kant* (Cornell University Press, 1991), *"Chatter": Language and History in Kierkegaard* (Stanford University Press, 1993), *Arresting Language: From Leibniz to Benjamin* (Stanford University Press, 2001), *Late Kant: Toward Another Law of the Earth* (Routledge, 2003; translated into German and Spanish), and *The Messianic Reduction: Walter Benjamin and the Shape of Time* (Stanford University Press, 2011; translated into Spanish). He is also the editor or coeditor of numerous volumes, including *Raising the Tone of Philosophy: Late Essays by Kant, Transformative Critique by Derrida* (Johns Hopkins University Press, 1993), *Two Essays on Friedrich Hölderlin* by Werner Hamacher (Stanford University Press, 2020), *Toward the Critique of Violence: A Critical Edition* by Walter Benjamin (Stanford University Press, 2021), *Synthesis und Systembegriff in der Philosophie* by Felix Noeggerath (Peter Lang, 2023), and *The Chaos in Cosmic Selection: An Attempt at a Critique of Cognition* by Felix Hausdorff (SUNY Press, forthcoming).

Kevin McLaughlin

Dean of the faculty at Brown University from 2011 to 2022, Kevin McLaughlin is currently George Hazard Crooker Professor of English, Comparative Literature, and German studies at Brown and the director of the John Nicholas Brown Center for Advanced Study. He is the author of *Writing in Parts: Imitation and Exchange in 19th-Century Literature* (Stanford University Press, 1995); *Paperwork: Literature and Mass Mediacy in the Age of Paper* (University of Pennsylvania Press, 2005); *Poetic Force: Poetry after Kant* (Stanford University Press, 2014); and *The Philology of Life: Walter Benjamin's Critical Program* (Fordham University Press, 2023). McLaughlin is also the cotranslator with Howard Eiland of Walter Benjamin's *Arcades Project* (Harvard University Press, 1999).

Jonas Rosenbrück

Assistant professor of German at Amherst College, Jonas Rosenbrück is the author of *Common Scents: Poetry, Modernity, and a Revolution of the Senses* (SUNY Press, 2024). His various articles on German and French literature, aesthetics, and philosophy have appeared in, among other venues, *Comparative Literature, CR: The New Centennial Review*, and the *Germanic Review*. His current research project is tentatively titled "Toward a Critique of *Geschlecht*."

Cultural Memory | *in the Present*

Elliot R. Wolfson, *Nocturnal Seeing: Hopelessness of Hope and Philosophical Gnosis in Susan Taubes, Gillian Rose, and Edith Wyschogrod*

Severo Sarduy, *Barroco and Other Writings*

David D. Kim, *Arendt's Solidarity: Anti-Semitism and Racism in the Atlantic World*

Hans Joas, *Why the Church? Self-Optimization or Community of Faith*

Jean-Luc Marion, *Revelation Comes from Elsewhere*

Peter Sloterdijk, *Out of the World*

Christopher J. Wild, *Descartes' Meditative Turn: Cartesian Thought as Spiritual Practice*

Eli Friedlander, *Walter Benjamin and the Idea of Natural History*

Helmut Puff, *The Antechamber: Toward a History of Waiting*

Raúl E. Zegarra, *A Revolutionary Faith: Liberation Theology between Public Religion and Public Reason*

David Simpson, *Engaging Violence: Civility and the Reach of Literature*

Michael Steinberg, *The Afterlife of Moses: Exile, Democracy, Renewal*

Alain Badiou, *Badiou by Badiou*, translated by Bruno Bosteels

Eric Song, *Love against Substitution: Seventeenth-Century English Literature and the Meaning of Marriage*

Niklaus Largier, *Figures of Possibility: Aesthetic Experience, Mysticism, and the Play of the Senses*

Mihaela Mihai, *Political Memory and the Aesthetics of Care: The Art of Complicity and Resistance*

Ethan Kleinberg, *Emmanuel Levinas's Talmudic Turn: Philosophy and Jewish Thought*

Willemien Otten, *Thinking Nature and the Nature of Thinking: From Eriugena to Emerson*

Michael Rothberg, *The Implicated Subject: Beyond Victims and Perpetrators*

Hans Ruin, *Being with the Dead: Burial, Ancestral Politics, and the Roots of Historical Consciousness*

Eric Oberle, *Theodor Adorno and the Century of Negative Identity*

David Marriott, *Whither Fanon? Studies in the Blackness of Being*

Reinhart Koselleck, *Sediments of Time: On Possible Histories*, translated and edited by Sean Franzel and Stefan-Ludwig Hoffmann

Devin Singh, *Divine Currency: The Theological Power of Money in the West*

Stefanos Geroulanos, *Transparency in Postwar France: A Critical History of the Present*

Sari Nusseibeh, *The Story of Reason in Islam*

Olivia C. Harrison, *Transcolonial Maghreb: Imagining Palestine in the Era of Decolonization*

Barbara Vinken, *Flaubert Postsecular: Modernity Crossed Out*

Aishwary Kumar, *Radical Equality: Ambedkar, Gandhi, and the Problem of Democracy*

Simona Forti, *New Demons: Rethinking Power and Evil Today*

Joseph Vogl, *The Specter of Capital*

Hans Joas, *Faith as an Option*

Michael Gubser, *The Far Reaches: Ethics, Phenomenology, and the Call for Social Renewal in Twentieth-Century Central Europe*

Françoise Davoine, *Mother Folly: A Tale*

Knox Peden, *Spinoza Contra Phenomenology: French Rationalism from Cavaillès to Deleuze*

Elizabeth A. Pritchard, *Locke's Political Theology: Public Religion and Sacred Rights*

Ankhi Mukherjee, *What Is a Classic? Postcolonial Rewriting and Invention of the Canon*

Jean-Pierre Dupuy, *The Mark of the Sacred*

Henri Atlan, *Fraud: The World of Ona'ah*

Niklas Luhmann, *Theory of Society*, volume 2

Ilit Ferber, *Philosophy and Melancholy: Benjamin's Early Reflections on Theater and Language*

Alexandre Lefebvre, *Human Rights as a Way of Life: On Bergson's Political Philosophy*

Theodore W. Jennings Jr., *Outlaw Justice: The Messianic Politics of Paul*

Alexander Etkind, *Warped Mourning: Stories of the Undead in the Land of the Unburied*

Denis Guénoun, *About Europe: Philosophical Hypotheses*

Maria Boletsi, *Barbarism and Its Discontents*

Sigrid Weigel, *Walter Benjamin: Images, the Creaturely, and the Holy*

Roberto Esposito, *Living Thought: The Origins and Actuality of Italian Philosophy*

Henri Atlan, *The Sparks of Randomness*, volume 2: *The Atheism of Scripture*

Rüdiger Campe, *The Game of Probability: Literature and Calculation from Pascal to Kleist*

Niklas Luhmann, *A Systems Theory of Religion*

Jean-Luc Marion, *In the Self's Place: The Approach of Saint Augustine*

Rodolphe Gasché, *Georges Bataille: Phenomenology and Phantasmatology*

Niklas Luhmann, *Theory of Society*, volume 1

Alessia Ricciardi, *After La Dolce Vita: A Cultural Prehistory of Berlusconi's Italy*

Daniel Innerarity, *The Future and Its Enemies: In Defense of Political Hope*

Patricia Pisters, *The Neuro-image: A Deleuzian Film-Philosophy of Digital Screen Culture*

François-David Sebbah, *Testing the Limit: Derrida, Henry, Levinas, and the Phenomenological Tradition*

Erik Peterson, *Theological Tractates*, edited by Michael J. Hollerich

Feisal G. Mohamed, *Milton and the Post-secular Present: Ethics, Politics, Terrorism*

Pierre Hadot, *The Present Alone Is Our Happiness, Second Edition: Conversations with Jeannie Carlier and Arnold I. Davidson*

For a complete listing of titles in this series, visit the Stanford University Press website, www.sup.org.